MW01487588

Yael Leibowitz

EZRA-NEHEMIAH

RETROGRADE REVOLUTION

Matan
Maggid Books

Ezra-Nehemiah
Retrograde Revolution

First Edition, 2025

Maggid Books
An imprint of Koren Publishers Jerusalem Ltd.

POB 8531, New Milford, CT 06776-8531, USA
& POB 4044, Jerusalem 9104001, Israel
www.korenpub.com

The publication of this book was made possible
through the generous support of *The Jewish Book Trust*.

ISBN 978-1-59264-707-1, *hardcover*

A CIP catalogue record for this title is
available from the British Library

Printed and bound in the United States

This book of Torah is dedicated to the memory of

Sadie Rennert z"l

A true angel, who established a home filled with Torah values and good deeds that have been passed down through the generations of her beloved family. We are forever grateful that Matan carries her name and that so many women are studying and teaching Torah in her merit.

פִּיהָ פָּתְחָה בְחָכְמָה וְתוֹרַת חֶסֶד עַל לְשׁוֹנָהּ

Her mouth is full of wisdom, Her tongue with kindly teaching.

And it is dedicated in honor of

Ira Leon and Ingeborg Hanna Rennert

their children

Tamara and Randall Winn
Yonina and Mitchell Davidson
Ari and Erynne Rennert

and grandchildren

Pillars and leaders of the Jewish world, living lives filled with Torah and gemilut chassadim, infusing the Jewish people with a beautiful light, and strengthening Medinat Yisrael. With thanks for helping Matan spread inspiring Torah learning to every corner of the world.

וּרְאֵה בָנִים לְבָנֶיךָ שָׁלוֹם עַל יִשְׂרָאֵל

And you will see your children's children. Peace upon **Israel**.

THE SADIE RENNERT WOMEN'S INSTITUTE FOR TORAH STUDIES

In the 1980s, Rabbanit Malke Bina began teaching a groundbreaking Talmud *shiur* for women, held around the dining room table of Lili Weil *z"l*. Inspired by this pioneering learning, Rabbanit Bina and her students envisioned an advanced Beit Midrash for women. This became a reality in 1988 with the establishment of Matan: The Sadie Rennert Women's Institute for Torah Studies. From its inception, Matan has been dedicated to cultivating high-level scholars, educators, and leaders, revolutionizing opportunities for women to engage deeply with Torah study.

Today, Matan has eleven branches, serving tens of thousands of students in Israel and worldwide. It offers intensive Beit Midrash programs in Bible, Talmud, Halakha and Jewish thought, continually raising the bar for women's Torah study. Additionally, there is a broad choice of weekly classes and series, Yemei Iyun in Israel and beyond, a summer learn-and-tour program, pre-holiday programming, an international mother-daughter bat mitzva program, and weekly *parasha* podcasts in Hebrew and English. Matan remains at the forefront of Torah study, inspiring and empowering the next generation through transformative Torah learning.

Kitvuni – Fellowship Program for Writing Torah Literature

In 2022 the Kitvuni Fellowship was launched, led by Dr. Yael Ziegler, a distinguished Matan graduate and senior lecturer. The initiative nurtures exceptional *talmidot ḥakhamim*, supporting them in writing and publishing books of Torah scholarship across diverse fields. Kitvuni provides a structured framework, mentorship, and professional support for every cohort, ensuring that each scholar's work reaches its highest potential. In collaboration with Koren Publishers, the program is producing books that will enrich the Jewish bookshelf for generations to come.

The first Matan Kitvuni publication in English, *Ezra-Nehemiah: Retrograde Revolution* by Yael Leibowitz, is part of the Maggid Studies in Tanakh series. The book explores the revolutionary strategies of Jewish leaders in the early Second Temple period as they navigated the challenges of restoration and rebuilding. Upcoming Kitvuni publications will feature works on Bible, Talmud, Halakha, Hassidut, and Kabbala, further enhancing contemporary Torah scholarship.

Contents

Preface

Calls for revolution these days do not seem to hold much promise, not because we doubt the conviction of those claiming dissatisfaction with the existing order, but because we doubt that they have a superior, implementable alternative. Revolutions, and the people who drive them, claim to want to break with the past and forge new, uncharted paths; to leave broken systems in the dustbins of history and enlighten the future with their sophisticated, upgraded ideals. Some revolutions succeed, while others fail. Historians, sociologists, and political scientists expend tremendous energy trying to discern what spells the difference between those outcomes. Many theories have been proposed; none is perfect.

The title of this book, *Retrograde Revolution*, speaks to a characteristically Jewish element of the watersheds that have shaped Jewish history. "Retrograde" means to move backward or revert to an earlier state. It softens the implications of the word "revolution," while, ironically in many cases, ensuring the success of its initiative. And while in our modern, progress-obsessed culture, the word itself may conjure negative connotations of regression and decline, what we will come to understand through studying the book of Ezra-Nehemiah is that true, lasting change manifests only when we are able, as a community, to move both backward and forward simultaneously. The past is not all bad, and all things new are not necessarily better; there are pieces of our past that we should want to recreate, occasions in which our system served the highest interests of our people, and instances in which we realized our shared potential. Identifying and endeavoring to return to those moments is vital to any true progress. For good reason, the book of Lamentations, written at one of the lowest points in Israelite history, concludes with the sentiment "Renew our days to be as they once were."[1]

That said, progress also demands that we identify how past systems have failed, how we have failed. Just as the past is not all bad, it is also, quite obviously, never all good. Being a self-conscious community means possessing both the ability and the desire to look at our past through an honest, critical lens and identify those components of our social and religious machinery that led to malfunctions. It is about knowing which parts need to be replaced, which need to be updated, which need lubrication to minimize unavoidable friction, and which are so antiquated as to be unsalvageable. New is not *necessarily* better, but sometimes it is. And that is where revolutions come in. Ezra-Nehemiah was written at a time when revolution was, on some level, unavoidable. The historical events that led to its writing compelled the Jewish people to reconsider their past and reflect upon what they wanted their future to look like.

But there is an additional reason this title was chosen for the study of Ezra-Nehemiah. The term "retrograde" also has astronomical connotations, which may serve as a helpful metaphor for understanding some important components of Ezra-Nehemiah, namely, studying, witnessing, and being Jewish in history. Astronomers claim that all planets move around the sun in the same direction, and that direction is referred to as "direct motion." But the speed at which a planet moves is contingent on its proximity to the sun. Planets closer to the sun move more quickly than those further away. So, when looking at the sky from Earth, planets moving at the same speed, or faster than us, appear to be moving in direct motion. But like the illusion experienced by runners on a track or drivers on a highway, those moving slower than us, despite moving in the same

---

1.   Lamentations 5:21.

direction, appear to be moving backward. This apparent motion is what astronomers call "retrograde." Of course, what is interesting to consider, and what astronomers are keen to point out, is the relative nature of the terms ascribed to the two motions. Celestial motion is neither direct nor retrograde; it is only our perspective that confers those designations.

In history, as in astronomical nomenclature, self-awareness is the key to appreciating the difference between direction and perceived direction. And Ezra-Nehemiah, perhaps more than any other book of the Bible, is cognizant of its orientation. It redraws the borders of national identity, revives ancient laws, and reconfigures society. But it does all that while carefully considering its community relative to those around it in space and relative to other eras in time. Ezra-Nehemiah is aware of the critical juncture at which it stands, and it employs that awareness to reshape our understanding of how Jews move through history. It does not use the speed at which things progress to gauge their course, and it does not assume that things that move differently are necessarily moving in opposition. Ezra-Nehemiah sees the direct motion of Jewish evolution, where others perceive retrograde motion and, in doing so, inspires its readers to do the same.

Acknowledgments

If I were to sit down and try to make a list of all the people to whom I owe thanks, the acknowledgments section of this book would no doubt be longer than the book itself. I have crossed paths with, and gleaned so much from, so many extraordinary individuals, and among the things I thank God for daily are the people He has brought into my life. So, if you are reading these words and we have a relationship, or even just a fleeting connection, please know, I am grateful for you.

For close to twenty-five years, I have had the privilege of learning Tanakh with students of different ages and from all walks of life. To those of you with whom I have been blessed to learn, whether you were in high school, college, or beyond, you have inspired me to broaden and deepen my knowledge; you have challenged my way of thinking; and, most importantly, you have made learning fun. The material in this book has been enhanced by the myriads of formal and informal conversations we have had, and I thank you for your contributions to my thinking. I am the teacher I am today because of the combined effect of having learned with each and every one of you.

Thank you to the administrators at the Upper School of Ramaz many years ago for taking a chance on a young, inexperienced educator, and thank you to my colleagues-turned-friends for showing me how it's done. To Yeshiva University, thank you for being my life-long academic anchor, and thank you for seven of the most enriching teaching years of my career.

After making aliya in 2014, I quickly found my intellectual and spiritual home at Matan. I do not take for granted the fact that I get to spend my days surrounded by *talmidot ḥakhamim* who are equal parts brilliant, humble, driven, and kind. To Rabbanit Malke Bina, thank you for having the foresight, over thirty-five years ago, to know how badly our community needed Matan, and thank you for having the resolve to transform your vision into reality. Because of you, we now have generations of sophisticated, erudite, female religious leaders, and, perhaps more importantly, we have young girls who don't even know the courage it once took to do what they now assume is their birthright.

The Kitvuni writing fellowship which Matan launched in 2022 defined the next frontier in women's learning, and I am deeply honored and grateful to have been a part of Kitvuni's first cohort. To Jordana Schoor, our collective community is a better place because your wellspring of ideas never dries up, nor does your selfless desire to see others excel. To Dr. Yael Ziegler, your breadth of knowledge and passion for teaching are a force to behold. Thank you for your example. To my fellow writers, Dr. Shifra Assulin, Dr. Sharon Galper-Grossman, Dr. Adina Sternberg, Dr. Merav Suisa, and Dr. Miriam Weitman, I cherish the time we spent together. Each of you came into the program with more wisdom than any one book can contain, and I grew by simply watching you spin your grand ideas into finite texts. Thank you for your support and your camaraderie. To Chaya Bina, I cannot think of anyone who works as tirelessly as you do to bring to life the programs others dream up. You are loyal, forthright, and indefatigable. Thank you, Chaya, for Matan, for Kitvuni, and for your friendship.

When I was told that the Kitvuni program included a mentor, I knew right away that I wanted Dr. Ari Mermelstein to guide me through the writing process. Ari's own scholarship combines meticulous research and a deep respect for our history and traditions, but, more notably, Ari is the consummate *mensch.* Thank you, Ari, for being so generous with your time, long after the fellowship ended, and thank you for making the writing of my first book such a heartening experience. Dr. Aaron Koller was kind enough to read through a manuscript of this book. Aaron, I cannot thank you enough for taking the time. Your feedback was characteristically discerning and thought-provoking, and I am most grateful for it. Thank you, Dr. Gillian Steinberg, for your warmth, your professionalism, and your easygoing manner that puts first-time authors at ease. Thank you Rabbi Jacob J. Schacter for your early review, your guidance, and more broadly speaking, for your ongoing support throughout the years. Dr. Diana Lipton, I don't know what I did to deserve being on the receiving end of your big-heartedness and intellectual rigor, but I am so grateful to you for both. To Saadya Schoor, editing references between calls to *miluim* is no simple feat. Thank you for what you did for this book, and, more importantly, for what you do for our country. And thank you Maayan Wertentheil for representing the "young, highly-educated, inquisitive, and spiritually inclined" demographic so eminently.

Thank you to Rabbi Reuven Ziegler, Matthew Miller, and Alex Drucker at Koren Publishers, and to their fantastic team of editors. Debbie Ismailoff and Esther Shafier, I have not yet gotten the chance to meet you in person, but I am so grateful for your scrupulous editing. Rabbi David Silverstein, you have been a sounding board from the inception of this project. Thank you, as always, for your candidness and your expertise. Caryn Meltz, working with you is an absolute pleasure. Thank you for taking care of every detail and for making it seem effortless in the process. Tani Bayer, thank you for so beautifully coupling artistic creativity and graciousness.

Thank you to my friends (and "framily") – to those who are an integral part of my daily life and those who have been with me from afar for the long haul; your love and laughter keep me sane. To my siblings (the ones I grew up with, and the ones I was gifted through marriage), thank you for your integrity and your dependability, for nurturing my children, and for always making fun of my dreams while secretly rooting for them. I love you all. To my in-laws, words will not suffice. Nonetheless, thank you Larry, for your calm, and thank you mom, one of the most graceful writers I know, for loving us marvelously and unconditionally. To my parents, who gave me everything. Abba, thank you for showing us that intellectual curiosity and pure faith can seamlessly co-exist and, like Ezra and Nehemiah, for always making sure that our religious experiences were simultaneously כתורת משה and thoroughly joyful. Mommy, your passion for the land of Israel inspired my own, and your unqualified devotion to those you love has taught me how to be.

To Azriel, Yair, and Nili, there are no words I can conjure to summarize in a sentence or two how much I love, respect, and enjoy each of you. (And, honestly, I hope you know, without having to read these pages!) So, I will simply thank you for being you. I am in perpetual awe of the human beings you are becoming. You are the first thing I thank Hashem for every morning and the last thing I thank Him for at night. You are my greatest blessing.

Lastly, to Aaron. Thank you for being my true partner in every sense of the word. You are the person I continue to learn the most from, and, after all this time, the best part of my day is still coming home to you. Thank you for what we have built.

All four of my grandparents *z"l* experienced *ḥurban* (destruction), and all four, in its wake, chose to rebuild. This book is dedicated in loving memory to them and to the ever-Jewish legacy they imparted.

While the bulk of this book was written before October 7th, 2023, large portions of it were edited and tweaked while we reeled as a people – searching for our missing, burying our dead, running to safe rooms, and sending those we love most in the world off to fight. As these words go to print, grief and fear still grip the country. Soldiers are still giving their lives to keep us safe, civilians are still being terrorized, and many are still unable to return to their homes. Most surrealistically, we still have innocent men, women, and babies being held by sadistic monsters. They are an hour's drive away from where I sit typing and we cannot get to them. Little about our new reality makes sense. Yet alongside the shock, horror, and overwhelming feelings of vulnerability and betrayal, exists a profound sense of Jewish nationalism, Jewish pride, and Jewish unity. For the first time in a long time, the country is unified by its convictions, and for the first time in a long time, Jews throughout the Diaspora are becoming increasingly vocal in support of their homeland. If Ezra-Nehemiah teaches us anything, it is that no matter the scope or the scale of tragedy, what we do is learn from our mistakes, and then, with broken hearts and battered bodies, we rebuild. We have done it countless times over our long and winding history, and we will do it again this time. We have no other choice; resilience is our imperative.

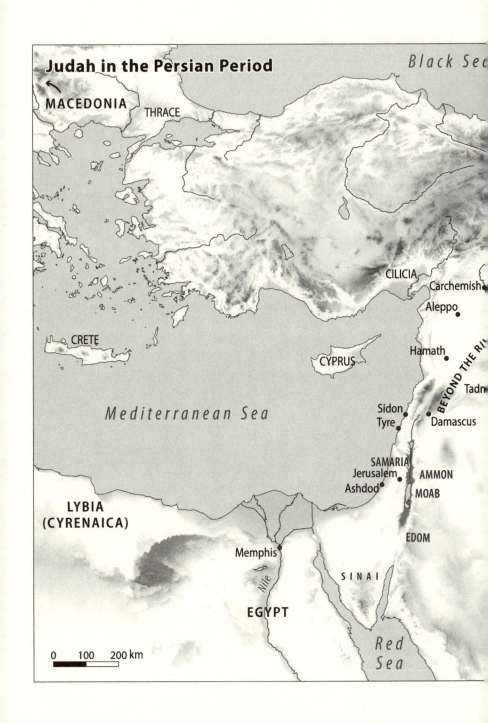

Judah in the Persian Period

MACEDONIA

THRACE

Black Sea

CILICIA

Carchemish

Aleppo

Hamath

CRETE

CYPRUS

BEYOND THE RIV

Tadm

Sidon

Tyre

Damascus

Mediterranean Sea

SAMARIA

Jerusalem

Ashdod

AMMON

MOAB

LYBIA
(CYRENAICA)

EDOM

Memphis

SINAI

Nile

EGYPT

Red
Sea

0   100   200 km

Caspian
Sea

ASSYRIA

Euphrates

Tigris (Chidekel)

MEDIA

PARTHIA

Ecbatana

BABYLONIA

KEDAR

Babylon

Susa

PERSIA

ARABIA

Persepolis

Persian
Gulf

Timeline

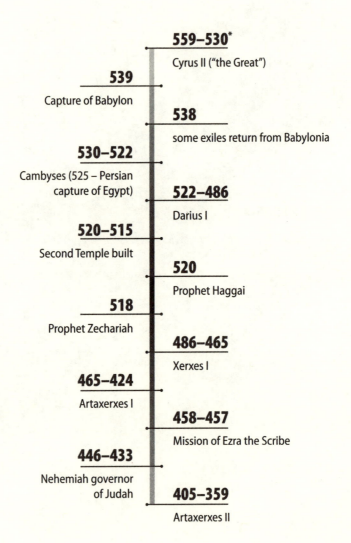

559–530[*]
Cyrus II ("the Great")

539
Capture of Babylon

538
some exiles return from Babylonia

530–522
Cambyses (525 – Persian capture of Egypt)

522–486
Darius I

520–515
Second Temple built

520
Prophet Haggai

518
Prophet Zechariah

486–465
Xerxes I

465–424
Artaxerxes I

458–457
Mission of Ezra the Scribe

446–433
Nehemiah governor of Judah

405–359
Artaxerxes II

* all years in BCE

Introduction

HISTORICAL BACKDROP

After the Exodus from Egypt and their wanderings in the desert, the people of Israel entered the land of Canaan in approximately 1250 BCE. Over the next six and a half centuries, the Israelites organized and built armies, cities, temples,[1] and empires. There were high points in the period, during which the Israelites flourished, but there was also no shortage of political and religious upheavals. In the late eighth century BCE, the northern Israelite kingdom was conquered by the invading Neo-Assyrian Empire,[2] and the majority of the twelve Israelite tribes were exiled from the land.[3]

---

1. In addition to Solomon's Temple in Jerusalem, there were also holy sites built in Shiloh (Josh. 18:1; Judges 21:19; Ps. 78:60; Jer. 7:12–15, 26:5–6), Dan (Judges 17–18; I Kings 12:28–29), Beth-El (I Sam. 10:3), Gilgal (I Sam. 13:4–5, 15:12–21, Hos. 4:15, 9:15, 12:12; Amos 4:4, 5:5), Mizpah (Judges 21:1–8; I Sam. 7:5–16, 10:17–25), Bethlehem (Judges 19:18; I Sam. 20:6, 28–29), and Nob (I Sam. 21:1–10, 22:16–19; Is. 10:32).

2. For a series of studies on the period of Neo-Assyrian conquest in Israel, see Shuichi Hasegawa, Christoph Levin, and Karen Radner, *The Last Days of the Kingdom of Israel* (Walter de Gruyter GmbH & Co KG, 2018).

3. Most, but not all, of the northerners were exiled, the implications of which will be felt in Ezra-Nehemiah and discussed in chapter seven.

The Southern Kingdom of Judah, comprised of the tribes of Judah and Benjamin, evaded Assyrian capture and remained in the land with its capital in Jerusalem. In 597 BCE, the Neo-Babylonian Empire exiled one of Judah's kings along with the kingdom's aristocrats. And then, in 586 BCE, the Babylonian king Nebuchadnezzar destroyed the Temple in Jerusalem and exiled most of the remaining populace to Babylon.[4] Most of the exiles went to Babylon. But then, in 539 BCE, after the Babylonian Empire fell to the Achaemenid dynasty, Cyrus, the first of the Achaemenid kings, released an edict allowing displaced peoples to return to their native lands and rebuild the temples the Babylonians had destroyed.

CONTENT AND STRUCTURE[5]

Ezra-Nehemiah depicts the activities of the Jewish community in the

---

4. II Kings 24:14–16 tells us that the first deportation in 597 saw seventeen thousand exiled. Although, according to Jeremiah 52:28, the number was only 3,023. Regarding the second deportation, both II Kings 25 and Chronicles 36 make clear that the deportation was definitive and the land was left desolate. In contrast, Jeremiah 52:29-30 tells us that 832 Judeans were exiled in the second deportation. Archaeological studies on Judah in the sixth century show that while the land was not left completely desolate, a sharp population collapse (likely from approximately 110,000 to about 15,000 to 40,000.) For more on this, see: T. Alstola, *Judeans in Babylonia: A Study of Deportees in the Sixth and Fifth Centuries BCE* (Brill, 2019).

5. Within the Hebrew Bible, Ezra and Nehemiah appear as two separate books. However, ancient Jewish sources point to the fact that the two were originally one literary unit, and it is under that assumption that we will be working throughout this study. The earliest hint of the work's initial integrity is the appearance of the Masoretic annotation for the midpoint of the work found in Nehemiah 3:21–22, which is in fact the midpoint of the two combined works. (The Masoretes, or *baalei hamesora*, refers to the group of Jewish scholars and scribes who compiled a system of vocalization, accents, and detailed technical notes to standardize the text of the Hebrew Bible.) The Septuagint (the third-to-second-century BCE Greek translation of the Bible, often abbreviated as LXX) similarly refers to the full text of Ezra-Nehemiah as 2 Esdras. In Josephus's first-century work (*Against Apion* 40), his enumeration of the biblical books seems to indicate that Ezra-Nehemiah was considered one work, and the Babylonian Talmud concurs that the books of Ezra and Nehemiah refer to the book of Ezra-Nehemiah (Bava Batra 15a; Sanhedrin 93b). There, the work is referred to simply as the book of Ezra, and the question why Nehemiah has no book called by his name is raised by the Rabbis. In the third and

Land of Israel in the aftermath of that edict.[6] The natural, overarching goal of the period was restoration, but, as we will see, that concept is charged and multifaceted. The restoration described in Ezra-Nehemiah entails a series of different movements.[7] The first movement, led by Sheshbazzar, Zerubbabel, and Jeshua the high priest (ca. 538–515 BCE), rebuilt the Temple complex and restored Temple ritual. The second movement, under the leadership of Ezra, reinstated religious law and Torah learning in the community (ca. 458–457 BCE.) And the third, led by Nehemiah, reconstructed the city walls around Jerusalem and repopulated the city itself (ca. 446–433 BCE).[8] Each movement included a leader, a mission, opposition to the mission, and the movement's

---

fourth centuries, a division was introduced by the church fathers and evidenced by the early church father Origen. The division is also found in the Vulgate edition of the Bible, and by the fifteenth century, Jewish printed versions of the Bible began adopting the division as well. For a sampling of modern scholars who address this topic, see Sara Japhet, *From the Rivers of Babylon to the Highlands of Judah: Collected Studies on the Restoration Period* (Eisenbrauns, 2006); Tamara Cohn Eskenazi, *In an Age of Prose: A Literary Approach to Ezra-Nehemiah* (Scholars, 1988); H. G. M. Williamson, *Ezra-Nehemiah*, vol. 16 (Zondervan Academic, 2018); Lester L. Grabbe, *Ezra-Nehemiah* (Psychology Press, 1998).

6. The work covers the events that occurred in the sixth and fifth centuries BCE.
7. Scholars voice different views on how the period the book covers should be divided. Sara Japhet, for example, argues that the work can be divided into two distinct periods, with each period led by two figureheads, one political and one religious, working side by side. In the first wave, those leaders are Zerubbabel and Jeshua, and in the second wave they are Ezra and Nehemiah (Sara Japhet, "Sheshbazzar and Zerubbabel – Against the Background of the Historical and Religious Tendencies of Ezra-Nehemiah," *Zeitschrift für die Alttestamentliche Wissenschaft* 95, no. 2 (January 1, 1983). Tamara Cohn Eskenazi, on the other hand, traces three distinct movements steered by groups of people and extending through the reign of three Persian monarchs. The three waves, according to Eskenazi, are bound together by adherence to God's will and royal decrees (Tamara Cohn Eskenazi, *In an Age of Prose*, 45.) Juha Pakkala identifies four distinct but interrelated movements. See J. K. Pakkala, "Centers and Peripheries in the Ezra Story," in E. Ben Zvi and C. Levin, eds., *Centres and Peripheries in the Early Second Temple Period* (Mohr Siebeck, 2016), 295–314.
8. These dates reflect the generally accepted dates, although some scholars have challenged them. For a survey of the different theories as to when each leader administered, see F. Charles Fensham, *The Books of Ezra and Nehemiah* (William B. Eerdmans, 1983), 6–9.

(partial) success. Thus, to understand Ezra-Nehemiah is to understand the facets of each movement in isolation and in their aggregate.

COMPOSITION AND STYLE

The Babylonian Talmud attributes the book of Ezra-Nehemiah to Ezra himself.[9] And while it is very possible that Ezra wrote significant portions of the text, internal clues lead us to believe that the compositional process was a more complicated one. There are sections of the work that date to a period later than Ezra,[10] and woven throughout the work are disparate literary genres. There are third-person narratives, extensive genealogical lists, official Aramaic documents, and first-person autobiographical sections written by both Ezra and Nehemiah, respectively. There are also chronological inconsistencies that break the flow of the narrative. For that reason, those accustomed to a straightforward writing style may initially feel disoriented and perhaps even overwhelmed by Ezra-Nehemiah's jarring stylistic shifts. Many have concluded, on account of these difficulties, that the book is simply a patchwork of disconnected sources.

In all likelihood, more than one pen did contribute to the formation of the book under discussion. And yet, as we explore the work, we will discover that *Ḥazal*'s attribution of the book to Ezra makes perfect sense because the book's internal coherence, even among the variegated sources, speaks to an underlying ideology that spans the work. That ideology proposes that unity and uniformity are not the same thing, and that a religiously conscious Jewish community is resilient enough to hold within it discord, mess, and heterogeneity. Disagreements do not undermine the whole, Ezra-Nehemiah's style proves; they shape it. As Tamara Cohn Eskenazi writes: "From a literary perspective, the divisions and fissures cease to be occasions to sever limbs but become, instead, clues to the book's overall intention."[11] So, taking into consideration the seemingly incongruous portions of the work, this study will look

---

9. Bava Batra 15a. But cooperation with Nehemiah is assumed.
10. The Talmud (ibid.) addresses some of the questions of this nature.
11. Eskenazi, *In an Age of Prose*, 13.

for those ideas, unique to Ezra-Nehemiah, that can be comprehended only within the artistic totality of the book.

THE FOCUS OF THIS STUDY

Many approaches to the study of Ezra-Nehemiah are possible. In this book, we will focus on those ways in which Ezra-Nehemiah shapes our understanding of the period of restoration in Israel. We will do so by identifying the challenges that arose due to the unique set of circumstances under which the book was written and the ways in which the historical actors of the time met those challenges. We will wade through what appear to be history and politics only to realize, time and again, that we are knee-deep in theology. But identifying how and why that happens requires that we first understand the broader phenomenon of history writing in Tanakh.

Every person who studies Tanakh does so with a set of working assumptions about what kind of work Tanakh constitutes. In some cases, the assumptions are conscious and in others they are unconscious, but in all cases they influence the way that we relate to the text in question. Religious beliefs, educational training, and internalized cultural codes all factor into the questions we ask of the text and the answers we expect to find.

The psychologically inclined, for example, may look to understand the complex inner workings of the mind of any given biblical personality. However, their inquiry will likely be based on conjecture, because, while biblical characters are not flat or uninteresting, Tanakh is concerned with the paradigmatic nature of its characters, not their fully-fledged psychological portraits.[12] In a similar vein, accounts of Israel in ancient Egypt will not help those looking for the engineering secrets

---

12. While there is certainly room for character analysis in the study of Tanakh, the manifold inner thoughts of the characters' minds are rarely revealed to the reader. What we know about biblical characters is primarily construed through narration and dialogue, which makes a true analysis challenging. For further reading, see Meir Sternberg, *The Poetics of Biblical Narrative: Ideological Literature and the Drama of Reading* (Indiana Press, 1987) and Robert Alter, *The Art of Biblical Narrative* (Basic Books, 2011).

behind the empire's impressive monoliths, just as the Tower of Babel story will not shed any light on the construction of ziggurats. Physicists will not understand *how* the world was created by reading the first two chapters of Genesis,[13] and those wondering about the otherworldly realm will not, after studying Tanakh, know what happens before or after we die. Those most likely to be frustrated, though, are historians looking for a comprehensive survey of the major and minor events of the periods Tanakh spans. Those who delve into the book of Kings eager to understand every detail of domestic life in the Judean Hills during the Late Iron Age will not find the answers, nor will those hoping to learn about the city-states that stood prior to Israel's entry into Canaan. An in-depth study of the book of Judges will yield an understanding of dangers of moral relativism, but it will not satisfy the curiosity of those looking for an exhaustive catalog of the events that took place during the 150-year period, because Tanakh is not a work of science or psychology, and, despite its facade, it is not simply a work of history either.[14]

Tanakh enables us to make sense of our individual place within society and the place of that society in relation to God. Tanakh contains wisdom literature that attempt to answer perennial questions about suffering and loss, love, and fulfillment.[15] It contains laments wailed into the hollows of devastation followed by lyrical balms of solace. Tanakh includes laws that curb our baser instincts and those that equip us to

---

13. Impressive attempts toward concordism of science and the Bible have been made in recent years. See, for example, Gerald Schroeder, *Genesis and the Big Bang Theory: The Discovery of Harmony Between Modern Science and the Bible* (Bantman, 2011); Nathan Aviezer, *In the Beginning: Biblical Creation and Science* (Ktav, 1990). For a critical perspective, see D. Shatz, "Is There Science in the Bible? An Assessment of Biblical Concordism," *Tradition* 41, no. 2 (2008): 198–244. Still, while the argument might be made that we can bring Genesis in line with what we know from scientific discovery, we could never glean those same scientific theories from a close reading of Genesis alone.

14. History writing as we think of it today did not exist as such in the ancient world. That said, Tanakh is one of the earliest examples of a work that blends factual reporting with theological and intellectual insights. For a discussion of the development and contributions of Biblical historiographical writing, see: Baruch Halpern, *The First Historians: The Hebrew Bible and History* (Penn State Press, 2010).

15. The term "wisdom literature" refers to the books of Proverbs, Ecclesiastes, and Job.

reach elevated states of spiritual connection. In Tanakh we can find poetry in its highest form and prose that expresses the profundity of the human experience. We may not find all we want to know about the people that populate its pages, but we find models of how Israel should and should not behave. We find models of heroes and cowards, mavericks and conformers. We find models of those who tried but failed because of a tragic flaw and those who were wildly successful despite their shortcomings. We will not learn about architecture from the massive building projects Tanakh records, but we will learn about hubris, tyranny, and the failings of state. We will not learn elaborate military strategy, but we will be reminded, time and again, that there exists a force more powerful than man-made weapons, and that it controls our battlefields.

We will not discover what exists before and after life on the pages of Tanakh, but we will learn how to live purposively and make our time on this Earth meaningful.

History, for Tanakh, is the medium through which these concepts are communicated. There is a historical context for the law giving and for prophetic critique. And the personalities central to our national self-understanding are born into specific historical circumstances. But the way history is shaped and told is always an intentional act.[16] It entails the selection of events and personas from a myriad of possibilities and the subsequent linking of those details to create a coherent, relevant narrative. That carefully curated narrative shapes not only our knowledge of the past but, perhaps more importantly, our understanding and interpretation of it. Tanakh outlines the parameters through which we understand history and, in doing so, infuses it with meaning. That meaning, construed through the events of our past, becomes the basis for our collective identity. To quote from the seminal work of Yosef Hayim Yerushalmi, "If Herodotus was the father of history, the fathers of meaning in history were the Jews."[17]

---

16. Intentionalism is seen on both the individual and collective levels. For an illuminating discussion of collective memory and historical consciousness, and the role it played in biblical (and Jewish historical) writing, see Amos Funkenstein, *Perceptions of Jewish History* (University of California Press, 1993).

17. Yosef Hayim Yerushalmi, *Zakhor: Jewish History and Jewish Memory* (University of Washington Press, 2011), 8.

Ezra-Nehemiah, like other historiographical works of Tanakh, sifts through the events of its time to create a cohesive narrative. It contextualizes what the community had endured and, by extension, why and how it became what it did. The author of Ezra-Nehemiah recounts the past in a conscious attempt to articulate the direction he believes his community should take. And as we read the work, we will begin to appreciate the subtle, creative, and artistic ways in which historical facts are spun into ideological truths.

Chapter One

Content Survey

EZRA 1
THE EDICT OF CYRUS

In 539 BCE, the first king of the Persian Empire, Cyrus II,[1] grants amnesty to captives of the newly vanquished Neo-Babylonian Empire, allowing them to return to their native lands and rebuild their shrines.[2] Those

---

1. The work begins with the words "In the first year of Cyrus, king of Persia." In fact, Cyrus ascended the throne in 559 BCE. In 539 BCE, the year in which Ezra-Nehemiah begins, Cyrus captured Babylon with, according to his own accounts, minimal effort. As such, the "first year" recalled at the outset of our work refers to his first year as king over Mesopotamia. For more on Cyrus's rise to power, see Matt Water, "Cyrus and the Achaemenids," *Iran* 42, no. 1 (2004): 91–102; Pierre Briant, *From Cyrus to Alexander: A History of the Persian Empire* (Penn State University Press, 2002), 31–61. The appellations attributed to the Achaemenid kings varied based on time and provenance. For a survey of the topic, see Elias J. Bickerman, "The Edict of Cyrus in Ezra," in *Studies in Jewish and Christian History* (Brill, 2007), 71–107.

2. Unearthed in 1879, what is known as the "Cyrus cylinder" speaks of Cyrus's appointment by the god Marduk as reprisal for the irreverence of Nabonidus (the last king of Babylon). The cylinder lists Cyrus's accomplishments, among them, his willingness to allow repatriation throughout his kingdom. Currently housed in the British Museum, the portion of the cylinder relevant for our chapter reads: "I am Cyrus, king of the universe, the great king, the powerful king, king of

former captives include the Jews who had been exiled, so the book of Ezra-Nehemiah begins with its version of that pronouncement.[3] In it, Cyrus proclaims that any Jews throughout his empire who want to

> Babylon, king of Sumer and Akkad, king of the four quarters of the world, son of Cambyses, the great king, king of the city of Anshan, grandson of Cyrus, the great king, ki[ng of the ci]ty of Anshan, descendant of Teispes, the great king, king of Anshan, the perpetual seed of kingship, whose reign Bel and Nabu love, and with whose kingship, to their joy, they concern themselves. When I went as harbinger of peace i[nt]o Babylon I founded my sovereign residence within the palace amid celebration and rejoicing. Marduk, the great lord, bestowed on me as my destiny the great magnanimity of one who loves Babylon, and I every day sought him out in awe. My vast troops marched peaceably in Babylon, and the whole of [Sumer] and Akkad had nothing to fear. I sought the welfare of the city of Babylon and all its sanctuaries. As for the population of Babylon [..., w]ho as if without div[ine intention] had endured a yoke not decreed for them, I soothed their weariness, I freed them from their bonds(?). Marduk, the great lord, rejoiced at [my good] deeds, and he pronounced a sweet blessing over me, Cyrus, the king who fears him, and over Cambyses, the son [my] issue, [and over] my all my troops, that we might proceed further at his exalted command. All kings who sit on thrones, from every quarter, from the Upper Sea to the Lower Sea, those who inhabit [remote distric]ts (and) the kings of the land of Amurru who live in tents, all of them, brought their weighty tribute into Shuanna, and kissed my feet. From [Shuanna] I sent back to their places to the city of Ashur and Susa, Akkad, the land of Eshnunna, the city of Zamban, the city of Meturnu, Der, as far as the border of the land of Qutu – the sanctuaries across the river Tigris – whose shrines had earlier become dilapidated, the gods who lived therein, and made permanent sanctuaries for them. I collected together all of their people and returned them to their settlements, and the gods of the land of Sumer and Akkad which Nabonidus – to the fury of the lord of the gods – had brought into Shuanna, at the command of Marduk, the great lord, I returned them unharmed to their cells, in the sanctuaries that make them happy. May all the gods that I returned to their sanctuaries, every day before Marduk and Nabu, ask for a long life for me, and mention my good deeds, and say to Marduk, my lord, this: "Cyrus, the king who fears you, and Cambyses his son, may their ... [...] [... ....]." The population of Babylon call blessings on my kingship, and I have enabled all the lands to live in peace." (New translation by Irving Finkel, Curator of Cuneiform Collections at the British Museum: https://www.britishmuseum. org/collection/object/W_1880-0617-1941)

3. The discrepancies between the narrative's retelling and extant documents from Persia that likely served as its basis should not trouble the reader. The author of Ezra-Nehemiah presents history through a theological lens, a practice characteristic of biblical writing. The Aramaic version of the pronouncement that appears in Ezra 6 (to be discussed below) is likely analogous to the original document. For

return to Jerusalem and rebuild the Temple are now free to do so.[4] And, the king further declares, any Jews who choose not to go are to donate to the cause.

So, laden with the contributions of those who remained behind,[5] the heads of Judah and Benjamin,[6] the priests, the Levites, and all "those whose spirit had been stirred by God" prepare for their journey back to their land. Cyrus removes the First Temple vessels from the storerooms where they had been held since the days of Nebuchadnezzar[7] and hands them over to Sheshbazzar, who is tasked with returning them to their rightful place in Jerusalem.[8] And thus begins what is referred to as the Jewish period of restoration. Its objective was established by Cyrus's

a comprehensive collection of sources from the Achaemenid period with accompanying annotations, see Amelie Kuhrt, *The Persian Empire: A Corpus of Sources from the Achaemenid Period* (Routledge, 2013).

4. Scholars speculate that the Temple in Jerusalem served the political and fiscal interests of the Persian throne and that the Persians were driven by motivations beyond those identified in Ezra-Nehemiah. See, for example, Briant, *From Cyrus to Alexander*, 48; and Joachim Schaper, "The Jerusalem Temple as an Instrument of the Achaemenid Fiscal Administration," *Vetus Testamentum* 45, no. 4 (1995): 528–39.

5. The image of Jews leaving a foreign land of captivity for Israel, replete with the riches from the locals, is evocative of the Exodus story (Exodus 3:21–22, 11:2, 12:35–36), a parallel that is threaded through much of the work.

6. After the exile of the northern tribes by Assyria in 722 BCE, Judah and Benjamin remained in the land. As such, they were exiled by the Babylonians in 597–586 BCE and on the receiving end of Cyrus's decree.

7. II Kings 25 tells us of the Temple plundering by Babylonians.

8. After his brief mention in chapter 1, Sheshbazzar is mentioned in the historical retrospective of Ezra 5:14, 16, where he is called "governor" and credited with laying the foundation of the Temple. But beyond that, nothing more is known of him. Some scholars have identified him with Shenazzar, the fourth son of Jehoiachin (I Chr. 3:18). Ezra 5 credits Sheshbazzar with laying the foundation of the Temple, while Ezra 3 credits Zerubbabel. Some attempt to harmonize the conflicting portraits by arguing that they are one and the same (Josephus, *Antiquities of the Jews*, 11.1.3). But there is little support for either of those approaches. In all likelihood, Sheshbazzar was one of the earliest Persian-appointed governors of Judah and the one responsible for laying the Temple's foundation. But because Zerubbabel was leader when the Temple was completed, he retained more space in the collective memory of the Judeans and is celebrated alongside Jeshua as leader of the first wave of return. For the intricacies of this discussion, see Sara Japhet, "Sheshbazzar and

opening decree, and the waves of return that follow marked the different phases toward the realization of that objective.

Orienting the monumental event theologically, Ezra-Nehemiah is quick to point out that historical changes transpire because the "end of exile" has arrived, just as the prophet Jeremiah had predicted. And the wording of the edict is likewise infused with monotheistic overtones, with the Persian king recognizing God's powers and universal sovereignty.[9] Still, students of Tanakh will notice that, in contrast to earlier phases of biblical history, in which prophets emphatically declared "so says the Lord," the opening of Ezra-Nehemiah presents a God who is active but silent.[10] His will is expressed indirectly through a foreign ruler rather than directly through a prophet. And, rather than being told emphatically what to do, the people are invited to return to the land should they so choose.[11] This obliqueness is emblematic of the era depicted in Ezra-Nehemiah and the root in many ways of both its challenges and opportunities.

Zerubbabel – Against the Background of the Historical and Religious Tendencies of Ezra-Nehemiah," in *From the Rivers of Babylon to the Highlands of Judah: Collected Studies on the Restoration Period* (Eisenbrauns, 2006), 66–98.

9.   God, in the declaration's opening sentence, is referred to as "The God of the heavens," an epithet ascribed in Persian to the Zoroastrian god Ahuramazda. Cyrus's ascription of the epithet to the God of Israel is part of an important theme that will be developed in chapter six. For more on Ahuramazda and Persian religion during the Achaemenid period, see William D. Davies and Louis Finkelstein, eds., *The Cambridge History of Judaism: Volume 1, The Persian Period* (Cambridge University Press, 1984), 279–307. And for a more thorough discussion of the Persian context of the apparent theological elements of the decree, see Bickerman, "Edict of Cyrus," 78–82.

10. For more on this rhetorical element, see Gordon F. Davies et al., *Berit Olam: Ezra and Nehemiah* (Liturgical Press, 1999), 6.

11. The verbs in the decree appear in the jussive (rather than command) form, leaving the choice up to the people.

EZRA 2
FIRST WAVE OF RETURN

The first group of people to return to the land, those referred to as "the people of the province" (*benei hamedina*),[12] are listed by name and tallied by family in Ezra 2.[13] This sort of extensive list of laypeople is uncharacteristic of Tanakh, and yet it is perfectly at home in Ezra-Nehemiah. In fact, each movement depicted in Ezra-Nehemiah is framed by a list of names at its beginning and another at its end.[14] As we will see,[15] that seemingly peculiar literary feature demonstrates how the author envisions the "newly improved" social structure of Judah, and who he believes its main characters to be. The two leaders who work in tandem and take center stage during this phase, Jeshua and Zerubbabel, are introduced in this chapter as well.

The bulk of Ezra 2 is a list of the names of laypeople, Temple priests, Levites, singers, gatekeepers, and Temple servants.[16] In some cases, spe-

---

12. One of the ways the Persian kings were able to maintain control over their vast empire was through the establishment of a system whereby the empire was divided into smaller satraps, all of which were connected to the Persian capitals through an intricate and efficient system of roads. Judah (Yehud) was a semiautonomous province within the larger Trans-Euphrates satrap aptly named "Beyond the River" (Abar Nahara). For the division and duties of satrapies within the Persian administrative context, see Briant, *From Cyrus to Alexander*, 63–66, 338–90 and Anson F. Rainey, "The Satrapy Beyond the River," *Australian Journal of Biblical Archaeology* (1969).

13. Some suggest that the impressively large total of over forty thousand includes tallies from subsequent returns as well. This theory is supported by the fact that certain names and places included in Ezra 2 become relevant only at later stages of the restoration. The scholarly literature dealing with the particulars of the Persian period–Judean population is vast and conflicting. For a sampling of the varied opinions, see Oded Lipschits, "Demographic Changes in Judah Between the Seventh and the Fifth Centuries BCE," in *Judah and the Judeans in the Neo-Babylonian Period* (2003), 323–76 and Gabriel Barkay, "Additional View of Jerusalem in Nehemiah Days," *New Studies in the Archaeology of Jerusalem and Its Region (Collected Papers)* 2 (2008): 48–54.

14. Ezra 8, 10; Nehemiah 3, 7, 10–12.

15. Chapter six.

16. The origins and role of these servants, known as *netinim* (נתינים), are not entirely clear. Internal evidence indicates that they were housed in their own quarters (Neh. 3:31) and that they were among the principal signers of the *amana* in Nehemiah 10

cific guilds are mentioned, adding an authentic and personal air to the lists, as well as a sense of dutiful cooperation toward a united goal. But just as we are beginning to assume the work is moving in the direction of "happily ever after," we discover that the Jewish status of several returnees is called into question because they are unable to provide documentation of their Jewish ancestral heritage.[17] In a similar development, we learn that some priests are disqualified from serving in the priesthood when written records of their genealogy cannot be found. The governor, weighing in on the matter, recommends that those priests abstain from partaking of the holy food offerings until the Urim and Thummim can be used to ascertain their status.[18] But, since the Urim and Thummim had either fallen out of use or had been lost with the destruction of the First Temple,[19] the permanent exclusion of those priests is, for all intents and purposes, a foregone conclusion. Still, despite the membership debates that surfaced, as the chapter draws to a close, we see the various strata of Judeans settling into their towns and the leaders making generous donations to the Temple building project, all of which point toward the commencement of that most important undertaking.

(v. 29) and listed as "heads of the province" (Neh. 11:3). For a survey of the suggested theories, see Baruch A. Levine, "The Netînîm," *Journal of Biblical Literature* (1963): 207–12.

17. This fact, mentioned offhandedly in chapter 2, foreshadows a much broader issue of Jewish identity that surfaces in this period. It is discussed at length in chapter seven.

18. In addition to their mention in Ezra-Nehemiah (they are mentioned again in Neh. 7:65), the Urim and Thummim are mentioned by name several times in Tanakh (Ex. 28:30; Lev. 8:8; Num. 27:21; I Sam. 28:6) and are likely implied in numerous other contexts as well; see, for example, I Samuel 14:41. While their role and function remain somewhat enigmatic to modern readers, what we do know is that they were used to "inquire of God" when the answer (often to a simple yes-or-no question) was being sought. For a careful study of the apparatus and phenomena associated with them, see Cornelis Van Dam, *The Urim and Thummim: A Means of Revelation in Ancient Israel* (Eisenbrauns, 1997); Irving L. Finkel, "In Black and White: Remarks on the Assur Psephomancy Ritual" *ZA* 85, (1995): 271–76; Victor Avigdor Hurowitz, "Urim and Thummim in Light of a Psephomancy Ritual from Assur (LKA 137)," *Journal of the Ancient Near Eastern Society* 21, no. 1 (1992).

19. The opinion of the Rabbis in Sota 48a is that the Urim and Thummim were not used beyond the era of the early prophets.

EZRA 3
LAYING THE TEMPLE'S FOUNDATIONS

By the time the seventh month arrives, the people are settled in their towns and ready to begin building the long-awaited Temple. They assemble in Jerusalem "as one,"[20] and then, on the very spot where Solomon's Temple stood for four centuries, Jeshua and the other priests, along with Zerubbabel and his comrades,[21] build an altar to God upon which they present burnt offerings morning and evening.[22] And lest anyone doubt the religious legitimacy of their worship, the text assures us that the offerings are all carried out "as prescribed in the Torah of Moses."

On the festival of Sukkot, the people bring the mandated sacrifices.[23] And after the festival's conclusion, they continue to bring all the offerings prescribed in the Torah.[24] We are reminded briefly that all of this happens despite the fact that the Temple had yet to be built.[25] But

20. The same words are used in Nehemiah 8:1 as well, highlighting the fact that at both central events of the era, the community participated in unison.
21. From other biblical works in which Jeshua and Zerubbabel are mentioned, we know that Jeshua was the high priest (Hag. 1:1, 12, 14, 2:2; Zech. 3:1) and that Zerubbabel held the title of governor (Hag. 1:1, 12, 2:2). We also know that Zerubbabel was the grandson of Jehoiachin, one of the last kings of Judah (I Chr. 3:16–19). The conspicuous absence of these details in Ezra 3 is not accidental and will be addressed in chapter six. Ezra 3, like Haggai 2:18 and Zechariah 4:9, credits Zerubbabel with laying the Temple's foundation, in contrast to Ezra 5:16. (See above note 8.)
22. The text briefly mentions the community's apprehensions regarding the "peoples of the land," a topic that will prove to be of great consequence in Ezra-Nehemiah. (See chapter seven.)
23. Numbers 29:12–38.
24. Ibid., chapter 28.
25. Trying to make sense of how such a situation came about, the Rabbis suggest that it was only a provisional measure sanctioned by a prophet (Zevaḥim 62a). That approach is further expanded upon in the Talmud with the claim that the sanctity of the First Temple "hallowed it for the nonce and for the future" (Zevaḥim 107b). Throughout the early biblical period, worship was not limited to the Temple in Jerusalem, although in his day Josiah attempted to centralize worship in Jerusalem (II Kings 23). Jeremiah seems to indicate that sacrifices continued in Jerusalem even after the destruction of the Temple (Jer. 41:5), and it is interesting to note that in the book of Jeremiah as well, the pilgrimage described took place in the seventh month. The books of Haggai (2:14–19) and Zechariah (7:2–3) both refer to the ritual system that was in place before the construction of the Temple. But Haggai,

in the same breath we are also informed that the leaders, with Cyrus's permission, are paying hewers, stonemasons, and workers to import building materials and facilitate the advancement of the program. In their second year, the people begin appointing priests and Levites to supervise the construction project, and leaders, including Kadmiel and the sons of Henadad, to supervise the builders.

Then, when the foundation is firmly established, the priests dress themselves in their vestments and, armed with trumpets, take up their positions, as do the Levites with their cymbals. They raise their voices and praise God and His goodness. But their shouts of happiness are not heard alone. They are fused, we are told, with the cries of those in the crowd who remember the First Temple in all its glory. And as the chapter concludes, the clamor created by the combination of those two experiences echoes into the distance.[26]

EZRA 4
THE "ADVERSARIES" OF JUDAH

If, until now, we were under the impression[27] that the restoration project progresses smoothly and unhindered, in Ezra 4 we learn that this is not the case. While we know from Ezra 1 that Cyrus gives the returnees permission to rebuild,[28] in Ezra 4 we discover that the construction is not completed until the days of Darius,[29] and that delay requires an explanation.

According to Ezra 4, those responsible for the stagnation of the process are labeled the "adversaries of Judah and Benjamin."[30] Those

---

as part of his attempts to encourage the construction, criticizes the impurity of the sacrifices, telling the people that only a purification will rectify the situation (Japhet, "The Temple in the Restoration Period: Reality and Ideology," in *From the Rivers of Babylon*, 183–232).

26. The depiction of this scene is emblematic of Ezra-Nehemiah's worldview and is discussed in full in chapter four.

27. As we saw in the previous chapter, this opposition is referred to (v. 3), but, without context, the import of the reference is not fully understood.

28. 539 BCE.

29. The Temple was completed in the sixth year of Darius's reign (516 BCE).

30. Not all early Second Temple authors blamed external forces for the delay.

adversaries, according to the text, initially approach the leaders of the Judeans claiming that they too worship God and want to participate in building His Temple.[31] But Zerubbabel and Jeshua swiftly reject their request. Only "our people," the leaders declare emphatically, shall build. The Judeans maintain that their rejection is in keeping with the directives of the Persian government.[32] But their harsh repudiation has consequences.

The "people of the land" who are refused[33] seek to weaken the Judeans and foil their building efforts through political maneuvering. They send letters to the Persian kings claiming that the Judeans are rebuilding their Temple and city in preparation for the uprising they are mounting against the empire[34] and warn the kings against sanctioning the building of that rebellious city.[35] In the letter quoted in Ezra 4,[36]

Ezra-Nehemiah's choice to fault the Judeans' adversaries is an intentional rhetorical decision and is discussed in chapter four.

31. The group claimed to worship the God of Israel since Esarhaddon, king of Assyria (681–669 BCE), brought them to the land. More on their claim and its veracity or lack thereof can be found in chapter seven.

32. Their rejection, one of the most complicated and important topics in the work, is discussed at length in chapter seven.

33. The Hebrew phrase used, *am haaretz* (עם הארץ), has a wide semantic range within the Bible. In Ezra-Nehemiah, it likely refers to the inhabitants of Judah who were not considered members by the *gola* community. For a survey of the phrase's uses and evolutions, see Shemaryahu Talmon, "The Judean Am Ha'ares in Historical Perspective," in *Fourth World Congress of Jewish Studies*, vol. 1 (1967), 71–76.

34. Artaxerxes's reign (465–424 BCE) was marked by numerous points of instability, beginning with the revolt of his brother Hystaspes in Bactria at the beginning of his time in power. In 460 BCE, a nationalistic revolt supported by the Athenians broke out in Egypt. It was put down in 445 BCE, but in 448 BCE, Megabyzus, the satrap of Abar Nahara, also rebelled. All of this points to a climate ripe for the king to take extra precautions in response to reports on potentially rebellious peoples within his empire, particularly those living in Abar Nahara, located not far from Egypt (Briant, *From Cyrus to Alexander*, 569–611).

35. In addition to the letter from the days of Artaxerxes, which comprises the bulk of the chapter, the text also mentions, without citing its content, that a letter was written in the time of Xerxes as well, giving readers the sense of unrelenting attempts at diplomatic subterfuge by the adversaries.

36. Ezra 4:8–6:18, along with 7:12–26, is written in Aramaic rather than Hebrew. And while we know that Achaemenid Judah was a bilingual society (Nehemiah 8:8) and

Rehum the chancellor and Shimshai the secretary urge Artaxerxes to refer back to older scrolls from the days of his predecessors.[37] In those

---

that there were even some children in Judah who, to their leaders' chagrin, did not speak Hebrew at all (Neh. 13:24), that does not explain the unusual narratological choice of the author. Scholars discuss this curious feature at length. Some suggest that maintaining the original language in which the documents were composed gives them an air of authenticity, which, when it comes to written documents, as we will see in chapter eight, is a central concern of the author. Others assert that the language itself is a literary tool used to denote the point of view being expressed (Bill T. Arnold, "The use of Aramaic in the Hebrew Bible: Another Look at Bilingualism in Ezra and Daniel," *Journal of Northwest Semitic Languages* 22, no. 2 [1996]: 1–16). For an interesting theory on what the intentional use of Aramaic in late biblical and early Jewish texts might reveal about the complexities of Jewish identity in an era of foreign domination, see: J. Berman, "The Narratological Purpose of Aramaic Prose in Ezra 4.8–6.18," *Aramaic Studies* 5, no. 2 (2007): 165–91.

37. The seemingly "misplaced" documents that appear in Ezra 4 have been a source of confusion and debate. In the middle of recounting the challenges of Temple building in the days of Cyrus and Darius, the book jumps to letters from the days of Xerxes and Artaxerxes, who ruled after Darius and, more importantly, well after the Temple had been completed. The simplest explanation for the seemingly disordered material is that, while on the topic of "adversarial opposition," the author thought to include other times throughout the period in which opposition of the sort surfaced. So, he skipped ahead to later reigns and told of those events as well. Since the "adversaries" tried to undermine the wall-building project in the days of Artaxerxes, just as they had with the Temple-building project in the days of Cyrus and Darius, the author includes those events. Ezra 4:24, which scholars categorize as "repetitive resumption," functions to bring the reader back to where the narrator had been chronologically before his thematic tangent. See Joseph Blenkinsopp, *Ezra-Nehemiah: A Commentary* (Westminster John Knox, 1988), 111. Tamara Cohn Eskenazi likewise contends that the letter from the time of Artaxerxes is not misplaced. She asserts that in the period of Ezra-Nehemiah, the House of God (which Eskenazi distinguishes from the word *heikhal*, temple), extended beyond the Temple to include the city and its walls. As such, any discussion about opposition to building the House of God would necessarily include opposition to building the city's walls, which is why, according to Eskenazi, the letter from Artaxerxes's time was not only perfectly in place but was also a carefully situated rhetorical device that drove home the author's conception of the House of God. See Eskenazi, *In an Age of Prose*, 55–56. Sara Japhet sees the documents in Ezra-Nehemiah as a structuring device that bracket off the subunits of the larger narrative. In her understanding, the author used documents to tell the story of the period, and, as such, when an authentic document could not be found, rather than forging one, he would simply "borrow" a similarly themed document and insert it into the missing

scrolls, the adversaries claim, the king will find records of Jerusalem's long history of insurrection and understand the dangers inherent in their current building. So the king does so, and his reply, in which he confirms the adversaries' allegations, demands that the Judeans terminate the building project.[38] Of course, as soon as the adversaries read the king's response, they waste no time getting to Jerusalem and enforcing the new decree. So, as the chapter ends, we learn that work on the Temple is frozen until the second year of King Darius.

---

document's place. Obvious anachronisms, according to Japhet, were less important to the author than the ideological concepts he sought to convey. See Japhet, "History and Literature in the Persian Period," in *From the Rivers of Babylon*, 152–68. In a most intriguing of theories, Richard Steiner posits that the source of the four letters in Ezra 4–6 is in fact one report sent to Artaxerxes by Bishlam, Mithredath, and Tabeel after an archival search done at the king's behest. Like an excavated *tel*, Steiner explains, the newest information would have been most accessible, and as such the information is recorded in what appears as reverse chronological order. The author "flashes forward," according to Steiner, mentioning events from the days of Xerxes and Artaxerxes as they correspond to the quoted documents, and then brings the discussion back to Darius at the end. See Richard C. Steiner, "Bishlam's Archival Search Report in Nehemiah's Archive: Multiple Introductions and Reverse Chronological Order as Clues to the Origin of the Aramaic letters in Ezra 4–6," *Journal of Biblical Literature* 125, no. 4 (2006): 641–85. While each theory has its strengths, all of these scholars seem to agree that the documents that appear out of place were not accidentally left by an uninformed author or sloppy editor. Rather, because written documents were revered in the restoration period (see chapter eight), the author incorporated them creatively into his storytelling. For more on the chronological issue, see Mark J. Boda, "Flashforward: Future Glimpses in the Past of Ezra 1–6," in *Let Us Go Up to Zion* (Brill, 2012), 245–60.

38. The previous records that they were told to consult included Persian as well as Babylonian (and possibly even Assyrian) records, as the Persians saw themselves as the legitimate successors of the Babylonians. As such, in the course of their search, they would have found records of the rebellions of Judah's kings and Jerusalem's eventual capture and destruction by Nebuchadnezzar. ANET, 288, 563–64; see also Williamson, *Ezra-Nehemiah*, 63.

EZRA 5
THE JUDEANS SEND COUNTERCLAIMS

How and why the building project is restarted in the days of Darius
is accounted for in Ezra 5. The chapter begins by mentioning the prophetic activities of Haggai and Zechariah,[39] which presumably result in
Zerubbabel and Jeshua rebuilding the Temple in earnest.[40] Of course,
when Persian officials get wind of what is happening, they demand to
know the names of those responsible for the apparent flouting of the
building ban.[41]

In the letter that they then send to King Darius, Tattenai,[42] Shetar
Bozenai,[43] and their associates report the details of the building that
they witnessed in Jerusalem. But in that same letter, they also include
a quotation from the Judean builders themselves, defending the legitimacy of their actions.[44] Readers of Ezra-Nehemiah are already familiar
with the content that serves as the basis for the Judean defense, but the

---

39. The content of their prophecies can be found in the books called by their respective
names.
40. This image of the prophets encouraging and working in tandem with the priests
and political leaders of the period gives readers, familiar with the tensions and
corruption that marked the First Temple period, reason to believe things will be
different this time.
41. The text informs us that while the adversaries were waiting for their letter to reach
Darius and for the king to respond, God's providence ensured that in the interim
the Judeans did not stop building.
42. The governor of the Province Beyond the River. According to Persian documents,
a man by the name of Ushtani was the governor of Abar Nahara at the time. It is
possible then that Tattenai was a high official responsible to the satrap but is referred
to here as governor because he assumed the office later in the reign of Darius. See
Charles F. Fensham, *The Books of Ezra and Nehemiah* (William. B. Eerdmans, 1982),
79–80. It is also possible that the word "governor" (פחה) was flexible and that more
than one person could have held the title at once, which explains why Zerubbabel
was also called governor at the time. Williamson, *Ezra-Nehemiah*, 77.
43. Likely the secretary. Williamson, *Ezra-Nehemiah*, 77.
44. There is no reason to lump Tattenai and his associates together with the "adversaries." As Persian officials, it was their job to determine whether the activities of
locals within their province were conforming to Persian legislation. Furthermore,
the early years of Darius's reign were marked by upheaval, and, as such, it is not
surprising that even years later, internal affairs of the provinces were being carefully
monitored.

narrative seems to imply that neither Darius nor the Persian officials overseeing the province were kept abreast of developments. So the text cites the Judeans' account of how their previous Temple was destroyed by the Babylonians when their ancestors angered God.[45] It tells of their exile to Babylon and of Cyrus's liberating decree that directed them to return to their land and rebuild the Temple. The citation even recalls the details of Cyrus's handing over of the Temple vessels to Sheshbazzar and his directive that they be brought back and placed in the restored Temple, which is to be built on its original site.

The Judeans then explain that while Sheshbazzar laid the Temple's foundation as instructed,[46] they are unable to finish what he started because those overseeing the province are unaware of Cyrus's decree. Contrary to what their adversaries have written about them, the letter insinuates, their desire to build the Temple is a purely religious act driven by respect and loyalty to Persia's great first king.

After quoting the Judeans, the letter ends with a humble request by its authors that the king search the royal archives in Babylon to determine the validity of the Judean claim and guide the officials in how to proceed.

EZRA 6
COMPLETION AND DEDICATION OF
THE TEMPLE IN JERUSALEM

As per the appeal of his officials, Darius requisitions a search of the archives in Babylon, and eventually one scroll is found that corroborates the Judeans' story.[47] It substantiates their claim that in the first year of his reign, Cyrus issued an edict that the Temple in Jerusalem be rebuilt and even includes details of the building's dimensions and features. It

---

45. This seemingly minor point strategically focuses on their religious offenses against their God rather than their political offenses against Babylon when attributing a reason for the destruction. It serves as a response to the claims made about them in the Rehum letter (Ezra 4:15).

46. As mentioned above (note 8), this account conflicts with Ezra 3, which credits Zerubbabel with laying the foundation.

47. The document was not found in Babylon itself but in Ecbatana, the summer residence of some later Persian kings.

records that Cyrus assumes the cost of the building and instructs that the vessels from the First Temple are to be returned.[48]

So, with the new information at hand, Darius pens an edict of his own and sends it to Tattenai, Shetar Bozenai, their associates, and the surveyors of Abar Nahara. In that new edict, he warns his officials to keep their distance from the Judeans and to stop interfering in their building project. They are to let the Judean governor and their elders build their Temple on its original site and finance the cost of the building with the taxes collected in Abar Nahara. All that is needed for the Temple's functioning, Darius continues, is to be provided daily and promptly by the officials,[49] so that the Judeans can offer fragrant sacrifices to God and pray for the life of the king and his children.[50] The decree ends with a threat of impalement for anyone who deviates from the decree as well as the ruin of the offender's house.[51] And that threat extends to kings and nations who might dare to harm the House of God in Jerusalem.

---

48. The version of the edict that appears in Ezra 6 differs in several ways from that which is recorded in Ezra 1. In addition to the language of composition, the most obvious of the differences, it is also significant that the proclamation in Ezra 1 connects the Jewish return with the building of the Temple, whereas Ezra 6 is only concerned with the details of the Temple's construction. Ezra 1 makes no mention of financial support from the Persian treasury, whereas Ezra 6 makes no demands on the Jews who remained behind in Babylon. These and other minor discrepancies have led some scholars to speculate about the authenticity of the different versions. In all probability, the differences between the documents reflect their different functions. While the first one was directed at a large audience and likely announced as a herald or placed as a placard in public spaces, the second was placed in the royal archives as an official "memorandum." The differences in their functions account for the differences in their language, style, and even content. For more on this, see Bickerman, "Edict of Cyrus" and Japhet, "The Temple in the Restoration Period."

49. Those provisions included bulls, rams, and sheep for offerings, as well as wheat, salt, wine, oil, and whatever else the priests in Jerusalem might request.

50. It was common practice at the time to pray for the king and other high officials. Jeremiah told the Jewish exiles to pray for the place to which they were exiled (Jer. 29:7). There is evidence that Cyrus requested prayers for his welfare and that of his son. And when the Jews of Elephantine wrote to Bagohi, the Persian governor of Judah, they assured him that if their Temple were rebuilt, as per their request, they would always pray for him. Fensham, *The Books of Ezra and Nehemiah*, 90.

51. The threat spoke of impalement using the very beams of the offender's house that would be removed upon violation of the decree. Impalement in the ancient Near

Tattenai, Shetar Bozenai, and their associates have no choice but to follow Darius's edict in full. So, with the backing of Darius and the encouragement of their prophets Haggai and Zechariah, the Judeans continue building. And, at long last, on the thirteenth day of Adar in the sixth year of the reign of Darius, the Temple is completed.[52] The Judeans,[53] the priests and Levites, and all the returning exiles celebrate the Temple's dedication[54] with sacrifices and offerings of atonement.[55]

On the fourteenth day of the following month, the returnees bring the Passover sacrifice, and the priests, Levites, and returnees all celebrate the festival together.[56] Those who had separated themselves from the impurity of the nations of the land are included in the worship as well. For seven days, they all celebrate the festival of Passover together in joy. The chapter ends with a theological notation acknowledging God's role

---

East was reserved for the most severe crimes, including sedition and violation of treaty oaths. The Assyrian reliefs that depict Sennacherib's attack on Lachish, for example, show impaled Israelites (ANEP, no. 373). As such, the threat of impalement by a foreign king, this time as a measure of protection for Israelites, must have been especially meaningful for the Judeans to hear (see note 59 below).

52. The verse also mentions Cyrus and Artaxerxes. For a suggested explanation of the seemingly misplaced mention of Artaxerxes, see the theory of Eskenazi in note 37 above. It is also possible that Artaxerxes was listed along with the other Persian kings even though he ruled after the Temple was completed because, like them, he evinced the important theological notion mentioned in the verse, that God was working through benevolent Persian kings.

53. It is possible that the term "Israelites" rather than "Jews" or "returnees" is used to express the hopeful vision that the Temple will once again belong to all twelve tribes (Ezra 6:16).

54. The significance of the designation *benei hagola* for the community is discussed in chapter seven.

55. Moses's legal authority is invoked at this point, as it is in other instances throughout the work, creating a sense of continuity with the cultic rituals of earlier periods.

56. Focus on the celebration of Passover is not coincidental. The celebrations created a temporal bridge between the Israelites of the past and the present. Both had left a foreign land, purified themselves, and separated from the impurities of the land, dedicating themselves to the worship of God. Timothy Langille, "Reshaping the Persistent Past: A Study of Collective Trauma and Memory in Second Temple Judaism" (PhD diss., University of Toronto, 2014), 66–71.

in changing the heart of the king of Assyria, thus enabling the Judeans to build His house.[57]

EZRA 7
THE APPOINTMENT OF EZRA

Ezra appears on the scene for the first time in Ezra 7, during the reign of Artaxerxes.[58] When we are first introduced to Ezra, we are given his full pedigree, tracing his lineage back to Aaron the high priest.[59] But in addition to that pedigree, we are also told that he is a scribe[60] and an expert in the Torah of Moses and that, because the hand of God is upon him, the king granted him his every wish. [61]

---

57. As mentioned above, the Persian kings assumed various titles, including "king" of empires they believed to have succeeded (see above note 1). Joseph Fleishman suggests that the specific use of the term "King of Assyria" is a metonymic expression meant to evoke thoughts of the first wave of Israelite exile in the eighth century BCE at the hands of the Assyrians. The comprehensiveness of the Assyrian and Babylonian exiles is expressed in statements such as that of Jeremiah 50:17: "A scattered sheep is Israel; lions have driven it away. The king of Assyria was the first to devour it, and now this last one, Nebuchadnezzar, king of Babylon, has gnawed its bones." Remembering the inception of the prolonged series of exiles at the Temple's dedication helped to drive home the sense of the event as the realization of the long-awaited redemption. See, for example, Nehemiah 9:32. Joseph Fleishman, "An Echo of Optimism in Ezra 6: 19–22," *Hebrew Union College Annual* (1998): 15–29.

58. The chapter begins with the words "after these events," creating the sense of a fluid transition from Ezra 6. In reality, there was a gap of over fifty years between the end of Ezra 6 and the beginning of Ezra 7 (515–458 BCE). But in the author's mind, Ezra's journey represented the next momentous step in the restoration, and as such, a line of continuity was drawn between the two.

59. Seraiah, who is listed as Ezra's father, could not have been his father, as Seraiah was killed by Nebuchadnezzar at Riblah in 587/6 BCE (II Kings 25:18; Jer. 52:24). Alternative genealogies are listed (I Chr. 5:27–41), but this telescoping of generations is not uncommon in Tanakh.

60. In pre-exilic times, the priests were the guardians and teachers of the law. As religion evolved in the Second Temple period, the role of scribes as students and teachers grew in prominence. Ezra was the link between these two phases in history. This important transition is discussed at length in chapter eight.

61. By linking Ezra's Aaronite lineage with his knowledge of the law of Moses, the author is ensuring we know that not only is his pedigree impeccable but also that Ezra's priestly family, despite being in Babylon for six or seven generations, retained

We then learn of the second wave of returnees who head toward Israel with Ezra in the seventh year of Artaxerxes's reign.[62] They leave on the first day of the first month, we are told, and arrive in Jerusalem four months later.[63] The swiftness with which they make their journey, the text tells us, is attributed to the divine providence granted to Ezra on account of his intent to spread God's Torah to Israel.[64]

In Ezra 7, a royal edict once again plays a central role in the narrative. This time, though, Ezra is bearing the edict sent by King Artaxerxes. In it, the king grants his permission to anyone from the nation of Israel within the Persian kingdom who wants to go to Jerusalem. The edict also charges Ezra, to whom it refers as an authority on God's law, with supervising Judah and Jerusalem in accordance with that law of God.[65] He is to transport the silver and gold, as well as capital acquired in Babylon and funds donated by the people and their priests, back to the Temple. Ezra is to use that money to buy items to offer to God on the altar in Jerusalem. And whatever silver and gold remain after Ezra purchases the necessary offerings is to be used as Ezra and his brothers see fit, according to the will of God. Ezra is given vessels for the Temple, which he is to transport, and he is assured that anything else needed for the Temple can be charged to the king's coffers.

The edict further proclaims that all treasurers in Abar Nahara are to grant Ezra's every request, within measure,[66] and that they are to meet

---

their priestly training and scribal expertise. As such, Ezra was perfectly qualified for the leadership with which he was endowed. Gary Knoppers, "Exile, Return and Diaspora. Expatriates and Repatriates in Late Biblical literature," in *Texts, Contexts and Readings in Postexilic Literature* (2011), 29–61.

62. The group included priests, Levites, singers, gatekeepers, and Netinim.

63. As mentioned in the previous chapter, the fact that they began their journey in the first month, just like their ancestors who left Egypt, is significant. In a similar vein, as Solomon's Temple was destroyed in the fifth month (II Kings 25), their return in that month marks the beginning of a new era.

64. The distance from Babylon to Jerusalem is only five hundred miles, but it has been suggested that due to the revolts that broke out in Egypt at the time, a direct route through the desert was less safe than through Syria, which is probably how they traveled. Fensham, *The Books of Ezra and Nehemiah*, 100.

65. The impetus behind this decree of Artaxerxes is explained in chapter eight.

66. There was a cap on the requests, which were recorded as up to the sum of one

those requests thoroughly and efficiently, lest God's anger lash out at the realm of the king and his sons. Temple officials in Jerusalem are exempted from taxes,[67] and Ezra is to use his wisdom to appoint judges and magistrates to help dispense justice and educate the people who do not know God's laws.

Much like Darius's edict, the edict in this chapter concludes with the threat of severe punishment for violators. Also like the previous chapter, Ezra 7 ends with an acknowledgment of God's influence on the benevolent decisions of the foreign king. This time, though, it is not the narrator who acknowledges God's intervention but Ezra himself. The end of chapter 7 is the beginning of a new genre of writing within Ezra-Nehemiah known as the "memoirs" of Ezra-Nehemiah. In the memoirs sections, the leader narrates the events of his day through his own recollections and reflections.[68]

EZRA 8
EZRA'S JOURNEY TOWARD THE LAND

Ezra opens chapter 8 by listing the names of the men and their families who go up with him from Babylon[69] and then describes the events that

---

hundred *kikar* of silver, one hundred *kor* of wheat, one hundred *bat* of wine, and one hundred *bat* of oil. Salt was unlimited. For an understanding of the Persian economic system and the modern-day equivalences of these measurements, see Briant, *From Cyrus to Alexander*, 388–471.

67. The specific taxes from which they were exempt included tributes, head taxes, and property taxes. As mentioned above, at the time of Ezra's mission, Egypt was in revolt. The Persian army that was sent to quell the revolt had been defeated and the satrap of Egypt had been killed. The possibility that the Egypt and Syro-Palestinian area of the empire might be lost to Persia was a real possibility, and thus the cooperation of the local deities was considered of critical importance to the king. Documents from this period demonstrate that one of the ways he tried to secure that cooperation was through exempting cultic personnel in those areas from taxation (Blenkinsopp, *Ezra-Nehemiah*, 150). Of course, within our chapter, such measures are grouped with the other benevolent acts of the king and attributed to God's intervention.

68. These portions have a different tone and ostensibly different perspective than the third-person narrator of the other sections.

69. Some suggest that the twelve families recorded serve to evoke the twelve tribes

punctuate their journey. He begins by telling of his assembly of fellow travelers by the Ahava River and how he notices during their three-day encampment that Israelites and priests are present but that no Levites are to be found. So he tasks the leaders and teachers present with requesting from Ido and his brother Netinim from Casiphia that they send Levites to serve in the Temple.[70] Ezra lists the names of the people who are sent, but before doing so, he clarifies that these specific people are sent because God's hand is upon Ezra and the travelers, implying his satisfaction with the people and the belief that God wants their mission to succeed.

After the arrival of the Levites, Ezra proclaims a fast as a form of supplication for a smooth journey.[71] Ezra explains that he had been ashamed to ask the king for a royal escort to protect the travelers since they had earlier told the king that God protects those who seek His favor.[72] But, seemingly apprehensive in the moment, Ezra and his co-travelers fast and pray to God, and God grants their request.

Ezra then sets aside twelve leading priests, in addition to two men named Sherebiah and Hashabiah and their ten kinsmen. He weighs the silver, gold, vessels, and all the donations received for the Temple[73]

---

that left Egypt and headed toward the Promised Land.

70. Scholars assume that Casiphia was a place with a major population of Jews. Some suggest that there was a training school of sorts there for Temple officials; others suggest that the word "place" (*makom*) as a descriptor implies that perhaps some sort of sanctuary stood there. (The word in Tanakh is used to refer to temples; cf. Deut. 12:5; I Kings 8:29; Jer. 7:3–7; Ezra 9:8). Fensham, *The Books of Ezra and Nehemiah*, 114.

71. It is possible that the words *derekh yeshara*, literally translated "straight path," that Ezra used, meant to recall Isaiah's vision about the return from exile: "Clear the Lord's way in the desert: smooth across the arid plain a road for our God" (40:3), reinforcing the idea that Ezra's return was a fulfillment of earlier prophecies. Psalms 107:7 also uses a similar phrase referring to the Exodus, once again generating a sense of parallels between this and the nation's past redemptive experiences.

72. Ezra's concern for God's reputation in exile puts him in good company with both Joseph and Daniel; see Genesis 41:15–16; Daniel 1–3, 5–6. John Kessler, "Images of Exile: Representations of the 'Exile' and 'Empty Land' in the Sixth to Fourth Century BCE Yehudite Literature," in *The Concept of Exile in Ancient Israel and Its Historical Contexts* (de Gruyter, 2010), 336.

73. Extant archival material from Nippur in Babylon dating to the second half of the

and then explains to the appointees that they, like the vessels and the precious metals, are consecrated.[74] As such, Ezra tells them, they are chosen to safeguard the wealth until it can be weighed publicly in front of the leaders, priests, Levites, and heads of the households in Jerusalem. The appointees agree and take it upon themselves to transport the entire amount to the Temple.

The travelers move on from the Ahava River on the twelfth day of the first month, and all along the way, Ezra records, God protects them from attacks and roadside ambushes. Upon arriving in Jerusalem and after resting for three days, they go up to the Temple in Jerusalem where they turn the valuables over to the priests and Levites to be weighed and put on record. Those who return present burnt offerings to God and deliver the king's orders to the satraps and governors of Abar Nahara, whom, we are told, hold the people and the House of God in great esteem.

EZRA 9
THE MIXED MARRIAGE CRISIS

After everything has been delivered to the appropriate people and locations,[75] the leaders of the people approach Ezra, bemoaning the fact that the Judeans had failed to separate from the peoples of the land. Even the priests and Levites, they tell him, are engaged in the abominations of foreigners.[76] According to the leaders, the Judeans are taking foreign

---

fifth century BCE gives insight into the financial affairs of a particularly wealthy Jewish family named the Murashu family. The archives help reinforce the sense alluded to in these chapters, that there were Jews in Babylon with the means to assist Ezra in his mission. Kuhrt, *The Persian Empire*, 12.

74. Removed from the mundane sphere and set aside for use in the Temple.

75. According to Ezra 10:9, these events took place in the ninth month. It is unlikely that four months after his arrival Ezra was unaware of the problem of mixed marriages. Whether he knew or not, though, is less significant than the fact that the people, not the singular leader, were the ones to initiate the religious revolution. For more on this shift in power dynamics highlighted in the work, see chapter six.

76. Many of the nations mentioned by the people no longer existed. Nevertheless, the anachronistic reference to Israel's traditional enemies is relevant for the point the

daughters as wives for themselves and their sons, and in doing so, they are mixing the "holy seed" with the people of the land.[77]

When Ezra hears the news, he tears his garments and rips out the hairs on his head and beard. Like the prophets of old, he then sits dumbfounded until the afternoon. Those who fear God slowly begin to gather around him until, at the time of the evening offering, Ezra rises from his fast in his torn garment and spreads out his hands to God in prayer.

In that prayer, Ezra declares his utter mortification at the degree of guilt the people had accrued through their relentless sinning. He recalls their ongoing sins since the days of their ancestors, and how, because of those sins, they, their priests, and their kings had been handed over to foreign rulers, the sword, captivity, pillage, and abject shame from which they continue to suffer. For a moment, Ezra emphasizes, God granted them a pardon, allowing a remnant to return and take a stake in His holy place. Ezra speaks of how God rekindled the light in their eyes by allowing them to sustain themselves in their bondage. They are "slaves,"[78] Ezra declares, but, nonetheless, God allowed them to exalt His House and build a wall in Judah and Jerusalem.

---

leaders were trying to make. For more on this, the use of the terms "holy seed" and "unfaithfulness," as well as the identity of the people under discussion, see chapter seven.

77. This topic is one of the primary points of contention within the work. For a full discussion of its import, see chapter seven.

78. The word "slave" (עֶבֶד) has been a source of confusion for many, as it seems incongruous with the attitude regarding the Persian rulers and their empire that pervades the rest of the work. On the whole, Ezra-Nehemiah indicates a relationship marked by the benevolence of foreign kings and the freedom of movement and religion they granted the Jews, which is why the reference to the Judeans as "slaves" of the Persian Empire in Ezra's prayer is surprising. But Manfred Oeming points out that in the Persian Empire, the word (from the Persian expression *bandaka*) carried the specific connotation of a title of honor for vassals who maintained orderly, positive relations with the king. As such, Ezra was not claiming that in this era in which God gave them a second chance they were slaves, but rather, "well-regarded allies of the Persian Empire." See Manfred Oeming, "See, We Are Serving Today" (Nehemiah 9: 36): Nehemiah 9 as a Rheological Interpretation of the Persian Period," in *Judah and the Judeans in the Persian Period* (2006), 571–88. Along similar lines, Oded Lipschits points out that the word belongs primarily in the context of royal court and that, rather than referring to a specific position, it

In his prayer, Ezra goes on to pose a rhetorical question. After all their ancestors had done, he wants to know, forsaking the warnings of God's prophets, what can the people now possibly be thinking? Before God brought them to the land, Ezra recalls, God warned them not to become impure from the abominations of the people who lived there. They were warned not to intermarry or seek the residents' peace or welfare. Only if they lived without polluting influences, God told them, could they hope to partake of the best of the land and bequeath it to their children. When they violate those commandments, Ezra goes on, God, in His mercy, punishes them far less than they deserve, which is why a remnant of them endures.[79] But if they repeat those same mistakes, God will rage against them, this time not leaving a remnant or trace. His prayer ends with a request that God deal with them righteously despite their unworthy status.

EZRA 10:
COMMUNAL REPENTANCE

Ezra continues to confess the sins of the people, kneeling in front of the Temple and weeping aloud, and as he does, large crowds of men, women, and children gather around him. A man by the name of Shecaniah speaks up on behalf of the people. He acknowledges the unfaithfulness Ezra is lamenting but ventures that there is still hope for the community. They could make a binding agreement with God, he proposes, agreeing to send away all the women and offspring from the mixed marriages. He encourages Ezra to rise up and take care of the matter while assuring him that the leaders will stand with him and back up any decisive actions he takes.

---

indicates a special closeness between certain individuals and the king. He compares the term to the phrase "servant of God" found throughout Tanakh to indicate an individual who is closely connected to God. Thus, rather than lamenting their slave status, the phrase comments on how, in God's kindness, He saved a remnant and put them in good standing with the Persian government. As such, the sentence is perfectly compatible with the outlook of the work. See Lipschits, "On the Titles *Abad Hamalak* and *Abad*," *Shnaton* 13 (2002): 157–71 [Hebrew].

79. This is an important theological assertion that is developed in chapter nine.

So, Ezra arises and makes the leaders of the priests, the Levites, and all of Israel take an oath that they will act upon this new idea. He leaves his place in front of the Temple and goes out to the chamber of Yohanan the son of Eliashib,[80] all the while still fasting and mourning the unfaithfulness of the returnees. A proclamation goes out to all of Judah and Jerusalem calling on the returnees to assemble in Jerusalem. Anyone who fails to come within three days as prescribed by the leaders and elders, they warn, will have his property confiscated and be shunned from the community of exiles.[81]

Within three days, as the leaders demand, Judah and Benjamin assemble in Jerusalem. And on the twentieth day of the ninth month, they gather in front of the Temple, trembling.[82] Ezra addresses the people, reminding them of the dangers of their transgressions and enjoining them to make amends by separating from the peoples of the land and the foreign women.[83] The assembly agrees but qualifies that, due to the rains, the size of the community, and the extent of the sinning, the initiative will take more than a few days to complete. They suggest that in the meantime the leaders stand in as the representatives of the community, and that, at appointed times, people come to undo their sins[84] until God is no longer angry with them. The chapter lists, almost as an aside, that there are those who object to the initiative, and it names each objector.[85]

---

80. Numerous options regarding the identity of Yohanan and his relevance at this juncture in the story have been suggested. In general, due to the frequency with which names occurred in the Persian period, caution should be exercised when linking two people with the same name. For a full range of the options, see Williamson, *Ezra-Nehemiah*, 151–54.

81. The lay leaders, rather than Ezra, were leading the charge. Also noteworthy in this chapter is the fact that as the people increasingly step in to lead, Ezra begins to recede into the background. This idea is part of a larger theme in Ezra-Nehemiah discussed in chapter six.

82. Both, the text tells us, because of the rains and because of what was happening.

83. The seemingly draconian measures that appear to go further than what biblical law demands are explained in chapter seven.

84. Literally speaking, this meant absolving the illegitimate marriages.

85. But it is not entirely clear from the text whether they were opposed to the divorce

On the first day of the tenth month, Ezra and the heads of families convene to identify the guilty parties within the community, and by the first day of the first month, the investigation is complete.[86] The chapter concludes with a detailed list of those who married foreign women. It lists the guilty priests[87] along with the sacrifices they pledge to give as part of the repentance process, and then moves on to other groups within the community, culminating with the guilty laypeople. The conclusion of the chapter leaves the reader with the sense that the issue had been dealt with sufficiently, but as we will see, that is not the case.

NEHEMIAH 1
NEHEMIAH'S PRAYER

We meet Nehemiah for the first time in Nehemiah 1. Just as Ezra narrates portions of his story, so too does Nehemiah, and Nehemiah 1 comprises the first portion of his memoirs.[88] The bulk of the chapter contains the prayer Nehemiah utters after learning of the plight of the Judean returnees.[89] According to his account, while in Susa in the twentieth year of Artaxerxes's reign,[90] Nehemiah inquires of a man named Hanani[91] and

---

of the foreign wives or the seemingly lenient compromise to which Ezra agreed. Still, the inclusion of opposing voices within the work is an important feature of Ezra-Nehemiah and carries didactic significance (see chapter eight).

86. This is the same date on which Ezra began his journey (Ezra 7:8–9), bringing a sense of closure at this juncture.

87. Jeshua's descendants are listed first, giving readers a vivid sense of the pervasiveness of the problem.

88. For an analysis of the literary significance of the memoirs within the work, see, David J. A. Clines, "The Nehemiah Memoir: The Perils of Autobiography," in *What Does Eve Do to Help? And Other Readerly Questions to the Old Testament* (1990), 124–64.

89. Nehemiah refers to them as "escaped remnant" (*peleita*), a term used elsewhere in Ezra-Nehemiah (Ezra 9:8, 13–15) and Chronicles (I Chr. 4:43; II Chr. 12:7, 20:24, 30:6). The term, while seemingly referring to the returnees, encompasses theological inferences derived from the earlier prophets, which are an important component of the narrative. For more on this, see chapter seven.

90. The text only says "the twentieth year," but the words likely refer to the twentieth year of Artaxerxes's reign (465–424 BCE). Cf. Nehemiah 2:1 and 5:14.

91. Hanani is introduced as Nehemiah's brother, which is certainly possible. But

a few others about the state of the people in Jerusalem. The men inform him of the degraded state and dire stress of the people and explain that Jerusalem's wall has been breached in numerous places and her gates have been burned.[92] Upon hearing the dismal report, Nehemiah tells us, he sits down and weeps, mourning for days, fasting, and praying.

His prayer, which begins by praising God,[93] acknowledges that along with the Israelites, he and his father's house have sinned, flouting the commandments, statutes, and laws that God gave through Moses.[94] But Nehemiah asks, specifically for that reason, that God remember the promise He made to Moses. In that promise, God predicted that the people would break their faith and that He would disperse them among the nations. But it also predicted that they would return to Him. And when they do, Nehemiah reminds God, He promised to gather them in from the farthest horizons, bringing them back to the place where He chose to house His name. Nehemiah ends his prayer by reminding God of His unique relationship with Israel and asking, on a personal level, that God grant him the mercy of the king so that he can be successful. At the very end of the section, we are told that Nehemiah is the official cupbearer to the king, a detail that becomes relevant in the coming chapter.[95]

"brother" can also be used to refer to kinsmen.

92. It is not clear whether the wall had been burned recently or it had been in that condition since the days of Nebuchadnezzar. Regardless, as is discussed in chapter seven, the wall around Jerusalem becomes an important metaphor within the work. Its dilapidated state was problematic, requiring a leader like Nehemiah to set things right.

93. The close link between the notion of covenant and God's love for His people tells us a lot about the theology of Ezra-Nehemiah. For more on this, see chapter nine.

94. This deep sense of the need to acknowledge past sins before restitution can happen is an important feature of Second Temple prayers. See Mark J. Boda, "Confession as Theological Expression: Ideological Origins of Penitential Prayer," in *Seeking the Favor of God*, vol. 1 (2006), 21–50.

95. The royal cupbearer constituted a high-ranking position in the palace and would have been an important point of access to the king. See Williamson, *Ezra-Nehemiah*, 174.

NEHEMIAH 2
NEHEMIAH'S JOURNEY

Nehemiah 2 begins with Nehemiah's recollection of the events that led to his move from Susa to Jerusalem. He recounts that while serving wine to King Artaxerxes in the twentieth year of his reign,[96] the king notices that Nehemiah's face looks downcast and inquires about his mood. Nehemiah explains that the city that houses his ancestral tombs is in ruins, and her gates are burned.[97] Therefore, when the king asks Nehemiah what he wants, Nehemiah tells the king of his wish to return to Judah to rebuild.[98] The king is pleased to send Nehemiah, but only after they agree on a date of return.

Concerned about the potential resistance he might encounter along the way, Nehemiah requests missives to present to the governors of Abar Nahara to ensure his passage, as well as one for Asaf the royal forester to ensure he receives the timber for the needed repairs.[99] The king provides Nehemiah with the requested letters, along with army captains and a cavalry.[100] As an aside, we find out that Sanballat the Horonite and Tobiah the Amonite, having learned of Nehemiah's arrival, are not happy.[101]

---

96. Nehemiah did not speak with the king immediately. He waited more than three months, perhaps indicating the precarious nature of the request. It is also possible that he simply waited for an opportune time, such as during the festivities described.
97. Respect for ancestral tombs was ubiquitous in the ancient Near East. But it is worth noting that Nehemiah kept his request personal, never mentioning Jerusalem by name.
98. In the text, Nehemiah first utters a quick prayer to God before voicing his request.
99. The repairs Nehemiah anticipated included the roof of the gates of the citadel house, the city wall, and the house he would inhabit.
100. Some see this point of contrast with Ezra indicating their different leadership styles. See, for example, Eskenazi, *In an Age of Prose,* 136–54.
101. Sanballat is Nehemiah's main nemesis in the narrative. His Babylonian name, which means "Sin the moon god gives life" (*Sin-uballit*), does not tell us very much about his origins, status, or faith, as many Jews at that time adopted foreign names. We know from the Elephantine papyri that he gave his sons names with Jewish theophoric elements (Delaiah and Shelemiah), which would indicate that he saw himself as an adherent of the Israelite religion. According to the papyri, he was the governor of Samaria in 408 BCE, but the records seem to indicate that by that year he was already quite elderly, and his sons were acting in his place. While it is possible that he was already governor by 445 BCE (the dialogue between him and

Nehemiah arrives in Jerusalem and is there for three days before arising at night, with a few others, to inspect the walls. Nehemiah keeps a low profile, bringing only the one animal he rides, and he does not tell anyone his plans.[102] He exits through the valley gate and sees that the walls everywhere were breached and that the gates were consumed by fire. When he arrives at the Spring Gate and the King's pool, there is not even room for his animal to pass, so he turns to the streambed to continue the survey and then reenters the city through the Valley Gate.

The officials have no idea where Nehemiah is or what he is doing, and he does not reveal his intentions to the priests, the nobles, officials, or even those who join him on the inspection. Only once he is ready does Nehemiah propose to those around him that they rebuild Jerusalem's walls. He tells them of how God's hand favored him and what the king said to him. Once convinced, the people agree to rise and rebuild.

Sanballat, Tobiah, and the newly introduced Geshem the Arab[103] mock and deride the builders, accusing them of rebelling against the king.

Nehemiah points to such a dynamic), Nehemiah never graces him with the title. Instead, Nehemiah consistently refers to him as the "Horonite," the etymology of which is disputed among scholars. What is relevant for us, and will be addressed in chapter seven, is the fact that regardless of how Sanballat identified, Nehemiah considered him an outsider. It is possible that Tobiah, who is often linked with the influential Tobiad family from later-Second Temple times, was the governor of Ammon, although some reject the idea that the province of Ammon would have had such close ties with Jerusalem. Nehemiah, though, calls him "servant" on more than one occasion which, as we saw (note 78), can mean "important official," but in this case was probably used derogatively. For a translation of the relevant papyri, see Bezalel Porten and Ada Yardeni, eds. *Textbook of Aramaic Documents from Ancient Egypt: Ostraca and Assorted Inscriptions*, vol. 4, no. 1. (Hebrew University, Department of the History of the Jewish People, 1999), 53, 69–76. For more suggestions as to the identity and origins of these men, see, Williamson, *Ezra-Nehemiah*, 168, 182–84; Blenkinsopp, *Ezra-Nehemiah*, 216–19.

102. Aware of the political climate, it is very possible Nehemiah did not want to stir up trouble until he had a better idea of the details he was to contend with.

103. The third opponent named in this chapter seems, from extant extrabiblical evidence, to have been a powerful monarch in the region. His name appears on a silver vessel from Lower Egypt, and there is another possible reference to him in a Lihyan (Dedan) inscription. While it is not entirely clear why he would have been hostile to Nehemiah, his sphere of influence would have posed a threat to Judah. Willamson, *Ezra-Nehemiah*, 192; Blenkinsopp, *Ezra-Nehemiah*, 225–26.

Nehemiah, undeterred, responds that God is the One who will grant them success. And as for Sanballat, Tobiah, and Geshem, Nehemiah points out, Jerusalem holds neither a share nor a memory for them.[104]

NEHEMIAH 3
REBUILDING JERUSALEM'S WALLS

In Nehemiah 3, Nehemiah lists the various individuals and groups of people who are involved in the wall-building process,[105] describing each section and component of the wall and giving credit where it is due.[106] But the industriousness that marks the bulk of the chapter is interrupted by Sanballat who, we are told, becomes furious when he hears about the project.[107] He mocks the Judeans in front of his kinsmen and the Samaritan forces,[108] asking whether the Judeans truly believe they are going to rebuild what had been destroyed. His jeers include vivid depictions of rubble and burned stones, and he contends that the Jews are being overly optimistic in assuming their venture will be successful. Tobiah chimes in as well, adding that even if the Jews finish the wall, it will be so flimsy that a climbing jackal could easily break through.

Their taunts, likely heard secondhand, inspire Nehemiah to pray to God once again. This time, he speaks of the shame the people experience

---

104. The antagonism between Nehemiah and these men is addressed in chapter seven. But what becomes evident from Nehemiah's memoirs is that by the fifth century BCE, Judah was surrounded by what he describes as hostile forces.

105. This is in keeping with the tendency already noted in Ezra-Nehemiah (and discussed more fully in chapter six) to focus on the laypeople and their collective efforts in bringing about the restoration.

106. He also mentions people such as the chieftains of the Tekoites, who did not submit to the work. It is not entirely clear why this group is singled out or why they resisted. It is possible that being so proximal and vulnerable to attack by Geshem, they were scared to join. It is also possible that they were simply resentful of Nehemiah's leadership. Either way, it is important to note that Nehemiah does not present an idealized portrait of a unified community; rather, he includes those details that reveal extant frictions.

107. The impression created in Nehemiah is that every time the community advanced toward its goal, their opponents set them back. See, for example, 2:10, 19; 4:1.

108. This suggests the possibility that Sanballat was in the early phases of planning an armed attack.

and asks God to throw their opponents' derision back on them and to punish them appropriately for their crimes.

The final verse of the chapter informs us that the wall is completed in length and built up to half its height by the people who, Nehemiah makes sure to add, act with a willing heart.[109] The more than forty sections of wall are rebuilt and repaired, supporting Nehemiah's evaluation. Likewise, the unity of purpose displayed by the builders reflects the organizational leadership of Nehemiah as well as the people's dedication to the project.

NEHEMIAH 4
WATCHING AND PRAYING OVER
THE WALL OF JERUSALEM

If Nehemiah 3 ends on the hopeful note that the wall is about to be rebuilt, Nehemiah 4 begins, not surprisingly, with pushback from Judah's opponents.[110] Nehemiah recalls how, when Sanballat, Tobiah, the Arabs, Ammonites, and Ashdodites hear that the wall project is succeeding, they become incensed and join forces to wage war upon Jerusalem and cause confusion.[111] Thereafter, the Judeans pray to God and set up a watch over the wall day and night.[112]

---

109. For a modern archaeological survey of what is believed by some to be Nehemiah's wall, see Eilat Mazar, "The Wall That Nehemiah Built," *Biblical Archaeology Review* 35, no. 2 (2009).

110. The impression created in this opening verse of the chapter is that the opposition was coming from all sides, with Sanballat in the north (Samaria), Geshem in the south, Tobiah in the east, and the Ashdodites in the west. (Geshem is not mentioned by name in that verse, but the Arabians are).

111. The word used to describe the restoration of the wall draws on the metaphor of a healing wound. It is an idiom used in other places (cf. Is. 58:8; Jer. 8:22, 30:17, 33:6; II Chr. 24:13) but particularly in this context it may reveal something about Nehemiah's view on the completed wall as essential for the Judeans' social and religious "health." For more on the metaphorical significance of the wall, see chapter seven.

112. Verse 4 has been understood by some as a poem that might have been chanted by the workers, a theme song of sorts, reflecting their dual feelings of inadequacy and hope. See Jacob M. Myers, "Ezra, Nehemiah: Introduction, Translation, and Notes," in *The Anchor Bible* (1965), 126.

The enemies, we learn, are plotting an impending attack. But the Jews who live among the enemies inform Nehemiah. So Nehemiah implements highly organized defense protocols, dispatching people according to their families to the vulnerable spaces in the wall. After doing so, he reassures the Judeans that with God on their side they have nothing to fear. The narrator corroborates Nehemiah's theological claim by informing us that the enemies' plots are foiled.[113]

Then, once war is no longer an imminent threat, the Judeans go back to their building efforts. But from that point on, half of them go to work on the construction project, while the other half remain armed and on guard. The scene Nehemiah depicts is one in which the people work with building utensils in one hand and weapons in the other. Nehemiah appoints a horn blower to stand next to him, and the people, who are scattered widely across the expanse of the wall, know that if the horn sounds, they are to gather at the spot from which the sound emanates. They also know, according to Nehemiah, that God will fight for them.[114] Nehemiah appoints a night guard as well, and he concludes the chapter by informing us that neither he nor his brothers nor the watchmen following him ever undress or let their guard down. Rather, as the situation demands, they remain constantly vigilant.

---

113. The expression used for God's frustrating of the enemies' plans is also used in Ezra 4:5 to describe the frustration of the Judeans' plans to rebuild the Temple. This phrase-borrowing points to the larger theological thrust of the chapter, which highlights God's role in the failures and successes of human endeavors.

114. In earlier times, the blowing of trumpets was a call to war (see Num. 10:9; Judges 3:27, 6:34, 7:18; I Sam. 13:3). Perhaps most famously, the Israelites blew trumpets prior to their invasion of Jericho. Joshua 6 tells us that when the Israelite trumpets were sounded, the walls of the otherwise impenetrable city collapsed. That story, which marks the beginning of the Israelite conquest of the land, would have resonated powerfully in Nehemiah's time when the Judeans once again felt vulnerable and outnumbered, and it is possible that he was evoking that earlier miracle. The theology that lay behind the story of Jericho is further emphasized by Nehemiah in his claim that God will fight for them. This characteristically biblical claim (see Ex. 14:14; Deut. 1:30, 3:22, 20:4; Josh. 10:14, 42, 23:10) points to an important theological principle that Nehemiah saw fit to evoke (cf. Ps. 127:1).

NEHEMIAH 5
ECONOMIC AND SOCIAL INSTABILITY

In Nehemiah 5, we learn of another problem that Nehemiah has to contend with. But this time, rather than being external and political, the problem is internal and economic.[115] The chapter begins with the outcry of some in Judah against their brethren, complaining that they have many children but such limited funds that they are forced to mortgage their fields and vineyards just to buy enough grain to stave off starvation.[116] Some claim to have had no choice but to borrow against their property to pay the king's levy,[117] while others admit to selling their own children into servitude.[118] Amid the list of desperate measures they take to survive, the complainers ask why they are any different from their brethren, alluding to the vast gap in wealth between the upper and lower strata of society.[119]

An appalled Nehemiah scolds the nobles and officials for the exorbitant payments they extracted from the people. He points out the self-contradictory nature of their behavior, noting that they were careful to buy back their brothers who were sold to other nations but have no problem causing those in the land to sell their own children. [120] The

---

115. Many of the problems enumerated in this chapter are referred to in Zechariah 8:10 and Malachi 3:5–15.

116. Extant evidence from Upper Egypt indicates that loans of grain during this time carried heavy interest rates and severe penalties for nonpayment (Bezalel Porten, "Archives from Elephantine," [1968], 78–79).

117. According to the Greek historian Herodotus, the burden of land taxation increased significantly from the days of Xerxes, making it almost impossible for subsistence farmers to meet their tax obligations. That reality led to a situation in which many were driven into the hands of middlemen or wealthy landowners. A majority of those who owed money ultimately defaulted and had their land expropriated, leading to the social unrest evident in this chapter (Blenkinsopp, *Ezra-Nehemiah*, 257).

118. The practice of debt slavery existed in earlier periods in Israel (see, for example, II Kings 4:1–2). However, biblical law prescribed a maximum of seven years of servitude (see Ex. 21:2–11; Deut. 15:12–18).

119. Their complaint is about the lack of "brotherhood" within the community. Not coincidentally, the laws found in Leviticus 25, which address the minimal rights of the very poor in Israel, repeatedly use the word "brother."

120. The practice of redeeming those sold to non-Israelites to which Nehemiah refers

nobles and officials are unable to reply, and Nehemiah then orders them to end the extractions. The people's fields, vineyards, olive groves, and homes are to be returned to them, and the money, grain, wine, and olive oil debts are all to be canceled.

The leaders agree to all of Nehemiah's demands, and the priests swear to act in accordance as well. In a symbolic act reminiscent of classical prophets, Nehemiah shakes out the pockets of his garment and declares that God should shake out from their homes those who do not comply, leaving those homes empty. The entire congregation says "Amen," praising God, and the people, we are told, abide by his policies.

Nehemiah points out that, in contrast to the governors who preceded him and took bread, wine, and money from the people, burdening them heavily, neither he nor his kinsmen ever partake of the governor's food for tribute.[121] He attributes his generous approach to his reverence for God and goes on to tell us that he and his kinsmen support the work on the wall and contribute to the enterprise without ever acquiring others' fields. Nehemiah ends the chapter with his request that God remember all the good he does for the people.[122]

---

is mentioned in Leviticus 25:47–48.

121. This was true, according to Nehemiah, for all twelve years of his governorship and despite the fact that, as he mentions, he had over 150 people eating at his table.

122. This portion of Nehemiah's memoir is stylistically similar to a late Egyptian inscription from the early years of Darius I. The similarities point to Nehemiah's knowledge and use of Persian conventions in his memoirs: "I was a good man in my city, rescuing my people from the very great turmoil which happened throughout the entire land, the like of which had never happened in this land. I protected the weak against the powerful; I rescued the timid person when it was his turn to suffer; I did for them whatever was to their advantage when the time came to act on their behalf.... O great gods who are in Sais! Remember all the useful things accomplished by the chief physician Udjahorresnet! May you do for him whatever is useful and make his name endure in this land forever!" (Briant, *From Cyrus to Alexaner*, 56–57; Blenkinsopp, *Ezra-Nehemiah*, 262).

NEHEMIAH 6
ATTEMPTED ATTACKS ON NEHEMIAH

When the wall is complete and only its doors are left to be erected, Sanballat and Geshem send a letter to Nehemiah requesting they convene in Kephirim in the valley of Ono.[123] Nehemiah, intuiting foul play, sends a letter back with messengers claiming that he is engaged in a large project and too busy to meet them. They attempt to get him to show up four separate times, and each time, Nehemiah tells us, he refuses. The fifth time, Sanballat sends a man with an open missive in his hand for Nehemiah to read. The missive states that there are rumors, confirmed by Gashmu, that the Jews are building their wall in preparation for a rebellion against Persia and that prophets have been set up in Jerusalem proclaiming Nehemiah king. They warn Nehemiah that Artaxerxes will undoubtedly get wind of these facts and that Nehemiah should deliberate with them about how to proceed.

Once again, though, Nehemiah proves not easily intimidated. He sends a response to the missive's authors, letting them know that not only are its claims fake but that he knows that his opponents fabricated the letter with the intent of drawing him out of Jerusalem and harming him. Rather than weakening him, though, their attempts only strengthen his conviction.

His memoir continues with an account of a similar attempt made by a man named Shemaiah, believed to be a prophet.[124] According to

---

123. The site is uncertain. Some suggest it was neutral territory between the province of Ashdod and Samaria, while others suggest that it was a remote area within the province of Judah, which is what might have roused Nehemiah's suspicions. Williamson, *Ezra-Nehemiah*, 255.

124. For a discussion of the relationship between Nehemiah and the prophets he disparages, see Matthew Korpman "Was Noadiah a Trustworthy Prophet? The Demise of Prophecy in the Second Temple Period," *Zeitschrift für die Alttestamentliche Wissenschaft* 135, no. 1 (2023): 52–70. The fact that Noadiah is mentioned by name speaks to her prominence within the community. Athalya Brenner-Idan, *The Israelite Women: Social Role and Literary Type in Biblical Narrative* (New York: Bloomsbury, 2015), 62. For a discussion of prophecy this far into the Second Temple period, see: Benjamin D. Sommer, "Did Prophecy Cease? Evaluating a Reevaluation," *Journal of Biblical Literature* 115/1 (1996): 31–47:32; and Frederick E. Greenspahn, "Why Prophecy Ceased," *Journal of Biblical Literature* 108/1 (1989): 37–49. According to

Nehemiah's account, Shemaiah is in seclusion,[125] and when Nehemiah pays him a visit, Shemaiah tells him that there are people trying to kill him. Shemaiah suggests that he and Nehemiah close themselves in the sanctuary. But, suspecting Shemaiah's nefarious intentions and collaboration with Tobiah and Sanballat, Nehemiah refuses. Nehemiah understands their intention to trick him into running into the sacred sanctuary so that the sin generated by such an infringement would defame him and cause him to be disgraced,[126] and he does not fall for their scheme.

He utters a prayer at this point in his memoirs, asking God to remember the actions of Tobiah and Sanballat,[127] adding to the list Noadiah the prophetess and the other prophets who are trying to intimidate him.[128] Then, presenting the Judeans' progress as the ultimate revenge against the attempts to undermine him, Nehemiah informs us that after fifty-two days, the wall was completed.[129]

Nehemiah describes the fearful reactions of the surrounding nations as they realized that such an endeavor could only have been successful if brought about by God. And yet, Nehemiah also recounts that despite

---

some of the talmudic Rabbis, the gift of prophecy had been moved formally from prophets to Sages at this time in Judah's history (cf. Bava Batra 12a; Seder Olam Rabba 30; Mishna Avot 1:1). For an interesting theory linking Nehemiah's reactions to the laws of false prophets outlined in Deuteronomy 32, see David Shepherd, "Prophetaphobia: Fear and False Prophecy in Nehemiah VI," *Vetus Testamentum* 55, no. 2 (2005): 232–50.

125. The meaning of "in seclusion" (עָצוּר) is not entirely clear. Some suggest it implies being detained or quarantined (cf. I Sam. 21:8; Jer. 36:5). Mordechai Zer-Kavod, *Ezra-Nehemiah* (Mossad HaRav Kook, 2001), 96.

126. The Bible acknowledges the need for a place of sanctuary within the land (Ex. 21:13–14), and we know that the altar that stood in the open court was used as such (I Kings 1:50). But Shemaiah was suggesting that Nehemiah seek asylum inside the Temple, where he was not permitted to enter (Num. 18:7).

127. The prayer he utters is similar to the prayer in Jeremiah 18:23. It is possible that Nehemiah's identification with a prophet's experiences is meant to ensure that the reader knows on which side of history he stands, lest they get confused by the appearance of prophets opposing his endeavors (Berakhot 13a calls Nehemiah a prophet).

128. While more about them is not known, Nehemiah's account gives us the impression that the Shemaiah incident was not an isolated one and that his enemies used prophetic channels to make numerous similar attempts.

129. It was completed on the twenty-fifth day of Elul.

that realization, ongoing familial relationships are being forged between the nobles in Judah and Tobiah.[130] The chapter ends with Nehemiah's description of the dual loyalties of the nobles and of Tobiah's ongoing attempts to use those loyalties to challenge Nehemiah.

NEHEMIAH 7
LIST OF THE WALL BUILDERS

Once the wall is built and its doors affixed, the gatekeepers, singers, and Levites are counted. Nehemiah puts Hanani, along with Hananiah, who has the reputation of being a true and God-fearing man, in charge of Jerusalem.[131] He gives orders to keep the gates of Jerusalem shut until midday[132] and to assign the inhabitants of Jerusalem to shifts, guarding the area. At the time, Nehemiah recalls, Jerusalem is large and extensive but few live there.[133]

Nehemiah tells us that God inspires him to register the genealogies of the nobles, officials, and the people, and that he finds the genealogical records of those that first came up.[134] So he registers what he finds, recording the names of the people who came up from Babylon and their

---

130. Tobiah had married the daughter of Shechania, a member of the family of Arah. And their son, Jehohanan, married a daughter of Meshullam, the leader of one of the repair groups. The chapter seems to be simultaneously telling us of the success of the wall-building project and of its inability to fully protect the Judeans. More on this in chapter seven.

131. The citadel over which Hananiah was put in charge was possibly the precursor to the Akra from the Hellenistic period, which played an important role in the Maccabean revolt. See 1 Maccabees 11:20.

132. As the conclusion of the previous chapter made clear, though the walls had been erected, there was still a need for watchfulness. As such, the citizens were conscripted for guard duty.

133. The claim that there were no built houses is likely hyperbolic, but it stresses the challenge of guarding a city with a sparse population. It is also possible that the term "houses" refers to "families" (cf. Ex. 1:21; Deut. 25:9; Ruth 4:11). Either way, the implications of the claim are similar.

134. It has been suggested that the use of earlier lists links Nehemiah's efforts to protect and repopulate Jerusalem with the original settlement of the city in the days of Ezra. See Grabbe, *Ezra-Nehemiah*, 51.

leaders.[135] The chapter details and counts the returnees and mentions at its conclusion that some of the clan leaders, the governor, and some of the people donate financially to the project. And when the seventh month arrives, Nehemiah tells us, the Israelites are settled in their towns.

NEHEMIAH 8
THE LAW GIVING

Ezra steps back onto the page in Nehemiah 8, which begins on the first day of the seventh month.[136] On that day, we are told, all the people assemble in the open area opposite the Water Gate in Jerusalem and request that Ezra bring out the Torah of Moses.[137] Ezra complies, and from sunrise through midday, he reads the Torah's words aloud to an attentive audience comprised of men, women, and children.[138]

Standing on a wooden platform[139] and flanked by Mattithiah, Shema, Anaiah, Uriah, Hilkiah, and Maaseiah to his right, and Pedaiah, Mishael, Malchijah, Hashum, Hashbadanah, Zechariah, and Meshullam to his left, Ezra unfurls the Torah scroll. As he does, the people rise to their feet. Ezra praises God, the people bow, and then the Levites, along with Jeshua, Bani, Sherebiah, Jamin, Akkub, Shabbethai, Hodiah, Maaseiah, Kelita, Azariah, Jozabad, Hanan, and Pelaiah, explain the Torah to the standing crowd.[140]

Upon learning what the Torah demands of them, though, the people begin to cry.[141] Ezra and Nehemiah, appearing in tandem for the first

---

135. There are some slight differences between the list here and that found in Ezra 2. Most of the differences have to do with numbers, the order of certain family names, and specific additions and omissions.

136. The first of Tishrei, *Yom Terua*, later to be known as Rosh HaShana, the Jewish new year (Lev. 23:23–25; Num. 29:1–6), was a fitting day for a new start.

137. It is worth noting that the reading did not take place at the Temple, making it accessible to all.

138. Like Moses, Ezra did not distinguish between men and women when it came to Torah learning.

139. Once again, the people receive credit for initiating the important moment. This theme will be elaborated upon in chapter six.

140. What they were explaining is discussed in chapter eight.

141. The reason for their tears is not explicit in the text, but, from context and a similar

time, are quoted as telling the crowd to neither mourn nor weep, for the day is sacred.[142] The leaders encourage the people to feast on delicacies, drink sweet things, and send servings of food to those in need. Rejoicing in the Lord, the leaders reinforce, *is* the people's strength and shelter.[143] The Levites, joining the cause, further encourage the people to celebrate the moment. And the people do as they are told.

On the second day, the clan leaders, along with the priests and Levites, gather around Ezra to continue learning. While doing so, they come across the verse in which God tells the Israelites to dwell in booths during the festival of the seventh month. They proclaim throughout their towns and in Jerusalem that the people are to go to the hills and gather thick, leafy branches from olive, pine, myrtle, and date trees and construct the booths the Torah prescribes.[144]

Once again, the people do as they learned, building booths on their rooftops, in their courtyards, in the courtyard of the Temple, and in the plaza of the Water and Ephraim Gates. The entire community of returnees sits in the booths they built, which had not been done since the days of Joshua. Ezra continues reading from the Torah, there is jubilant rejoicing for seven days, and on the eighth day the people assemble as prescribed in the Torah.

---

scenario found in II Kings 22:11–13, we can assume that they were disappointed in their own failures in fulfilling the Torah's demands.

142. The sacredness of the day is known from Leviticus 23:24 and Numbers 29:1–6. If the ceremony was modeled after the ritual mentioned in Deuteronomy 31:9–13, then that, too, would have been sacred. The weeping of the people and the response of their leaders represents an important idea threaded through the work and is discussed in chapter four.

143. Cf. I Chronicles 16:27; Psalms 96:6.

144. The sacrificial component of the festival (Numbers 29) is not addressed, only the obligation to sit in booths. This is in keeping with the book's focus on the laity and their reacquaintance with the Torah rather than the inner workings of the rebuilt Temple.

NEHEMIAH 9
CONFESSIONS OF PAST SINFUL PATTERNS

Nehemiah 9 tells of a convention of engaging in fasting, confessions, and prostrations on the twenty-fourth of that month, when the people read from the Torah, separate from foreigners, and confess their sins.[145] Standing atop the platform, a group of Levites listed by name cry out in loud voices to God, followed by another group that praise and exalt God above all else. God, the Creator of the heavens, earth, seas, and all that the world contains, they proclaim, gives life to all, and the hosts of heaven prostrate before Him. [146]

Their praise then leads into a historical retrospective that highlights certain episodes in Israelite history that inform their current relationship with God.[147] They speak of how God chose Abram and took him out of Ur, changing his name to Abraham. They then tell how, finding Abraham's heart to be faithful, God forged a covenant with him, vowing to give his descendants the land of the Canaanites, Hittites, Amorites, Perizzites, Jebusites, and Girgashites. And because God is just, they contend, He kept His word.[148]

God saw their ancestors suffering in Egypt and heard their cries at the Sea of Reeds, they recall. And knowing how cruelly the Egyptians had treated His people, God performed wonders against Pharaoh, his

---

145. While the connection to the previous chapter is not obvious at first, it seems that after Nehemiah 8, the people continued learning and understanding their history through the lens of the Torah. The prayer itself indicates a thorough knowledge of many of the Torah's teachings. For a list of the biblical sources upon which their words seem to be based, see Myers, *Ezra, Nehemiah*, 167–69.

146. The "penitential prayer" that comprises this chapter constitutes a form of prayer in which an individual or group confesses sins and petitions for forgiveness as an act of repentance. Scholars contend that this specific formulation was the product of the Babylonian and Persian periods, and that, when read correctly, it can shed important light on the theological and ideological orientations of the communities that produced them. For a sampling of important essays on the subject, see Boda, *Seeking the Favor of God*.

147. The significance of the episodes chosen is discussed in chapter nine.

148. Of all the biblical covenants, only the one made with Abraham is mentioned, keeping the focus of the chapter on the inheritance of the land and nationhood. Blenkinsopp, *Ezra-Nehemiah*, 304.

servants, and all the people of his land, making a permanent name for Himself. He guided the Israelites through the wilderness with a cloud column during the day and a column of fire at night and spoke to them from heaven on Mount Sinai, giving them good and true commandments. God taught them about Shabbat and charged them with all His laws and statutes. He gave them food from heaven and water from rocks, and He told them to enter and inherit the land they were promised.

Yet despite all that God did for them, the speakers confess, their ancestors acted in willful wickedness, stiffening their necks and disobeying God's commands. They did not listen to His commandments, nor did they remember the miracles He performed for them, and, in their stubbornness, they considered turning back to slavery.[149] Because God is compassionate, though, He did not forsake them. Even after they made a molten calf and declared it their god, He did not forsake them. The columns of cloud and fire remained, illuminating the way for them. God never withheld the food or water He provided, and for forty years in the desert, the Israelites lacked for nothing.

God brought their ancestors into the land and enabled them to take possession of it by subduing the peoples that lived there.[150] The Israelites captured fortified cities and rich fertile land, and they inherited houses full of hewn cisterns, vineyards, olive groves, and plentiful fruit orchards. Naturally, they ate and were satisfied, and they grew rich and fat while luxuriating in God's goodness. Still, despite having everything they could have possibly wanted, the people rebelled against God. They cast His Torah aside and murdered His prophets. In his fury, God turned the Israelites over into the hands of their enemies, who oppressed them. But every time they were oppressed, the speakers recall, the Israelites cried out to God, and in His infinite mercy, God rescued them. Then,

---

149. Gordon Davies points out that the first act of disobedience has nothing to do with the violation of specific laws but rather a refusal to attach themselves to God, which is, in his opinion, the overarching theme of these chapters. Davies et al., *Ezra and Nehemiah*, 121.

150. There is no mention of Joshua or the early wars of conquest; rather, the prayer focuses on God as the One who conquers and confers land in history. That portrayal of God as "God of history" is an important theme in Ezra-Nehemiah. Fensham, *The Books of Ezra and Nehemiah*, 231.

as soon as they grew comfortable again, the Israelites fell back into their old patterns, and God again punished them. This pattern of sin, punishment, repentance, and salvation persisted for years, yet because of His compassion, God never fully annihilated His people.[151]

After recounting their ancestors' problematic history, the speakers focus on their own, recent experiences. They ask God not to discount the hardships they have been enduring since the days of the Assyrian kings.[152] And they speak of the fact that, while back on the land promised to their ancestors, they are still servants in that land, with all the bounty and goodness the land provides going to the kings who God has appointed over them.[153] The chapter ends with the people claiming to be in dire trouble and distress.

NEHEMIAH 10
FORGING A NEW COVENANT

Picking up where Nehemiah 9 leaves off, Nehemiah 10 begins with a list of signatories representing the people who now understood their history and the destructive patterns of their ancestors. The signatories, Nehemiah 10 tells us, want something different for themselves and their descendants, so they forge a new covenant with God.[154] In that covenant, they bind themselves anew to God and vow, under the penalty of curse, to follow all the laws and precepts He revealed through Moses.[155]

---

151. The prayer traces the cycle, evident in the book of Judges, throughout their early history, beginning with the Exodus and all the way through the Babylonian exile.

152. This may be a reference to the Assyrian kings Tiglat-Pileser III, Shalmaneser V, Sargon II, and Sennacherib, or simply a pseudonym for the Persian kings (cf. Ezra 6:22).

153. This claim, which seems to conflict with the overall attitude of the work vis-à-vis its foreign rulers, is addressed in note 78.

154. In place of the word "covenant" (ברית), the people use the word *amana* (אמנה) meaning "something firm, true, or faithful." For a thorough analysis of the covenant and its implications, see Michael W. Duggan, *The Covenant Renewal in Ezra-Nehemiah: (Neh. 7: 72b–10:40); An Exegetical, Literary, and Theological Study* (Society of Biblical Literature, 2001).

155. The content, structure, and specific stipulations of this new covenant, which represent an important phase in the development of the community, is discussed in

The people swear off intermarriage[156] and further promise not to
purchase merchandise or food from the peoples of the land on Shabbat
and holy days.[157] They vow to keep the laws of *Shemitta*, forgoing land
cultivation and canceling all debts every seventh year. And they take it
upon themselves to pay a third of a shekel annually to the Temple for
an assortment of uses. The people further commit to bringing the wood
offering,[158] the first fruits, and their firstborn of their sons and animals to
the Temple, as well as the first offerings of dough and choice donations
from all their fruit tree, wine, and olive oil. A tenth of their land will be
left for the Levites, which will also go toward the Temple, and they will
never again, they swear, forsake the House of God.[159]

NEHEMIAH 11
THE INHABITANTS OF JERUSALEM

Nehemiah 11 contains another settlement list, focusing on, but not limited to, those who settled in Jerusalem.[160] We are told that the Judean

---

chapter nine.

156. The topic, which is first addressed in Ezra 9–10 and mentioned again in Nehemiah
13, is discussed in this work in chapter seven.

157. While not explicitly biblical, the Shabbat laws were already understood to include
the prohibition against trading (Amos 8:5; Jer. 17:21; Is. 58:13).

158. The scarcity of wood in the province is likely what made this pledge both burden-
some and important. Wood was needed to fulfill the priestly requirement to keep
the fire for the morning and evening sacrifices burning continuously (Lev. 6:2, 5–6).
In earlier times, it had been the responsibility of the Gibeonites (Josh. 9:27), but
now new measures had to be instituted. The list of families that contributed and the
times at which the contributions were to be made, can be found in Mishna Taanit
4:5, Taanit 28a. For more on this development, see Blenkinsopp, *Ezra-Nehemiah*,
317.

159. The particulars of the covenant seem to indicate those areas in which the community felt it had lapsed (cf. Neh. 13). It is also interesting to note that many of
the requirements reflect interpretations and expansions of preexisting biblical laws,
indicating a continuation of the process that began in Nehemiah 8.

160. The list has many similarities with and differences from I Chronicles 9. It has
been suggested that both were based on similar archival materials (Myers, *Ezra-
Nehemiah*, 185). For conjectured explanations for the differences, see Blenkinsopp,
Ezra-Nehemiah, 324.

officials live in Jerusalem but that, due to the obvious hardships that living there entailed, very few citizens opt to live within the city. So, one-tenth of the population is asked to move to the city.[161] Lots are drawn to determine who those people will be,[162] and the rest of the people remain in their rural towns. The people praise those who volunteer to stay.[163]

NEHEMIAH 12
DEDICATION OF JERUSALEM'S WALL

As the book of Nehemiah draws to a close, it once again lists the original priests, Levites, and their descendants who return to the land.[164] The people, we are told, had to gather the Levites from all the surrounding villages in which they settled, bringing them to Jerusalem to celebrate

---

161. The city is referred to as "the holy city" (עיר הקדש). This phrase is primarily used in postexilic works (cf. Is. 48:2, 52:1; Neh. 11:18; Dan. 9:24). Tamara Cohn Eskenazi argues that Ezra-Nehemiah espouses that a Temple-like sanctity extended beyond the Temple and encompassed the city as well. She uses that assertion to explain some of the particularities found throughout the work, including the implicit connection between the Temple and the city walls in Ezra 4, the parallels between the building accounts in Ezra 1–6 and Nehemiah 1–7, and the fact that singers and Levites were appointed to guard the city gates (Neh. 7:1, 13:22). For more on her theory, see Eskenazi, *In an Age of Prose*, 83–87.

162. Lot casting was a common practice used to reveal the divine will (Num. 26:55; Josh. 7:14–18, 14:2, 18:6–8; I Sam. 10:20–21, 14:41–22; Prov. 16:33). For more on this practice in its ancient Near Eastern context, see W. Hallo, "The First Purim," *Biblical Archaeologist* 46, no. 1 (Winter 1983): 19–29; and Ron Beeri and Dror Ben-Yosef, "Gaming Dice and Dice for Prognostication in the Ancient East in Light of the Finds from Mount Ebal," *Revue Biblique* 117, no. 3 (2010): 410–29.

163. The problem of a sparsely populated Jerusalem was first raised in Nehemiah 7. In Nehemiah 8–10, the city is firmly established as the space where Torah reading and liturgical and cultic feasts take place, and where religious covenants are enacted and signed. It is fitting, then, that in Nehemiah 11, the people are expected to populate that center. For more on the evolution of the city's significance during this period, see Maria Häusl, "Jerusalem, the Holy City: The Meaning of the City of Jerusalem in the Books of Ezra-Nehemiah" (2013).

164. The use of older lists here creates a sense of seamless continuity between the different periods that appear in the work. For more on how the work links different historical periods, see chapter five. For a clarification of the list and an analysis of those places in which it overlaps with and differs from extant parallel records, see Blenkinsopp, *Ezra-Nehemiah*, 333–41.

the dedication of its wall.[165] Upon their arrival, the people celebrate with thanksgiving and music, and then the priests and Levites purify themselves, the people, the gates, and the wall.[166]

Nehemiah, who resumes speaking in this chapter,[167] describes how he brought the leaders to the top of the wall, where he had two large choirs waiting. Some of the leaders, as well as those playing musical instruments, are mentioned by name. Ezra is depicted as leading a procession that finds its way to the Temple.[168] There, more music is being played, and communal sacrifices are being offered by an elated community. The jubilation of Jerusalem, Nehemiah tells us, is heard from afar.[169]

On that day, men are appointed to different positions. Some are to supervise the changes, while others are to collect contributions, including first fruit and tithes. The people rejoice in the priests and Levites who carry out the rituals, and Nehemiah mentions that they fulfill their duties just as was done in the days of David and Asaf. Nehemiah ends with a sweeping statement linking the different phases of the restoration

---

165. Nehemiah 13 gives further insight into why the Levites had to be "summoned" from where they were living. But for the sake of this chapter, the sense we get is that because music is both an expression of and an elicitor of joy, it was important that the Levites, the primary musicians and singers, be present in significant numbers to create the atmosphere described in the chapter.

166. Purification marks the start of other biblical dedication ceremonies (cf. Ex. 19:10–15; Num. 8:5–8; Ezra 6:20), but purification of the walls of the city is unprecedented. This innovation likely corresponds to the sense in Ezra-Nehemiah that the sanctity of the Temple extended through the entire city. See note 161 above. Some suggest that because so many people had died on the wall during the attempted defense of the city against the Babylonians, the purification was similar to the practice of cleansing private houses prescribed in Leviticus 14:49–53. Williamson, *Ezra-Nehemiah*, 373.

167. Verse 31.

168. Discussing the ancient practice of circumambulating city walls, Mircea Eliade explains how the act reaffirmed the enclosure around the sacred center, which protected that center from the chaotic forces beyond. This idea is likely alluded to in Psalms 48:13–15 (Mircea Eliade, *Patterns in Comparative Religion* [University of Nebraska Press], 371).

169. The unadulterated joy surpasses both the consecration of the site of the Temple (Ezra 3:12–13) and the presentation of the law (Neh. 8:12, 17), both of which were marked by a mix of joy *and* weeping.

period. He tells us that in the days of Zerubbabel and Nehemiah, all Israel provide daily portions for the Levites, and that the Levites in turn dedicate portions to the priests.

NEHEMIAH 13
THE CLOSING ARGUMENT

The final chapter of Nehemiah provides a smattering of episodes that take place at different points during the period.[170] First we learn that while the Torah is being read aloud, those listening come across the verses describing the Ammonites and Moabites' refusal to provide water to the Israelites.[171] They learn about the nations' hiring of Balaam to curse the Israelites and of God's reversing that curse into a blessing. Owing to those events, the people learn, the Torah forbids the entry of any Ammonite or Moabite into the congregation. So the newly educated Judeans separate from those with mixed lineage.

But the focus of the narrative then switches to Nehemiah's reactions to events that unfolded in his absence.[172] We are told about how shocked he is to find that Eliashib, the priest with a connection to Tobiah, occupies a chamber in the Temple that had previously been used as a storage chamber for Temple donations. Nehemiah casts out all the vessels of the house of Tobiah from the chamber and gives orders to purify the chamber. Only once it is purified are the vessels returned to their rightful place.

---

170. The first episode mentioned is said to have occurred "on that day." It is possible that the verse is picking up on the previous chapter, in which case it would be referring to the day the wall was dedicated. But it is also possible that it is not referring to any particular day because by that point the Torah was being read regularly.

171. Numbers 22–24 and Deuteronomy 23:4–7.

172. Nehemiah was governor from the twentieth to the thirty-second year of Artaxerxes's reign (445–433 BCE) but was then called back to Persia. According to his account, Nehemiah requested a second leave of absence, and this chapter tells of the challenges he confronted during his second term in the land. A somewhat comparable although more severe scenario happened in Egypt during the reign of Darius II. There, opponents of the Jewish community in Elephantine took advantage of the absence of its governor Arsames and destroyed the temple. Bezalel Porten, "Aramaic Papyri and Parchments: A New Look," *Biblical Archaeologist* 42, no. 2 (1979): 74–104.

But that is not the only thing Nehemiah is disappointed by upon his return. He also tells us that when he gets back, he discovers that the Levites hadn't received their allotted portions, leaving many Levites and singers no choice but to return to their fields rather than perform their ritual duties.[173] Nehemiah reproaches the officials in Judah,[174] demanding to know how and why the Temple was forsaken. He reassembles the Levites, restoring them to their posts. And from that point on, we learn, Judah brings their tithes. Nehemiah appoints treasurers over the storerooms, and each one is listed by name.

Nehemiah then utters another prayer to God in which he requests that God remember the loyal actions he performs for the Temple and its service. He mentions that he witnessed people treading in winepresses and bringing produce into Jerusalem on Shabbat[175] and that he admonished them for it. He reprimands the nobles, demanding to know how they allowed Shabbat desecration to take place in the very city that had been destroyed for similar reasons and ordered the gates shut before Shabbat. Nehemiah insists that they are not to be opened until after Shabbat, and he even stations men at the gates to ensure no loads are brought in. On a few occasions, Nehemiah recollects, traders and vendors camp outside Jerusalem overnight, but they stop when Nehemiah threatens them with violence. After their purification, Nehemiah brings the Levites to sanctify Shabbat by guarding the gates. And then he again begs God to remember his efforts and be merciful.

---

173. Levites were completely dependent on tithes, and so when the people stopped donating, they were forced to work the land. In theory, of course, Levites did not own land (Num. 18:21–24; Deut. 14:29, 18:1). However, Ezra-Nehemiah seems to indicate that, by that time, many had already departed from such an ideal (see Neh. 7:72, 11:20, 12:28–29).

174. Nehemiah seems to have felt that, in his absence, the leaders should have been enforcing the laws.

175. Nehemiah mentions the Phoenician merchants who were selling fish and other wares to Judeans on Shabbat. The Phoenicians (Sidonians and Tyrians) were famous navigators and traders in the ancient world and mentioned frequently in the Bible. By the Persian period, they were well established along the entire coastal region. So it is not surprising that one of their main inland trading stations would have been Jerusalem. Blenkinsopp, *Ezra-Nehemiah*, 359–60.

Nehemiah laments the fact that there are still Jews at that time who bring home foreign wives and whose children cannot even speak Hebrew.[176] He reprimands them as well and even goes so far as to strike some of them and rip out their hair, forcing them to swear an oath to God that they will desist from such behaviors. Nehemiah reminds them of Solomon's sin of intermarrying, asking them how they expect the people to tolerate such evil. He mentions that even the grandson of Eliashib the high priest is married to the daughter of Sanballat,[177] so Nehemiah expels him as well. In the final words of the work, Nehemiah requests that God remember how some defiled the covenant of the priesthood and the Levites, and how he, Nehemiah, purified them.[178]

---

176. For a historical survey of the Hebrew language and the interplay of language, land, and people, see William M. Schniedewind, *A Social History of Hebrew: Its Origins through the Rabbinic Period* (Yale University Press, 2013).

177. One of the sons of Joiada, the son of Eliashib. Leviticus 21:13–15 prohibits a priest from marrying a foreign woman. Malachi seems to echo Nehemiah's condemning sentiments (Mal. 2:1–9).

178. The metaphor that God keeps a ledger of people's deeds is found in Isaiah 65:6 and Daniel 7:10.

Chapter Two

"The Black Hole"

(FALSE?) IMPRESSIONS

If we were to limit our study of Tanakh to the historiographical works, as they are known, we would walk away with a distinct impression of the evolution of Jewish history in the sixth through fifth centuries BCE. In fact, in the previous chapter, when we surveyed the historical context of Ezra-Nehemiah, we subscribed to that very impression: The Israelites lived in the land for a long time. Then for a brief hiatus in which nothing particularly significant happened, they did not. Then they did again, and Jewish history continued. Our impression would derive from the way the historiographical works construct the Israelites' story. We know a tremendous amount about what happened when they lived in the land both the first and second times. But we know virtually nothing about the approximately fifty-year period in between.[1] The book of Kings ends with the account of the destruction of the community in Judah and the deportation of its residents, and Ezra-Nehemiah begins with their

---

1. Even Josephus is compelled to cull from extrabiblical sources to supplement his knowledge of the period. See Rainer Albertz, *Israel in Exile: The History and Literature of the Sixth Century B.C.E.* (Society of Biblical Literature, 2003), 4.

return.[2] A similar sense of history is fashioned in the book of Chronicles, which recounts Israelite history from the origins of humanity through Cyrus's decree. In the last chapter of the work, II Chronicles 36, we are told of the Babylonian destruction: "They burned down the House of God and tore down the wall of Jerusalem; they burned all its palaces with fire and destroyed all its treasures. He exiled the remnant who had survived the sword to Babylon, and they became slaves for him and his sons," and then, without missing a beat, the same verse continues: "until the Persian Empire rose to power – fulfilling the word of the Lord as pronounced by Jeremiah: until the land had paid back its Sabbatical years, it lay Sabbath-fallow all the days of its desolation until seventy years were fulfilled. In the first year of Cyrus, king of Persia, when the Lord's word pronounced by Jeremiah had come to pass, the Lord stirred the spirit of Cyrus, king of Persia, and he issued a proclamation throughout his kingdom by word of mouth and written word as well."[3] The exile is not dwelt on, and the focus shifts almost immediately to the return to the land. Therefore, the historiographical works, if read independently, create the sense of a seamless transition from one period of existence in the land to the next. The intervening years, referred to but not recorded, are but a blip on the screen of history, a mere nuisance to bide out.[4]

Of course, it goes without saying that the period of exile was much more than a blip. It was a formative period in many ways. So, as students of Tanakh, our job is twofold. First, we must use all the resources at our disposal to reconstruct what happened between the end of Kings and the beginning of Ezra-Nehemiah. And, second, we must attempt to understand why, even though the historiographers undoubtedly knew

---

2. Details of the exile can be gleaned from references in post-exilic prophecies, but those prophecies are not meant to be historiographic.

3. Verses 19–22.

4. It is interesting to note that while we are told that the Israelites were in Egypt for four hundred years, and much textual space is allotted to both the Exodus and the ensuing forty-year journey in the wilderness, virtually nothing is known about their time spent in Egypt itself. For more on this, see Gary Knoppers, "Exile, Return, and Diaspora: Expatriates and Repatriates in Late Biblical Literature," in Louis C. Jonker, *Texts, Contexts, and Readings in Postexilic Literature: Explorations into Historiography and Identity Negotiations in Hebrew Bible and Related Texts* (2011), 29–61.

what we know (and more), they nonetheless chose to gloss over the Babylonian exile. Our first job will be addressed here; the second will be part of a larger discussion in chapter five.

Unfortunately, the paucity of biblical evidence from the exilic period is compounded by the fact that there is also minimal extra-biblical evidence to help fill the lacuna. There are few references to Judah in the neo-Babylonian records and, as we will see, a handful of extant Jewish documents from the community of Babylonian exiles. We also have archaeological surveys from the Land of Israel that look at the cities that were ostensibly destroyed or deserted after the Babylonian invasion and in-depth studies of neo-Babylonian imperial policy.[5] Still, taken together, the information we have enables us to speculate about certain aspects of inter-Temple circumstances but is nowhere near comprehensive enough for us to get a clear picture of the situation. That said, understanding what happened in the years before the period of restoration is critical to understanding the restoration itself. So, with the evidence that we do have, we will do our best to understand the character of three different Jewish communities that emerged in the shadow of the Temple's destruction.[6]

LIFE IN THE LAND IN THE AFTERMATH OF DESTRUCTION

The first community was comprised of those who managed to evade the exile and remain in the land. Excavations of Jerusalem and the southern part of the former Kingdom of Judah confirm the Tanakh's claim of a sweeping destruction in 586 BCE.[7] However, excavations of the area

---

5.   See Jill Middlemas, *The Troubles of Templeless Judah* (OUP Oxford, 2005), 39–48.

6.   The Jews in Egypt lived hundreds of miles apart, and so the term "community" may not be completely apt. Nonetheless, for the sake of this study, we will refer to the Egyptian Jewish communities as a cohesive whole.

7.   See Oded Lipschits, "Judah, Jerusalem and the Temple (586–539 BC)," *Transeuphratène* 22 (2001): 129–42; Nitsan Shalom et al., "Destruction by Fire: Reconstructing the Evidence of the 586 BCE Babylonian Destruction in a Monumental Building in Jerusalem," *Journal of Archaeological Science* (January 1, 2023), https://doi.org/10.2139/ssrn.4441154.

north of Jerusalem, the territory that had been assigned to the tribe of Benjamin, show signs of continued life in the region.[8] What daily and political life looked like in the areas where people remained is not entirely clear. There are those who contend that a significant community continued to exist but only as a neglected periphery. Others suggest that the community that remained was sizable, resilient, supported by Babylon, and a trader of wine and oil.[9] What we do know is that, due to its military limitations, what was originally left of Judah shrank and fragmented over time. It was forced to deal with ongoing clashes with foreigners that took advantage of its vulnerable situation, and the "territorial social integrity" it once enjoyed no longer existed.[10] And so, while Jewish life persisted on the land, it did so under less-than ideal conditions.

BABYLONIAN *GOLA*

The second community, created by force, consisted of the Jews who were led out to Babylon. The community, as expected, struggled with the emotional fallout of the calamity. And yet, available evidence also indicates a resilience and adjustment to their new reality. Ezekiel 1:1–3 tells us that the exiled Jews settled beside the "River Chebar" that flowed through Nippur. Documents from the fifth century BCE evince the existence of twenty-eight different Jewish settlements in the Nippur area, including one of the best known, the Al-Yahudu village ("the village of Judah"). The name of the village reflects a well-attested Babylonian tradition of naming areas for the place from which most of its inhabitants originate, indicating the tendency of Babylonian Jews to cluster together.

---

8. These excavations substantiate the offhanded statement made in Kings and repeated in Jeremiah, that the poor were left to tend the land (to be addressed below). Joseph Blenkinsopp, "The Babylonian Gap Revisited. There Was No Gap," *Biblical Archaeology Review* 28, no. 3 (2002); Efraim Stern, "The Babylonian Gap Revisited. Yes There Was," *Biblical Archaeology Review* 28, no. 3 (2002).

9. See Oded Lipschits, *The Fall and Rise of Jerusalem: Judah Under Babylonian Rule* (Eisenbrauns, 2005); Eric Meyers, "Exile and Restoration in Light of Recent Archaeology and Demographic Studies," in Gary N. Knoppers and Lester L. Grabbe, *Exile and Restoration Revisited: Essays on the Babylonian and Persian Periods in Memory or Peter R. Ackroyd* (Bloomsbury, 2011), 166–73.

10. See Albertz, *Israel in Exile*, 96.

A cache of documents discovered in Al-Yahudu gives us further insight into the daily lives of the exiles.[11] The documents record agricultural and commercial activities, including land leases, payment receipts, sale of livestock, house rentals, silver loans, and slavery transactions. They tell of Jews paying taxes, settling matters of inheritance within the family, and receiving workable land from the king of Babylon in return for military service and corvée labor. The documents seem to indicate that within a relatively short time after their arrival, the exiles and their descendants had adopted the language, script, and legal traditions of Babylon.[12] Many Hebrew names appear in the documents, and yet the degree to which Jews lived Jewishly remains unclear. On the one hand, marriages between women of Judean descent and Babylonian men are occasionally attested.[13] On the other hand, scholars note that none of the documents issued were drafted during Jewish holidays, suggesting that the holy days continued to be consecrated.[14]

The documents seem to indicate that there was no discrimination against the Jews despite their foreign status,[15] and, in fact, there is even evidence that certain Jews held positions of prestige in Babylon.[16] The

---

11.   The documents span the years 572–477 BCE, from soon after the Jews' arrival until well after Cyrus's decree.

12.   For a translation and helpful guide to the relevant Jewish documents from Assyria and Babylon, see Mordechai Cogan, *Bound for Exile: Israelites and Judeans Under Imperial Yoke: Documents from Assyria and Babylonia* (Carta Jerusalem, 2013).

13.   For a discussion regarding the observance or lack of observance of Shabbat and Jewish holidays during this period, see Yigal Bloch, "Was the Sabbath Observed in Āl-Yāḫūdu in the Early Decades of the Babylonian Exile?" *Zeitschrift für die Alttestamentliche Wissenschaft* 132 (2020): 117–20.

14.   An additional support for this assumption is the appearance of the name Haggai, based on the word *ḥag* (festival). However, not all scholars agree that such leaps can be made.

15.   They drew up the same contracts, and at the same interest rates as natives, for example. Indications from the book of Daniel seem to imply that Nabonidus (556–539 BCE) attempted to impose religious uniformity in Babylon, but extant evidence from the period does not seem to support this notion. Likely, the author of Daniel superimposed from the political situation under which he was living onto the past.

16.   See Tero Alstola, *Judeans in Babylonia: A Study of Deportees in the Sixth and Fifth Centuries BCE* (2020). Alstola's work includes, among other topics, discussions of Judean royalty, merchants, and the now-famous Murashu archives.

apparent leniency with which the exiles were treated is further supported by evidence found discussing the fate of the one of the last Davidic kings, Jehoiachin.[17] In a staircase of a basement storeroom in Nebuchadnezzar's South Palace in Babylon, a large archive of cuneiform texts was discovered, dating from the tenth to the thirty-fifth year of Nebuchadnezzar's reign (597–570 BCE). Among the records of receipt and distribution of foods including oil, barley, dates, and spices, Jehoiachin is listed as one of the dependents who received food from the throne. And, from the quality of rations provided for his family and the fact that his royal title was maintained, it seems that initially at least, Jehoiachin was treated fairly well.[18]

That relatively benevolent attitude displayed by Babylonians is further corroborated by the near absence of anti-Babylon hostility found in the prophetic texts of the time.[19] But even more important than arguments from silence are the explicitly positive statements sent by Jeremiah to

---

17. II Kings 24:6–15 tells of Jehoiachin's short rule, which ended abruptly when he and his family were exiled to Babylon along with Jerusalem's elite.

18. Some scholars suggest that Jehoiachin was subsequently sent to prison for reasons that are not entirely clear. It is possible that he was sent to prison in 595–594 BCE as a punitive measure for the rebellions in Babylon or in 582 after Gedaliah's assassination. Not everyone agrees with this time line. Some contend he was under house arrest from the time of his original exile. Either way, by 562 BCE, with the accession of Evil-Merodach to the throne, Jehoiachin was "released" (see II Kings 25:27–30). What his imprisonment and subsequent release must have meant for the Jews living in Babylon, we can only speculate (see chapter three), but there is no doubt that both would have been significant events for the fresh exiles. For more on the events, see Peter R. Ackroyd, *Exile and Restoration: A Commentary* (Westminster John Knox, 1968), 18; Albertz, *Israel in Exile*, 104.

19. The prophecies transmitted just before and during the exile are noticeably less antagonistic than those such as Isaiah 13–14, 21, which were transmitted earlier. In later prophecies, such as Isaiah 46, there is a ridiculing of Babylon's gods, but the rhetorical goals of such a prophecy are theological rather than political or psychological. Jeremiah 50–51 does articulate a harsh condemnation of Babylon's cruelty and their downfall that will ensue as a result, but those chapters belong to the prophecies known as "Oracles Against the Nations" in which Jeremiah makes clear that God's judgment will come full circle and that those responsible for Judah's loss will be held accountable. Still, the tone is theological, which stands in stark contrast to Jeremiah 29, for example, which advises amicable relations between the exiles and their host.

the "remaining elders of the exiles, and to the priests and the prophets, and to all the people that Nebuchadnezzar had exiled from Jerusalem to Babylon"[20] in 597 BCE. The letter encourages the exiles to "build houses and dwell in them; plant gardens and eat their fruit. Take wives, and beget sons and daughters. Take wives for your sons and give your daughters to husbands so that they may give birth to sons and daughters. Multiply there; do not be diminished. Seek the welfare of the city to which I have exiled you, and pray on its behalf to the Lord, for in its peace there shall be peace for you."[21] In outlining a practical approach to exile,[22] Jeremiah encourages the displaced Jews to act congenially toward their overlords and accept their reality of dislocation despite the emotional challenges it presents.

JUDEANS IN EGYPT

The third and final area where Jews lived during this period was Egypt. Three of the places in which they settled, Migdol, Daphne, and Memphis, were well-known Egyptian garrison cities. And so, while we cannot be sure, there is good reason to assume that the Jews who resettled in Egypt did so as soldiers in Egyptian service.[23]

In the late nineteenth and early twentieth centuries, a trove of documents dating to the late fifth century BCE were discovered on Elephantine, an island along the upper part of the Nile. The documents are what remain of a community that may have arrived one to two centuries earlier and provide tremendous insight into the political, economic, social, and

---

20. Jeremiah 29:1.
21. Ibid. 29:5–7.
22. More on the theology of the letter to be discussed in chapter three.
23. Judeans arrived and settled in Egypt in several waves during the history of the Kingdom of Judah, and Jeremiah 44 describes the decision of Judahites to flee to Egypt in the aftermath of Gedaliah's murder. For a discussion of the waves and dates of arrival of the various groups, see Dan'el Kahn, "The Date of the Arrival of the Judeans at Elephantine and the Foundation of Their Colony," *Journal of Near Eastern Studies* 81, no. 1 (2022): 139–64. Kahn contends that the foundation of the colony in Elephantine should be dated to the reign of Josiah (640–609 BCE). Rainer Albertz suggests that some Judahites may even have gone there as early as 716 BCE with the Assyrian army (Albertz, *Israel in Exile*, 97).

religious life of a Jewish Diaspora community in Egypt.[24] The Elephantine Jews observed Shabbat and celebrated Passover, and while their spoken language was Aramaic, some continued to give their children Hebrew names. Intermarriage with Egyptians occurred, but when it did, the Egyptians were assimilated into the Jewish community rather than the reverse. Some legal and economic practices seem to have been very similar to Egyptian ones, while other social practices remained distinctly Jewish. The community at Elephantine maintained contact with other Jewish communities, and their leaders displayed great concern for the welfare of their Jewish brethren throughout the Persian Empire.[25]

One of the most unique features of the community was a temple, known in the Aramaic documents as an "altar house." In that temple, which is remembered by Jewish worshippers as having been magnificent, with a cedar roof and stone gateways, the community sacrificed to Hashem, the God of Israel.[26] Some suggest that in building the temple, the community was attempting to fulfill the words of Isaiah, who prophesied that "on that day, in Egypt's heartlands, an altar to the Lord will stand; at her borders a pillar to the Lord."[27] Others think that a temple

---

24. Even though the majority of the documents date to a time when Jews had already returned to the land and the Temple in Jerusalem was standing, the community was established and functioning before that stage and so is still relevant for a discussion of the Diaspora situation in the inter-Temple period.

25. This model resembles the figure of Mordekhai in the Book of Esther, and, as we will see, it characterized Nehemiah as well.

26. In 410 BCE, the Egyptian Khnum priests (who worshipped the god Khnum in the same fortress) requested and were granted permission from Persia to destroy that temple. The Jews in Elephantine mourned the destruction and requested assistance from the Jews in Jerusalem and Samaria interceding with the Persian authorities. Their letters seem to indicate that they did not see themselves as schismatic or existing in opposition to the Temple in Jerusalem. That said, their first letter remained unanswered by the nobles and high priest in Jerusalem. There is evidence that a response eventually arrived and that the temple was rebuilt. We cannot help but wonder, though, what the lack of initial response says about how the community in Judah viewed the temple. Bezalel Porten, "Elephantine," *Shalvi/Hyman Encyclopedia of Jewish Women*, 31 December 1999, Jewish Women's Archive.

27. Isaiah 19:19. The prophecy to Egypt is part of a larger collection of "prophecies to the nations." In chapter 19, Isaiah describes a time when the Egyptians will come to recognize God and, reflecting a new world order, serve Him as true monotheists.

in Egypt tells us that Egyptian Jewry had accepted their life and no longer harbored hopes of a return to Jerusalem.[28]

While we may never know why they built their temple, an interesting feature of the Egyptian community becomes evident through a careful reading of the biblical texts. And that feature needs to be considered in our discussion, as it sheds light on the emerging Diaspora in the period preceding and during Ezra-Nehemiah.

CONFLICTING BIBLICAL ACCOUNTS

If we carefully examine biblical descriptions of what happened to the people who remained in the land after the destruction of the Temple, we find overlapping but subtly different portraits of the situation.

The book of Lamentations describes a dire situation in the immediate aftermath of the destruction, including severe famine that at times led to cannibalism[29] and the heavy-handed cruelty of the ruling Babylonians. "Slaves now rule over us; none will release us from their hands. We risk our lives for bread under the sword in desert lands. Our skin burns like an oven with the fevers of starvation. They raped women in Zion, virgin girls in the towns of Judah. Princes were hung up by their hands; no regard was shown to elders."[30] The exile devastates the land, and life for the small fragment that remains is unbearable.

II Kings 25:8–9 tells a similar story: "And on the seventh day of the fifth month, in the nineteenth year of the reign of Nebuchadnezzar, king of Babylon, Nebuzaradan, chief of the guard, the king of Babylon's official, entered Jerusalem." In the verses that follow, we are given the

---

Some claim that the verses are referring to the Jewish communities in Egypt from the postexilic period, in which case the building of the Temple would be conceived as a fulfillment of the prophecy. The Talmud Menaḥot 109b, in a similar vein, understands the section as predicting the Jewish temple that was built in Leontopolis in 160 BCE.

28. Shemaryahu Talmon, "'Exile' and 'Restoration' in the Conceptual World of Ancient Judaism," in James M. Scott, *Restoration: Old Testament, Jewish, and Christian Perspectives* (Brill, 2001), 107–46.

29. Lamentations 1:1, 2:12.

30. Ibid. 5:8–13.

details of the devastation. We are told about the burning of the Temple, the tearing down of the city walls, the destruction and pillaging of the Temple vessels,[31] and the gory fate of perceived political offenders.[32] Verse 12 mentions that some of the poorest of the land were retained by "the chief of the guard" to serve "as vinedressers and field workers."[33] And yet, the statement that follows in verse 21 seems to render that fact negligible, as it claims, "Thus Judah was exiled from its own soil." The book of Kings, then, like Lamentations, leaves us with the impression that the national import of what happened eclipses the significance of the landed remnant. Individuals may have remained, but their experience is irrelevant within the larger portrait of exile.

As such, when we are told in that same chapter that Gedaliah the son of Ahikam is appointed governor over the people who remain in the land,[34] we do not hold out much hope for him. Gedaliah may have believed that the people could evade exile,[35] but students of Kings know that the fate of the people had already been sealed. Therefore, we are not surprised when, after Gedaliah's assassination,[36] "all the people – from

---

31. More on the significance of these acts in chapter five.

32. "The chief of the guard seized Seraiah, the head priest, and Zephaniah, the deputy priest, and the three guardians of the threshold. And from the city, he took one official who was in charge of the military men and five men among the king's personal attendants who were left in the city, and the scribe of the army commander whose duty was to rally the people of the land, and sixty of the people of the land who were left in the city. Nebuzaradan, the chief of the guard, took them and led them to the king of Babylon in Riblah, and the king of Babylon struck them down and put them to death in Riblah, in the land of Hamath" (II Kings 25:18–21).

33. Ibid. 25:12.

34. His headquarters were in Mizpah, about 12 kilometers north of Jerusalem. According to Oded Lipschits, the Babylonians were in the process of establishing Mizpah as an administrative center prior to the destruction of Jerusalem. Lipschits suggests that there was an organized group of pro-Babylonian Judahites associated with the territory and involved in the process. Lipschits, *The Fall and Rise of Jerusalem*, 476–82.

35. "'Do not fear the Chaldean officials,' Gedaliah promised them and their men. 'Stay in the land and serve the king of Babylon, and all will be well for you'" (II Kings 25:24).

36. Gedaliah was murdered by Ishmael son of Netanya in the seventh month. Some suggest that the third deportation of 582 BCE referred to in II Chronicles 36:6–7 was a punitive action taken by Babylon for the assassination of their appointed.

the smallest to the greatest and the army officers – set out and came to Egypt, for they were afraid of the Chaldeans."[37] The exile described in Kings is comprehensive, and the land is left desolate because the people, through no choice of their own, are exiled or forced to flee.

Interestingly, the book of Jeremiah contains similar facts but with a different thrust. To begin with, the merciless Nebuchadnezzar of the book of Kings is the very man responsible for the prophet's rescue in the book of Jeremiah. In chapter 39, Jeremiah records Nebuchadnezzar's words that set him free: "Release him and treat him with care. Do nothing harmful to him; rather, do for him whatever he asks of you." And in the verses that follow, we learn that "Nebuzaradan, chief of the guard, sent word along with Nebushazban the Rab-Saris, Nergal-sarezer the Rab-mag, and all the commanders of the king of Babylon. They sent word and had Jeremiah released from the prison courtyard. They entrusted him to Gedaliah son of Ahikam son of Shaphan so that he would be taken to his house. He stayed among the people."[38] The evil Babylonians depicted in Kings and Lamentations, Jeremiah suggests, are also responsible for certain positive developments, which help Jeremiah but extend beyond him as well.

Whereas the book of Kings mentions Gedaliah's leadership as a milestone on the way to the irrevocable exile, Jeremiah 40 gives the impression, at least initially, that Gedaliah's appointment signals the potential for continued existence on the land, albeit for the small percentage that remain. We are told that when "all the army officers who were scattered in the countryside, they and their men, heard that the king of Babylon had appointed Gedaliah son of Ahikam over the land and that he had entrusted him with the men, women, and children who were among the poor of the land who were not exiled to Babylon, they came to Gedaliah at Mizpah."[39] The portion that remained go to their new leader in Mizpah and there, at his headquarters, echoing the message Jeremiah had tried for years to convey,[40] Gedaliah tells the people, "Do not be

---

37. II Kings 25:26.
38. Jeremiah 39:12–14.
39. Ibid. 40:7–8.
40. See for example, Jeremiah 37:9–10, 38:2, 17–18.

afraid to serve the Chaldeans.... Stay in the land and serve the king of Babylon, and all will be well for you. I intend to remain in Mizpah to represent you before the Chaldeans when they come for us. As for you, gather wine and summer fruit and oil and store them in your vessels, and settle in the towns that you have accepted."[41]

In contrast to Kings and Lamentations, Jeremiah seems to indicate that the Israelites who remain in the land stand a real chance of sustaining components of what was. That prospect is buttressed by Jeremiah's description of the people's willingness to rally around the new leadership model. We are told that "when all the people of Judah who were in Moab and among the Ammonites and in Edom and in all other lands heard that the king of Babylon had granted a remnant in Judah and had appointed Gedaliah son of Ahikam son of Shaphan over them, all the people of Judah returned from all the places where they had been dispersed and came to the land of Judah, to Gedaliah in Mizpah. They gathered a great deal of wine and summer fruit."[42] The depiction of an ingathering of Jewish people, with the bounty signaling God's blessing, paints a hopeful, potential-filled picture of the community that remains in the aftermath of the Temple's destruction.

In addition to the potential for sustained life on the land, Jeremiah seems to imply that sacrificial worship continues there as well. In chapter 41, we are told that in the seventh month, a group of men "had grain offerings and incense with them to bring to the House of the Lord."[43] We cannot say with certainty whether this account reflects a onetime event or an ongoing state of affairs. We also do not know if the sacrifices brought are limited to grain and incense or whether meat is brought as well. All we can deduce is the possibility that sacrificial worship continues where the Temple had stood even after the building itself is

---

41. Ibid. 40:9–10.
42. Ibid., vv. 11–12.
43. Ibid. 41:5. It has been suggested that mention of the seventh month implies that the men were making a pilgrimage for Sukkot. Their outward signs of mourning indicate that they were aware the Temple had been destroyed and were going to sacrifice nonetheless.

destroyed.[44] And so, for a moment in Jeremiah, despite the destruction, readers are hopeful that, for a small group, life in the land could endure.

Even after Gedaliah's murder and the internecine bloody rampage that followed, Jeremiah's insistence that the people remain in Judah is unwavering. He brings the word of God to them, saying, "If you will indeed dwell in this land, I will rebuild you and not tear you down. I will plant you and not uproot you, for I have come to regret the disaster that I inflicted upon you. No longer fear the king of Babylon as you fear him now. Do not fear him, declares the Lord, for I am with you to save you and to rescue you from his hands. I will grant you mercy, and he will show mercy toward you and return you to your land."[45] Jeremiah even goes so far as to forewarn those who remain of the consequences of leaving. If they say, "No! We will go to Egypt, where we will not see war, nor hear the sound of trumpets, and not hunger for bread. There we shall dwell!" Jeremiah cautioned that "in that case...the sword that you fear will overtake you in the land of Egypt, and the famine that you worry over shall pursue you there in Egypt, and there you shall die.... Just as My anger and My wrath poured out upon the inhabitants of Jerusalem, so will My wrath pour out upon you when you arrive in Egypt. You will become an object of swearing and horror, of curses and vilification. You shall never see this place again. The Lord has told you, remnant of Judah: Do not go to Egypt."[46] Tragically, most people ignore Jeremiah's threats, and many depart for Egypt, leaving us with an overwhelming sense of opportunity lost. In stark contrast to the book of Kings, Jeremiah offers a hypothetical future for those who remain after the destruction. As readers, we understand that had the people chosen to listen to their prophet, who had proven himself trustworthy through the destruction itself, they could have remained and even flourished in the land.

---

44. For more on this assumption, see Sara Japhet, "The Temple in the Restoration Period," in *From the Rivers of Babylon to the Highlands of Judah: Collected Studies on the Restoration Period* (Eisenbrauns, 2006), 183–232.
45. Jeremiah 42:10–12.
46. Ibid., vv. 14–22.

THE SIGNIFICANCE OF DIFFERING ACCOUNTS

Of course, the discrepancies between these books can be explained by their different objectives. While Kings traces the failure of the first commonwealth and the inescapable exile that failure wrought, Jeremiah focuses on the endless opportunities God gave the people and their obstinate refusal to listen to the clarity and wisdom of His prophets. But what is important for our understanding of Ezra-Nehemiah is the fact that, according to Jeremiah's account, the Diaspora community that develops in Egypt is not forcibly displaced. Fear may factor into their decision, and they may believe that fleeing is their only option. But fleeing despite being told unequivocally by a prophet that staying is the better alternative means that their displacement is voluntary. The people of the Egyptian Diaspora community are not led out in fetters nor prodded in the direction of Egypt with Babylonian swords at their necks. They choose to leave because they believe that life elsewhere will be better than life in the land.

That volition highlighted by Jeremiah calls into question the indiscriminate application of the word "exiles" to the emerging Diaspora communities.[47] It also adds dimensions to the questions we ask about those communities. We mentioned earlier, for example, that a Jewish temple stood in Elephantine and that it was in use well into the Second Temple period. Knowing what we do about that community, we may ask how the community thought of and experienced Diaspora and whether the experience was shaped by their living outside of the land by choice rather than compulsion. Did the community attribute primacy to the Temple in Jerusalem despite the existence of their own? Or did they see the two as equal in prominence and sanctity? How did location influence their relationship with God and the nature of Jewish life? Did they see a need, more broadly speaking, for a Jewish homeland?[48] While we cannot definitively answer any of these questions, and none of them are

---

47. The words "refugee" or "expatriate" might be more appropriate. See Middlemas, *The Troubles of Templeless Judah*, 4.

48. Similar questions can be raised about the Jewish Temple of Onias established at Heliopolis (Leontopolis) in Egypt in the mid-second century BCE, but because we are concerned with communities that serve as the backdrop for Ezra-Nehemiah, that Hellenistic temple, while fascinating, is beyond the scope of this discussion.

asked explicitly in Ezra-Nehemiah, the apprehension felt about Diaspora communities factors into the writing of Ezra-Nehemiah, and, as we will see, into their conception of Jewish history.

THREE DISTINCT REALITIES

What remains, then, are three distinct post-Temple communities that serve as the backdrop for Ezra-Nehemiah. One community, small as it may have been, remains in the land, perhaps even maintaining traditional ritual worship in some capacity. A second community relocates to Egypt by choice and finds, in that new reality, ways of maintaining Jewish identity and sacrificial worship. And a third community is forcibly exiled to Babylon but, due to the conducive reality fostered by its host country and the urging of some of its prophets, endeavors to live amicably with its neighbors while still retaining a degree of ethnic, and perhaps religious, distinction from them.

While the reality of all three communities plays a role in the worldview of Ezra-Nehemiah, voices from the Babylonian community become most influential in shaping post-exilic biblical thought. Despite the varied nature of the post-Temple communities, our discussion of exile in the coming chapter focuses primarily on the experience of the Babylonian Jews. That is not to say that many of the concepts addressed do not apply to the other communities, but we are working toward an understanding of the ideology of Ezra-Nehemiah, and, to reach it, we must understand the roots of the exilic experience that led to its production.

To do so, though, we must go back in time a bit because the impact of exile on Israelite thought does not begin in 586 BCE. It does not even begin in 597 BCE. The impact of exile on Israelite thought can be traced all the way back to the very beginnings of Israel's story.

Chapter Three

Understanding Exile

JOURNEYS INWARD AND BACK OUT

Exile serves as the backdrop for Ezra-Nehemiah. The work's heroes always move in the direction from exile toward the land, and reestablishing what was lost on account of exile is the prime motivating force behind the restoration. Ezra-Nehemiah begins with the charge "go," and that charge sets the work in motion. Of course, sixth-century Babylonian Jews are not the first biblical persons told to leave Mesopotamia and head toward the Land of Israel. Genesis 12 begins with the words "Go – from your land, your birthplace, and your father's house – to the land that I will show you. I will make you a great nation, and I will bless you and make your name great. You will become a blessing. And I will bless those who bless you, and those who curse you I will curse. And through you, all the families of the earth will be blessed."[1] God tells Israel's founding father Abraham to go to Canaan, and Abraham "went, as the Lord had told him."[2] This fact is taken as a given by those well versed in biblical narrative. But as we study Ezra-Nehemiah, we must continue to think about how movement toward the land features in Tanakh.

---

1.   Genesis 12:1–3.
2.   Ibid., v. 4.

Abraham moves from the outside of the land inward, so, by definition, Israel's founder is an immigrant. Unlike the "Canaanites [that] were then in the land,"[3] Abraham is not indigenous. That fact, as we will see, is critical to Israel's national self-perception. But to understand its import, alternatives to that reality are worth considering. God, for example, could have chosen an inhabitant of the land to be Israel's founder, someone with deep roots in Canaan whose family had been living there for generations and who knew nothing of life outside its borders. Perhaps that choice would have been the more natural one. Or, in the reverse hypothetical, we might see Abraham as founder but in his native land of Haran. He could have stayed where he was and built a nation from within. But neither of these scenarios occurs. Instead, God chooses an outsider and then demands that that outsider migrate inward. In doing so, two interrelated precepts of biblical thought are established: the pairing of Chosen People with Chosen Land,[4] and the structural conception of a biblical center and periphery. These precepts give form to the conception of exile that dominates biblical thought and drive the progression of Ezra-Nehemiah.

THE LOOMING CLOUD OF EXILE

We noted in the previous chapter that there is a dearth of biblical information about what happened during the Babylonian exile. While this is true, a careful reading of Tanakh reveals a preoccupation with the *concept* of exile.[5] Already at the outset of Abraham's story, exile is introduced as that which would delay the realization of God's promise of land.

---

3. Ibid., v. 6.
4. Lot, for example, chose to move beyond the boundaries of the land (Gen. 13:12–15). It seems from the text and the reassurance God provided Abraham after Lot's choice that Abraham assumed that, in leaving the land, Lot had forfeited his chance to be the beneficiary of God's promise.
5. The book of Kings, for example, creates the sense that all Israelite history in the land led toward exile, and the books of the later prophets were written either in anticipation of or in response to the exile, not to mention the books of Writings, including Lamentations, Esther, and Daniel, which wrestle with the aftereffects of the travesty.

Abraham's descendants would inherit the land, but not before their sojourn in a foreign one. "Know with certainty," God informs him, "that your descendants will be migrants in a land not their own, and there they will be enslaved and oppressed for four hundred years. But I will bring judgment on the nation they will serve, and afterward they will go free with great wealth."[6] Abraham moves to the land, but his foothold there is necessarily impermanent. His descendants, God decrees, would move out again, and only once they emerged from exile would the promises of nation and land materialize. Yet even that development is not as clear or as final as we might initially think.

Following the Exodus narrative, the Israelites wander in the desert for forty years, maturing psychologically and religiously in preparation for life in the land. While there, they receive laws delineating the lives they are expected to live. Appropriately, many of those laws are preceded by the refrain "when you enter the land." The ceremony of the Passover sacrifice, for example, shall be done "when you enter the land the Lord will give you as He has promised."[7] The same holds true for numerous other sacrificial practices,[8] certain purity laws,[9] agricultural imperatives,[10] wartime procedures,[11] and kingship regulation.[12] The very formulation of the laws received outside the land make it clear to the Israelites that a fully conceived religious life can be lived only inside the land to which they were headed.

At the same time, though, the formulation makes it equally clear that while God is bringing them to the land, their continued existence on it is not guaranteed. Rather, it is contingent on their willingness to adhere to the covenant to which they agreed at Sinai. On more than one occasion, God warns the Israelites that "if...you...do not listen to Me – if still you walk contrary to Me – then I, in My fury, will walk contrary to you.... I shall scatter you among the nations; I will draw My sword

---

6.   Genesis 15:13–14.
7.   Exodus 12:25.
8.   Numbers 15:1–31.
9.   Leviticus 14:34.
10. Ibid. 19:23, 23:10, 25:1–3.
11. Numbers 10:9.
12. Deuteronomy 17:14.

against you. Your land will be desolate; your cities, ruins."[13] An assortment of punishments for those who defy the covenant can be found throughout Deuteronomy, but exile is always foremost among them: "You will be torn away from the land that you are now coming into to possess. The Lord will scatter you among all nations, from one end of the earth to the other, and there you will serve other gods, of wood and of stone, which neither you nor your ancestors have known. Yet even among those nations you shall find no ease, no resting place for the sole of your foot. There the Lord will give you a trembling heart, pining eyes, and a languishing spirit. Your life will hang suspended before you; you will dread both night and day, never sure you will survive."[14] In the wilderness, while pining for a settled existence, the Israelites are warned that the life they are headed toward hangs in the balance. The covenant makes clear that Israel's adherence to the laws stipulated in the Torah would be the sole determining factor of whether they retain their right to live on the land.

So, just like their forefather Abraham, Israel's story begins outside, on the periphery. Like Abraham, they are enjoined to move toward the center with the promise that life there will be qualitatively different. But also like him, it is made clear from the start that exile is a constant, looming prospect. Living on the land, they are told, is not a given. And inhabitancy, once achieved, is not guaranteed but a right that must be perpetually earned.

WHAT IS SO BAD ABOUT EXILE?

But if exile is an ever-present threat embedded in Israel's covenantal system, why is that threat effective? What about being forced off the land worries the Israelites, and why is physical distance from the land a prospect daunting enough to serve as a deterrent to bad behavior? The answer to that fundamental question will help us understand what return to the land in the period of Ezra-Nehemiah means to the people and why it is worth the considerable efforts it demands. It is inextricably

---

13.   Leviticus 26:27–33.
14.   Deuteronomy 28:63–66.

linked to how Israel conceives of her relationship with God both in and outside the land. And while perhaps different from modern conceptions of God, the answer also reflects a central component of Israelite faith prior to the exile.

GOD'S OMNIPRESENCE AND IMMANENCE

For the Israelites, God's relationship to the land is complicated. On the one hand, they were taught that God had dominion over the entire world.[15] On the other hand, they were also taught that God chooses to dwell in the land and among the people of Israel. Deuteronomy addresses this complicated theological construct in the following words: "Look: the heavens, even the highest heavens, belong to the Lord your God, with the earth and all it contains. Yet it was on your ancestors alone that the Lord set His heart in love, and it was you, their descendants after them, that He chose among all the peoples."[16] A similar tension is found in the chapter of Kings describing the dedication of God's Temple in Jerusalem. After spending years building a Temple in which God would be worshipped, Solomon poses the following query: "For will God truly dwell on earth? If the heavens – the highest heavens – cannot contain You, how will this House that I have built?"[17] And yet, just a few verses earlier in the same chapter, we are told that the "priests brought the Ark of the Lord's Covenant to its place – to the House's Inner Sanctuary, the Holy of Holies, to under the shade of the wings of the cherubim.... And as the priests left the holy place, a cloud filled the House of the Lord; the priests could not stand and serve because of the cloud, for the glory of the Lord had filled the House of the Lord. Then Solomon declared: 'The Lord promised that He would dwell in deep mist; I have now built You an exalted House, a permanent place for Your abode.'"[18] Steven Grosby summarizes this interplay between these dual theological notions: "The one, true God whose jurisdiction

---

15. As can be seen in statements such as "the whole earth is Mine" (Ex. 19:5).
16. Deuteronomy 10:14–16. See also Exodus 19:5–6.
17. I Kings 8:27.
18. Ibid., vv. 6–13.

is the entire world, has, despite his universal distinction, an enduringly narrowed focus on a particular people and a particular land."[19] The entire world is God's dominion, but a different level of consideration is reserved for the Land of Israel.

THE INFLUENCE OF SURROUNDING ASSUMPTIONS ON ISRAELITE THEOLOGY

As with all conceptions that consist of more than one feature, depending on the historical, cultural, and emotional needs of a people, certain aspects of the whole become more dominant than others. Regarding the theology of the Israelites in the pre-exilic period, the territorial conception of God becomes more prominent than the universal one, which might be explained by the fact that the Israelites lived among well-established ancient Near Eastern cultures that subscribed to the notion of localized, territorial deities. That meant that gods were believed to have jurisdiction over specific lands, and, as such, temples were built to gods in territories they were believed to rule.[20]

An important piece of this theological system was the belief that while gods ruled over large territories, for worshippers to receive their blessings, gods needed to be immanent, and that immanence needed to be experienced in a concrete way. People needed to know where their god was dwelling and where they could find him (or her) to worship him (or her). For that reason, every ancient society, Israel included, had a temple that was believed to be a microcosm of their deity's dwelling place on earth.[21] As Baruch Levine explains, "Divine beings are viewed as the source of life and power. Power, in turn, is thought to be conducted

---

19. Steven E. Gros, "Once Again, Nationality and Religion," *Genealogy* 3, no. 3 (2019): 48.

20. Some suggest that Absalom's declaration in II Samuel that "I will now go and fulfill the vow that I pledged to the Lord in Hebron" (15:7) reflects such a belief. Absalom had previously been in Geshur, not Hebron, making the words "in Hebron" not self-descriptive but rather an epithet of God. For more textual and archaeological evidence for this belief in Israel, see Robert Karl Gnuse, *No Other Gods: Emergent Monotheism in Israel* (A & C Black, 1997), 183.

21. For a contextualized understanding of the phenomenon of temples in Israel and

from the source to that which is infused with it, and man invariably expresses concern with identifying the channels through which power is conducted. He reasons that the closer the source, the more certain and plentiful the power."[22] Temples enabled man to edge near that power.

This need to experience and be assured of God's immanence plays a major role in the early phases of Israel's trek in the wilderness. There, the Israelites demand to know, "Is the Lord among us or not?"[23] Immediately following the ten plagues and the Splitting of the Sea, the people do not doubt God's existence wholesale. Rather, they fear that in the wilderness, God is not in their midst. And if that is the case, they worry, they will not be privy to His providence.[24] So, in addition to the numerous miracles performed on their behalf in the desert, God "went ahead of them by day in a column of cloud to guide them, and at night in a column of fire to give them light,"[25] providing them with a constant

---

the ancient world, see Victor Hurowitz, *I have Built You an Exalted House: Temple Building in Light of Mesopotamia and North-West Semitic Writings* (A & C Black, 1992).

22. Baruch Levine, "On the Presence of God in Biblical Religion," in *Religions in Antiquity: Essays in Memory of Erwin Ramsdell Goodenough*, ed. Jacob Neusner (1968), 68–87. We also learn from numerous instances in Tanakh that God's presence was lethal, which is why approaching Him required that proper precautions and protocol were taken. See, for example, Exodus 19:12; Leviticus 10, 16:2–3; Judges 13:22; II Samuel 6:7.

23. Exodus 17:7.

24. Gideon, the charismatic leader from the period of Judges, expressed a similar fear when he responded to the angel's declaration that "the Lord is with you." Having seen the suffering of the Israelites at the hand of the Midianites, Gideon said, "If the Lord is with us, then why has all this befallen us? Where are all the wonders our ancestors have told us about.... The Lord has forsaken us and given us over to the clutches of Midian." (Judges 6:12–14). Moses acknowledged the validity of this conception. After the punishment of a forty-year delay had been decreed on those who participated in the sin of the spies, a band of warriors wanted to go to Canaan anyway. Moses warned: "Why are you transgressing the Lord's command? It will not work. Do not go up; the Lord is not with you. Do not be struck down by your enemies. Ahead of you are the Amalekites and Canaanites, and you will fall by the sword. Because you have turned away from following the Lord, *the Lord will not be with you*" (Num. 14:41–43).

25. Exodus 13:21–22.

visual confirmation of His presence.[26] Once the Israelites enter the land, of course, knowing that it is God's territory, that fear dissipates, so the cloud and pillar cease to manifest.

THE LIMITATIONS OF A LOCALIZED CONCEPTION OF GOD

This localized, territorial conception of God is helpful because it provides a tangible, centralized way of conceiving of God. But it also generates significant limitations. Worshipping a god outside of "his land" was often considered impossible, and traces of this understanding can be seen in several places in Tanakh. In the Book of Ruth, when Naomi tries to convince her daughter-in-law to return to Moab, she urges her to join her sister-in-law who has already "turned back to her people, to her gods."[27] An extreme and perhaps satirical example of this belief is found in II Kings. There, we find that Naaman, the commander of Aram's army, is miraculously cured of a skin ailment with the help of Elisha the prophet. In gratitude, Naaman declares that he will "no longer offer burnt offerings or sacrifice to other gods, but only to the Lord." However, he lives in Aram, not Israel, so the commander requests that "two mule loads' worth of soil" be brought back to Aram so that he can worship the God to whom he had pledged his allegiance.[28]

While both of these examples appear in non-Israelite contexts, we find a similar assumption about God's exclusive dwelling in Israel articulated by Israelites as well. In the book of Joshua, when the Israelites discover that the Transjordanian tribes of Reuben, Gad, and half of Menashe are building an altar outside the bordered Land of Israel, they send the following angry message: "Thus says the entire community of the Lord: Why have you broken faith with the God of Israel, turning away from the Lord today by building yourselves an altar to rebel today

---

26. The Tabernacle was constructed in the desert so that God could "dwell in their midst." For a discussion of the different ways God was conceived of in the wilderness period, see Benjamin D. Sommer, *The Bodies of God and the World of Ancient Israel* (Cambridge University Press, 2009).

27. Ruth 1:15.

28. II Kings 5:17.

against the Lord?... If the land of your holding is unclean, then cross over to the land of the Lord's holding where the Lord's Tabernacle dwells, and take possession among us. But do not rebel against the Lord or rebel against us by building yourselves any altar besides an altar for the Lord our God."[29] The assumption underlying the diatribe is clear. God cannot possibly be worshipped outside the Land of Israel. So, if an altar is constructed outside of Israel, it must be for a foreign god, and that, of course, is an inexcusable form of rebellion. David articulates a similar assumption when he begs Saul to stop pursuing him and forcing him to flee to foreign lands: "If the Lord has incited you against me, may He savor an offering, but if it was mere men, then may they be cursed before the Lord, for they have driven me out today from sharing in the Lord's estate, saying, 'Go serve other gods.'"[30] In David's mind, the God of Israel can be worshipped only in His territory. In his dire requests that Saul call off his manhunt, David explains that constantly being on the run outside the land has made worship of God impossible.[31]

At its core, then, what we find is that Israelite theology entails belief in a God who is simultaneously omnipresent and local.[32] But those two aspects are not always counterbalanced. Since, for most of Israel's pre-exilic history, the people are confined to the Land of Israel where they build Temples and believe God dwelled, over time, God's locative aspect begins to occupy more space in their collective imagination than His universality. God is sought in the Temple and He accepts sacrifices there, and the Temple is believed to be the seat of His power.

---

29. Joshua 22:16.

30. I Samuel 26:19.

31. Epigraphic evidence from Kuntillet Ajrud, a ninth-to-eighth century BCE site excavated near the Negev-Sinai border, also seems to indicate that God was associated with specific places. For a survey of the site's finds, see S. Aḥituv et al., "The Inscriptions," in *Kuntillet 'Ajrud* [N 15]:73–142. For an interesting interpretation of the implications of some of those finds, see Nadav Na'aman, "A New Outlook at Kuntillet 'Ajrud and Its Inscriptions," *Maarav* 20, no. 1 (2013): 39–51.

32. The book of Jonah, for example, seems to suggest that the prophet mistakenly assumed that God only has a locative aspect but learned otherwise.

AN OVERWEENING FAITH IN GOD'S
PRESENCE IN JERUSALEM

This sense of God's proximity is not inherently problematic. But the pre-exilic Israelite belief that God dwells in Israel, and more specifically Jerusalem, does lead to a false sense of security that they, and God, would remain there unconditionally and indefinitely. As the people themselves had been taught, their continued right to bask in God's presence was contingent on their adherence to the covenant. Somehow, though, their focus on how and where to find God obscured their provisional presence in the land. And, in time, despite the prophets' warnings of impending destruction and exile, no one believed such things would transpire. If God were in the land, the people reasoned, He would not let it fall.

This is the sentiment throughout Israel, but it intensifies in Jerusalem after the capital evades capture numerous times while other Israelite cities fall to the enemy.[33] In 722 BCE, Jerusalem remains standing after the Northern Kingdom has been defeated,[34] and in 701 BCE, after Lachish and a substantial portion of the remaining territory of Judah are captured by the Neo-Assyrians, Jerusalem miraculously evades capture when "an angel of the Lord went out and struck down 185,000 in the Assyrian camp."[35] But the seeming imperviousness of Jerusalem is misconstrued. There is a pervasive sense among the people remaining in Jerusalem and its surrounding areas that, because God dwells there, He would never allow the city to fall.[36] Prophets like Micah speak out against the hubris.[37] Jeremiah, too, does his best to push back against the false rhetoric.[38] But Jeremiah, Micah, and the other pre-exilic prophets fail to reorient the people and, ultimately, the destruction materializes.

---

33. I Kings 14:25; II Kings 15:37, 16:5.
34. II Kings 17.
35. Ibid. 19:35–36.
36. See Psalms 46:5–6, for example: "The holy dwelling place of the Most High. God is in its midst; it will never crumble."
37. Micah 3:11–12.
38. Jeremiah 7:4.

THE CRISIS OF EXILE: COULD GOD
HAVE BEEN ABDUCTED?

When we think of exile, we think primarily of geographical displacement. But while expulsion from the land undoubtedly generates significant practical and emotional challenges, perhaps most traumatic is the theological crisis it provokes. If the people conceive of God as localized and assume that God's dwelling in Jerusalem means it will not fall, then the most pressing question generated by the shock of destruction is, first and foremost, where has God gone? Based on what we know of Israelite thought at the time, two potential answers to that critical question likely surface. Both are theologically problematic, and both, as we will see, are rejected by the prophets.

If gods in the ancient Near East are believed to dwell in their temples and protect their allotted territories, then it stands to reason that military defeat means that the local deity has been overpowered. Thus, in their boasts of military success, in addition to listing treasures and deportees they carry off, ancient kings are also known to brag of their successful "god-napping."[39] The Assyrian King Tiglat-Pileser III,[40] for example, records: "I captured the cities of Tarbaṣu and Yaballu. I carried off thirty thousand people, together with their possessions, their property, their goods, and their gods. I destroyed those cities, together with cities in their environs, making them like the tells after the Deluge."[41] Gods of sacked territories in the ancient world are taken, often in a royal procession, and placed in the temples of the conquerors for safekeeping. Sometimes they are kept by the victors as a testament to the humiliating defeat of their enemy. At other times, they are held hostage until negotiations are conducted.

---

39. For a brief overview of this phenomenon, see Shana Zaia, "Godnapping in the Ancient Near East," *ASOR* (2016).
40. 745–727 BCE.
41. Zaia, "Godnapping." See also Michael B. Hundley, *Gods in Dwellings: Temples and Divine Presence in the Ancient Near East* (Society of Biblical Literature, 2013), 358–61.

BIBLICAL PRECEDENTS OF GOD-NAPPING

This fear of god-napping among Israelites is demonstrated in the famous ark narrative at the beginning of I Samuel. There we learn that after successfully defeating the Israelites at Afek, the Philistines capture the Ark of God and carry it off to their land, where it is placed in the temple of their god Dagon. The event is exceptionally troubling to the Israelites because, in Israel, the Ark is construed as God's throne or footstool. In Exodus, God tells the people that "from above the cover, between the two cherubim, above the Ark of the Testimony, I will meet with you and speak with you, and give you all My commands,"[42] and when the Ark is on the move, Moses declares: "Arise, Lord; let Your enemies be scattered, and Your foes flee before You."[43] On more than one occasion, God is designated "Lord of Hosts Enthroned upon the Cherubim."[44] And just as covenants in the ancient world are placed under the king's throne for safekeeping, the tablets Moses brought down from Sinai were placed in the Ark.[45] That conception of the Ark is likely why the sons of Eli brought it out to war with them, but it also explains the impact of the Ark's capture. Upon hearing of the capture, the high priest Eli dies from shock. The scope of the tragedy of the Ark's loss is expressed by Eli's daughter-in-law, who says, "Glory is gone from Israel...for the Ark of God has been taken."[46] As long as the Ark remained in Philistine territory, numerous curses befell the Philistines, leading them to conclude that the "Ark of Israel's God must not remain among us, for His hand is harsh against us and against our god Dagon."[47] The Philistines, believed to have captured the God of Israel when they stole the Ark, ultimately return it because of their fear of Him. And while this particular god-napping episode ends well for Israel, it lays the groundwork for the religious trauma that is experienced once the Temple in Jerusalem has been destroyed and the Ark permanently lost.[48] Their God, the Israel-

---

42. Exodus 25:22.
43. Numbers 10:35.
44. I Samuel 4:4. See also I Chronicles 13:6; Psalms 99:1, 132:7–8.
45. Deuteronomy 10:1–7.
46. I Samuel 4:22.
47. Ibid. 5:7.
48. For a survey of the different theories regarding the fate of the Ark after the

ites must have imagined, has been overpowered and taken captive, just like they have been.

IF GOD IS NOT CAPTURED, HAS HE ABANDONED THEM?

Of course, potentially more crushing than the belief that their God has been defeated is the belief that He has abandoned them.[49] But this, too, would have been a logical conclusion for the Israelites to draw. After all, Israel's relationship with God is a covenantal one in which God vowed to protect and provide for them within the land. But that protection has disappeared. And so, understandably, many Israelites assume that God must have relinquished His responsibilities toward them.[50]

The prospects that God has been defeated or that He is angry enough to abandon His people are both terrifying for the exiles, because both suggest that the nation of Israel has run its course. Echoes of the desperation and fear that set in once the people have been forcibly removed from their land reverberate in the words "How can we sing the Lord's song on foreign soil?"[51] Being severed from the land, in their minds, means being severed from God. It means that the matrix linking the people, the land, and God no longer holds.

If what the Israelites imagine is true, then they will go the way of other ancient nations, fading into the vicissitudes of history. If they no longer have a God to worship, their national identity will disappear, as will they. But they do not disappear. And that is because before the Israelites can give up, the prophets speak.

---

destruction of the First Temple, see Daniel Shalom Fisher, *Memories of the Ark: Texts, Objects, and the Construction of the Biblical Past* (2018).

49. Steven E. Grosby, "Once Again, Nationality and Religion," *Genealogy* 3, no. 3 (2019): 48.

50. Of course, students of the Bible know that in Deuteronomy, God has already assured the Israelites that even if He sent them into exile, He would never fully desert them (see, for example, Deuteronomy 4:25–40). Still, by virtue of the fact that the people had earned exile, it is safe to assume that the majority of the Sinaitic covenant had been forgotten or was being actively ignored.

51. Psalms 137:4.

PROPHETIC FAILURE AND PROPHETIC SUCCESS

The job of the biblical prophet is to orient his rebellious audience toward proper religious behaviors,[52] and the most common strategy is a warning of the consequences they will suffer if they ignore his instruction. As such, the measure of a biblical prophet's success is the degree to which he can prevent his own words from coming true.[53] And yet, ironically, it is the very failure of his mission that indisputably establishes his divine appointment.[54] Thus, in the aftermath of destruction, the prophetic voices that were ignored for decades suddenly resound with a renewed strength and clarity, having been vindicated by the most horrific event to befall the Israelite people until that point. And, perhaps more importantly, they resound because they provide the people with a strategy to recreate their faith.

The previous chapter mentioned the letter that Jeremiah pens to the fresh exiles in 597 BCE, in which he outlines a pragmatic coping strategy for the bewildered deportees. But it does something else, too. At the outset, Jeremiah quotes God introducing Himself in a subtle but profound sentence: "This is what the Lord of Hosts, God of Israel, said to all the exiles that I have exiled from Jerusalem to Babylon."[55] God exiled the people. *He* sent them there. The Israelites were not taken to Babylon because their God had abandoned them or been rendered powerless; they were exiled because their still-powerful God decided that was what they deserved.

---

52. For the sake of simplicity, the singular male pronoun is used, but that should not lead to the false impression that only males were prophets. Numerous female prophets are mentioned throughout the Bible.

53. Biblical prophets were not soothsayers who made a living predicting the future. Biblical prophets warned of the evils that would befall the people if they did not modify their immoral behaviors and generate change.

54. Shemaryahu Talmon explains that Jonah was the only example of a biblical prophet "who failed to grasp the intrinsic task of his mission, namely to prevail upon the sinful inhabitants of Nineveh to repent. However, when they did show penitence, and their city was saved, Jonah complained that his prestige as a prophet was jeopardized. His story proves by a negative example the basic conditional nature of true biblical prophecy." Shemaryahu Talmon, *Literary Motifs and Patterns in the Hebrew Bible: Collected Essays* (Penn State University Press, 2013).

55. Jeremiah 29:4.

Like Jeremiah, Ezekiel also frames the exile as a consequence of divine punishment and, as such, a sign of God's enduring power. In chapter 8, Ezekiel is lifted "between the land and the heavens and brought [me] to Jerusalem in a Godly vision,"[56] where he witnesses the "great abominations" that are being committed in the Temple just before its destruction.[57] In chapter 9, Ezekiel sees God authorizing the slaughter of Jerusalem's inhabitants. God tells the Babylonian invaders to "strike – do not let your eye pity, do not show mercy. The elderly, young men, young girls, small children, women – kill, destroy."[58] As haunting as this image is, Ezekiel makes clear that the massacre is on account of "the iniquity of the House of Israel and Yehuda is extremely great; the land is filled with blood, and the city is full of corruption."[59] In chapter 11, Ezekiel describes how the "cherubim lifted up their wings with the wheels beside them, and above, upon them," and how the "glory of the Lord rose from within the city and stood upon the mountain east of the city."[60] Only after God's intentional departure from the city, according to Ezekiel, do the Babylonians take over, further supporting the notion that God is angry but still very much in control.[61]

If earlier prophets tried to prevent the destruction by encouraging the people to repent, Ezekiel, like Jeremiah, tries to make theological sense of the destruction after it happens. They both do so by focusing on the culpability of the people. In short, they remind the people of the Sinaitic covenant and of their failures to uphold their end of the deal. While the excruciating day-to-day reality of the exiles may not be immediately mollified by the prophets' words, a key component of their religious crisis is. But the prophets' job is still not done.

---

56. Ezekiel 8:3.
57. Ibid., v. 6.
58. Ibid.
59. Ibid., v. 9.
60. Ibid., vv. 22–23.
61. For more on this subject, see Daniel I. Block, "Divine Abandonment: Ezekiel's Adaptation of an Ancient Near Eastern Motif," *The Book of Ezekiel: Theological and Anthropological Perspectives*, ed. Margaret S. Odell and John T. Strong (Atlanta: SBL, 2020); and John F. Kutsko, *Between Heaven and Earth: Divine Presence and Absence in the Book of Ezekiel* (1999).

GOD'S ALTERED BUT ONGOING PRESENCE

If God's immanence is believed to be a prerequisite to worship, then even if God was not defeated, the people have no idea where to find Him in exile, which is why they weep over their inability to worship God "by the rivers of Babylon."[62] If they cannot find God, their lament seems to indicate, they do not know how they can worship Him. Once again, the prophets provide succor. In that same letter in chapter 29, Jeremiah relays God's message to the people: "Then, when you call upon Me and follow and pray to Me, I will hear you. And when you search you will find Me, if you seek Me with all your heart. I shall be accessible to you."[63] They do not have to be in Jerusalem, Jeremiah reassures them; if they reach out to God, from wherever they are, He will hear them. Because of Jeremiah's words, God's omnipresence, the aspect of divine devotion that was overshadowed for so many centuries by a locative perspective, begins to echo with newfound relevance outside of His land.

Ezekiel goes a step further and, in doing so, brings immeasurable reassurance to the exiles. Describing God's chariot in all its majesty coming to him by the Chebar River,[64] Ezekiel makes a very important claim about the scope of God's presence. God comes to His people, Ezekiel's prophecies attest, even in the distant place of exile. In chapters 8–12, Ezekiel describes God's gradual departure from Jerusalem, a scene that would have initially horrified his audience. But, as Ezekiel goes on to explain, God remains close to His people in Babylon because of His departure from Jerusalem. In chapter 11, Ezekiel transmits God's novel claim to the exiles: "Though I have placed them far away among the nations, though I have scattered them over the lands and am but a small sanctuary for them in whichever lands they come to."[65] God exiled His people, and then He went to exile with them.

---

62. Psalms 137:1.
63. Jeremiah 29:12–14.
64. Ezekiel 1–3. In Psalms 18:11 and 68:18, the Ark is referred to as a "chariot." As we saw in the Ark narrative from Samuel, God was believed to move with the Ark. See also Numbers 10:35.
65. Ezekiel 11:16.

INSIGHTS GLEANED FROM EXILE

With the comfort of knowing that God is with them in exile, the people do their time. The process is understood as purifying the people from their sinful behaviors and giving the land, which had rejected the people, respite from their polluting influence. "In its desolation," we are told, "the land will have the rest it did not have during the Sabbaths when you were dwelling there."[66] The exile is thus seen as a time when the people atone and the land recuperates.

Taken together, the exilic prophets facilitate Jewish survival by providing a lens through which to process seemingly incongruous realities. It enables them to see their exile *and* their God as powerful. It also enables them to process the shame that naturally accompanies retribution without releasing their sense of collective worth. As David Aberbach explains, "Trauma, rather than overwhelming the Jewish people and leading to their disappearance, as was the case with most other peoples in the premodern world, stimulated creative cultural processes of adaptation."[67] The Babylonian exile is one such trauma. It induces the people to remember the truth they had forgotten, the truth that is inaugurated in the paradigmatic story of Abraham and reiterated in the Sinaitic covenant. This truth is that their existence in the chosen land has to be merited. If it is not, they will lose their right. But it is also true that that loss will never be permanent.

HOPE FOR THE FUTURE

The prophets Jeremiah, Ezekiel, and Isaiah all assert from the outset that the exile will last for a finite period. Just as God removed the people from the land, He would bring them back. Once refined, the prophets assure, the Chosen People will make their way from the periphery to God's chosen land again. And because the prophets depict the exile itself as a second wilderness experience, in which the sins of the people

---

66. Leviticus 26:35.

67. David Aberbach, *Major Turning Points in Jewish Intellectual History* (Springer, 2003), xii.

are being purged,[68] it makes perfect sense that the movement back to the land is similarly envisioned as a second Exodus; a grand, sweeping migration that will bring honor to both God and His people. "For I am making something new; even now it grows...I shall make a way through desert land and rivers across the wilderness.... for I have given the desert water and rivers in the wilderness to give My people, My chosen one, to drink."[69] Of course, as with the original Exodus, the one from Babylon would be sealed with a covenant. "Days are soon coming, declares the Lord, when I will make a new covenant with the House of Israel and the House of Judah."[70] But, unlike the first time, this new covenant that God planned to forge would be observed because, as God claims, "I will deliver My teaching into their midst and inscribe it upon their hearts, and I will be their God, and they will be My people. No longer will each person teach a neighbor and each person a brother, saying, 'Know the Lord!' For they will all know Me, from the least of them to their greatest, declares the Lord."[71] God promises, this time around, to safeguard His covenant so that the returning people will know Him and worship Him properly. Of course, that covenant guarantees the returnees protection so that they can "live securely and sleep in the forests,"[72] with rain "at its right time," and the trees to "bear their fruit."[73]

In the future envisioned by the prophets, the twelve tribes will be reunited, and foreign hostile powers will be defeated by God.[74] A Davidic leader will emerge, but, unlike the failed kings before him, the future, ideal leader will lead the people gently. He will be like a "shepherd to them,"[75] urging them along the path of the righteous. Then, with the

---

68. Ezekiel 20:36–37 reads, "Just as I entered into judgment with your fathers in the wilderness of the land of Egypt, so will I enter into judgment with you, declares the Lord God. I will make you pass beneath the rod." See also Isaiah 40:2, 50:1.

69. Isaiah 43:19–20. See also Isaiah 40:3–6, 48:20–21.

70. Jeremiah 31:31.

71. Ibid., vv. 32–33.

72. Ezekiel 34:25.

73. Ibid., vv. 26–27.

74. See, for example, Jeremiah 31:20; Ezekiel 37:15–23, 47:13; and the famous Gog and Magog oracles of Ezekiel 38–39. Isaiah 51:9–11 invokes God's defeat of the primeval forces of chaos as a template for what God would do in the future.

75. Ezekiel 34:23.

people back where they belong and the covenant restored, God will once again settle in their midst. But this time, it will be forever. "I will place My Sanctuary among them for eternity. My presence will be upon them; I will be their God, and they will be My people. And the nations will know that I the Lord make Israel holy when My Sanctuary is among them for all eternity."[76] The Temple in Ezekiel's vision is both expanded and redesigned, coming about without human initiative, thus creating a sense of God's will miraculously manifesting. From the envisioned Temple on the mountain, a stream of God's life-giving forces will flow, and God's returned presence to Jerusalem will be so obvious to everyone that the city itself will be renamed "The Lord is there."[77]

EXPECTATIONS SET

The words of the exilic prophets stirred the hearts and minds of the people, giving them hope that everything that had been lost would be fully restored and a reason to believe in the future. But while this hope saves those who would have otherwise been broken by exile, it projects a future that, as we will see, does not match reality. These promises set the bar by which all programs of restoration are measured, creating significant challenges for the post-exilic community. How Ezra-Nehemiah deals with those challenges is the fulcrum around which the work revolves.

---

76. Ibid. 37:26–28.
77. Ibid. 48:35.

Chapter Four

Optimism and Opportunity

REALITY BITES

Knowing what we do about biblical covenants, ties to the land, and the prophetic promises of a restored Temple, Cyrus's grant of return seems like the biblical equivalent of "they lived happily ever after." Yet the reality that confronts those who heed Cyrus's pronouncement is far from a fairy-tale ending.

A group of Jews do return from Babylon, but their contingent is nowhere near the mass migration from "all four edges of the world" envisioned by the prophets.[1] As part of the Persian province known as Abar Nahara,[2] the land of Judah remains firmly under Persian control. In

---

1. Isaiah 11:12.

2. According to the Greek historian Herodotus (*The Histories* 3.89), Darius divided the Persian Empire into twenty satrapies. One of these was known as the territory of "Beyond the (Euphrates) River." In Aramaic it was called 'Abar Naharaa and in Babylonian Ebir Naari (Albertz, *Israel in Exile*, 118). The term is used fifteen times in Ezra-Nehemiah. The phrase likely dates to the period of Assyrian conquest, when the region between the Euphrates and Egypt was united into one political and territorial unit. For more on the origins and significance of the term, see Lipschits,

keeping with Persian policy, Jews are appointed as proxy leaders within the land, but a Davidic king is not reinstated on any throne.[3] The miraculous, grandiose Temple described by Ezekiel is nowhere to be found. In its stead stands a meager edifice that takes more than twenty years to build, and though the Judeans do not have to actively fight off threats from foreign powers, they do have to counter forces from within that try to undermine their national efforts at renewal. That, in addition to the drought and onerous Persian taxation policies that supplant the bounty and prosperity they had been promised, made the dream of everlasting peace seem out of reach.[4] To make matters worse, prophecy as it was experienced in the pre-exilic and exilic eras was waning[5] and with it, or so it seemed, the ability to ascertain God's will.

These disappointments raise a series of important questions for early Second Temple Jews. What, for example, do these setbacks say about the people's relationship with God? Are they still His Chosen People? Has the covenant been restored? If it has been, why are they not experiencing its implicit blessings? If it has not, how can it be reestablished? Is sovereignty in the form of a Davidic king still an ideal? If so, what should their political aspirations look like? If not, what should fill the

---

The Fall and Rise of Jerusalem, 2. For a discussion of how geography, particularly Abar Nahara, played a role in the organization and thematic development of Ezra-Nehemiah, see Thomas B. Dozeman, "Geography and History in Herodotus and in Ezra-Nehemiah," *Journal of Biblical Literature* 122, no.3 (2003): 449–66.

3. Zerubbabel's connection to the Davidic kingdom will be discussed in chapter six.

4. Ezra-Nehemiah does not mention a drought explicitly, but Haggai speaks of the barrenness of the land during that period (1:6).

5. According to the Rabbis (Sanhedrin 11a, b; Yoma 9b; Sota 48b; Y. Sota 9:13), from the time of the later prophets Haggai, Zechariah, and Malachi, the holy spirit was withdrawn from Israel. Yoma 21b and Y. Taanit 2:1 identify the holy spirit as one of the five things that existed during the First Temple but not during the second. Seder Olam Rabba (ch. 30) teaches that "Alexander of Macedonia reigned for twelve years. Until that time prophets spoke prophecies through the holy spirit' from that time on, 'Incline your ear and listen to the words of the Sages.'" Other hints as to early Jewish traditions on the matter can be found in the I Maccabees (9:27) and Josephus (*The Wars of the Jews* 78:2, 113, 159, *The Antiquities of the Jews* 15:373–79). For an analysis of these traditions regarding the "waning" process, see Benjamin D. Sommer, "Did Prophecy Cease? Evaluating a Reevaluation," *Journal of Biblical Literature* 115, no.1 (1996): 31–47.

leadership void? If a majority of the Jewish people live outside the land, is Israel, particularly Jerusalem, still the center? And how should cohesion be maintained between the various Jewish communities if the land no longer delimits them? The character of the newly re-established Judean community depends on the answers to these questions. But Second Temple authors do not always agree on what those answers are.

AN ONGOING EXILE

For some early Second Temple authors, the rationale for the difficulties they experience is simple: the redemption has not yet occurred. Despite Cyrus's decree, some authors maintain, the exile had not actually ended. The book of Chronicles, for example, concludes with these words: "Thus says Cyrus, king of Persia: The Lord, God of the heavens, has granted me all the kingdoms of the earth, and He has charged me to build Him a House in Jerusalem in Judah. Whoever is among you from all His people, may the Lord his God be with him, and let him go up!"[6] Although written in the mid- to late-fourth century BCE, two centuries after the decree itself, the shifts in fortune expected from redemption had not yet manifested. And so, as Sara Japhet suggests, by ending with the potential for redemption but not its realization, the author of Chronicles makes clear that "the restoration of Israel's destiny is not a matter of the past but a program for the future – it has not yet occurred, but is to be expected and awaited"[7] For the Chronicler, according to this reading, the ongoing exile explains the people's current conditions. They are on the cusp but have not yet moved into the next phase of their history.[8]

The prophet Haggai reflects that precarity: "This people says, 'The time has not come – the time for the Lord's House to be built.'"[9] His

---

6. II Chronicles 36:23.
7. Japhet, *From the Rivers of Babylon*, 340.
8. This belief became widespread in the Second Temple period and is evident in many Jewish works produced during that time. See Paul D. Hanson, *The Dawn of the Apocalyptic* (Fortress, 1975) and Michael A. Knibb, "The Exile in the Literature of the Intertestamental Period," in Michael A. Knibb, *Essays on the Book of Enoch and Other Early Jewish Texts and Traditions* (Brill, 2009), 191–212.
9. Haggai 1:2. This prophecy was spoken in the year 520 BCE, the period between the

audience is waiting for an improvement in their circumstances to signal that the "appointed time" to build the Temple had arrived. The lack of a Davidic king and the challenging economic circumstances mentioned in Haggai are both privations that the redemption is supposed to have reversed. As such, they are two of the factors contributing to the people's hesitation. Pushing back at their reluctance, Haggai encourages the people to begin building despite the inadequacies of their current reality. Ultimately, he is successful, but perhaps more importantly for our discussion, his recorded efforts reveal a good deal about the prevailing attitude of the Judean community during those early, difficult years.

Those misgivings persist throughout the Second Temple period, as can be seen, for example, in the book of Daniel.[10] In chapter 9, Daniel is described as wrestling with the fact that the Jewish people are still suffering after Jeremiah's seventy-year cap on exile expired.[11] The angel Gabriel appears to Daniel and explains that Jeremiah's words remain true; Daniel simply misunderstood them and miscalculated. "Seventy cycles of a week of years are decreed upon your people and on your holy city to complete the transgressions," the angel clarifies, "to finish the sins and to atone for iniquity, and to bring everlasting justice, to validate the vision and the prophet, and to anoint a holy of holies."[12] The exile, Gabriel explains, is not predestined to be seventy years but rather seventy weeks (sabbaticals) of years, equaling 490 years.[13] In one sentence, Daniel simultaneously insists on the veracity of Jeremiah's prophecy and accounts for the fact that it has not come to fruition. The exile, according to these authors, is not a past historical event but an enduring

---

laying of the Temple's foundation and its construction.

10. While set in earlier periods, the final composition of the book of Daniel was probably ca. 164 BCE, during the time of the Maccabean revolt.

11. In both Jeremiah 25 and 29, the prophet assures the people that the exile will last for seventy years.

12. Daniel 9:24.

13. Various explanations have been offered for Daniel's reinterpretation of Jeremiah's prophecy. Many include reference to Leviticus 26:34–35, which depicts the exile as a "Sabbath for the land," and Leviticus 26:18, in which God threatens to punish the people sevenfold for their sins. For a full discussion of the vision's historical context and other possible explanations, see John J. Collins, *Daniel: A Commentary on the Book of Daniel* (Hermeneia, 1993).

reality awaiting its conclusion. It is, as Adele Berlin puts it, "an existential mode of being."[14]

UTOPIAN THINKING AS COPING MECHANISM

While that mindset helps preserve the integrity of past prophecies, it does not suffice to reconcile the disillusionments of the period. The emotional toll of the disappointment for those who had returned brimming with expectations is something the leaders had no choice but to address, which is where utopian thinking comes in. Utopia, as Northrop Frye explains, "presents an imaginative vision of the telos or end at which social life aims."[15] The need for an imagined utopia is triggered by the reality of a present that fails to measure up to the imagined ideals of the community. It presents its audience with a fantastical alternative that is better than that of the author's present.[16]

Biblical utopian prophecies are, by definition, assured by the very fact of God's omnipotence. But for that reason, they also cannot be rushed. The realization of a utopian future in the Bible, as does its timing, depends on God. There is nothing the community can do to precipitate it.[17] Zechariah, for example,[18] quotes God as saying that "once again My city will brim over with good, and the Lord will again comfort

---

14. Adele Berlin, "The Exile: Biblical Ideology and Its Postmodern Ideological Interpretation," in *Literary Construction of Identity in the Ancient World* (2010), 341–56. For more on the interpretations of Jeremiah's prophecies and what they reveal about Jewish attitudes toward the end of exile, see Steven M. Bryan, "The End of Exile: The Reception of Jeremiah's Prediction of a Seventy-Year Exile," *Journal of Biblical Literature* 137, no. 1 (2018): 107–26.
15. Northrop Frye, "Varieties of Literary Utopias," *Daedalus* (1965): 323–47.
16. Steven J. Schweitzer and Frauke Uhlenbrush, "Exile, Empire, and Prophecy: Reframing Utopian Concerns in Chronicles," in *Worlds That Could Not Be: Utopia in Chronicles, Ezra and Nehemiah* (Bloomsbury, 2016).
17. Haggai, Zechariah, and Malachi address aspects of the community's behavior that needed to change, including their apathy vis-à-vis the building project and issues of impurity. But the changes are a precondition for the utopian future to manifest, not a guarantee of its immediacy.
18. Zechariah is set in the same period as the book of Haggai, during the early years of Darius I.

Zion; again He will choose Jerusalem."[19] But there is no indication that the people can turn that vision into a reality. All they can do is wait. A biblically grounded, utopian-oriented community, then, is left with two key features: the ability to cope with the status quo by dissociating from it and a paradoxical mix of hope and powerlessness. That approach might have come to dominate Jewish thought had it not been for the drastically different outlook expressed in the work of Ezra-Nehemiah.

EZRA-NEHEMIAH'S REJECTION OF "ONGOING EXILE" AND "UTOPIAN THINKING" MODELS

Ezra-Nehemiah begins with the words "In the first year of Cyrus, king of Persia, when the Lord's word pronounced by Jeremiah had come to pass, the Lord stirred the spirit of Cyrus, king of Persia, and he issued a proclamation throughout his kingdom, by word of mouth and written word as well."[20] The assertion is unequivocal: Jeremiah's prophecy of redemption has materialized. That is not to say that the author of Ezra-Nehemiah is unaware of the difficulties posed by the Persian period. He is well aware of them, and those difficulties are addressed throughout the book. But rather than comforting his audience, the author of Ezra-Nehemiah chooses to embolden them. He encourages them, as we will see, to mine their reality for its latent potential rather than focus on its deficiencies and wait for perfection. Instead of painting portraits of what could be, the author of Ezra-Nehemiah urges his audience to accept what is. And then, he tells them: *make it better.*

CONSCIOUS OPTIMISM

Two scenes depicted in Ezra-Nehemiah capture the attitude that stands in stark contrast to utopian thought. Not coincidentally, the scenes take place during the seminal events of the period: the commencement of the Temple building project and the law giving.

---

19. Zechariah 1:17.
20. Ezra 1:1.

Ezra 3 tells us that "after the builders had laid the foundation for the Temple of the Lord, the priests took up their positions in their vestments with trumpets, and the Levites, the sons of Asaf, with cymbals, to praise the Lord, as David, king of Israel, had ordained. The Levites chanted hymns of praise thanking the Lord, 'For He is good; for His kindness to Israel is forever.' And all the people raised a great shout in praise of the Lord, for the House of the Lord had been established."[21] But a sadness punctures the joy. Ezra-Nehemiah, like Haggai, mentions a contingent that remembers the glory of the First Temple and begins to mourn the evident disparity. We are told that "when many of the older priests, Levites, and family heads who had seen the first House upon its foundations laid their eyes on this House, they wept with loud voices, while the crowds raised their voices in a shout of joy."[22] But unlike Haggai, the author of Ezra-Nehemiah does not combat their tears with utopian promises.[23] Those crying are not encouraged to fantasize about an alternative future to make the present bearable. What we find instead is a simple narration of the scene's outcome. "The people could not distinguish the sound of the shout of joy from the voices of those who wept; for the people raised a great shout, and the sound was heard from afar."[24] Disappointment is acknowledged in Ezra-Nehemiah, but discontent and gratitude, we are shown, can coexist. The difficulties of the period are conceded, but the sorrow generated by those difficulties is not granted the power to drown out the joy of its triumphs. The community described in Ezra-Nehemiah savors the historic moments it is witness to, imperfect as they may be.

Nehemiah 8 similarly depicts accepting the complexities of the religious-historical experience. In an open plaza opposite the Water Gate in Jerusalem, the people assemble around Ezra to study the Torah of Moses. Men, women, and anyone old enough to learn gather around the wooden platform upon which Ezra stands, and they clamor to hear every word he utters. But the people "were all weeping as they listened

---

21. Ibid. 3:10–11.
22. Ibid., v. 12.
23. They also are not met with the rebuke that Haggai delivers (Hag. 1:3–6).
24. Ezra 3:13.

to the words of the Torah."[25] Realizing how little Torah they know and how many sins they have inadvertently committed, the people begin to cry. They are not, as a religious community, where they now understand they should be. Once again, the community in Ezra-Nehemiah confronts a chasm between a biblical ideal and their current reality. Once again, their response to that disparity reflects the author's outlook: "Today is sacred to the Lord, your God," the leaders proclaim, "You should neither mourn nor weep."[26] Ezra then continues, "Now go and feast on delicacies, drink sweet things, and send servings of food to those who have none – for this day is sacred to our Lord. Do not be sorrowful, for rejoicing in the Lord is your strength and shelter."[27] Ezra is not absolving the people of their responsibility to fortify their religious observance. His critique of the community's sins is explicit on multiple occasions.[28] He is also not simply telling them to "cheer up." Without denying their flaws, Ezra reminds his audience that the instrument of change is in their hands. The laws that would lead them toward the ideal are now theirs. Ezra tells them to replace their weeping and self-flagellation with Torah learning by studying the books that have been preserved and passed down to them and in that way to transform into the community they want to be. And that is exactly what the people do. They return the next day to "ponder the words of the Torah."[29] They learn about long-forgotten festivals and then renew those festivals, and there is "jubilant rejoicing."[30]

THEOLOGY AT THE ROOT OF EZRA-NEHEMIAH'S OPTIMISM

The optimism evident in Ezra-Nehemiah is not borne of naivete but of a conscious choice. Numerous factors including personality, upbringing, and cultural conditioning can play a role in an individual or community's choice to assume an optimistic approach to life. And while we

---

25. Nehemiah 8:9.
26. Ibid.
27. Ibid., v. 10.
28. Ezra 9–10.
29. Nehemiah 8:13.
30. Ibid., v. 17.

cannot speak to the personality or upbringing of the author of Ezra-Nehemiah, we can trace the theology of the work that seems to anchor its optimism. This theology is already evident in the opening verse of the book. "In the first year of Cyrus, king of Persia, when the Lord's word pronounced by Jeremiah had come to pass, the Lord stirred the spirit of Cyrus, king of Persia, and he issued a proclamation throughout his kingdom, by word of mouth and written word as well."[31] The author is not simply telling us *what* happened in 539 BCE; he is telling us *why* it happened. Cyrus's proclamation, according to the author, is a manifestation of God's intervention in and management of history. And while students of the Bible may take the fact of God's mediation in history as a given, the same may not necessarily be said for the original audience of Ezra-Nehemiah, as indicated by the author's choice to introduce his work with such an explicitly theological claim.[32]

While God's control of the universe and ability to intervene in history are biblical doctrine, His intervention is not always evinced. The Book of Esther, for example, set in the Persian period as well, makes no such claims about God's direct intervention in history. The Jewish actors in the Book of Esther, like the Jews in Ezra-Nehemiah, are at the whim of foreign rulers. The fates of both communities depend on the decisions and – as is the case in Esther – the unstable impulses of those in charge. But the Jews in the Book of Esther need to survive completely on their own. God is famously excluded from their story. Of course, the series of serendipitous events around which the plot of Esther unfolds leads its reader to question whether a higher power orchestrates the lucky coincidences. But while Esther insinuates the possibility of God's involvement, the book never explicitly asserts it. As Michael V. Fox explains, the theology of Esther is "like an optical illusion that shifts orientation as you stare at it."[33] That very lack of certainty, the author of Esther seems to suggest, is the quintessential exilic experience. The fear and vulnerability

---

31. Ezra 1:1.

32. If we compare this verse to Ezra 6:3, which, as we explained in chapter one, likely contains a version of the decree that more closely resembles the original, the insertion of God becomes even more noteworthy.

33. Michael V. Fox, *Character and Ideology in the Book of Esther*, 246.

that come with not knowing just how, or even if, God is intervening in history, and the actions the Jewish community must take in light of that uncertainty, lie at the heart of the work. Ezra-Nehemiah, on the other hand, makes clear from its first sentence that God is pulling the strings of history. Behind the power of the Persian throne lies the ultimate power.

Of course, this understanding of divine intervention is not new in the Bible, and Ezra-Nehemiah is certainly not the first biblical book to claim that God controls international affairs. What distinguishes Ezra-Nehemiah's theology from that of other biblical works is the question that prompts it.

THEOLOGICAL TRADITIONS

Theology in the Bible is not synonymous with modern, Western theology. Biblical theology is not interested in proving or disproving the existence of God; He is taken as a given. As such, the Bible does not engage in epistemological exercises or question how and what we know about God. Biblical theology is driven instead by the desire to understand how God interacts with humanity and what those interactions tell us about the human experience. Depictions of God's primordial acts, characteristics ascribed to Him, and recollections of His intervention in human affairs all serve to delineate to the biblical audience what they can expect of God and what God expects of them.

The book of Genesis, for example, teaches us about God's omnipotence and supremacy. God as described in Genesis did not have to battle other deities or malevolent forces to gain preeminence.[34] He simply speaks His will, and, as He does, an ordered world is fashioned from unformed potential. That is important because, just a few verses later, readers of Genesis learn that they are expected to partner with the omnipotent God of creation in the perpetuation of human life on

---

34. This depiction of God stands in stark contrast to the ancient Near Eastern creation myths prevalent at the time. For more on this topic, see Nahum M. Sarna, *Understanding Genesis: The World in Light of History* (Schocken Books, 1970) and Avigdor Shinan and Yair Zakovitch, *From Gods to God: How the Bible Debunked, Suppressed, or Changed Ancient Myths and Legends* (University of Nebraska Press, 2012).

this planet[35] and maintain the order established during creation. That maintenance is accomplished when humans respect the value of human life and manifest their potential by constructing their societies around that premise.[36]

In Exodus through Deuteronomy, God particularizes His expectations of His chosen people, and the minutiae of what Israel's ordered society should look like are further explicated. But the system of reward and punishment embedded in those books, while seemingly straightforward, can also beget a uniquely monotheistic problem.[37]

THEODICY

If God is omnipotent, in which case, by definition, only He controls the materialization of evil in this world, the tacit assumption is that if the Israelites do as they are told, they will not suffer. But, as we know, they suffer plenty, both on the individual and national levels. Therefore, what we find throughout the Bible is an attempt to account for that suffering without surrendering belief in a just God. Job may be the most famous expression of this tension, better known as theodicy, but in fact almost every book in the Bible relates to this overarching theological challenge, in some cases more obliquely than others. That said, not all biblical works pose an identical solution to the problem of theodicy.

Some works explicitly invoke the framework of reward and punishment in their storytelling. In the book of Judges, for example, each time an enemy surfaces and persecutes Israel, the reader is reminded that the persecution is punishment from God for the moral deterioration of Israel's fragmented society.[38] In a similar vein, the book of Kings invokes the instances of Israel's religious failings to preemptively account for

---

35. Genesis 1:28.

36. This concept is made most evident in the single directive humanity received after it descended into chaos and was nearly wiped out by the flood. (Gen. 9:1–11).

37. For a discussion of theodicy challenges in polytheistic societies, see Antti Laato and Johannes C. De Moor, *Theodicy in the World of the Bible* (Brill E-Books, 2003), https://ci.nii.ac.jp/ncid/BA67809329, xxii.

38. This plotline is outlined in Judges 2:6–22.

the forced exiles wrought by invading empires.[39] The bulk of classical prophecy warns Israel that her actions will incur punishment, so when that punishment eventually comes to pass, God's justness has already been accounted for.[40] But other works relay alternative perspectives.

In some of the psalms, for example, we find the notion of delayed justice. Psalm 37 proclaims, "Do not be incensed at the wicked or let your envy be kindled by evildoers, for they will soon wither like grass and fade away like greenery....Wait for the Lord silently, patiently.... For the wicked will be cut off, while those who hope for the Lord shall inherit the earth."[41] The psalmist suggests that our questions about God's justness arise from our lack of awareness of an extended time line. That timeline, he claims, is just, and we simply need to recognize that our experiences are but a point on it, not its entirety. This belief in *eventual* justice diffuses the problem of present injustices. The book of Job, less temporally focused, claims that the injustices we perceive belong to a larger divine order that we cannot comprehend. In fact, Job himself admits as much to God at the end of the book when he says, "I know that You can do anything, that no plan is beyond You. 'Who dares obscure wisdom when he himself knows nothing?' Indeed, I have spoken but did not understand. There are wonders beyond me I did not know."[42]

These are but a few of the approaches the Bible offers to the perennial question. Ultimately, though, as Michael Fox explains, regardless of the approach, the "essence of theodicy is to see things differently. Seen in a different perspective, incidents of injustice become insignificant or subordinated to a greater, more meaningful whole."[43]

---

39. II Kings 17:7–41, 21:12–18, 22:16–20.
40. It is not uncommon for the Rabbis to offer explanations for suffering in their midrashic expansions on narratives where no reason is explicit. See, for example, Megilla 12a, where a reason for the near-Holocaust of the Jews is offered. Similarly, Bava Batra 91b offers an explanation for the deaths of Elimelech, Mahlon, and Kilyon at the beginning of the Book of Ruth.
41. Psalms 37:1–9.
42. Job 42:2–3.
43. See Michael V. Fox, *A Time to Tear Down and a Time to Build Up: A Rereading of Ecclesiastes* (Wipf and Stock, 2010), 63.

THEODICY IN EZRA-NEHEMIAH

Like many of its biblical counterparts, Ezra-Nehemiah claims that Israel's past sins are the reason for her exile and, as such, defends the notion of God's justice. When the elders of Judah explain the historical context of their building project to the Persian inspectors in Ezra 5, for example, they declare: "We are the servants of the God of the heavens and the earth. We are rebuilding the House which was built many years ago; a great king of Israel built it and completed it. But because our ancestors angered the God of the heavens, He placed them in the power of Nebuchadnezzar, the Chaldean, king of Babylon, who destroyed the House and exiled the people to Babylon."[44] Ezra's proclamation during his prayer in Ezra 9 reflects that same contention: "O Lord, God of Israel, You have dealt with us righteously."[45]

Nehemiah makes a similar declaration in his prayer in Nehemiah 9 when he says that God fulfilled his promises to Abraham because He is "just"[46] and recapitulates in verses 32–33 that "from the days of the Assyrian kings until today. You have been just throughout all that has come upon us." Perhaps most succinctly, Nehemiah says to God, "You have dealt in truth while we have committed evil. Our kings and our princes, our priests, and our ancestors did not act according to Your Torah; they heeded neither Your commands nor the warnings through which You admonished them. Despite their sovereign rule and the bountiful goodness You had bestowed upon them in the expansive and rich land You had given them, they did not serve You, nor did they repent or turn away from their evil deeds."[47] In a world where God's justice rules, Nehemiah puts very plainly that the Israelites deserve what is coming to them. He refers to God's justice in Nehemiah 13 as well, this time as an implicit warning to his audience. Rebuking the nobles of Jerusalem for not properly observing Shabbat, Nehemiah poses the following rhetorical question: "What is this evil thing you are doing, desecrating the Sabbath day? Your ancestors acted just like this, so that our God

---

44. Verses 11–12.
45. Ezra 9:15.
46. Nehemiah 9:8.
47. Ibid., vv. 33–35.

brought all this evil upon us and upon this city, and now you are stoking anger against Israel by desecrating the Sabbath."[48] If Shabbat desecration wrought punishment in the past, why would they risk making the same mistake again?

An additional component of God's justice is stressed in Ezra-Nehemiah as well.[49] Before he departs for Jerusalem, Nehemiah prays: "Please, Lord, God of the heavens, the great and awesome God.... We have injured You grievously and have not kept the commandments, statutes, and laws with which You charged Moses, Your servant. Remember, please, what You charged Moses, Your servant, saying, 'You will break faith; I will disperse you among the nations.'"[50] But then, as his prayer continues, the notion of God's justice is extended to the end of the exile as well. Paraphrasing God's promise, Nehemiah proclaims, "Yet you will return to Me; you will keep My commandments and observe them. If you should be expelled to the farthest of horizons, even from there I will gather them, bringing them to the place where I have chosen to house My name."[51] If their past sins earned them the exile, Nehemiah points out, then their past repentance and good deeds likewise earned their return. God's application of justice is consistent and therefore equally evident in Israel's suffering and good fortune.

GOD'S COMPASSION

We mentioned earlier that Ezra-Nehemiah's theology gives rise to its optimism but that theology is not rooted in the belief in God's justice alone. In fact, what distinguishes Ezra-Nehemiah's theology is the very lack of attention paid to God's contemporary justice. Both Ezra and Nehemiah refer to those ways in which God's justice was demonstrated in the past, but, interestingly, neither of them refers to God's current application of justice. When God's justice is mentioned in their speeches, it is always in

---

48. Ibid. 13:17–18.
49. This component is not unique to Ezra-Nehemiah, but it is emphasized in the work as part of its broader theological framework.
50. Nehemiah 1:5–8.
51. Ibid., v. 9.

retrospect. His justice was evident in Israel's past, but neither Ezra nor Nehemiah claim that God's justice continues to regulate the events of their time. That obvious omission suggests that something else is at play.

If other biblical works ask how to make sense of a just God in the context of Israel's suffering and cite Israel's sins as the answer, Ezra-Nehemiah asks how to make sense of a just God considering Israel's undeserved blessings. The answer offered in Ezra-Nehemiah is that while God is just and has demonstrated that justness in the past, He is also compassionate. And in the era through which they are living, God's compassion reigns.[52]

Ezra speaks to this compassion in his prayer in Ezra 9. After mentioning the sins of their past that led to exile, Ezra continues: "But now, for a short moment we have been granted a pardon by the Lord our God, who has left us a remnant and has given us a stake in His holy place. Our God has rekindled the light in our eyes, allowing us to sustain ourselves.... He has shown us kindness through the kings of Persia, allowing us to sustain ourselves, to exalt the House of our God and rebuild its ruins; He has built us a wall in Judah and Jerusalem."[53] Because God is compassionate, Ezra explains, they are experiencing the blessing of return. Because God is merciful, He is allowing them unprecedented opportunities. In Ezra 9, Ezra claims that "after all that has befallen us due to our evil deeds and our great guilt, You, our God, have punished us for less than the worth of our sins, having given us this remnant."[54] God's justice, Ezra asserts, is fact. But if God so pleases, His compassion can trump strict justice. Ezra clarifies that his audience experiences the benefits of that dominant divine attribute, but how they utilize that moment is up to them.

Like other biblical authors, the author of Ezra-Nehemiah uses the interface between God and Israel to explain the circumstances in which his audience finds itself. But unlike so many others, he locates

---

52. Sara Japhet formulates this understanding of theodicy in the book of Ezra-Nehemiah in an article titled "Theodicy in Ezra-Nehemiah and Chronicles," in Laato and De Moor, *Theodicy in the World of the Bible,* 429–69.
53. Ezra 9:8–9.
54. Ibid., v. 13.

that interface amid positive experiences and hope. He chooses to view those events that illuminate God's ongoing kindness. Rather than ask why things are so bad, the author wants to know why things are so good. He wants to know why "God has rekindled the light in our eyes."[55] This focus drives the optimism of the book. The theological contours of the work create space for a traumatized people to feel safe once again in their relationship with God while motivating them to effect change. Ezra-Nehemiah's audience understands that it must work to repair the community and ensure that it does not repeat the mistakes of its past, but its faith also rests on trust in God's munificence and, by extension, the success of its endeavors.

REMAINING QUESTION

This chapter began by listing the adversities the returnees to Jerusalem faced. Ezra-Nehemiah's optimism does not entail its disregard for the very real problems the people confronted. Poverty, foreign political pressure, and antagonism toward the building project are all addressed in the work. But if it does not attribute those challenges to the reality of an ongoing exile or to God's punishment of His people as we might have expected, then to what can they be ascribed? And if, as logic dictates, the solution to the problems is not patience or repentance, then what is it? The answers to those questions will be more complex and more profound than we might have initially assumed. But they will also contain within them a road map for generations of Jews to follow.

---

55. Ibid., v. 8.

Chapter Five

History Uninterrupted

MISPLACED PRIORITIES

The delay in the building project, which comprises a large part of Ezra 1–6, was undoubtedly frustrating to the Judeans at the time. And yet, as we saw in the previous chapters, while those difficulties are presented, they are not dwelled upon. In the historical retrospective of those early chapters, for example, we learn about the hurdles the community had to surmount in order to complete the Temple's construction, but the community in those chapters is presented as proactive, resourceful, and successful.[1] The dire economic straits later in the work are likewise presented as a significant difficulty, but one for which solutions could be implemented.[2] At no point in Ezra-Nehemiah, though, do we get the sense that these challenges lead the people to question the veracity of their mission or the possibility of its ultimate success. That outlook is an important component of Ezra-Nehemiah's ideology, and it differs from some Second Temple prophets. So, in what follows, we will look

---

1. The success is also explicitly attributed to God's interference and assistance (see Ezra 6:22).
2. Nehemiah 5.

more closely at Ezra-Nehemiah's pragmatic, empowering outlook and try to understand from where it derives.

To begin with a point of contrast, the prophet Haggai seems to indicate that the Judeans were to blame for the challenges that arose during the rebuilding process. To borrow from a contemporary psychological model, if one were to rank Temple building according to Maslow's famous hierarchy of needs, it would probably be consigned to one of the last categories of human priorities. Built to meet the spiritual needs of the people, the Temple would be sought only after more basic physiological needs, such as food and shelter, were already secured. Haggai seems to indicate that this is exactly what happens when the people return to the land. Before they start building the Temple, he claims, they make sure that, among other comforts, they have homes in which to dwell. But Haggai, unlike modern psychologists, rejects this seemingly instinctive human phenomenon. Eighteen years after Cyrus's declaration,[3] with the Temple still incomplete, Haggai criticizes the people for putting their personal wants before the Temple-building project. In his first oracle, the prophet proclaims God's message to the people: "Is it the time for you yourselves to sit under roofs in your homes while this House lies desolate?"[4] The people, Haggai declares, care more about their physical indulgences than they do about building an appropriate space for God in their midst. Those disordered priorities, the prophet goes on, are to blame for the drought and economic challenges they suffer. "You sow much but bring in little, eat but are not satisfied, drink but remain sober. You clothe yourselves but are not warmed, and anyone who earns wages receives them into a pouch full of holes…. You expect much but receive little. You bring it home; I cause it to wither. Why? Because of My House which remains desolate while each of you keeps running back to his own house, says the Lord of Hosts. Therefore, the skies lock up

---

3. Haggai's first prophecy is dated to the second year of the reign of Darius I (522–485 BCE).

4. Haggai 1:4. The verse is reminiscent of the discomfort King David expressed to the prophet Nathan, "Look now – I am dwelling in a cedarwood palace while the Ark of God is dwelling in a tent," before announcing his intentions to build a Temple (II Sam. 7:2). Haggai critiques the people for their lack of a comparable discomfort.

the dew above you; the land locks up its produce."[5] Relief from their anguish, God tells them through the prophet, will only come when they "go up onto the mountain, bring wood, and build My House."[6] The economic difficulties they face are retribution for the fact that they delight in their houses before the Temple is constructed. Likewise, the delay of the building project, Haggai makes clear, is a result of that apathy.[7]

A GUILTLESS PEOPLE

In Ezra 5:1–2, the efforts of Haggai and Zechariah to rouse the determination of the people is mentioned,[8] and in 6:14 the prophets are credited in part with the success of the project:[9] "And the elders of the Jews went on with the building successfully encouraged by the prophecy of Haggai the prophet and Zechariah son of Ido; they built the House and completed it according to the command of the God of Israel and in keeping with the edict of Cyrus, Darius, and King Artaxerxes of Persia." But while the prophets themselves are mentioned by name, the attitude apparent in their texts is not. Ezra-Nehemiah acknowledges both the poverty of the people and the delay of the Temple project, but nowhere is the indifference of the people invoked. If anything, we are told that "some of the clan leaders, when they arrived at the House of the Lord in Jerusalem, willingly contributed to fix the House of God back on its

5. Haggai 1:5–10.
6. Ibid., v. 8.
7. As mentioned in chapter four, there are those who claim, based on Haggai 1–2, that the people did not believe the seventy years of exile had reached their conclusion. For more on this theory, see, for example, Hayim Tadmor, "'The Appointed Time Has Not Yet Arrived': the Historical Background of Haggai 1:2," in *Ki Baruch Hu: Ancient Near Eastern, Biblical, and Judaic Studies in Honor of Baruch A. Levine*, ed. Robert Chazan et al. (Winona Lake: Eisenbrauns, 1999), 401–8.
8. "And the prophets Haggai the prophet and Zechariah son of Ido prophesied to the Jews in Judah and Jerusalem in the name of the God of Israel. So Zerubbabel son of Shealtiel and Jeshua son of Jozadak arose and began to rebuild the House of God in Jerusalem with God's prophets supporting them."
9. The book of Zechariah, set in the same period as Haggai, addresses similar issues pertaining to the restoration of the Temple and the community.

foundations, each giving what they could."[10] In addition, we learn that in "the second year of their arrival in Jerusalem, for the House of God, in the second month, Zerubbabel son of Shealtiel and Jeshua son of Jozadak and the rest of their brothers – the priests and the Levites, and all those who had come from the exile to Jerusalem – began by appointing the Levites, twenty years of age and above, to supervise the work of constructing the Lord's House."[11] In contrast to the book of Haggai, Ezra-Nehemiah conveys a sense of unanimous commitment to the project. The indifference addressed in Haggai's oracles is contrasted with the enthusiasm evident in Ezra-Nehemiah's recollection of the period, and the building project in Ezra-Nehemiah seems to be a top priority of the people. As such, the delay is ascribed to a very different explanation.

EXTERNAL FACTORS

In Ezra 3, we read about the eagerness of the people to build the Temple, and in the next chapter we come to understand what thwarted that eagerness. Ezra 4:1 introduces the "adversaries of Judah and Benjamin" for the first time.[12] These adversaries, we are told, "undermined the people of Judah, and made them afraid to build. They employed advisors to foil their plans throughout the reign of Cyrus, king of Persia, and through the reign of Darius, king of Persia."[13] The adversaries "wrote an accusation against the people of Judah and Jerusalem"[14] and succeed in convincing the Persian authorities to issue a royal order to halt the project, which remains in effect "until the second year of the reign of Darius, king of Persia."[15] Ezra-Nehemiah does not blame a lazy or ambivalent community for the setbacks experienced in the early phases of restoration. Instead, it blames Judah's adversaries, who set out to undermine the project, and the Persian emperors, who unwittingly go along with the ruse.

---

10. Ezra 2:68–69.
11. Ibid. 3:8.
12. The identity of these "adversaries" constitutes a central theme of the work and is addressed at length in chapter seven.
13. Ezra 4:4–5.
14. Ibid., v. 6.
15. Ibid., v. 24.

The assessment that external factors rather than internal deficits are to blame makes its way into Nehemiah's explanation for the community's economic struggles seventy-five years later as well. In Nehemiah 2, for example, Nehemiah blames the "dismal state" of Jerusalem on the unrelenting attacks of the Judean's adversaries.[16] And in Nehemiah 5, he addresses the impact of the heavy taxation burden imposed by the Persian Empire.[17] In contrast to the prophets of the early restoration period, Ezra-Nehemiah presents the challenges it faces as fallout of external opposition, not internal failures.

WHEN TANAKH PRESENTS MORE THAN ONE EXPLANATION

When internal-biblical discrepancies such as this one arise, it is tempting to try to discern which account is "truer" or which explanation is *the* explanation. But that reflex is beside the point in the study of Tanakh. When it comes to biblical interpretation of historical events, there is rarely one truth. Instead, the Tanakh reveals time and again the existence of multiple, simultaneous truths. It shows us that there are numerous facets to every reality and that the specific ideology of a given work determines which facet of its reality is highlighted. Our job as readers is not to ask which book got it "right," but rather to scrutinize what a given work is trying to communicate through its choices, arrangement, and presentation of facts. Seemingly incongruous biblical portraits lead to a richer, more holistic understanding of our past.

As such, the prophets' portrayal of the difficulties of their time in these various ways is not surprising. Haggai simultaneously censures and inspires his audience, which is exactly what a biblical prophet is meant to do. He urges the people to consider how their behaviors contribute to the scenarios in which they find themselves and encourages

---

16. Nehemiah 2:19.
17. Ibid. 5:4–5. In the same chapter, Nehemiah criticizes some of the elites for not canceling debts in a time of such dire poverty, a topic that will be addressed fully in chapter nine. But his criticism is restricted to a specific segment of the population and to specific behaviors, and we don't get the sense, as we do in Haggai, that the people on the whole were the root cause of the retributive poverty.

penitence and action. And, in fact, as explored in the previous chapter, the cause and effect through which the prophets frame the challenges of the period seem to have worked: the building project that had lain dormant for close to two decades was complete within four years of Haggai's first oracle.

But the author of Ezra-Nehemiah has different objectives. Writing when the Temple is already built, the author of Ezra-Nehemiah does not have to rouse the people from their stasis or motivate them to build a Temple. Instead, he can focus on those elements that once interfered with the building project and continue to be a problem in his time. The author of Ezra-Nehemiah focuses on the "opponents of Judah" and the occasional unjust Persian policy, because this approach serves the dual purpose of uniting his audience against a common enemy and encouraging them to do what is politically necessary to resolve their ongoing struggles.[18] Like the prophets, the author of Ezra-Nehemiah wants to galvanize the people around his social agenda. But because his agenda differs from Haggai's, so does the way he recalls and sketches their early difficulties. As Jeremiah Cataldo pithily puts it, "My concerns of today shape my memories of the past."[19]

In addition to rallying its audience, Ezra-Nehemiah's conception of the era's setbacks is also steered by its understanding of history and the way in which history progresses. Memory, as Eviatar Zerubavel explains, is "patterned in a highly structured manner that both shapes and distorts what we actually come to mentally retain from the past."[20] The structures of those memories give "shape" to history as well. Where other works see beginnings and ends of eras, Ezra-Nehemiah sees an unending flow of history, which has direct bearing on the work's response to adversity.[21]

We have already considered how memory of the exile shaped the character of post-exilic communities and the literature they produced.

---

18. We will see in chapter seven that unanimity was never fully achieved.

19. Jeremiah Cataldo, "Utopia in Agony: The Role of Prejudice in Ezra-Nehemiah's Idea for Restoration," in *Worlds That Could Not Be. Utopia in Chronicles, Ezra and Nehemiah* (2016), 147.

20. Eviatar Zerubavel, *Time Maps: Collective Memory and the Social Shape of the Past* (University of Chicago Press, 2003), 11.

21. Penelope J. Corfield, *Time and Shape of History* (Yale University Press, 2007).

But if other biblical works present the exile as a violent rupture with the past,[22] Ezra-Nehemiah presents the exile as one event within a series of ongoing movements and countermovements, at home in the ebb and flow of Jewish history. While that perspective is not explicit, it is communicated through Ezra-Nehemiah's deliberate use of motifs. Biblical motifs, as Shemaryahu Talmon explains, are employed for the "formative messages" they convey. They are "meant to assist their readers in reliving the intrinsic sentiments and reactions which inspired the individuals and collectivities that had actually experienced the primal situations or conditions."[23] Ezra-Nehemiah uses motifs to communicate themes that are central to the work and to its understanding of time. But rather than simply recycling biblical motifs, Ezra-Nehemiah alters preexisting ones just enough to shift how exile and the period that followed are registered in the imagination of its readers. Two motifs in particular, the Temple vessels and the royal table, are excellent examples of this literary technique.

THE MOTIF OF TEMPLE VESSELS

The final chapters of the book of Kings describe the destruction of the Temple in vivid detail. In II Kings 24, we are told that Nebuchadnezzar "carried off all the treasures of the House of the Lord and the treasures of the palace, and he stripped off all the golden vessels that Solomon, king of Israel, had made in the Sanctuary of the Lord."[24] In the next chapter, we learn that "the Chaldeans broke down the bronze pillars from the House of the Lord, the stands, and the Bronze Sea that was in the House of the Lord and carried the bronze off to Babylon. They took the pots, shovels, shears, and spoons and all the bronze vessels that had been used in service, while the chief of the guard took the fire pans and the basins – whatever was of gold, and whatever was of silver. The two pillars, the Molten Sea, and the stands that Solomon had made for

---

22. See for example, the end of II Kings and the Book of Lamentations.
23. Shemaryahu Talmon, *Literary Motifs and Patterns in the Hebrew Bible: Collected Essays* (Penn State University Press, 2013), 5.
24. II Kings 24:13.

the House of the Lord – the weight in bronze of all these vessels was incalculable. Each pillar was eighteen cubits high, and its capital was of bronze – the capital was three cubits high – and meshwork and pomegranates surrounded the capital, all of bronze; and the same on top of the second pillar atop the meshwork."[25] As we read the words, we cannot help but think of an earlier, idyllic time, when Solomon carefully and lovingly erected those very pillars and inaugurated the vessels that are now stripped and smelted for their monetary value.[26] It is likely that the author of Kings intends to convey this discord, the difference between the beginning and the end of the era, between the vessels in their proper place in Jerusalem's center and their displacement in the foreign land of their enemies. Like the people who once utilized them, the vessels in the book of Kings had been forcibly removed from where they belong.

Ample material and textual evidence from the ancient Near East bears witness to the fact that statues and monuments removed from temples were often treated with violence.[27] As Jacob Wright explains, "Given their spatial-symbolic valence, the demolition of temples – along with the deportation and/or destruction of gods and other cultic items found within them – constitutes one of the most effective methods of conquering and remapping territories."[28] Or, as Natalie May puts it, "The ultimate case of demolition of figurative complexes is attested for empires, which created the most powerful imagery and semantic semiotic systems that reflect and propagandize their might. The destruction of imperial power was the destruction of the semiotic system created by it – destruction of the art of the empire, hence of the art and empire."[29] The focus in Kings on the vessels' confiscation indicates that the author understands the gravity of the act. Knowing what we do about their symbolism within the program of imperialism, readers assume that the vessels are at worst

---

25. Ibid. 25:13–17.

26. I Kings 6.

27. For examples, see Brad E. Kelle et al., *Interpreting Exile: Displacement and Deportation in Biblical Modern Contexts* (Brill, 2012), 121–24.

28. Ibid.

29. Natalie Naomi May, ed., *Iconoclasm and Text Destruction in the Ancient Near East and Beyond*, vol. 8 (Oriental Institute of the University of Chicago, 2012), 6.

destroyed, at best mishandled and profaned.[30] Either way, as the author of Kings intends, their removal feels final.[31]

The opening of Ezra-Nehemiah tells us that "King Cyrus took out the vessels of the House of the Lord that Nebuchadnezzar had removed from Jerusalem and placed in the house of his gods. Cyrus, king of Persia, had them taken out by Mithredath, keeper of the treasures, who counted them for Sheshbazzar, prince of Judah."[32] The symbol of finality and rupture in Kings becomes, in Ezra-Nehemiah, a sign of continuity. The vessels, to our pleasant surprise, are not destroyed; they are simply detained temporarily in the temple of Babylon and are now returning with their rightful owners to Jerusalem.[33] Babylon is not the vessels' final resting place according to Ezra-Nehemiah; it is simply a stop on their journey through history. And the vessels' lot, while perhaps insignificant to the modern reader, is of crucial import to the work's original audience. At no point, the vessels demonstrate, is there complete severance from the past. Thorough annihilation of what once was, according to Ezra-Nehemiah, never occurs. The auspicious fate of the vessels depicted in Ezra-Nehemiah pushes back at the notion of exile as a "radical discontinuity"[34] and presents it instead as a stage in an ongoing progression that encompasses both life in the land and life beyond. As Yael Zerubavel speaks of relics as "tangible evidence" that serves to connect people with their otherwise elusive past.[35] The

---

30. Their mistreatment is alluded to in Daniel 5, in which King Belshazzar ordered the vessels brought for use at his banquet where foreign gods were being praised. It is a shocking image, but, as it turns out, Belshazzar was appropriately punished for his brazen misuse of the vessels, reinforcing the message of the work. Along similar lines, the tradition to read the words "vessels unlike any other" (Est. 1:7) to the tune of Lamentations also seems to imply that the vessels used at the feast of Xerxes were from the Jerusalem Temple.

31. II Chronicles 36:10 tells us that vessels were also brought to Babylon with Jehoiachin.

32. Ezra 1: 7–8.

33. In Isaiah 52:11, the vessels are also used, poetically, as a symbol of return. However, as is explicit in Ezra-Nehemiah, not all the vessels were returned (Ezra 2:63; Neh. 7:65).

34. Kelle, *Interpreting Exile*, 106.

35. Yael Zerubavel, *Recovered Roots: Collective Memory and the Making of Israeli National Tradition* (University of Chicago Press, 1995), 67. In an earlier chapter, she quotes

vessels returned from the First Temple link the returnees in a tangible way with what came before.[36]

THE MAGNITUDE OF THE KING'S TABLE

Like the vessels, the motif of the "king's table" plays an important role at the end of the book of Kings. Also like the vessels, it is transformed in Ezra-Nehemiah to expose newfound significance. The final scene in the book of Kings tells us that King Jehoiachin is released from prison by order of the Babylonian king Evil-Merodach and that "he dined in his [Evil-Merodach's] presence for the rest of his life."[37] On its most basic level, the scene ends the book on a hopeful note. It leaves the reader with the sense that, while the Temple was destroyed and the last of the Judean kings were either killed or exiled with the people, there remains a glimmer of hope that the situation will improve. The release of the Davidic heir and the benevolent treatment he receives could be interpreted as a sign of better things to come. While there certainly is something to be said for the encouragement the scene provides, its significance is still greater.

Sitting at a king's table can symbolize camaraderie and intimacy, but it can also signal distrust, mostly on the part of the king toward his guest. "Keep your enemies close" is probably the adage most apt to describe a king's motivation in such a scenario. In the book of Samuel, for example, we learn that Saul uses his table as the place to monitor suspected enemies and, as such, becomes paranoid when David unexpectedly vacates

---

the famed Israeli archaeologist Yigal Yadin describing his work at excavation sites in Israel. "[W]e found that our emotions were a mixture of tension and awe, astonishment and pride at being part of the reborn State of Israel after a Diaspora of eighteen hundred years. Here we were, living in tents erected by the Israel Defense Forces, walking every day through the ruins of a Roman camp which caused the death of our forefathers. Nothing remains here today of the Romans save a heap of stones on the face of the desert, but here the descendants of the besieged were returning to salvage their ancestors' precious belongings" (p. 59).

36. References to the vessels are made several times throughout the work in addition to Ezra 1, always in this context of continuity and building. See, for example, Ezra 5:14 and 6:5.

37. II Kings 25:30.

his assigned seat.[38] Later on, after he has assumed the throne, David similarly decrees that Mephibosheth, one of the only surviving heirs of Saul's household and a potential threat, would remain in Jerusalem and "always dined at the king's table."[39] Of course, there are circumstances in which being invited to dine with the king is a sign of royal benevolence or gratitude,[40] but even in those cases, the table "serves as a symbol of monarchic power."[41] Eating at the table of a foreign king means eating under his watchful gaze, so the symbolism of Jehoiachin as guest at the table of a Babylonian king is multivalent.

This is why, just as the account of the vessels' destruction at the end of Kings evokes memories of a better time, Jehoiachin's dining also brings readers back to earlier, safer times, when Davidic kings dined under very different circumstances. The opening chapters of the book of Kings depict the grandeur and autonomy that Solomon's reign symbolizes. His reign is described as a time when Solomon "ruled over all the kingdoms from the River to the land of the Philistines, up to the border of Egypt"[42] and "had peace on every surrounding border; from Dan to Be'er Sheba; Judah and Israel dwelled in safety, each person beneath his grapevine and fig tree."[43] Most importantly for our discussion, Solomon makes a "feast for all his servants."[44] The reaction of the Queen of Sheba to the feasts of Solomon is perhaps most indicative of his prosperity and power: "When the Queen of Sheba saw all of Solomon's wisdom and the House he had built, and the fare of his table and how his subjects were seated and his servants' attendance and attire, and his cupbearers and the burnt offerings he offered up in the House of the Lord, she was left breathless."[45] While Jehoiachin's eating at the table of the Babylonian king is certainly better than eating in prison, readers of

---

38. I Samuel 20:27.
39. II Samuel 9:13. Esther, too, used the king's table as the setting to sabotage Haman (Est. 7:1–6).
40. I Kings 2:7, 5:7.
41. Kelle, *Interpreting Exile*, 112.
42. I Kings 5:1.
43. Ibid., vv. 4–5.
44. Ibid. 3:15.
45. Ibid. 10:4–5.

Kings cannot help but also fixate on just how much has changed since the days of Solomon. If the table at the beginning of the work depicts an independent Davidic king, exerting absolute control from the heart of his empire, the table at the end signals a Davidic king displaced, likely demoralized, and utterly dependent on the inclinations of a foreign ruler. Like the Temple vessels, the motif of the king's table signals a conclusive end to the First Commonwealth.

But just as Ezra-Nehemiah redefines the symbolism of the Temple vessels, it likewise reformulates the significance of the king's table. At the king's table in Nehemiah 2, "while wine was before him,"[46] Nehemiah's request to return to Jerusalem is granted. Nehemiah, the royal cupbearer, is depicted as having a personal relationship with the king, and, in Nehemiah's words, "It pleased the king to send me."[47] Rather than a sign of capture and confinement, the king's table in Ezra-Nehemiah is a portal back to the Land of Israel, which is why Nehemiah's requests of the king – "Let me be given missives to the governors beyond the River granting me passage so that I may come to Judah"[48] – was gladly met by Artaxerxes. Nehemiah is not being held under arrest at the king's table. He is not trapped by foreign authority. Rather, the king's table in Ezra-Nehemiah is where the transport of Judah's leader is granted and financed.[49] In addition to securing his own passage, Nehemiah also asks for a "missive to Asaf, the royal forester, so that he will provide me with timber to roof the gates of the citadel of the House, the city wall, and the residence to which I will come." Of course, as per his request, "the king endowed me in accordance with the good hand of my God upon me."[50] In Ezra-Nehemiah, Judah's leaders are dispatched and empowered to lead effectively from the foreign king's table. So, rather than

---

46. Nehemiah 2:1.
47. Ibid., v. 6.
48. Ibid., v. 7.
49. We are not ignoring the fact that Nehemiah needed the king's permission to leave his post, but the generous reaction of the king, as well as his personal concern for Nehemiah, make the request feel like a formality. The focus in the scene is less on the permission of the king and more on the movement that originates from his table.
50. Nehemiah 2:8.

symbolizing the conclusion to Israel's grand era in the land as it does at the end of Kings, the royal table in Ezra-Nehemiah is the mechanism through which that grand era picks up from where it left off.

CONTINUITY IN HISTORY AND WHY IT MATTERS

This sense of continuity created by the motifs of the vessels and the king's table is carried through the entirety of the work. In that first chapter, there is a sense that the personae mentioned seamlessly flow from one to the next even though time and geography kept them far apart. Jeremiah, who had never been to Babylon, textually encounters Cyrus in verse 1.[51] Cyrus, living decades after Nebuchadnezzar, annuls Nebuchadnezzar's earlier actions. What would otherwise be classified as pre-exilic, exilic, and post-exilic personalities are woven together in chapter 1, erasing the space between the "periods" in which they lived.

It is not only the human agents who create the illusion of an uninterrupted history. God Himself in Ezra 1:3 seems to be waiting in Jerusalem for His House to be built: "Whoever is among you from all His people, may his God be with him, and let him go up to Jerusalem, in Judah, and build the House of the Lord, God of Israel, who is the God in Jerusalem." No mention is made of God's departure or return to the land;[52] He is simply, according to Ezra 1, where He has always been. And if the Jews so choose, they can join Him.

Time continues to be telescoped in this manner in Ezra 2, where we hear about "Solomon's servants" and the "sons of Solomon's servants" in the tally of returnees.[53] Readers, aware of the number of years that have elapsed from the days of Solomon, assume the text is referring to the servants' descendants and not their actual sons. But regardless of

---

51. "In the first year of Cyrus, king of Persia, when the Lord's word pronounced by Jeremiah had come to pass." Ezra-Nehemiah is far from the only work of Tanakh that creates the sense of an unbroken flow of history. Many of the latter prophets, including Isaiah and Ezekiel generate a similar impression. In Ezra-Nehemiah however, this sense of continuity is germane to the theological and ideological ideas the work is espousing.

52. Cf. Ezekiel 10.

53. Ezra 2:55–58.

our computations, like the mention of Solomon's vessels, the mention of his servants merges the two otherwise distinct Temple periods. As Eviatar Zerubavel explains, "The various mnemonic strategies we use to help us create the illusion of historical continuity typically involve some mental bridging. A prototypical facilitator of integrating noncontiguous spaces, the bridge is a perfect metaphor for the mnemonic effort to integrate temporally noncontiguous manifestations of what we nevertheless consider 'the same' entity (person, organization, nation)…. we also use various mental bridging techniques to produce the 'connecting historical tissue' that helps us fill any historical gaps between the past and the present."[54] Solomon's servants, in this case, serve as that bridge.

This sense of contiguity continues to emerge in the text even as readers know that a lapse in time has occurred. When Ezra 2 describes those who heed Cyrus's call, it tells us that the people "returned to Jerusalem and Judah, each to his own town."[55] Despite how complicated the process of resettlement must have been, as we read those words, we imagine the returnees simply entering their old towns, walking up to their once–front doors, unlocking them, and moving right back in. In addition to their homes being filled, we also get the impression from the end of the chapter that the various positions of Temple personnel are similarly, effortlessly, reoccupied. In verse 70, we read that "the priests, Levites, and others of the people, the singers, gatekeepers, and the Netinim, settled in their towns, so that all Israel were in their towns." It is likely that many of those assuming the posts were from a younger generation and never served in the First Temple, but the text does not mention any learning curve or training process that reality would have necessitated. Such an allusion would disturb the impression of an uninterrupted refilling of Temple posts that the text cultivates.

This sense of continuity manifests not only in the positive aspects of the restoration project. The sins of the people are similarly conceived as persisting from earlier times. In the beginning of Ezra 9, for example, the leaders of the community report to Ezra that "the people Israel, and even the priests and Levites, have failed to separate themselves from the

---

54. Zerubavel, *Time Maps,* 40.
55. Ezra 2:1.

people of the land. They engage in abominations in the manner of the Canaanites, the Hittites, the Perizzites, the Jebusites, the Amonites, the Moabites, the Egyptians, and the Amorites. For they have taken some of their daughters as wives for themselves and for their sons."[56] Most of the nations listed in their complaint had long ceased to exist by the time of Ezra-Nehemiah. Even if some of their descendants did remain, they certainly were not the "people of the land" anymore. And yet, the anachronistic reference has the effect of fusing the wrongdoings of Ezra's generation with those of generations past.[57] A "symbolic synchrony of 'now' and 'then'" is reflective of the "urge to do away with the very distinction between them."[58] As such, a fluidity is created between what their ancestors did and what they are doing, suggesting an unending chronological sequence.

"PERIODIZING" HISTORY

This brings us back to the significance of Ezra-Nehemiah's perception of history and how it ties into the distinctive way in which the work construes the challenges of their day. Historiographers often periodize history, which involves bracketing off one period from another in the interest of creating order from infinitude.[59] By compartmentalizing history and naming each discrete time block according to aspects of the period by which historians feel it is best defined, history is made intelligible. Terms such as "the Stone Age," "the medieval era," "the Renaissance," and "the post-industrial age" are all such examples. [60]

---

56. Ibid. 9:1–2.
57. An additional explanation for this anachronism appears in chapter seven.
58. Zerubavel, *Time Maps*, 47.
59. Within Tanakh, the periods are most explicitly bracketed by the books that cover them. The period of Joshua, for example, is distinct from those of Judges, Kings, and so forth.
60. There is always a risk of overcompartmentalizing. But, more importantly, the terms coined by modern historians often do not adequately reflect the experiences of those who lived through the given period. Rather, they express modern associations with and notions of the period.

If periodizing helps organize history, it also invites comparisons between the very eras it configures. As David Glatt-Gilad puts it, "Periodization enables writers of history to paint the broad sweep of the contours of their subject matter, highlighting the uniqueness of a particular period while contrasting it with another."[61] In those comparisons, though, the past is often idealized. Some prophets, for example, paint idyllic portraits of the wilderness period, recalling Israel's youthful devotion and willingness to follow God into the unknown.[62] The book of Chronicles presents some of Israel's kings in an excessively favorable light, creating the impression of a bygone era in which flawless, righteous kings ruled over a glorious empire that maintained stability, peace, and prosperity.[63] Of course, these glorifications of the past do not necessarily reflect an attempt to conceal or misrepresent it. They simply demonstrate the natural tendency of history tellers to offer their audience a gold standard to inspire future generations. Creating that touchstone, though, requires the intentional act of forgetting alongside remembering. By distilling memories from the past, prophets and biblical authors tacitly charge those listening to recreate the romanticized version of what was. Unfortunately, the present does not always reach the benchmarks set by those memories. And, in such cases, the past frustrates rather than inspires.

EZRA-NEHEMIAH'S LACK OF IDEALIZATION

Because Ezra-Nehemiah interlaces the period it describes with earlier, imperfect periods, comparisons that often result from periodizing do not surface in Ezra-Nehemiah. If Ezra-Nehemiah does not subscribe to the notion of a utopian vision of the future, it likewise does not subscribe

---

61. David A. Glatt-Gilad, "The Root Kn' and Historiographic Periodization in Chronicles," *Catholic Biblical Quarterly* 64, no. 2 (April 2002): 248–57.
62. See, for example, Hosea 2:16–17 and Jeremiah 2:2.
63. See Sara Japhet, *The Ideology of the Book of Chronicles and Its place in Biblical Thought* (Penn State University Press, 2009), 364–83. Of course, not all the kings of Israel are presented in this light. The book of Chronicles enumerates the various sins of other kings who ruled and the ways in which their sins impacted their reigns and the fates of the people they ruled. See, for example, II Chronicles 10–36.

to an idealized vision of the past. Instead, its reality is understood as another iteration of what has been and what will always be.

In both Ezra and Nehemiah's historical retrospectives that are pronounced in the context of prayers, Israel's past is presented as checkered and imperfect.[64] In contrast to the blemish-free biography of Solomon found in Chronicles, for example,[65] Nehemiah 13:26 is forthright about the king's sins. As such, his rule and its effects are de-romanticized and, by extension, disqualified as a flawless precedent to reenact. In contrast to Hosea and Jeremiah, Nehemiah describes the Israelites' time in the wilderness as one in which their "fathers acted in willful wickedness, stiffening their necks and disobeying Your commands. Refusing to listen, they did not remember Your marvels which You performed for them. They stiffened their necks and rebelliously turned their heads to return to their slavery."[66] Nehemiah 8:17 is equally candid about the people's lack of religious observance when it notes that they had not constructed or dwelt in sukkot "since the days of Joshua son of Nun."[67] The people were never perfect, and neither was their life in the land. There is no moment in history that is presented in Ezra-Nehemiah as *the* moment to which its audience should strive to return. History, as understood in Ezra-Nehemiah, has always been multidimensional.[68]

---

64. Ezra 9 and Nehemiah 9.

65. I Chronicles 29; II Chronicles 9. See also Ehud Ben Zvi, "The Book of Chronicles: Another Look," in *History, Literature and Theology in the Book of Chronicles* (Routledge, 2014), 20–41.

66. Nehemiah 9:16–17.

67. Ibid. 8:17. There are many other instances in Tanakh in which Israel's past sins are recounted. See for example, Judges 2, I Samuel 12, II Kings 23:13, Jeremiah 32:31. Unlike Chronicles, Ezra-Nehemiah consciously echoes those earlier, critical sentiments rather than idealizing its past.

68. Internally, as well, there is a sense of fluid progression rather than disjointed periods within the broader period of restoration. Introducing the arrival of Ezra in 7:1, for example, the text begins with the words "Some time after this, during the reign of Artaxerxes." Ezra's arrival was, in fact, fifty-seven years after the dedication of the Temple with which chapter 6 concludes, but the opening words to chapter 7 create the illusion of a continuous narrative. According to Gary Knoppers, of the approximately 112 years covered in the book, there are gaps totaling eighty-nine years. And yet those gaps are almost imperceptible from the narratological perspective. Gary

This is one of the reasons that Ezra-Nehemiah renders the challenges of its time as it does. Rather than seeing the exile as a breach with a romanticized past and the restoration as an attempt to recover that imagined, pristine period, Ezra-Nehemiah sees the times its audience is living through as another point on the continuum of Israel's imperfect history. Difficulties that present themselves, according to Ezra-Nehemiah, are par for history's course. If there are challenges to the building project, Ezra-Nehemiah responds to them through practical and political channels. The same holds true for economic difficulties. But the challenges in Ezra-Nehemiah do not compel those contending with them to question the entirety of their enterprise. The Judeans in Ezra-Nehemiah are not blamed for the building delays or for their poverty, because difficulties in Ezra-Nehemiah are not synonymous with failure. If their initiative is not failing, there is no reason to search for internal faults and shortcomings.

This is not to suggest that Ezra-Nehemiah is not religiously and theologically conscious. Much of the work centers on the people's need for, and implementation of, religious improvement. Those reforms will be dealt with in future chapters. But Ezra-Nehemiah displays a confidence that God "keeps His covenant of love with those who love Him"[69] and that, just as the people surmounted their complicated past, they can do so again.

WHERE WE STAND

What we are left with thus far is a work that consciously shapes its audience's sense of past and future. In the last chapter, we noted that Ezra-Nehemiah does not allow an imagined future the power to undermine the community's current sense of gratitude for, and obligation to, the present. In a similar vein, the work also prevents the people getting mired in or hindered by idealized portraits of a severed past. Taken together, its audience is left with a deep appreciation for the present's paramount

---

N. Knoppers, "Periodization in Ancient Israelite Historiography," in *Periodisierung und Epochenbewusstsein im Alten Testament und seinem Umfeld,* ed. Josef Wiesehöfer and Thomas Krüger (Stuttgart: Franz Steiner, 2012), 121–45.

69. Nehemiah 1:5.

import, coupled with an understanding that it is accountable for how that present plays out.

If, as we have argued, Ezra-Nehemiah creates the sense of a flow in history, that sense naturally coincides with an expectation of stability and constancy. There is an assumption, embedded in Ezra-Nehemiah's conception of history, that all that is should continue to be. Like the priests "resuming" their posts and the people "returning" to their homes, Ezra-Nehemiah sets up an unspoken expectation that all institutions that existed before will continue to exist. But while the Temple in Ezra-Nehemiah is rebuilt and the city is resettled, the throne in the palace of David remains glaringly empty. It is to that emptiness that we turn in the next chapter.

Chapter Six

With or Without a King

THE DESIRE FOR AUTONOMY, OR NOT

In the previous chapter, we discussed Ezra-Nehemiah's fluid conception of history and noted that most of the institutions that had been suspended due to exile are depicted as seamlessly resuming once the exiled returned to the land. But we also noted that kingship, one of the most central of Israel's past institutions, does not. While the Jews are permitted to return to their land and restore the ritual practices of their ancestors, they remain a province of the Persian Empire. This means that they pay taxes to Persia, their leaders are chosen by the Persians, and their internal governance is constantly monitored by Persian-appointed governors.[1] Thus, while they are granted cultural and religious freedoms,[2] the Jews are certainly not autonomous.

Autonomy is no small matter. The ability to self-govern rather than be controlled by external forces is a basic human desire. Few nation states –

---

1.   For a full discussion of the implications of Achaemenid rule on life in the land, see Jon. L. Berquist, "A History of the Jews and Judaism in the Second Temple Period. Volume 1, Yehud: A History of the Persian Province of Judah," *Journal of Biblical Literature* 125, no. 3 (October 1, 2006).

2.   There were occasions when religious worship was misconstrued as political insurgency, as in Ezra 4, and in those instances some of the freedoms were curbed.

even those that have been under the proverbial thumbs of nations more powerful than them for decades or even centuries – ever fully relinquish the desire for independence and self-rule. That resolve is evident in some early Second Temple works. Yet a cursory reading of Ezra-Nehemiah seems to point to an acceptance, without any misgivings, of a lack of Jewish autonomy. How this acceptance can be explained and whether it is a valid attitude is the subject of this chapter.

PROVINCIAL STATUS AND ITS DISCONTENTS

To appreciate the exceptionality of Ezra-Nehemiah's take on political matters, we must first tune into some of the frustrated voices that emerged from the period. When we do, we find that other early Second Temple writers express their longings for autonomy through sanitized memories of, and ongoing hopes for, the Davidic dynasty. The book of Chronicles, for example, prunes from its memoirs the sins for which both David and Solomon are explicitly rebuked in the books of Samuel and Kings.[3] Of course, the author of Chronicles is not ignorant of the facts he excludes, nor does he aim to whitewash historical personalities. Rather, as Moshe Reiss and David Zucker explain, the depictions of David and Solomon in Chronicles "create and consolidate the permanent institutions that would be forever binding; the institutions … are more important than their human (and flawed) creators/consolidators."[4] For the author of Chronicles, the restoration of the Davidic dynasty is contingent on its audience's commitment to it, and that surpasses in importance the details of its founder's flaws.

This commitment to the dynasty's restoration is not limited to the narrative portions of the works alone. For example, I Chronicles 3:1–24, the longest genealogy in the Bible, traces David's descendants from David through the Persian period. Such a centuries-long genealogy may seem excessive, unless, as is the case with the chronicler, the royal pedigree remains relevant well into the Persian period. The lengthy

---

3.   I Chronicles 11–29; II Chronicles 1–9.
4.   Moshe Reiss and David J. Zucker, "Chronicles as Revisionist Religious History," *Asbury Journal* 68, no. 2 (2013): 9.

genealogy, and the fact that David is the focus of the lineage of Judah, displays what Gary Knoppers refers to as a "scribal attentiveness to the Davidic house in postmonarchic times."[5] Such attentiveness, he argues, reveals the yearnings of some within the post-exilic community for the restitution of a Davidic dynasty. If they can keep track of David's descendants, the thinking goes, they will be ready when the time comes to anoint their new king.

These harbored hopes are given full expression through one individual in Chronicles's genealogy. Zerubbabel, whom we encounter in Ezra-Nehemiah as one of the leaders of the restoration project, is listed in Chronicles as a direct descendant of King Jehoiachin.[6] This familial tie undoubtedly lends Zerubbabel gravitas, but as we see in Haggai and Zechariah, it also gives form to the people's dynastic aspirations. In Haggai 2, for example, God instructs the prophet to deliver the following message to Zerubbabel: "I am going to shake the heavens and earth, I will overturn the thrones of kingdoms, and I will destroy the mighty dominion of nations; I will overturn the chariot and its riders. ... I will take you, Zerubbabel son of Shealtiel, My servant ... and wear you close like a signet ring, for it is you whom I have chosen."[7] The verses imply the impending overthrow of the existing political order and, quite naturally, Zerubbabel as its alternative.

Allusions to kingship are less overt in Zechariah, and yet readers, likely including the prophet's original audience, still walk away with a profound sense that on Zerubbabel were pinned expectations for an improved political reality. In Zechariah 4:7, the prophet tells Zerubbabel that the "great mountain" before him "will become a level plain," referring to the ease with which Zerubbabel will accomplish his feats. In that same chapter, God explains to the prophet that the "two olive branches"

---

5.   Gary N. Knoppers, *Prophets, Priests, and Promises: Essays on the Deuteronomistic History, Chronicles, and Ezra-Nehemiah*, vol. 186 (Brill, 2021), 388.

6.   I Chronicles 3:17–24.

7.   Haggai 2:21–23. The signet ring as a sign of royal power is recognized throughout Tanakh, the stories of Joseph and Mordekhai being two such examples. But in this case, it is also possible that the reference to the ring hints even more specifically at a reversal of the episode in Jeremiah 22:24–30 that led to the removal of Jehoiachin's ring.

he sees represent the "two sons of the anointed ones," referring, according to most scholars, to the collaborative leadership of Joshua the high priest and Zerubbabel, the ostensible royal figure.[8]

ROOTS OF BELIEF IN A RESTORED MONARCHY

This expectation, embodied by Zerubbabel, for a restored monarchy does not emerge out of thin air. The tradition of an eternal Davidic dynasty is deeply embedded in Israel's collective memory, and for good reason. In II Samuel, God makes an unconditional covenant with David in which He promises to "establish his kingdom" and "firmly establish his royal throne forever."[9] Even if David were to sin, God guarantees His "loyalties shall not move from him" and David's "throne will be secure forever."[10] The eternal nature of the covenant is sung about in Psalms,[11] and even after the Temple is destroyed and the last of the Davidic kings dethroned, prophets such as Jeremiah speak of a future in which the yoke of foreign kings will be broken and the people will once again "serve the Lord their God, and David their king, whom I shall raise up for them."[12]

Such beliefs are rooted in both textual and practical grounds. Historically, the Davidic line and the Temple institution were inextricably linked. David initiates the enterprise,[13] and his son Solomon designs and oversees the building's construction and dedication.[14] The founding of the Second Temple reinforces assumptions that the event is a portent of the re-founding of the Davidic dynasty. In addition, the Achaemenid administration tolerates a vast array of polities, including, in some cases, native monarchies under Persian authority.[15] Therefore, the returnees

---

8. Zechariah 4:12–14.
9. II Samuel 7:11–14.
10. Ibid., 15–16.
11. In Psalms 89, for example, Ethan the Ezrahite, a Temple musician, sings of God's loyalty to David and how God has sworn to His servant David: "I will establish your seed forever; I have built your throne for all generations" (vv. 4–5).
12. Jeremiah 30:8–9. See also Jeremiah 33:14–18; Ezekiel 34:23–24, 37:24–25.
13. II Samuel 7.
14. I Kings 5:16–8:66.
15. Lester L. Grabbe, "A History of the Jews and Judaism in the Second Temple Period," in *A History of the Jews and Judaism in the Second Temple Period* (2021), 1–544;

have reason to assume that if the desired arrangement facilitates stability for the imperial regime, such a model will be possible.[16]

Bearing in mind the natural desire for autonomy, combined with expectations set by the earlier prophets and the fact that the Israelites lived under their own king for nearly five hundred years, the hope expressed in the early years of the Second Temple period for the restoration of a Jewish king is not surprising.

EZRA-NEHEMIAH'S CONTENTMENT

What *is* surprising, however, is the fact that Ezra-Nehemiah seems to be perfectly content with a lack of autonomy. The pining for change evident in other Second Temple works is absent in Ezra-Nehemiah. And not only are Davidic figures less accentuated, but as we will see, the whole Davidic line is downplayed. Zerubbabel, for example, is remembered for the role he played in the Temple project, but his illustrious bloodline is never mentioned. In fact, a reader of Ezra-Nehemiah who does not encounter Zerubbabel in other works would never know of his royal lineage. This omission becomes even starker considering the priestly and Levitical genealogies that appear at the end of Nehemiah.[17] Ezra-Nehemiah, it seems, is not disinterested in genealogies altogether; it is simply disinterested in David's.

This disinterest extends beyond genealogies. God's promise to David is reiterated and takes up significant space in Chronicles.[18] In Ezra-Nehemiah, it is never mentioned. David is not glorified as he is in Chronicles, nor is Solomon. In fact, the one recollection of Solomon in Ezra-Nehemiah is found in the context of rebuke for intermarriage,

---

Vadim S. Jigoulov, "Administration of Achaemenid Phoenicia: A Case for Managed Autonomy," in *Exile and Restoration Revisited: Essays in Memory of Peter R. Ackroyd*, ed. G. N. Knoppers et al., Fulton, LSTS 73 (London: T & T Clark Continuum, 2009), 138–51.

16. For a fuller discussion of this topic with footnotes, see Knoppers, *Prophets, Priests, and Promises*, 369–71.

17. Nehemiah 11:1–12:26.

18. I Chronicles 17.

a sin for which he was guilty and in which Nehemiah's audience persists.[19] The few references to David that appear in Ezra-Nehemiah are in the context of the "City" and "graves of David,"[20] as well as his legacy as a cultic musician.[21] After the Temple foundation has been laid and the priests and Levites commence their melodious praise of God, we are told that they are stationed "as David, king of Israel, had ordained."[22] David is thus known in Ezra-Nehemiah for the historic city that bears his name and for the religious norms he establishes that are later integrated into Temple worship. But David is not celebrated as the initiator of the First Temple building project, and nowhere is there even the slightest hint of hope for the reestablishment of his dynasty.

All of this begs the obvious question: Why, in contrast to other early Second Temple works, does Ezra-Nehemiah seem disinterested in the dynasty and its reemergence? There are two dovetailing answers to this question, but comprehending those answers requires historical context and an understanding of the ever-changing Israelite views regarding monarchy.

PRE-MONARCHIC INSTITUTIONS

While monarchy is the longest standing governing structure in Israel during the early biblical period, it is not the only one. After Joshua's death, Israel enters what is later coined "the period of Judges." For that 150-year period, the people survive as a tribal confederacy led by charismatic rulers whose chief priority is staving off local enemy threats. In addition to their military function, some judges also perform traditional judicial tasks and even receive prophecy. But as the book of Judges repeatedly points out, the lack of centralized leadership and smooth succession of power prompts a chaotic situation dominated by internecine warfare, summarized by the recurrent refrain and closing argument of the book:

---

19. Solomon's name appears throughout the work as a progenitor in the name lists, but his persona and activities as king are mentioned only once, in Nehemiah 13:26.
20. Nehemiah 3:15–16.
21. Ibid. 12:24, 45–46.
22. Ezra 3:10.

"In those days, there was no king in Israel; everyone did what was right in his own eyes."[23] This theme also seems to point toward kingship as the obvious, superior solution, which is why the people's request that their prophet Samuel "appoint a king for us to govern us like any other nation" seems to make perfect sense. As Moshe Halbertal and Stephen Holmes put it, "The monarchy for which they were pleading would thus answer the people's two most pressing and existential political concerns: the need for unity and the need for continuity."[24] And yet, rational as their request may have been, both God and His prophet disapprove.

PROBLEMS GENERATED BY THE MONARCHY

Samuel immediately condemns their appeal and "prayed to the Lord"[25] to ask for direction. Rather than reject the people's request, though, God tells the prophet to "heed the voice of the people," making clear that it is not the prophet the people are rejecting but God Himself. "For it is not you they have rejected," God tells Samuel, "it is Me they have rejected, from reigning over them."[26] In one simple sentence, the Tanakh establishes an opposition between monarchy and divine kingship.[27] The ideal system, we learn from the verse, is one in which God is King over Israel. This is a system in which God is the invisible warrior who fights their battles and whose laws keep society in check.[28] But the people, we also learn, prefer a flesh-and-blood king. They want a king who "shall govern

---

23. Judges 21:25.
24. Moshe Halbertal and Stephen Holmes, *The Beginning of Politics: Power in the Biblical Book of Samuel.* (Princeton University Press, 2017), 8.
25. I Samuel 8:6.
26. Ibid., v. 7.
27. In the ancient Near East, kings were either believed to be a god, an incarnation of a god, or a semi-divine being chosen by the gods to mediate between the divine and human realms. As such, the Bible's claim that "God is King," rather than "the king is god," created a scenario in which "the sole or exclusive kingship of God was irreconcilable with a consolidated political monarchy" (Halbertal and Holmes, *The Beginning of Politics,* 5).
28. For a fuller discussion of this concept, see Gary V. Smith, "The Concept of God/the Gods as King in the Ancient Near East and the Bible." *Trinity Journal* 3, no. 1 (1982): 18–38.

us and go out before us and fight our battles."[29] The people express the desire to experience their king tangibly and to have someone they can see leading them to battle, discharging punishments for civil offenses, and rewarding their allegiance. But the Tanakh makes clear that a king they can see and a divine king cannot coexist; once people watch their human king fulfilling his kingly duties, they will forget about God entirely.[30]

DAVID AS MODEL KING?

That risk is one reason that David's slaying of Goliath serves as the most famous backstory to his reign, proving his worth as future king. The story takes place when Saul still rules over Israel, but the Israelites have lost faith in their king and God to protect them from Philistine onslaught. David bravely fights Goliath, the Philistine giant. But the scene is most known not for David's physical prowess or his military tactics. In fact, David is described as young, feeble, and at a significant disadvantage due to his lack of training. Instead, David's shouted words on the way out to the confrontation become etched in the legendary tales of the battle. "You come at me with sword and spear and javelin," he calls out, "but I come at you in the name of the Lord of Hosts, the God of the ranks of Israel, whom you taunted. This very day, the Lord will deliver you into my hands, and I will strike you down and sever your head from your body. And I will dole out the corpses of the Philistine camp for the birds of the sky and the beasts of the land, on this very day. Then all the land will know that there is a God over Israel; and all this crowd will know that the Lord does not grant victory by sword or

---

29. I Samuel 8:20.
30. This is not the first time such a demand is made in Tanakh, nor is it the first time the demand is met with theologically lined resistance. In the book of Judges, after Gideon has proven himself to be both a valiant warrior and an effective diplomat, the people say to him, "Rule over us, you and your son and the son of your son – for you have saved us from Midian's hand!" Gideon's response is quick and concise: "I shall not rule over you," he says to them, "nor shall my son rule over you – the Lord shall rule over you" (Judges 8:22–23). Gideon and Samuel express identical doubts. The difference is that Gideon's refusal was final, while in Samuel God told the prophet to acquiesce to the people's request despite its troubling nature. In Judges 9, "Jotham's fable" further maligns the institution.

by spear – for the battle is the Lord's, and He will deliver you into our hands."[31] David's swift and improbable victory not only enables the Israelites to rout the Philistines, but it also restores the people's faith in God's ability to protect them. David, who they can see fighting their battle, makes clear that he is simply an instrument in God's hand and that the true war hero is God. David never allows his accomplishments to divert the people's attention from God, and he maintains this attitude for the entirety of his career. In fact, David's ability to redirect the people's attention toward God is likely the reason he becomes, within Tanakh, the barometer for all future kings.[32]

Nonetheless, the book of Samuel is also clear that while David never allows his kingly power to obscure divine kingship, he does fall prey to the second occupational hazard of kingship. As his career progresses, David abuses the power he was granted, and the ripple effects of his greed engulf the people.[33]

THE KING'S ABUSE OF POWER

David's sins should not have shocked the people. Before Samuel appoints their first king, he warns the people of the abuses they will inevitably suffer at the hands of a leader whose power is not circumscribed. He warns them that their sons and daughters will be conscripted for royal service and that their land and those who work on it will be seized in the name of the throne. Most ominously, he warns them that when those times come, there will be nothing they can do to stop it. "On that day," Samuel says, "you will cry out because of your own king, whom you yourselves chose, but the Lord will not answer you on that day."[34] In fact, the second book of Samuel traces the corrosion of David's reign and attributes it to his abuses of power. As such, the reader of Samuel walks away with

---

31. I Samuel 17:45–47.
32. According to some interpretations, Moses's failure to do just that led to the punishment that prevented his entry into the land (Num. 20:1–13, and see, for example, Ramban, Ibn Ezra, and Rabbeinu Ḥananel ad loc.).
33. The ripple effects are traced from chapter 11, in which David sins with Bathsheba, through the end of his reign.
34. I Samuel 8:18.

the impression that if someone as virtuous as David cannot resist the temptations of unrestricted power, then the model itself must be faulty.

This impression is further reinforced when readers of the next book in the Bible, the book of Kings, learn that despite his extensive contributions to the security and prestige of Israel, Solomon "did what was evil in the Lord's sight and was not fully with the Lord, as his father David was."[35] Of course, following Solomon, the remainder of the book of Kings is brimming with stories of monarchs whose misuse of power and lack of monotheistic integrity have a damaging effect on the populace. On more than one occasion, the book of Kings makes clear that the challenges the Israelites face during the First Temple period and their eventual exile are punishment for the sins of their kings.[36]

Thus, the Tanakh asserts from the Davidic monarchy's inception that embedded in the institution are two inherent threats. The first, a theological threat, is that a human king will eclipse the true Divine King. And the second, a practical threat, is that power unchecked will inevitably lead to abuse.[37]

EZRA-NEHEMIAH'S RECOGNITION OF THE FAILURES OF KINGSHIP

The author of Ezra-Nehemiah, knowing what he does about Israel's history, does not identify with the early Second Temple voices that advocate for the institution's restoration. As we have already seen, Ezra-Nehemiah does not romanticize the past, an underlying position that

---

35. I Kings 11:6. David remained a paragon of religious righteousness, despite his failures.

36. See, for example, I Kings 11:9–11, 14:15–16; II Kings 10:31–32, 13:1–3, 15:17–20, 27–29, 16:1–6, 17:1–3, 21:1–15, 23:26–27, 24:1–3.

37. This disinclination toward kingship set Israelite thought apart from that of its neighbors. As Ehud Ben Zvi explains, "Problematizing monarchy as an institution to such a degree and in multiple ways represents somewhat of an anomaly within the common political thought that characterized the area for millennia. It is not only that 'all the nations' had kings…but that monarchy was usually considered a necessity and a gift from the gods." Ehud Ben Zvi, "Memory and Political Thought in the Late Persian/Early Hellenistic Yehud/Judah: Some Observations," in *Leadership, Social Memory and Judean Discourse in the Fifth–Second Centuries BCE* (2016), 9–26.

is important to remember here as well. Because while Ezra-Nehemiah does not explicitly denounce the monarchy, the text's clear lack of interest in its restoration seems to reflect a historically honest understanding of the monarchy when it stood. That is not to say that the author of Ezra-Nehemiah does not recognize the monarchy's contributions to the history of the people. In the letter sent to Darius in Ezra 5, for example, the people mention that the Temple they are attempting to rebuild had been "built many years ago; a great king of Israel built it and completed it."[38] But Ezra-Nehemiah envisions a different leadership model, one that, in theory, would bypass at least some of the pitfalls into which the Davidic monarchy fell. Therefore, the obvious next question is what Ezra-Nehemiah's new, preferred model of leadership looks like.

As with everything in Ezra-Nehemiah, the answer to that seemingly simple question is multifaceted and profoundly ideological. It does not consist of one alternative but rather a fusion of alternatives that consider two very important ideas: the theological implications of a foreign, benevolent ruler and the leadership potential of the people themselves. As we will see, the blending of those ideas leads to the promotion of a system in which God, a foreign king, and the laypeople in Judah all work in tandem. But to understand why Ezra-Nehemiah prefers and promotes this system, we need to understand each element individually.

THEOLOGICAL IMPLICATIONS OF FOREIGN RULERS IN TANAKH

A survey of foreign rulers prior to the period of Ezra-Nehemiah reveals their two primary functions within Tanakh. Either God proves His power and His preference for the Israelites through the defeat of a foreign ruler that is oppressing Israel,[39] or God sends a foreign ruler to punish a disobedient, sinful Israel. Foreign rulers, we learn, are simultaneously God's tool and Israel's nemesis. While this may initially strike us as paradoxical, if we consider the origins of the relationship

---

38. Ezra 5:11.
39. This function can be detected even before Israel becomes a nation. See, for example, God's protection of Abraham and Sarah from Pharaoh (Gen. 12:10–20).

between God and Israel, the paradigm makes perfect sense. God introduces Himself to Israel and proves His incomparable powers through
His miraculous defeat of Pharaoh in Egypt. Then, on the heels of
those miracles, He establishes Himself as Israel's God in a covenant
to which Israel agreed at Sinai. Not coincidentally, the first words of
the covenant read, "I am the Lord your God who brought you out of
the land of Egypt, out of the house of slaves. Have no other gods than
Me."[40] Israel's relationship with God and obligation to worship Him
exclusively are predicated on the fact that God vanquishes a foreign,
oppressive ruler and leads Israel to freedom.

But God's omnipotence is a double-edged sword. If He has the
power to defeat foreign rulers for Israel's gain, then He can also give
those same leaders free rein to attack Israel should she so deserve.
That's where the second function of foreign rulers arises. This function is perhaps most explicit in the book of Judges, where the cycle
of violence that pervades the era is explained through a theological
lens: "When the Israelites did what was evil in the eyes of the Lord.…
They abandoned the Lord, the God of their ancestors, who had taken
them out of the land of Egypt, and embraced other gods…. The Lord's
wrath raged against Israel, and He abandoned them to the hands of
marauders who oppressed them. He handed them over to the foes
that surrounded them – no longer could they withstand their foes."[41]
The theological messaging could not be clearer: Foreign rulers are a
threat to Israel, so God holds them at bay for as long as Israel earns
His protection. But when Israel defies God, He no longer restrains
the threat, and foreign rulers do as they please. We also learn from
the book of Judges that when the oppression becomes unbearable,
the people "cried out to the Lord."[42] This pattern affirms that, at the
very least, for a brief time before they resume their sinful behavior,
the Israelites remember Who is in control.

---

40. Exodus 20:1–2.
41. Judges 2:11–14.
42. See, for example, Judges 3:9.

THE EXPANSION OF GOD'S ROLE

Interestingly, in these earlier phases of Israelite history, as in the example above, God is depicted as removing His protection of Israel, resulting in their oppression at the hands of neighboring enemies,[43] but God is not depicted as directly controlling the military actions of foreign kings. He restrains them, but He does not directly guide their military campaigns. As regional empires grow in scope and influence, though, the extent of God's interference shifts subtly, resulting in an expanded image of God as supreme manager of international affairs. We see the earliest evidence of this depiction in the Neo-Assyrian period, but it endures well into the Babylonian period. The adoption of this depiction, with slight revisions, is the basis for Ezra-Nehemiah's approach to monarchy in the Persian period as well.

Baruch Levine explains the development as follows: "The immediacy and inescapable force of the Assyrian threat demanded a God-idea broad enough to measure up to empire. First Isaiah expounded just such a concept for the first time in biblical literature. He preached that international events, albeit catastrophic, were going according to the plan of the God of Israel for the whole earth."[44] If in earlier periods, the foreign rulers Israel encounters were local kings, then the depiction of God in Israel holding the enemies at bay sufficed to give Israel a sense of security. But as imperialism rises and international affairs are dictated by monarchs who claim to be empowered by their deities to take over "the world," the way the prophets speak of God has to evolve accordingly.[45] Therefore, the language intentionally employed by the Israelite prophets of that period portrays God as unequivocally in control and the bombastic imperialists as nothing but a mechanism of His universal hegemony.[46]

---

43. During the periods of Joshua and the Judges, the Israelites primarily fought with Canaanites, Philistines, Ammonites, Moabites, Edomites, and Midianites.

44. Baruch A. Levine, "Assyrian Ideology and Israelite Monotheism," *Iraq* 67, no. 1 (2005): 411–27.

45. For a discussion of the ways in which Israel's prophets responded to the theological claims that lay behind Assyria's imperial tactics, see Levine, "Assyrian Ideology."

46. These ideas are not new to Tanakh. God's hardening of Pharaoh's heart in Exodus (9:12, 10:1, 20, 11:10), for example, displayed at the outset of Israel's history that

The Neo-Assyrian Empire in Isaiah 10, for example, is referred to as the "staff" of God's fury, which God plans to set "loose upon a vile nation and command them against the people of My wrath to plunder for plunder, to ravage for spoils, to leave them to be trampled like street mud."[47] The Assyrians, the prophet seems to say, are not the ones the Israelites should fear; God is. For the Assyrians are nothing but God's implement. They are but one device in the toolbox from which God draws in His management of world history. And since the Israelites rebelled against God time and again, He will dispatch that device, and it will ravage them.

THE FATE OF INTERNATIONAL EMPIRES DEPENDS ON ISRAEL

Since God's control of foreign rulers is absolute, He decides whether they succeed or fail in their expansionist goals, a decision that is contingent on Israelite conduct. This is seen most clearly in the contrasting fates of the northern and southern empires to the Neo-Assyrian invasions of Israel. Of the northern empire, we are told that "the king of Assyria captured Shomron. He exiled Israel to Assyria....This came to pass because the Israelites had sinned against the Lord their God – who had brought them out from the land of Egypt and the oppression of Pharaoh, king of Egypt – by revering other gods."[48] Cause and effect are clear. The northern empire defies God, so God sends a foreign power to destroy them. In the south, though, when King Hezekiah learns of an impending Assyrian attack, he "rent his clothes and covered himself in sackcloth and came to the House of the Lord."[49] Hezekiah prays to God and consults with the prophet Isaiah, who reassures him that the "king of Assyria will not enter this city; he will not shoot one arrow

---

God is in control of and employs foreign rulers to carry out His plans. Similarly, the Israelites are warned in Deuteronomy that nations will avenge their wrongdoings (see, for example, Deuteronomy 32:21). But the need, in the age of expanding empires, to reiterate the idea is reflected in the prophets' language.

47. Isaiah 10:5–6.
48. II Kings 17:6–7.
49. Ibid. 19:1.

there. He will not advance upon her with the shield, nor pile up a siege mound against her. The way he came he will return, but this city he will not enter."[50] The righteous King Hezekiah does everything in his power to atone for the sins of Israel, and as a result, the Tanakh tells us, the Assyrian troops that were poised to destroy Jerusalem are "struck down" by an angel of God.[51]

When the southern empire is eventually destroyed, this task too is understood as having been carried out by God's minions. Prior to Nebuchadnezzar's invasion of Jerusalem, Jeremiah refers to him as God's "servant." In doing so, Jeremiah establishes an understanding that in Nebuchadnezzar's invasion and transformation of Jerusalem into "a wasteland and a place of shrieking, an eternal ruin,"[52] he is doing God's bidding. Where others see imperialist expansion, Israelite prophets see reward, punishment, and God's dominion.

Of course, foreign rulers not only rise at God's behest, but they also fall as well. If they exercise excessive cruelty, as is the case with Nebuchadnezzar,[53] or if they become overly self-impressed and undermine rather than garner reverence for God, God tears them down as quickly as He promoted them.[54] Taken together, then, the message emphasized by late First Temple prophets is clear: "Empires rise and fall, but it is God who grants kings their transient power and retains possession of true kingship."[55] The Israelites hear this message on the eve of the destruction of their own kingdom. It is also the message that the author of Ezra-Nehemiah draws from when he formulates a modified political idea for the Judean people.

---

50. Ibid., vv. 32–33.
51. Ibid., v. 35.
52. Jeremiah 25:8–10.
53. Ibid., chs. 50–51.
54. See, for example, the oracle Isaiah delivers about Sennacherib's downfall, which he attributes to Sennacherib's arrogance and disrespect toward God (Is. 37:21–35).
55. Levine, "Assyrian Ideology," 424.

A NEW MODEL OF FOREIGN RULE

That modified idea explains that God, as Supreme Ruler, utilizes human monarchs to carry out His historical agendas. But Ezra-Nehemiah adds a new, critical feature to the long-established template. If, in the past, all rulers that held sway over Israel were, by default, enemy rulers,[56] that binary is erased in Ezra-Nehemiah. In Ezra-Nehemiah, foreign rulers can both control and serve the interests of the Jewish people. In this new model, they can work in tandem with, not in opposition to, the Jewish people. This model is laid out gracefully in the book's opening verses: "In the first year of Cyrus, king of Persia, when the Lord's word pronounced by Jeremiah had come to pass. The Lord stirred the spirit of Cyrus, king of Persia, and he issued a proclamation throughout his kingdom, by word of mouth and written word as well. Thus says Cyrus, king of Persia: The Lord, God of the heavens, has granted me all the kingdoms of the earth, and He has charged me to build Him a House in Jerusalem, in Judah."[57] A far cry from those who profane God and ravage the Temple, Cyrus is introduced as a man who venerates God and His Temple.

This intentional characterization is underscored by the analogous quote in chapter six. There, Cyrus's announcement, whose wording is likely derived from the original proclamation,[58] reads as follows: "In the first year of the reign of King Cyrus, King Cyrus issued an edict regarding the House of God in Jerusalem. He ordered that the House be rebuilt – a place where sacrifices are offered – its foundations shall be fortified. Its height shall be sixty cubits and its width sixty cubits. It shall have three courses of smoothed stones and one course of wood, and the cost shall be paid out of the king's coffers. Additionally, the gold and silver vessels of the House of God that Nebuchadnezzar had taken from the

---

56. That is not the same as saying that all foreign rulers were thought to be enemies. Hiram, the king of Tyre, for example, graciously supplied Solomon with builders and materials for the Temple (I Kings 5–10). But kings that held political sway over Israel were considered problematic.

57. Ezra 1:1–2. Compare the focus of this verse with that of Haggai in which God also "arouses the spirit" of the prophet, Zerubbabel, Jeshua, and the people to build, but not the foreign king (Hag. 1:1, 14).

58. For more on this, see Japhet, *From the Rivers of Babylon*, 190–204.

Sanctuary in Jerusalem and brought to Babylon shall be returned. Each one shall be replaced in the Temple in Jerusalem; you shall deposit it in the House of God."[59] Chapters 1 and 6 both cite documents that grant permission to build, but the dry, uninspired tone in chapter 6 helps us appreciate the artistic license employed by the author of Ezra-Nehemiah in his shaping of the persona of Cyrus in chapter 1. The Cyrus we meet in chapter 1 recognizes God's power and unabashedly proclaims it to anyone willing to listen. Knowing what we do about human kings' abilities to either detract from or restore God's glory, this quality cannot be overstated. Interestingly, this rendering is unique to Ezra-Nehemiah.

While other biblical works share aspects of Ezra-Nehemiah's portrait of Persian kings, none include the combination of positive legislation and awareness of God. Isaiah, for example, designates Cyrus as God's "servant," "shepherd," and "anointed one," but he maintains in the words "and I gird you though you do not know Me" that Cyrus himself was not aware of the role God played in his ascent to the Persian throne.[60] In Daniel, some Persian kings are portrayed as recognizing God's power, but their appreciation is limited in scope and only surfaces after God proves Himself through miraculous means.[61] Ezra-Nehemiah is the only biblical work in which the Persian monarch is portrayed as intuitively understanding that his vast successes are all a tribute to God's ultimate power. Cyrus's lucid articulation of this awareness places him in a distinct category. Featuring as the opening of the work, it seems to herald a new, promising era in Jewish religio-political history.

This sense only intensifies when, in addition to acknowledging God's power, the Persian kings encourage Jewish fidelity to God's laws. When Ezra is first sent to Jerusalem, he bears a message from King Artaxerxes empowering him to "use the wisdom of your God to appoint judges and magistrates who will dispense judgment to all the people in the province beyond the River." The letter further warns that "anyone who fails

---

59. Ezra 6:3–5.
60. Isaiah 44:26–45:5. This language of "not knowing God" is reminiscent of Pharaoh (Ex. 5:2), resulting in a very different impression of Cyrus than the one created in Ezra-Nehemiah.
61. See, for example, Darius's reaction to God's saving of Daniel in the lion's den (Dan. 6).

to obey the laws of your God and the laws of the king shall be sentenced promptly to death, corporal punishment, fine, or imprisonment."[62] Jewish law is now being backed and enforced by a foreign ruler.

HERALDING A NEW ERA

That is why, in contrast to its literary counterparts, Ezra-Nehemiah does not pine for a Davidic monarchy.[63] If, as established in earlier biblical works, God seats and unseats rulers, and the king currently in control publicly recognizes God's supreme control, accepts the task for which he has been divinely chosen, and charges the exiles to rally around his call to build a religious center in God's chosen city, then from the perspective of Ezra-Nehemiah, the Jewish people already have their king. As Gary Knoppers puts it: "If Judean society in the Second Commonwealth is a theocratic monarchy, the monarchy is Persian in nature."[64]

That being the case, it goes without saying that, as God's obedient elect, the Persian monarch warrants the reverence and support of the Jewish people. And so, in addition to their political loyalty, the Jews were also expected to "pray for the life of the king and his children."[65] No Persian monarch is ever derided in Ezra-Nehemiah, and no nefarious intentions are ever attributed to them.[66] On the rare occasion that the interests of a Persian monarch conflict with those of the Judeans, the work is quick to show that the conflict was a result of the monarch being misled by Judah's enemies.[67] Once the misunderstanding is cleared up, though, the Persian monarch resumes his place among the other virtuous kings.

---

62. Ezra 7:25–26.
63. There are those who argue that Ezra 9:9 and Nehemiah 9:36 indicate a yearning for independence. But see note 78 in chapter one, where that claim is addressed.
64. Knoppers, *Prophets, Priests, and Promises*, 382.
65. Ezra 6:10.
66. This stands in contrast to other works set in the Persian period, namely Esther and Daniel, whose portrayal of Persian kings is significantly less flattering.
67. Artaxerxes's cessation of the building project due to pressure and libels from the enemies of Judah is an example of such an occurrence.

What we are left with in Ezra-Nehemiah, then, is not the reestablishment of the Davidic dynasty as envisioned in other biblical works, but the embrace of a monarchic system that seems to correct those ways in which earlier political institutions failed. Ezra-Nehemiah sees in its new world order the potential for God's name and power to be universally acknowledged and for the Jewish people to benefit from leaders who smoothly succeed one another and use their power judiciously for the good of the people throughout their empire.[68]

REDEFINING RESTORATION

By adopting this outlook, Ezra-Nehemiah essentially redefined restoration. David Aune and Eric Stewart explain that "the concept of 'restoration' is rooted in the pre-modern perception of culture which explicitly and implicitly regarded the imagined past as the sole legitimate basis for appraising the legitimacy of the present and envisioning or shaping the future."[69] But Ezra-Nehemiah, as we have seen, rejects this sweeping definition. It does not seek to restore what was simply because it was. Rather, Ezra-Nehemiah looks at the motivations behind the establishment of past institutions, as well as the factors that contributed to their failure, and then articulates a vision that moderates both.[70] By letting go of the rigid expectations of what restoration should look like, Ezra-Nehemiah is able to identify within its lived reality viable and even preferable alternatives to the past.

---

68. It goes without saying that the impression created by the author of Ezra-Nehemiah is oversimplified. The Achaemenid Empire, like every empire, dealt with internal politics and conspiracies (see Briant, *From Cyrus to Alexander*, 125–38).

69. David E. Aune, and Eric Stewart, "From the Idealized Past to the Imaginary Future: Eschatological Restoration in Jewish Apocalyptic Literature," in *Restoration* (Brill, 2001), 147–77.

70. Iain Duguid makes a compelling argument that while there was no king during the period of Ezra-Nehemiah, Nehemiah himself is reminiscent of ideal pre-exilic kings. To support his claim, Duguid looks at those features of Nehemiah's leaderships, including his prayers on behalf of the people, building accomplishments, insistence on just rule, and reformation of the cult. Iain Duguid, "Nehemiah – The Best King Judah Never Had," in *Let Us Go Up to Zion* (Brill, 2012), 261–71.

This approach is apparent in its understanding of monarchy, as we have seen. But it is also discernible in the way Ezra-Nehemiah perceives the people in Judah themselves and the role they play within the broader leadership dynamic, which differs significantly from earlier biblical periods. Ezra-Nehemiah contends that God chose the Persian kings, and thus the Persian throne was the site from which legislation derived. But it is the laypeople in Judah who are credited with executing the kings' orders and seeing that the royal vision is achieved, making the laypeople the third and final piece of the leadership puzzle.

GRASSROOTS LEADERSHIP

We have already seen that Zerubbabel's royal pedigree is ignored in Ezra-Nehemiah as part of a larger tendency to downplay pro-Davidic sentiments. But a closer look at the description of Zerubbabel in Ezra-Nehemiah shows that it is not just his pedigree but his job description altogether which is downplayed. We know from Haggai that Zerubbabel was a governor,[71] but nowhere in Ezra-Nehemiah is that fact revealed. The same goes for Sheshbazzar, who is simply called "the leader" when he is introduced,[72] even though we know from the official documents quoted that he, too, was a governor.[73] Even Nehemiah, with all the space he occupies in the text, is granted the title "governor" only once by the narrator and once in his first-person memoirs.[74]

"Governor" is not the only title to have been deleted from the narrative portions of Ezra-Nehemiah. Jeshua the priest is never referred to as "high priest" or "chief priest,"[75] a title that Haggai and Zechariah confirm he held.[76] Even Ezra himself is referred to only as either "priest" or "priest and scribe,"[77] despite the fact that his lineage leads directly to

---

71. The phrase *paḥat Yehuda* appears in Haggai 1:14, 2:2, 21.
72. Ezra 1:8 uses the term *nasi*.
73. Ezra 5:14–16.
74. Nehemiah 12:28, 5:14.
75. Ezra 2:2, 3:8,4:3, 5:2, 10:18; Nehemiah 7:7, 12:1. 7, 10, 26.
76. Haggai 1:1, 12, 14:2:2, 4; Zechariah 3:1, 8, 6:11.
77. Ezra is referred to simply as priest in Ezra 10:10, 16 and Nehemiah 8:2, and as "priest and scribe" in Ezra 7:11, and Nehemiah 8:9, 12:26.

Seraiah, the last high priest to serve in the First Temple.[78] The only mention of a contemporary high priest is Eliashib, again found exclusively in Nehemiah's memoirs.[79] The author maintains these titles as they appeared in the original documents or memoirs, which highlights his decision to rarely use them in the narrative portions he constructs.[80] The author is not trying to conceal these leadership titles; he simply does not consider them germane to the story he tells.

The author of Ezra-Nehemiah is not telling the story of Persian kings and solitary Jewish leaders. Rather, the story of the Jews during this period, according to Ezra-Nehemiah, consists of Persian kings working in tandem with the entire community of Jewish leaders. Gone are the days in which one Jewish king or judge is the focus of the biblical text. In the mind of the author of Ezra-Nehemiah, it is the entirety of the Jewish people and their cooperative, grassroots efforts that will shape their fortunes.

THE PRIMACY OF JUDAH'S LAYPEOPLE

Cyrus's initial proclamation is addressed to "whoever is among you from all His people."[81] It is not spoken in private chambers to one Jewish leader chosen to lead the masses back to their land. It is aimed at all the Jews throughout the Persian Empire. As such, we are told that it is embraced by "all of the heads of the ancestral Houses of Judah and Benjamin and the priests and the Levites, and all those whose spirit had been stirred by God."[82] The following chapter, which traces that migration back to the land, contains an extensive list of names of Jewish returnees. Names of people who ostensibly held leadership positions are mentioned in the beginning of the chapter, but their titles are not

---

78. Ezra 7:1 and II Kings 25:18.
79. Nehemiah 3:1, 20, 13:28.
80. As Sara Japhet explains: "The tension between the point of view of the author and the period which he is describing is expressed among other ways in the tension between his own composition and the other sources of contemporary or earlier writers," Japhet, *From the Rivers of Babylon*, 75.
81. Ezra 1:3.
82. Ibid., v. 5.

enumerated, and at no point are we given the impression that the fate of the people rests in their hands. The list, uncharacteristically detailed for any biblical census, includes "the entire community" in its count.[83] All the people from that community, we are then told, "willingly contributed to fix the House of God back on its foundations. Each giving what they could, they donated to the project."[84]

In Ezra 3, we are told that the "people assembled in Jerusalem as one" to begin work on the Temple, and only after that does the text add that Jeshua the priest and Zerubbabel "rose up and built an altar for the God of Israel."[85] The official leaders play a role, but the initiative is indisputably that of the people. Likewise, it is "the people," not the leaders, who "celebrated the festival of Tabernacles as prescribed, performing the designated number of daily offerings each day in accordance with the law for each day," and the people that "continued to present the regular offerings, the offerings of the New Month and all of the Lord's sacred assemblies, and the voluntary offerings brought for the Lord." Only in the seventh month do the priests begin to "present burnt offerings to the Lord."[86] If the First Temple project was initiated by Solomon, who invited foreign architects and craftsmen to import wood and help design and build the Temple,[87] this time around it is the lay leaders who "paid the hewers and stone masons in silver, and the Sidonians and Tyrians were given food and drink and oil to bring cedarwood from Lebanon to the Sea of Jaffa."[88] Fittingly, it is the "Israelites, the priests and the Levites, and all the other returning exiles [who] celebrated the dedication of the House of God with joy."[89] In stark contrast to Zechariah's claim that "Zerubbabel's hands founded this House, and his hands will complete it,"[90] Ezra-Nehemiah makes it clear that the Temple building project, from beginning to end, is a cumulative effort by the entire

---

83. Ibid. 2:64.
84. Ibid., vv. 68–69.
85. Ibid. 3:1–2.
86. Ibid., vv. 4–6.
87. I Kings 6:1–8:66; II Chronicles 3:1–7:11.
88. Ezra 3:7.
89. Ibid. 6:16.
90. Zechariah 4:9.

community of returnees. As Tamara Cohn Eskenazi puts it, "The return was a return of a great multitude, composed of the major categories within Judean society.... The people who will build the House of God are the central focus of the book. They are the ones who went up to Jerusalem, in compliance with divine and royal decree, to restore Jewish life. Leaders will emerge (e.g., Zerubbabel and Jeshua); these leaders also fade. The people themselves complete the task and celebrate. They are consequently presented in detail. Ezra-Nehemiah firmly established before the readers' eyes the fact that a multiplicity of individuals, families, and classes combine to make up this entity called '*am*,' the people of Israel. It is these people – listed fully with tiresome specificity whose story Ezra-Nehemiah narrates."[91] Individuals with titles no longer make up the bulk of biblical historical writing. Ezra-Nehemiah redefines the main characters in the new Jewish drama. This time around, it claims, the entire community and their efforts take center stage.

This focus on the people does not change once Ezra and Nehemiah are introduced. When Ezra heads to Jerusalem, he does so with a group of "pilgrims" who include "some of the Israelites, priests, Levites, singers, gatekeepers, and Netinim."[92] Those returnees, like the cohort who returned with Sheshbazzar and Zerubbabel, are enumerated by name. It is they, not Ezra, who "delivered the king's orders to the king's viceroys and to the governors."[93] It is the people in Ezra 9 and 10 who instigate religious reforms, as "a very large crowd of Israelites gathered around him: men, women, and children, weeping a great deal."[94] Likewise, the people, divided by guild in Nehemiah "acted with a willing heart"[95] and rally to rebuild the wall around Jerusalem. "All the people assembled together in the open plaza opposite the Water Gate" and call upon Ezra to teach them Torah.[96] And in Nehemiah 9, prior to renewing their covenant with God, "the Israelites convened, fasting and in sackcloth with earth on themselves" and "confessed their sins and the wrongdoings

---

91. Eskenazi, *In An Age of Prose*, 49.
92. Ezra 7:7–9.
93. Ibid. 8:36.
94. Ibid. 10:1.
95. Nehemiah 3:38.
96. Ibid. 8:1.

of their ancestors."[97] Of course, there were authorized leaders in Judah, and those leaders are mentioned on more than one occasion. But every leader mentioned appears "within a web of social, religious, and kinship relations."[98] The reader of Ezra-Nehemiah understands that, in contrast to earlier periods, the restoration period is not about individual accomplishments but about collective ones. While leaders are present at various events and occasions, the people are consistently presented as initiating and implementing the positive developments of the period.

THE IDEAL INTERPLAY OF POWER

Having put all three pieces of the puzzle together, we can now appreciate the verses that appear at the conclusion of the Temple building project and perfectly encapsulate Ezra-Nehemiah's newly imagined amalgam of leaders. The verses read: "So Tattenai, governor of the province beyond the River, and Shetar Bozenai and their associates followed Darius's edict in full. And the elders of the Jews went on with the building successfully encouraged by the prophecy of Haggai the prophet and Zechariah son of Ido; they built the House and completed it according to the command of the God of Israel and in keeping with the edict of Cyrus, Darius, and King Artaxerxes of Persia."[99] This, according to Ezra-Nehemiah, is the new ideal. Persian kings relay orders in line with the aspirations of Jewish prophets. Their orders are dispatched by local leaders in Judah and fulfilled by the cooperative Jewish populace. The project is linked to the terms of three Persian kings, creating the sense of an all-embracing imperial support of this most important project. And, of course, at the head of the chain of command is none other than God Himself.

These principal verses appear within a specific context, but their implications apply equally to all the relevant phases of the period. By embracing a more flexible definition of restoration and encouraging its audience to draw from the past while refining it, Ezra-Nehemiah empowers its audience to simultaneously restore and reimagine. In the

---

97. Ibid. 9:1–2.
98. Knoppers, *Prophets, Priests, and Promises,* 377.
99. Ezra 6:13–14.

case of leadership, it reimagines a new dynamic. But this dual-pronged approach lies at the heart of the work and at the heart of Jewish continuity. Only when a community can do both simultaneously can it endure.

That said, as we will see in the coming chapter, the process of reimagining is not always straightforward or unanimously accepted. Ezra-Nehemiah presents the laypeople that comprise its community as the central component in its development. But just who they are has yet to be defined. So, in the coming chapter, we will explore one of the most contentious and formative issues of the early Second Temple period: the question of Jewish identity.

Chapter Seven

Who Is a Jew?

REEVALUATING JEWISH IDENTITY

Ezra-Nehemiah promotes reconstructing aspects of the past while conforming to the needs of the present, and nowhere is this view more apparent than in the restoration of the Jewish community itself. When we think of restoration, we likely imagine tangible or quantifiable aspects of society. In the case of the Persian period, we might picture some of the elements we have considered thus far: the return of the holy vessels, the reconstruction of the Temple complex, or the reestablishment of internal governance. We know that restoration necessarily demands a return of the exiled people, but rarely do we consider the rebuilding of the actual community and communal identity. Perhaps this is because we envision Jewish identity as a fixed phenomenon and, by extension, we consider the character of the Jewish community to be self-evident. As we will see, though, that was not the case in Ezra-Nehemiah, when the leaders of the restoration were forced to reevaluate and redefine what belonging to the Jewish community meant. To understand that process and its consequences, we return again to the opening of the work.

REACTIONS TO A PARTIAL RETURN

In that opening, Cyrus addresses his decree to all the people throughout his empire who worship the God of Israel. Some respond in the affirmative and head back to Jerusalem, but many do not. For some Second Temple authors, this partial return is problematic. Earlier prophets spoke of a comprehensive return in which God would "gather in the scattered ones of Israel from all four edges of the world,"[1] and "the children of Judah and the children of Israel will gather together."[2] They envisioned a time when both Israel and Judah would be gathered by God "from the ends of the earth"[3] and Jerusalem would once again be "densely populated" by the "whole House of Israel."[4] These expectations made the partial return of exiles disappointing.

Not surprisingly, speaking to the small, disenchanted segment that did return, Zechariah attempts to console his audience with claims that in the future God will "strengthen the House of Judah and deliver the House of Joseph."[5] Some have returned, Zechariah acknowledges, but the true, ultimate return has yet to come. When it does, he proclaims, "the city squares will be full and alive with young boys and girls playing," because God will bring His people back "from the land of Egypt; from Assyria ... gather them in and bring them to the land of Gilad and Lebanon."[6] Once again, we see an early Second Temple prophet attempting to contextualize and thereby minimize his audience's disappointment.

And once again as well, Ezra-Nehemiah makes no such attempt: "Thus says Cyrus, king of Persia: 'The Lord, God of the heavens, has granted me all the kingdoms of the earth, and He has charged me to build Him a House in Jerusalem, in Judah. Whoever is among you from

---

1. Isaiah 11:11–12. In those verses, Jeremiah speaks of the ingathering of "those who remain, from Assyria and Egypt, from Patros and from Kush, from Eilam and from Shinar, Hamat and the islands of the sea," referring to places as far as Egypt, Iran, Mesopotamia, and Syria.
2. Hosea 2:2.
3. Jeremiah 30–31 envisions a mass return marked by divine blessing, repopulation, prosperity, and national unity.
4. Ezekiel 36:10. See also chapters 37, 47–48.
5. The prophet does not necessarily envision a restored northern empire, but he does envision the people of the north returning to the land.
6. Zechariah 8:5–8, 10:6–12.

all His people, may his God be with him, and let him go up to Jerusalem, in Judah.... As for anyone left behind in the place where he lives, his townsmen shall aid him with silver, gold, supplies, and beasts of burden, as well as gifts for the House of God in Jerusalem.' So all of the heads of the ancestral Houses of Judah and Benjamin and the priests and the Levites, and all those whose spirit had been stirred by God, prepared to go up and to build the House of the Lord, in Jerusalem. And their neighbors supported them with vessels of silver, gold, supplies, beasts of burden, and precious goods, aside from gifts which had been donated."[7]

Ezra-Nehemiah informs us matter-of-factly that only a portion of those who heard Cyrus's decree went back to the land. Some Jews returned and others Jews stayed where they were, but nowhere is there any indication that the partial nature of the return hinders the program of restoration or calls its legitimacy into question. That said, while the incomplete return does not seem to bother the author of Ezra-Nehemiah, we do find indications that the new reality created by those who stayed behind has significant ramifications. One such ramification manifests in the need to formally redefine what it means to belong to the nation of Israel.[8] To understand why a partial return would provoke such a need requires an understanding of what "being an Israelite" means in the pre-exilic period.

---

7. Ezra 1:6.
8. The evolving nature of the terms "Israelite," "Judean," and "Jew" is both complex and important, as are the distinctions between concepts such as nation, ethnos, and religion. Scholarly considerations of these issues rely on biblical, Second Temple, and early Jewish writings. See, for example, Daniel R. Schwartz, *Studies in the Jewish Background of Christianity* (Tübingen: Mohr-Siebeck, 1992); Shaye J. D. Cohen, *The Beginnings of Jewishness: Boundaries, Varieties, Uncertainties* vol. 31 (University of California Press, 1999); Steve Mason, "Jews, Judeans, Judaizing, Judaism: Problems of Categorization in Ancient History," *Journal for the Study of Judaism* 38, nos. 4–5 (2007): 457–512; Daniel Boyarin, "Rethinking Jewish Christianity: An Argument for Dismantling a Dubious Category (to which is Appended a Correction of my *Border Lines*)," *Jewish Quarterly Review* 99, no. 1 (2009): 7–36; Seth Schwartz, "How Many Judaisms Were There?: A Critique of Neusner and Smith on Definition and Mason and Boyarin on Categorization," *Journal of Ancient Judaism* 2, no. 2 (2011): 208–38.

BEING ISRAELITE BEFORE THE EXILE

Prior to the exile, Israelite identity consisted of several potential qualifying factors, the most obvious being genealogical association. But even if an individual or community lacked pedigree, the Tanakh indicates, there were other ways to gain inclusion within the community. Most simply, one could choose to join.[9] Ruth, the quintessential example of a biblical *ger*, illustrates what that choice looks like. Rather than remaining in her native land, Ruth the Moabitess chooses to accompany her Israelite mother-in-law to the Land of Israel and join its people. At the literal and figurative crossroads that appear at the end of the first chapter of the Megilla, Ruth makes the following declaration: "Do not entreat me to leave you, to turn back, not to walk after you. For wherever you walk, I shall walk, and wherever you stay, there I stay. Your people is my people; your God is my God. Wherever you die, there I die, and there shall I be buried."[10] Choosing to live in the Land of Israel, identifying with the people of Israel, and worshipping the God of Israel are thus the three critical components for acceptance within the nation of Israel. Of course, not all *ger* stories are as dramatic as Ruth's, and not all *gerim* consciously choose to make such a move. In fact, most references to *gerim* in Tanakh simply refer to people living in the Land of Israel who are not of Israelite descent but become, over time, part of its society. These *gerim*, a classification taken as a given in the legal texts of Tanakh, are not automatically obligated in all the positive commandments of the Torah, but they are obligated to prepare themselves appropriately for worship should they choose to participate. Exodus 12, for example, tells us that "if a stranger lives among you and wishes to offer a Passover sacrifice to the Lord, every male in his household must be circumcised. Then he

---

9.   Certain people and nations were barred from participating in Israelite communal life (Deut. 23:2–9). The Sages distinguish between the categories they label *ger toshav* and *ger tzedek*, the implications of which are vast. For a discussion of this rabbinic binary as well as other rabbinic conceptions of *ger*, see Ishay Rosen-Zvi and Adi Ophir, "Goy: Toward a Genealogy," *Dine Israel* 28 (2011): 69–122; Eliezer Hadad, *The Status of Minorities in the Jewish State: Halakhic Aspects* (2010); Raanan Mallek, "Historical Developments of the Term Ger Toshav and the Halakhic Implications Therein for Relating to Non-Jews," in *Jews in Dialogue* (Brill, 2020).

10.   Ruth 1:16–17.

may join in observing it and be like a native born. But no uncircumcised man may eat of it. There shall be one and the same law for the native born and the stranger who lives among you."[11] Unlike a native Israelite, the *ger* is not obligated to bring the Passover sacrifice, but like a native Israelite, if he does so, he must be circumcised.[12] This freedom of choice that is unique to *gerim*, however, does not apply in all cases. Regarding Passover, Exodus tells us that "during these seven days, leaven must not be found in your houses. Anyone, whether newcomer or native born, who eats leavened food will have his soul severed from the community of Israel."[13] Similarly, a *ger*, just like an Israelite who ingests the blood of an animal, will be cut off from the people.[14] A critical point thus emerges from these injunctions and their attendant threats. *Gerim* are obligated to uphold negative commandments because they are part of the community.[15] And as part of the community, the onus falls equally on them, as for native Israelites, to ensure the ritual and moral well-being of the community. As such, *gerim* are enjoined to rest on Shabbat,[16] to "afflict" themselves on Yom Kippur,[17] and to abstain from "abhorrent acts,"[18] from child sacrifice,[19] from working the land during the Sabbatical year,[20] and

---

11. Exodus 12:48–49.
12. The Torah distinguishes the *ger* from the "stranger" (*toshav* and *sachir*), who is prohibited from bringing a sacrifice altogether, further elucidating the unique status of a *ger* (see verse 45 in that same chapter).
13. Exodus 12:19–20.
14. Leviticus 17:10.
15. An interesting exception to this rule seems to appear in Deuteronomy 14:21, where the Israelites are commanded to give carrion to the *ger* rather than partake of it. But this seeming discrepancy is explained by the simple fact that carrion is forbidden for its unclean status, not because there is still blood in the carrion. And a *ger* is under no obligation to remain clean unless he or she wants to partake in cultic ceremonies. For more on this and the biblical laws pertaining to the *ger*, see Hans-Georg Wuench, "The Stranger in God's Land – Foreigners, Stranger, Guest: What Can We Learn from Israel's Attitude Towards Strangers?" in *Old Testament Essays* 27, no. 3 (2014): 1129–54.
16. Exodus 20:9, 23:12; Deuteronomy 5:13–14.
17. Leviticus 16:29.
18. Ibid. 18:26.
19. Ibid. 20:2.
20. Ibid. 25:6.

from entering the camp in an impure state.[21] When the Israelites receive the guidelines for fire offerings, they are told that the migrant "shall do just as you do," because there "shall be one law for the congregation."[22] And when the priest offers sacrifices to atone for the inadvertent sins of the community, "the community of Israel and the migrants living among them will all be forgiven, because all the people acted in error."[23] The actions of *gerim,* like the actions of native-born Israelites, affect the whole of the community, and, as such, they are held responsible for the choices they make.

But just as the *gerim* share in the obligations of the community, they also share in its delights. Like the Israelite, the *ger* was to "rejoice before the Lord" during Passover, Shavuot,[24] and Sukkot. And like the Israelites, he is guaranteed one of the most coveted promises in the ancient world: "Blessing in all your harvest and in all the work of your hands."[25]

What we find throughout the early biblical period, then, is an understanding that Israelite identity is determined by one of two factors: genealogy or geography. One could be born Israelite and automatically obligated in the covenantal requirements of the Israelite people, or one could remain within the borders of Israel, embrace the biblical laws that govern the land, and become Israelite that way.[26] And while this two-

---

21. Numbers 19:10.
22. Ibid. 15:15–16.
23. Ibid. 15:26.
24. The script for the first-fruit ritual (Deut. 26:1–15) contains a first-person historical retrospective that recalls God's choice of Abraham and the Israelites' journey toward the Promised Land. Interestingly, there is no separate script for the *ger,* seemingly implying that becoming a *ger* meant integrating the collective memory of the Israelites in addition to their practices.
25. Deuteronomy 16:15.
26. The *ger* was such a fundamental component of Israelite society that in his vision of restoration, Ezekiel grants those who join the community equal space within it. In chapter 47, he proclaims, "You shall divide this land for yourselves according to the tribes of Israel. You shall allot it as an inheritance for yourselves and for the strangers who live amongst you, who bear children in your midst. These shall be considered by you as citizens among the children of Israel. They shall be allotted an inheritance among the tribes of Israel. It shall be that in whatever tribe's territory the stranger lives, there shall you give him his inheritance" (Ezek. 47:21–23).

pronged system held in Israel for most of its pre-exilic history, in Ezra-Nehemiah, things begin to change.[27]

EARLY EVIDENCE THAT THE FORMER
SYSTEM NO LONGER APPLIES

Evidence of this change is first seen in Ezra 4, where we learn that a group of people who identify with the community want to assist in the building project. The group, we are told, "heard that the returned exiles were building a Sanctuary for the Lord, God of Israel. So they approached Zerubbabel and the family heads and said to them: 'Let us join you in building it, for we too worship your God and have been sacrificing to Him ever since the days of Esarhaddon king of Assyria, who brought us here.'"[28] But the leaders in Israel would hear nothing of it, and the episode continues: "But Zerubbabel and Jeshua and the rest of the family heads of Israel replied: 'You shall have no part with us building a House for our God; rather, it is our people who, alone, shall build a House for the Lord, God of Israel, as Cyrus, king of Persia, has commanded us to do.'"[29] The rejection is not well received, and "the people of the land undermined the people of Judah and made them afraid to build. They employed advisors to foil their plans throughout the reign of Cyrus, king of Persia, and through the reign of Darius, king of Persia."[30] Not surprisingly, the book of Ezra-Nehemiah, written in retrospect, refers to this group as the "adversaries of Judah and Benjamin."[31]

The obvious question that surfaces from this episode is: Why are they rejected? They live in the land and claim to worship the God of Israel. Moreover, their desire to help rebuild the Temple speaks to their commitment to the reestablishment of the Israelite worship and

---

27. Ezra-Nehemiah's approach to the outsider differs significantly from that of Chronicles. See, for example, Japhet, *The Ideology of the Book of Chronicles*, 241–48; David A. Glatt-Gilad, "Chronicles as Consensus Literature," in *What Was Authoritative for Chronicles* (2011), 67–75.
28. Ezra 4:1–2.
29. Ibid., v. 3.
30. Ibid., vv. 4–5.
31. Ibid., v. 1.

its associated laws. For all intents and purposes, they would have been considered *gerim* prior to the exile. But now, in the post-exilic period, they are barred from joining the community. What has changed?

The simplest explanation, based on the origin story of this group,[32] is that nothing changed. The people are rejected because they are not actually dedicated to God, which, even in First Temple times, would have disqualified them. Evidence of this claim is traced to II Kings, where we are told that after the Assyrian king Shalmaneser exiles the Northern Kingdom,[33] he "brought in people from Babylon, Kuta, Ava, Hamat, and Sefarvites, and he settled them in the towns of Shomron instead of the Israelites. They took possession of Shomron and settled its cities." But we are also told that when "they first settled there, they had no reverence for the Lord, so the Lord sent forth against them lions who killed some of them." To prevent an ongoing bloodbath within his newly conquered territories, the king of Assyria commands the people to bring an Israelite priest back from exile so that he can "settle there and teach them the customs of the local God," in the hopes that if they learn the proper way to worship Him, the lion attacks will stop. However, the book of Kings is very clear about the fact that while "these nations revered the Lord," ultimately, "they continued to serve their idols – and their children and their children's children do just as their ancestors did

---

32. II Kings 17. For a suggested reconstruction of the history of these people, see Yigal Levin, "Bi-Directional Forced Deportations in the Neo-Assyrian Empire and the Origins of the Samaritans: Colonialism and Hybridity," *Archaeological Review from Cambridge* 28 (2013): 217–40.

33. The conquest of Samaria is attributed (in cuneiform documents) to both Shalmaneser V and Sargon, but Kings attributes it solely to Shalmaneser. *The Revised New Jerusalem Bible: Study Edition* (Image, 2019), 758. As Yigal Levin explains, "2 Kgs 17.24 is in any case a partial summary, since it does not include the Arabs whom Sargon himself claims to have settled in Samerina, and of course it ignores the Persians, Erechites, and Elamites whom Ezra 4.2, 9–10 states were brought in the reigns of Esarhaddon and 'Osnappar' (presumably Assurbanipal). So, it would seem that only some of the deportations that actually occurred are mentioned in the existing sources." See Yigal Levin, "Judea, Samaria and Idumea: Three Models of Ethnicity and Administration in the Persian Period," in *Judah to Judaea, Socio-Economic Structures and Processes in the Persian Period* (2012), 4–53.

to this day."[34] If the group that approaches the Jewish leaders in Ezra 4 are descendants of the group denigrated in Kings, then the argument can be made that they are not true *gerim* and, as such, have not earned their place within the community. The fact that when they speak to the Judeans, they refer to God as "your God"[35] is used as a further proof that the issue at stake is a flawed theology.[36]

Interestingly, while the argument that the group is not sufficiently monotheistic would likely have been known to the author of Ezra-Nehemiah, it is not cited in the work. The Judean leaders in Ezra-Nehemiah do not question the integrity of the group's theology. In fact, their integrity seems to be irrelevant. The people who approach the leaders in Ezra-Nehemiah are plainly assumed to be outsiders, which is why the response of the leaders emphasizes that "it is our people who, alone, shall build a House for the Lord, God of Israel, as Cyrus, king of Persia, has commanded us to do."[37] This brings us back to the previous question: If, in earlier times, the group that wanted to join the Temple building project would have been included within the Israelite community, why now are they being excluded?

---

34. II Kings 17:24–41.
35. Ezra 4:2.
36. If we look at the verse quoted earlier from Ruth, she, too, calls Naomi's God "your God," and, in doing so, acknowledges the choice she makes to align herself with a deity that is not hers by birth but by choice. It would make little sense to impose a different meaning on the same claim made by a group of *gerim*. Like Ruth, the group is essentially saying, "He was originally your God, but now He is ours, too." Furthermore, while the "importees" may have been rightly accused of syncretistic worship in the pre-exilic period, that makes them no different from the pre-exilic Israelites. The book of Kings is clear about the fact that foreign worship is chief among those sins for which the Israelites were exiled. If the group of returnees was accused of worshipping foreign gods in the past but are now a different, repented people, then on what grounds are they refusing to accept the importees' claim that they too, now, exclusively worship God?
37. Ezra 4:3.

WHEN BOUNDARIES NEED TO BE REDRAWN

The answer lies in a reality that arises before the repatriates begin rebuilding but only becomes pressing once they return. For much of the early biblical period, as we see above, Israelite identity is demarcated by genealogy or geography, and that twofold system makes sense as long as Israel is a "land-based national entity."[38] People with long-standing residence within the Land of Israel are expected to behave like Israelites, and as such, the geographical boundaries of the land also function as the figurative boundaries around Israelite identity.

But exile changes that. Exile creates a reality in which, for the first time, the majority of the once-Israelites live outside of the land. As we see in chapter two, sizable Jewish communities exist in Egypt, Babylon, and other regions in the Levant.[39] That means that the geographical boundaries and indigenous politics that once guaranteed cohesion no longer do. The implicit danger, which is never explicitly articulated in the work but underlies its position, is that if the boundaries of the land define the boundaries of peoplehood, most of the once-Israelites would be lost. A new, shared quality between those inside and those outside the land needs to be established. As Lawrence Schiffman explains, because the exile "caused Judaism to adapt to a new, extraterritorial existence, the importance of genealogy increased."[40] When the reality of life outside the land renders the criterion of geography obsolete, genealogy becomes the primary determinant.[41]

The question of whether geography could still be a qualifying factor for those living in the land but not genealogically tied to the community plays out in the scene between the returnees and those who want

---

38. Lawrence H. Schiffman, "Jewish Identity and Jewish Descent," *Judaism* 34, no. 1 (1985): 78–84.
39. For a survey of the communities that existed in light of recent investigations, see Oded Lipschitz and Manfred Oeming, *Judah and the Judeans in the Persian Period* (Eisenbrauns, 2006), 94–98.
40. Schiffman, "Jewish Identity," 82.
41. By linking the behavioral component with that of the "holy seed," Ezra-Nehemiah makes clear that the revolution was a religious, not a racial, one. Genealogy was simply the tangible means by which the leaders drew boundaries around their redefined community.

to join the building project. Clearly, those who want to join feel that their presence on the land and their pronounced loyalty to God suffice. But the rejection voiced by the leaders of Judah reveals their unequivocal opposition, which asserts that genealogy has become necessary in determining Jewish identity. The leaders who voice that contention, we must remember, had recently returned from exile. Thus, their agenda is likely fueled by the belief that to maintain consistency throughout the now geographically fragmented Jewish nation, a single criterion for belonging is necessary. By extension, the formerly acceptable premise that "living in Israel and behaving like an Israelite makes you Israelite" had to be renounced.

The broad-sweeping term *amei haaretz*, "peoples of the land," which is used to refer to all the local ethnic groups with whom the protagonists in Ezra-Nehemiah interact and to whom entry is denied,[42] reflects this new identity politics. Since any ethnicity other than Judean is rendered non-Judean, the specific ethnicity to which one belongs is irrelevant.[43] Instead, the simple binary of "insider" and "outsider" is applied across the board. Jewish lineage makes one an insider, while lack of it renders one an outsider. And while that assertion is not automatically or unanimously accepted by all Judeans at the time,[44] it is certainly the approach espoused by the author of Ezra-Nehemiah. It is apparent in the episode quoted above, in which people with long-standing residence in Israel but no Jewish lineage are disqualified from the community despite their claims to worship Israel's God, and it is alluded to in the records of returnees when families are singled out because they "could not prove whether their ancestral house or descent were of Israel."[45]

---

42. Ezra 3:3, 4:4, 9:1–2, 11, 10:2, 11; Nehemiah 10:29–32.
43. Specific ethnicities are mentioned at different points. See, for example, Ezra 9:1 and Nehemiah 13:1. But according to Ezra-Nehemiah, those details are of no consequence within the new system.
44. Alternative perspectives are evident within the text of Ezra-Nehemiah itself and other post-exilic Biblical works. For a discussion of the biblical voices that push back at this particularistic view, see Moshe Weinfeld, "Universalistic and Particularistic Trends During the Exile and Restoration," in *Normative and Sectarian Judaism in the Second Temple Period* (2005), 251–66.
45. Ezra 2:59. Those same families are remembered as outliers in the days of Nehemiah as well (Neh. 7:5).

These changes, seen in the first wave of return, are upheld in later waves as well. Nehemiah rejects two of his three main opponents, Sanballat and Tobiah, even though they both seem to self-identify as belonging to the Judean community. Sanballat, the governor of Samaria, gives his children theophoric names and is regarded by the Elephantine Jews as belonging to the same community as the Jerusalem priests.[46] Tobiah, too, whose name means "(the) God (of Israel) is good," names his son Yohanan,[47] meaning "God has been compassionate."[48] Still, regardless of how they view themselves and even how they may have been perceived in other Jewish communities, from the perspective of Ezra-Nehemiah, they are categorically outsiders. They are grouped with "our other enemies" throughout the work,[49] and when Sanballat attempts to gain access by aligning himself with Nehemiah, his attempts prove futile.[50]

Still, despite his best attempts, Sanballat, like Tobiah and their followers, are deemed inexorable outsiders. Nehemiah refers to Sanballat, Tobiah, and an additional opponent, Geshem, as the Horonite, the Ammonite, and the Arab, respectively, and in doing so makes clear that

---

46. See: Bezalel Porten, *The Elephantine Papyri in English: Three Millennia of Cross-Cultural Continuity and Change* (Brill, 1996), 79, n91.

47. Nehemiah 6:18.

48. It could be argued that names alone do not guarantee ethnic affiliation. Zerubbabel, for example, has a Babylonian name and yet he returns as the Judean leader. Still, someone who does not identify as Judean is less likely to incorporate Israel's God into his (or his child's) name than a Judean in Babylon is to adopt a local name.

49. See, for example, Nehemiah 6:1.

50. The missive Sanballat sends to Nehemiah, for example, says: "It is rumored among the nations and confirmed by Gashmu that you and the Jews plan to rebel, and that is why you are building the wall, intending to be their king, and additional such reports. Furthermore, you have set up prophets to proclaim of you in Jerusalem, 'A king in Judah.' Now the king will hear such reports! Come, let us deliberate together"(Neh. 6:6). The words "you and the Jews" clearly mark Sanballat as an outsider. By reporting what the *goyim*, "the nations," are saying about the Judeans and offering to "deliberate together," it becomes clear that Sanballat attempts to align himself with the Jewish community and perhaps gain acceptance. Borrowing a page from Ezra-Nehemiah's playbook, he broadly groups all outsiders in contrast to himself. The word *goy* could refer to Israel, but it is never used as such in Ezra-Nehemiah. Lipschits, Oded, Gary N. Knoppers, and Rainer Albertz, eds. *Judah and the Judeans in the Fourth Century BCE.* (Penn State Press, 2007), 156.

none of them is to be granted entry into the community.[51] Still, while
the narrative portions and the name lists emphatically clarify the *stance*
assumed in Ezra-Nehemiah vis-à-vis outsiders, the *rationale* behind that
stance is only fully articulated in the discussions of intermarriage that
arise in the period of Ezra.

INTERMARRIAGE BEFORE THE
TIME OF EZRA-NEHEMIAH

Intermarriage is the first crisis Ezra addresses upon arriving in Judah.
He is first apprised of the problem when the leaders there approach
him bemoaning the fact that "the people of Israel, and even the priests
and Levites, have failed to separate themselves from the people of the
land. They engage in abominations in the manner of the Canaanites,
the Hittites, the Perizzites, the Jebusites, the Ammonites, the Moabites,
the Egyptians, and the Amorites. For they have taken some of their
daughters as wives for themselves and for their sons."[52] Ezra reacts with
outward signs of mourning and prayer as well as a demand that the
people who had been "unfaithful by marrying foreign women," separate
themselves "from the peoples of the land and from foreign women."[53]
Although bans never succeed in fully eradicating behaviors, there is certainly a sense in Ezra 10 that while the problem is widespread, so is support for its rectification. Still, more significant than the overt storyline
is the expansive nature of Ezra's initiative.

Until Ezra, the prohibition against intermarriage was predicated on
the fear that intimate contact with nations of low moral standing would
lead Israel to imitate their idolatrous and immoral ways. In Deuteronomy, for example, the prohibition against intermarriage with the seven
Canaanite nations is couched in explicit warnings: "Do not intermarry
with them," the Israelites are told. And "do not give your daughters to
their sons in marriage or take their daughters for your sons. For they

---

51. As we discover in Nehemiah 6 and 13, though, Nehemiah's efforts are never fully
successful.
52. Ezra 9:1.
53. Ibid. 10:10–11.

will turn your children away from walking after Me, and bring them to serve other gods."[54] The warnings reveal a fear of exogamy's destructive social and religious influences.[55]

This moral-religious rationale, as Christine Hayes points out, "can be used to broaden the scope of the prohibition because it can be argued that intermarriage with any Gentile (not just one from the seven Canaanite nations) who turns an Israelite to idolatry should be prohibited." At the same time, though, "it does not render the law of universal application. On the contrary, the clear implication of this rationale is that only those exogamous unions that result in the moral or religious alienation of the Israelite partner are prohibited."[56] For that reason, the prohibition against intermarriage in the early biblical period is limited in scope.[57] It applies only to those peoples who constitute a perceived threat to the religious character or welfare of Israel. If an Israelite man wants to marry a foreign woman caught in war, for example, assuming she is not a religious threat and that he follows the prescribed protocol, he is permitted to do so.[58]

WHAT INTERMARRIAGE BECAME AND HOW

But in Ezra-Nehemiah, norms begin to change. The people who update Ezra on the perceived intermarriage epidemic bring two charges before him. They begin with the complaint that the Judeans "engage in

---

54. Deuteronomy 7:3–4. See also Exodus 34:15–16 and Deuteronomy 20:18 for similar sentiments.
55. In addition to the seven Canaanite nations with whom intermarriage is prohibited for fear of religious and cultural diffusion, the Ammonites and Moabites are prohibited as well, seemingly because their cruel character was anathema to Israel (see Deuteronomy 23:4–5). Deuteronomy 23:8–9 also prohibits the entry of Edomites and Egyptians for three generations, and the language there seems to indicate the prohibition is related to intermarriage as well. For other exceptional cases of barred entry, see Deuteronomy 23:2–3.
56. Christine Hayes, "Intermarriage and Impurity in Ancient Jewish Sources," *Harvard Theological Review* 92, no. 1 (1999): 3–36.
57. Shaye Cohen, "From the Bible to the Talmud: The Prohibition of Intermarriage," *Hebrew Annual Review* 7 (1983): 23–39.
58. Deuteronomy 21:10–14.

abominations," hearkening back to the moral-religious threat posed by intermarriage.[59] Then, to bolster their claim, they anachronistically invoke the names of no-longer-extant but once morally repugnant nations alongside the up-to-date list of nations with whom intermarriage is taking place.[60] In doing so, they make clear that just as the idol worship of those nations once threatened the viability of the Israelite community, the current behaviors of the nations with whom they are now intermarrying pose an equally grave threat. But their register of offending nations does something else as well. By listing the seven Canaanite nations with whom intermarriage is prohibited on behavioral grounds,[61] alongside the Ammonites and Moabites, two nations to whom entry into the community is permanently and unconditionally prohibited,[62] they establish an equivalence between the two. Like the Ammonites and Moabites, the work seems to say, all foreign nations are permanently and unconditionally forbidden from entering the community.[63]

---

59. The concept of "abominations" is not found in the context of the intermarriage prohibition in Deuteronomy 7, but it is used to classify the problematic behaviors of the Canaanite nations in Leviticus 18. As we will see below and in the coming chapter, the act of weaving together distinct biblical ideas lies at the heart of Ezra's reforms.

60. Ezra 9:1 lists the defunct Canaanite, Hittite, Perizzite, Jebusite, and Amorite nations alongside the extant Ammonites, Moabites, and Egyptians.

61. Deuteronomy 7:1–3.

62. Ibid. 23:4–7. The reason for their permanent exclusion, "For they would not greet you with food and water on your way when you came out of Egypt; and in hostility against you they hired Balaam son of Beor from Petor of Aram Naharayim to curse you," seems to imply that their national character, which is marked by cruelty, cannot be reconciled with the national character of Israel. The Ammonites and Moabites are listed alongside other groups of people that are not to be "admitted to the congregation of the Lord" (Deut. 23:2–7).

63. This assertion is further supported at the end of Nehemiah where the people's comprehension that "no Ammonite or Moabite shall be admitted to the congregation of God," is followed by "they separated all those of mixed lineage from Israel" (Neh. 13:1–3). According to Gary Knoppers, this extension of the ban is likely inspired by I Kings 11:1–2, which states that "King Solomon loved many foreign women besides the daughter of Pharaoh – Moabite women, Ammonite women, Edomite women, Sidonian women, Hittite women – from the nations of which the Lord had warned the Israelites: 'You must not join with them, nor must they join with

Then, in addition to linking two previously distinct verses, the people also append to their first grievance the complaint that "the holy seed has been mixed up with that of the people of the land."[64] Intermarriage, they seemed to say, carries more than just behavioral costs. It also affects the holiness of Israel. Of course, the notion that Israelites are a "holy people" is deeply ingrained in earlier textual traditions. In Leviticus, for example, God tells the Israelites to "be holy, for I am holy,"[65] and in Deuteronomy, twice they are reminded that they are "a holy people to the Lord your God."[66] That holiness, the Torah makes clear, must be sustained through proper behavior, and so, by definition, intermarriage with foreigners that "will turn your children away... and bring them to serve other gods,"[67] poses a threat to that holy status. But in these verses, it is the sinful behaviors generated by intermarriage that poses a threat to Israel's holiness, not the act of intermarriage itself. In Ezra-Nehemiah, though, we find for the first time the contention that intermarriage itself profanes Israel's holy status.

This creative application of "holy seed" to intermarriage marks an additional means by which the prohibition of outsiders joining the community becomes comprehensive in Ezra-Nehemiah. As Saul Olyan explains, the "purity ideology of Ezra-Nehemiah functions as one of several significant tools used to reconfigure the Judean community through the definition of who is a Judean and expulsion of those classed as aliens."[68] The concept, in its most basic configuration, is likely borrowed from priestly marriage laws.[69] Priests, who are considered to have a holy status conferred by God, are prohibited from marrying women who would profane that status.[70] But in some Second Temple prophetic

---

you, for they will turn your hearts astray after their own gods." See G. N. Knoppers, "Sex, Religion, and Politics: The Deuteronomist on Intermarriage," *Hebrew Annual Review* 14 (1994): 121–14

64. Ezra 9:2.
65. Leviticus 19:1.
66. Deuteronomy 7:6, 14:2. See also 14:21, 28:9.
67. Ibid. 7:4.
68. Saul Olyan, "Purity Ideology in Ezra-Nehemiah as a Tool to Reconstitute the Community," *Journal for the Study of Judaism* 35, no. 1 (2004): 1–16.
69. Hayes, "Intermarriage and Impurity."
70. Leviticus 21:7–9. The binary of "holy" and "profane" is not to be confused with that

writings, we begin to see this rationale applied to ordinary Israelites as well. Malachi, for example, laments the fact that "Judah has been faithless, and an abomination has been perpetrated in Israel and Jerusalem. For Judah, whom He loves, has desecrated that which is holy to the Lord and married the daughter of a foreign god." [71] If Israel has been consecrated to God, then marriage with non-consecrated, profane people desecrates that holy status. In a similar vein, the verse from Ezra 9 that mentions the sin of intermarriage uses the term *maal* which, within the Temple lexicon, refers to the sin of profaning that which is holy.[72] As a result, Ezra instructs the people who intermarried to bring a guilt offering,[73] the very offering prescribed in Leviticus for the offense of profanation.[74]

This link constructed between intermarriage and profanation, while novel, is likely rooted in the biblical juxtaposition of the concepts of intermarriage and holiness.[75] The prohibition against intermarriage with the seven Canaanite nations mentioned above[76] is immediately followed by the words "For you are a holy people to the Lord your God."[77] The word *ki*, translated as "for" or "because," seems to imply that the Israel's consecration is the rationale behind the prohibition. If that is the case,

---

of "pure" and "impure." "Impure" denotes a state of "cultic disability" and as such is the antonym of "pure." The term "holy," on the other hand, denotes someone or something that has been consecrated to God. Such a person or thing can be desecrated by an ordinary/profane/non-holy person, activity, or object. Becoming impure is not sinful and is easily rectified through the variously prescribed rituals of purification. Desecration, on the other hand, must be avoided. This distinction is critical, as nowhere does the work of Ezra-Nehemiah see non-Judeans as inherently impure; they are simply construed as not holy, having never been consecrated by God the way Israel was. For a full discussion of the distinctions between these concepts, see Jonathan Klawans, *Impurity and Sin in Ancient Judaism* (Oxford University Press, 2000); Christine Hayes, *Gentile Impurities and Jewish Identities: Intermarriage and Conversion from the Bible to the Talmud* (Oxford University Press, USA, 2002).

71. Malachi 2:11.
72. Ezra 9:2.
73. Ibid. 10:19.
74. Leviticus 5:14–16.
75. For a more detailed explanation of this link, see Jacob Milgrom, *Leviticus/[1] 1–16* (Doubleday, 1991), 359–36.
76. Deuteronomy 7:1–5.
77. Ibid., v. 6.

then the moral-religious rationale, while still relevant, is no longer the sole rationale. Added to it is the notion that, as a holy nation, Israel alone generates "holy seed." Because that holiness is inherited, not earned, marriage and procreation with non-holy peoples profane that holiness and cannot be tolerated. So, at the behest of Ezra, the Judeans vow to separate "from the peoples of the land and from the foreign women."[78]

THE NEW REALITY CREATED IN JUDAH

The new ban on joining the community in Ezra-Nehemiah seems both absolute and irrevocable. Once-acceptable ways for non-Judeans to join the community had been rendered invalid.[79] We glean from Ezra-Nehemiah that to ensure a coherent identity for homeland and Diaspora Jews alike, the Judean leaders employ painstaking measures to close all portals of entry to outsiders. Lines of distinction become sharper, the work seems to argue, and the once-fluid boundaries between "us" and "them" are hermetically sealed.

Of course, the work attests to the fact that the leaders' efforts are never fully successful and that Ezra's categorical legislations are not adopted.[80] We are told that specific individuals who had been barred, for example, nonetheless remain fixtures within the narrative, reflecting their staying power within the community. On more than one occasion, Nehemiah laments the support and familial ties his "enemies" are able to accumulate from within the community. The final chapter of the work tells us that intermarriage continues to be a problem. Still, while the work openly acknowledges the pushback against Ezra and Nehemiah's

---

78. Ezra 10:11.

79. Ezra 6:21 tells us that they "separated themselves from the impurity of the nations of the land and came to worship the Lord, God of Israel," leading some to suggest that while they were not permitted to join the building project, they were allowed to participate in the Passover celebration (Kiddushin 70a). But it is also possible that the verse in Ezra, like the verse in Nehemiah 10:29 that speaks of "all those who had separated themselves from the peoples of the lands to be with God's Torah" is telling us that those people separated from their foreign spouses.

80. For a discussion of the impact of his legislations on Second Temple literature and practice, see Hayes, *Gentile Impurities*, 27–44.

reforms, it is also clearly sympathetic to those reforms. Furthermore, it does not seem to question the harsh exclusivist measures employed by the work's leaders because their conviction is based on a truth that is deeply embedded in biblical thought, which needs to be understood if we are to fully appreciate the challenge those leaders believed they were facing.

IDENTITY FORMATION

Group identities, like individual identities, are predicated on the assumption of "self" as distinct from "other." As Jeremiah Cataldo explains, "The subject, the self, the I, exists in relation to the object or individual who is simultaneously rejected and a necessary component of the subject's self."[81] If a person or group defines itself based on specific biological, cultural, or religious traits, then anyone who does not possess that trait will necessarily be excluded, an exclusion that demarcates the boundaries around the identity. Cataldo elaborates that "it is the causalities of difference that generate the foundation of society.... We are recognizable as ourselves because we recognize that we are different from someone or something else."[82] Identity cannot exist without the quintessential other because to know who we are we must first know who we are not.

This concept is introduced on its most elemental level in the primordial episodes of Genesis. There, Creation occurs through the dual process of declaration and distinction. God says, "Let there be light" and then "separated the light from the darkness."[83] He separates the waters above from the waters below and the seas from dry land, and He distinguishes the varieties of vegetation and living creatures according to their species. Entities only exist, Genesis seems to be telling us, when they can be distinguished from that which is around them. As such, those distinctions must be maintained.[84]

---

81. Jeremiah W. Cataldo, *Imagined Worlds and Constructed Differences in the Hebrew Bible* (Bloomsbury, 2019), 15.
82. Ibid.
83. Genesis 1:3–4.
84. Divine beings, for example, cannot mix with mortals (Gen. 6:1–4), seeds of different trees cannot be grafted, and animals cannot be crossbred (Lev. 19:19; Deut.

The entity of Israel is no different. From the outset, Israel's identity is rooted in the belief that she is chosen to follow a distinct set of divinely revealed laws in a chosen land.[85] The charge "Be holy to Me, for I the Lord am holy, and I have set you apart from all other peoples to be My own"[86] can only be understood in the context of the law giving in which it appears. As a fledgling nation in the desert, poised between the dominant cultures of Egypt and Canaan, Israel is told: "You shall not do as they do in the land of Egypt where you lived. Nor shall you do as they do in the land of Canaan where I am bringing you; do not follow their practices. Observe My laws, keep My statutes and follow them; I am the Lord your God."[87] Like the process described in Genesis, Israel's creation too comes about through distinction. To continue to exist, she must know where to draw the boundaries around her identity and how to preserve them. But in Ezra-Nehemiah, that preservation proves particularly challenging.

VULNERABILITY OF THE JUDEAN COMMUNITY

The geographical boundaries of the Land of Israel no longer suffice as identity determinants in the post-exilic reality. Once, they delimited the Israelite nation, but with the enduring reality of Diaspora Jewry, that is no longer the case. So alterations are made, and "holy seed" becomes the qualifying criterion.

As with all changes in history, however, this change takes longer to become convention than its creators might have liked. Throughout Ezra-Nehemiah, we find evidence that marriages with those deemed

---

22:9–11).

85. This concept of chosenness is a central tenet of Israelite identity. As Tikva Frymer-Kensky puts it, "As an alternative to any idea of superiority, the Bible proposed the idea of election. The biblical idea of election, 'chosen-ness,' is the alternative to an idea of natural superiority; as Deuteronomy says, it is not because Israel is bigger or smarter that God is in covenant with it but because God chose it." (Tikva Frymer-Kensky, "Judaism and Pluralism," *Journal of Ecumenical Studies* 52, no. 1 [2017]: 34–38).

86. Leviticus 20:26.

87. Ibid. 18:3–4.

"foreigners" by Ezra-Nehemiah continues. We also find attempts by those rejected to breach the barriers that render them outsiders. Ezra-Nehemiah describes those attempted breaches by alternating seamlessly between the physical and metaphorical barriers under threat, revealing the vulnerable position in which the Judean leaders believed their community to be and explaining the draconian measures undertaken to safeguard insiders.

From the perspective of Ezra-Nehemiah, that which is inside needs safeguarding because, at least initially, it is operating from a place of fragility. The word *peleita*, remnant, used repeatedly by the Judean leaders to describe the community,[88] conveys their sense that the returnees are a paltry representation of the glorious nation that once lived in the land. Numerically, they are not wrong. But their concern goes beyond numbers. Their word choice discloses their fear that the survival of the Judean community *as* a Judean community is in jeopardy. That fear is not unfounded because ultimately, as Tamara Cohn Eskenazi explains, "There is no such thing as cultural unspecificity. In cases of a minority, such as the community as it portrays itself in Ezra-Nehemiah, lack of boundaries means merging with the dominant culture. That culture could be the wider Persian Empire or that of its neighbour Samaria." Of course, the leaders fiercely resist such a merger, and "Ezra-Nehemiah's ethnocentric agenda can be understood, therefore, as a struggle for identity in the midst of a sea of more powerful nationalities."[89]

In addition, according to the work's accounts, some of those nationalities, particularly those living within the land, have nefarious intentions. Accordingly, both the Judeans and their leaders worry that the attempts of those adversaries to infiltrate and destabilize what they are working

---

88. Ezra 9:8, 13–15; Nehemiah 1:2. For a full discussion of the use of this word within the text, see Tamara Cohn Eskenazi, "Imagining the Other in the Construction of Judahite Identity in Ezra-Nehemiah," in *Imagining the Other and Constructing Israelite Identity in the Early Second Temple Period* (2014), 230–56.

89. Tamara Cohn Eskenazi, "From Exile and Restoration to Exile and Reconstruction," in *Exile and Restoration Revisited: Essays on the Babylonian Persian Period in Memory of Peter R. Ackroyd* (2009), 78–93.

so hard to build might succeed.[90] As such, they treat every word and action of their opponents with a "hermeneutic of suspicion."[91]

Even before the building of the Temple officially commences, we are told that the Judeans are "fearful of the peoples of the land."[92] That fear is validated once the building begins and "the people of the land undermined the people of Judah, and made them afraid to build. They employed advisors to foil their plans throughout the reign of Cyrus, king of Persia, and through the reign of Darius, king of Persia."[93] When Ezra comes to Judah with the Torah of Moses, primed to revive the community's religious commitment, he makes it clear that intermarriage with the people of the land poses an existential threat to those revivification efforts. He also understands that the Judeans' good fortune and return to the land are not guaranteed. The historical retrospective he lays out for his audience, in which he recounts Israel's existence on the land and banishment from it, culminates in his rhetorical question for God: "Shall we then disobey Your commandments yet again by intermarrying with these peoples who are replete with these abominations? Would You not rage against us to the end, not leaving a remnant (*peleita*) or a trace?"[94] The success of the small remnant under his purview, Ezra understands, is highly precarious. To rebuild effectively, the community has no choice but to separate completely from those who are anathema to everything they are trying to accomplish.

Nehemiah is similarly depicted as having to contend with parties that were his complete inverse. Nehemiah, who goes to Judah out of

---

90. It is important to note that not all non-Judeans are presented as enemies of Judah. As we see in the previous chapter, Ezra-Nehemiah consistently speaks positively of its Persian leaders, as it does about the hewers and stonemasons from Sidon and Tyre, who assist in the preparations for the building project (Ezra 3:7). Only those who assume an adversarial position vis-à-vis Judah and behave like foes are treated as such. As Tamara Cohn Eskenazi claims, "More than any other Biblical Book, Ezra-Nehemiah posits foreigners as other not only as foe but also as friend." Eskenazi, "Imagining the Other," 236.
91. Knoppers, *Prophets, Priests, and Promises*, 68.
92. Ezra 3:3. For suggested explanations of their fears, see Jacob M. Myers, *The Anchor Bible: Ezra Nehemiah* (1965), 25.
93. Ezra 4:4–5.
94. Ibid. 9:14.

concern for the welfare of his people, faces, upon arrival, those who "took it exceedingly ill that someone had come seeking the good of the Israelites."[95] Those men, we are told, "mocked and derided" Nehemiah's efforts to fortify the city, and, like the group rejected in Ezra 4, accuse him of "rebelling against the king."[96] They try intimidating Nehemiah and his supporters and, when that fails, they embark on an obstruction campaign, joining forces to "wage war upon Jerusalem and cause confusion there."[97] Gary Knoppers encapsulates the impression created by Nehemiah's memoirs as follows: "The first-person accounts thus present matters in a clear-cut fashion. The proponent, Nehemiah, drives the action and seeks to implement positive change on behalf of God for the Judeans, while his adversaries, the neighboring nations and their leaders, try to frustrate, if not undo, these good reforms at every step."[98]

Historically, it is difficult to determine whether those branded "adversaries" or "enemies" of Judah and Benjamin were averse to the goals of the Judean community from the outset or whether their hostility grew from a sense of rejection or even out of competing political interests.[99] Regardless, the picture painted in Ezra-Nehemiah is one of a foreign ethnicity intertwined with behaviors that seem to stand in the way of the Judean community's social and religious progress. Those barred entry are not simply born to the wrong parents, Ezra-Nehemiah argues; they are also behaving wrongly. They are presented time and again as standing "diametrically opposed to the well-being of the Jerusalem community,"[100]

95. Nehemiah 2:10.
96. Ibid., vv. 19–20.
97. Ibid. 4:1–2. When those attempts to impede the Judeans' progress fails as well, Nehemiah's opponents conspire to attack Nehemiah himself (Neh. 6:1–2, 10–14).
98. Gary N. Knoppers, "Nehemiah and Sanballat: The Enemy Without or Within?" in *Judah and the Judeans*, 305–22.
99. For different suggested explanations to account for their opposition, see Lisbeth S. Fried, "Something There Is That Doesn't Love a Wall (around Jerusalem) – Why Would a Simple Wall Create Such a Crisis?" *Transeuphratene* 39 (2010): 79–89.
100. Knoppers, "Nehemiah and Sanballat," 313. Blenkinsopp sees the sentence as an ironic pun on Tobiah's name, highlighting the contrast between the one named "Tob-iah" and the one who truly seeks to do good (*tob*) for his people. Blenkinsopp, *Ezra-Nehemiah*, 219.

and their opposition is presented as capable of decimating the restoration enterprise.

FORTIFYING (BOTH) WALL(S) AROUND THE COMMUNITY

For that reason, a substantial portion of Ezra-Nehemiah deals with construction of boundaries around the Judean community. Zerubbabel erects a boundary between the community of Temple builders and those beyond. Through his intermarriage ban, Ezra reinforces that boundary, shielding Judean families and, by extension, the entire community from foreign influences. Only a short while later, Nehemiah extends this project by both solidifying the community from within and reconstructing the wall around Jerusalem that had been left in shambles.[101] The rebuilding of that physical wall epitomizes in many ways the earlier phases of distinction and is granted significant space within the narrative.

We first hear about the wall at the beginning of Nehemiah while Nehemiah is still in Persia. There, Nehemiah enquires about the *peleita* and about Jerusalem, and he discovers that "those remaining from the captivity in the province are degraded and in dire distress while Jerusalem's wall has been everywhere broken through, and her gates have been put to the torch."[102] The distress of the community in his account is directly linked to its permeability, and by extension, its vulnerability. Nehemiah's first action upon reaching Jerusalem is to repair what was broken, because the wall is both practically important and symbolically significant. It lends credence to the perception that there is a remnant inside trying to rehabilitate itself by protecting its fragile identity and those just outside eager to crack it open.

In response, the Judeans band together, and the grassroots leadership reinforces the boundary between themselves and those who seek to undermine their agenda. The individuals, clans, and guilds are recalled by name, and each is acknowledged for the section of the wall

---

101. For insights into the wall from modern archaeological excavations, see E. Mazar, "The Wall That Nehemiah Built," *Biblical Archaeology Review* 35, no. 2 (2009).
102. Nehemiah 1:2–3.

for which it is responsible. Predictably, their opponents are infuriated by the headway they are making, and in a jeer that casts Sanballat as the unmistakable enemy of the restoration, he asks, "What are the miserable Jews doing? Will they plaster, offer the consecration sacrifices, and reach the completion day? Will they revive the stones from the rubble heaps after they have been burned?"[103] Questioning the Judean community's ability to rebuild that which was destroyed is tantamount to questioning its existence. Nehemiah and his supporters believe that, like their community, scorched rocks can be extracted from the rubble and reconstructed to form something stable and grand. Sanballat's cynicism is a direct affront to that conviction.

As we read Nehemiah's account of the wall project, we understand that his words communicate so much more than a mere building strategy to his audience. When, likely intimidated by their enemies, the builders are ready to give up, crying that their "strength is sapped" and they are "simply unable to build the wall," Nehemiah encourages them to "fight for your kinsmen, for your sons, and daughters, your wives, and your homes."[104] Their enemies are God's enemies, Nehemiah assures them, further sharpening the points of divergence between the Judeans and their adversaries. In an exhortation reminiscent of Moses at the Sea of Reeds just prior to the defeat of the Egyptians,[105] Nehemiah proclaims, "our God will fight for us."[106] So, "with one hand doing the work and the other holding a weapon," the community under Nehemiah's leadership simultaneously builds the wall that demarcates it and defends that demarcation from those who want it effaced.

THE WALL METAPHOR AND ITS SIGNIFICANCE

This chapter begins by noting that the identity of the Judean community was, by necessity, redefined in the restoration period. But identity will always be contested, as the author of Ezra-Nehemiah conveys through

---

103. Ibid. 3:34.
104. Ibid. 4:4–8.
105. Exodus 14:14.
106. Nehemiah 4:14.

the wall metaphor. Like Jerusalem's wall, the community will inevitably have sections that are "broken through."[107] It is through those fissures that foreign influences seep in. That seepage, the leaders in Ezra-Nehemiah contend, is a risk the *peleita* cannot afford to take, so what was erected also had to be continually reinforced and safeguarded.

Of course, Ezra-Nehemiah also reflects an acute understanding that leaders alone cannot generate lasting change; they certainly cannot single-handedly guarantee that the walls surrounding the community remain strong. Such a venture requires the concerted efforts of its members. It requires that some "make repairs" to the wall, others erect "doors, bolts, and bars," and still others ensure that porous sections are "plastered."[108] More than anything, though, the efforts to restore communal identity require a unity of purpose. Nehemiah tells the men who are "scattered.... spread along the wall, far away from each other,"[109] to listen for the "sound of the horn"[110] that will ring out if their brethren are in trouble. And when they hear it, he tells them, they should band together because only united will they prevail.

Thus, alongside the word *peleita* that we noted earlier, the word *ḥazak*, meaning strength or power, appears throughout the account of the building of the wall. Tamara Cohn Eskenazi explains the seeming incongruity as follows: "Strength then, is tied to this building, not because the wall itself is invulnerable, which it apparently is not, but because in building it, the people strengthened one another.... Building the wall is building an identity rooted in strength, with the capacity to stand one's ground and with readiness to fight."[111] The very process of rebuilding the wall physically protects the Judeans from enemies who are planning to "come among them and slaughter them,"[112] while mentally preparing them to do what it takes to ensure the community's future.

---

107. Ibid. 2:13.
108. Nehemiah 3:1–32.
109. Ibid. 4:14.
110. Ibid.
111. She notes that the word *ḥazak* appears forty-two times in Nehemiah 1–7 alone and forty-eight times total in Ezra-Nehemiah, far more than any biblical book besides Chronicles. Eskenazi, "Imagining the Other," 255.
112. Nehemiah 4:5.

KNOWING WHO YOU ARE NOT IS NOT ENOUGH

Manfred Oeming sums up the magnitude of the wall project as follows: "In the heads and hearts of those who built the wall, there existed a multifaceted complex of theological ideas: for them, the wall was a highly symbolic sign of the activity and the presence of God in history, for the end of God's judgment, for the return of God's name to His chosen dwelling place, for the beginning of the return of the Diaspora, for the holy space where Torah was reigning. Israel regained its identity only within this wall."[113] The initial step toward communal renewal for the Judean community entails distinguishing itself from what it is not. But to truly reestablish itself, a community also needs to know what it is, what its values are, and what makes it unique. Fighting to keep outsiders out is meaningful only if those inside know what they stand for; building walls is worthwhile only if what they enclose is worth protecting. Therefore, in the coming chapter we will watch the second and perhaps most essential phase of identity rebuilding: the community will fill the space within their wall with meaning. We will watch it ask hard questions, search for new ways to answer them, and come to an enhanced understanding of what it is fighting so hard to protect.

---

113. Manfred Oeming, "The Real History: The Theological Ideas Behind Nehemiah's Wall," in *New Perspectives on Ezra-Nehemiah: History and Historiography, Text, Literature, and Interpretation*, ed. Isaac Kalimi (2013), 131–50.

Chapter Eight

A Second *Matan Torah*

A TURNING POINT IN JEWISH HISTORY

The leaders of the restoration period, in contending with unprecedented questions of Jewish identity, reference and expand upon biblical verses and constructs. Their approach does not surprise their constituents, and while adherence to their rulings is not always unanimous, there is no indication in Ezra-Nehemiah that their methodology is ever disputed. On more than one occasion, the rulings enacted in the days of Ezra are said to derive from the Torah,[1] but that claim is not as simple as it appears. Understanding Ezra's claim and its implications is essential to appreciating the seminal moment in religious history through which the repatriates live. The moment is marked by a staunch commitment to the fixed text of the Torah coupled with an implicit appreciation for its interpretive dimensions. Pioneering policies of the Persian Empire and the shifting needs of the Jewish community coalesce to fuel that decisive moment. What emerges from it lays the groundwork for the millennia of Jewish history that follow. But, as with all turning points, to understand what is unique, we must first understand what precedes it.

---

1. Ezra 10:3; Nehemiah 8:14, 9:14, 10:35.

ORAL TRANSMISSION OF TORAH IN
THE EARLY-BIBLICAL PERIOD

In Deuteronomy, just prior to Israel's entry into the land, Moses recounts the nation's short, tumultuous history, and then proclaims, "Listen, Israel, to the decrees and laws that I shall declare in your hearing today; learn them and carefully observe them."[2] He enjoins them to "let these words that I charge you with today remain impressed upon your heart. Teach them to your children, speaking of them when you sit at home and when you travel on the way, when you lie down and when you rise."[3] The people, Moses tells them, must remain engaged in an ongoing educational venture, passing on to their children the stipulations of the covenant that, if upheld, will guarantee blessing. That venture seems to be primarily an oral one. The verses speak of the Israelites teaching their children the written words through verbal recitation, over and over, until the ideas are impressed upon their children's hearts as on their own. As David Carr puts it, "The mind stood at the center of the often discussed oral-written interface. The focus was on inscribing a culture's most precious traditions on the insides of people."[4] So when children request explanations for the laws, their parents are told to answer them verbally. In Deuteronomy, for example, Moses tells the people, "And in the future, when your child asks you, 'What is the meaning of the testimonies, decrees, and laws that the Lord our God has commanded you?' tell him, 'We were slaves to Pharaoh in Egypt, but the Lord brought us out of Egypt with a mighty hand...and awesome signs and wonders.... He freed us from there, to bring us in and give us the land that He promised.... The Lord commanded us to keep all these decrees...so that we might always prosper.'"[5] A text is not consulted during this imagined exchange. Instead, verbal questions are met with verbal answers based on written words that have been internalized.

---

2. Deuteronomy 5:1.
3. Ibid. 6:4–7.
4. David M. Carr, *Writing on the Tablet of the Heart: Origins of Scripture and Literature* (Oxford University Press, 2005), 6.
5. Deuteronomy 6:20–24. A similar dialogue revolving around the sacrifice of the firstborn is imagined earlier in the chapter (vv. 4–7).

In addition to the role that parents play in imparting the laws and stipulations, the priests, too, are directed "to teach the Israelites all the statutes that the Lord has spoken to them through Moses."[6] And they too seem to transmit their wisdom orally. "If a case is beyond your judgment," the Israelites are told, then they should "approach the Levitical priests or the judge who is in office at that time. Inquire of them," the people are instructed, "and they will give you the verdict."[7] In situations where the verdict is not self-evident and rituals of ordeal are enacted,[8] the priests play a vital role. For example, in the case of an unsolved murder, the elders and judges help determine guilt, but it is "the priests, sons of Levi" who "shall step forward, for it is them the Lord your God has chosen to minister to Him, to give blessing in the Lord's name, and to decide all cases of dispute and assault."[9] As such, God tells the Israelites to "carefully do whatever the Levitical priests instruct you, as I have commanded them,"[10] suggesting a dialogue of sorts that takes place between the lay Israelites and the priestly experts in God's laws.

SYMBOLIC SIGNIFICANCE OF THE WRITTEN TEXT

The laws that were to be communicated orally from one generation to the next were written down. Once inscribed, the written text seems to assume a value that extends beyond the role played by standard texts. After "Moses wrote down this Law," for example, he "gave it to the priests…and to all the elders of Israel."[11] That written law is to be taken out and read publicly "at the end of every seventh year, the year of remission, during the festival of Tabernacles, when all of Israel comes

---

6. Leviticus 10:11.
7. Deuteronomy 17:8–9.
8. "Ritual of ordeal" refers to a ritual in the form of a trial or test whose outcome is believed to determine a person's fate, innocence, or purity. Perhaps the most famous biblical example is the *sota* ritual, the ritual of bitter waters enacted in the case of the suspected adulteress (Num. 5:11–31).
9. Deuteronomy 21:1–9.
10. Ibid. 24:8.
11. Ibid. 31:9.

to appear before the Lord your God at the place that He will choose."[12] But until that time, Moses entrusts the text to the Levites. "Take this scroll of the Law," he commands them, "and place it beside the Ark of the Covenant of the Lord your God. Let it *remain there* as a *witness* to you."[13] The words contained in that scroll are memorized, internalized, and transmitted. But the scroll itself, brought out every seven years, serves as a tangible symbol of the covenant. The Ten Commandments that God inscribes "on two tablets of stone"[14] are similarly placed in the aptly named "Ark of the Testimony" where they remain as physical evidence of the covenant between God and Israel.[15] In a similar vein, the commandments the Israelites are enjoined to speak of incessantly, impressing them on the minds of their children, are to be written "on the doorposts of your house and on your gates" and bound as "a sign on your arm and an emblem between your eyes."[16] Before Moses's death, he and the elders charge the people, "On the day that you cross the Jordan to the land that the Lord your God is giving you, set up large boulders, and coat them with plaster, and write on them all the words of this Law."[17] Those engraved, immobile stones become standing symbols of the choice the people are to make, between a blessed life of following the Torah or a cursed life without it. Taken together, we find that smaller sections of the law in some cases and the entire Torah in others serve as a concrete, physical symbol of the law itself.[18]

Nowhere is this association between the written and the spoken text clearer than in the chapters leading up to the death of Moses, the law bearer himself. After "Moses finished writing down in a scroll the words of this law to the very end" and requests that the Levites place it

---

12. Ibid. 31:10–11.
13. Ibid. 31:26.
14. Ibid. 4:13, 9:10.
15. Exodus 26:34, 30:26, 40:3, 5, 21; Joshua 4:6.
16. Deuteronomy 6:7–9.
17. Ibid. 27:2–3.
18. In primarily oral cultures, the written word often takes on a "numinous" character, and traces of this are found, for example, in Numbers 5:23, 17:16–28. Susan Niditch, *Oral World and Written Word: Ancient Israelite Literature* (Westminster John Knox, 1996), 44.

beside the ark "as a witness," Moses stands in front of the entire nation and proclaims the poem known as *Haazinu*.[19] Summarizing in poetic form the basic outlines of the God-Israel relationship, Moses encourages his audience to *"ask* your father, and he will *tell* you; your elders, and they will *speak."*[20] With the Torah scroll preserved for posterity, Moses reminds the people that a true understanding of its subject matter is contained in the wisdom passed down orally from one generation to the next. This "dual phenomenon of speech and writing,"[21] is similarly seen in the aftermath of the battle with Amalek, when God commands Moses to "write this as a memorial on a scroll, and commit it to Joshua's ears."[22]

In keeping with this message, when Joshua assumes the mantle of leadership after Moses's death, God tells him, the "book of Torah must never leave your lips; contemplate it day and night, so that you will faithfully uphold all that is written within it."[23] This image of the Torah never leaving Joshua's lips echoes the command we saw earlier, that parents teach their children Torah by "speaking of them when you sit at home and when you travel on the way."[24] On Mount Ebal, Joshua "read out all the words of the Torah, blessing and curse, exactly as written in the book of the Torah." The book of Joshua is quick to point out that "there was not a single word Moses had commanded that Joshua failed to read before the whole congregation of Israel."[25] Once Moses is no longer around, the words he had committed to writing are read

---

19. Deuteronomy 31:24–32:43. The fact of poetry itself seems to indicate that the verses are to be memorized and recited rather than read.

20. Ibid. 32:7. That verse is likely referring to Israel's stories of the past rather than specific laws. But as the structure of the Torah seems to indicate through its interlacing of stories and laws, to adhere to the latter, the people must first know the former. So their stories too, like their laws, Moses tells them, need to be passed down orally.

21. For more on this interplay, see Victor Hurowitz, "Spanning the Generations: Aspects of Oral and Written Transmission in the Bible and Ancient Mesopotamia," in Rela M. Geffen and Marsha Bryan Edelman, *Freedom and Responsibility: Exploring the Challenges of Jewish Continuity* (1988), 11–30.

22. Exodus 17:14.

23. Joshua 1:8.

24. Deuteronomy 6:7.

25. Joshua 8:34–35.

aloud by his protégé and successor, exemplifying how the Torah is to be preserved in Israel.

Not surprisingly, the expectation that the leader of Israel be well versed in Torah is found in the biblical prognostications about kingship as well. Their future king, the people are told in Deuteronomy, "must inscribe a copy of this Law for himself upon a scroll in the presence of the Levitical priests. It must always be with him, and he shall read from it all the days of his life, so that he may learn to revere the Lord his God, taking care to keep all the words of this commandment and these decrees, not considering himself superior to his people, or straying from the commandments to the right or to the left."[26] But the king's internalization of the Torah's teachings, Deuteronomy seems to suggest, is not for the sake of adjudication but rather to regulate the king's moral integrity. As Christine Hayes puts it, "The king is instructed to read from the Torah each day of his life, making him not the chief law teacher but rather the first law student."[27] This distinction is important because while Israel's leaders are expected to know the text of the Torah, reading the text does not seem to be the primary means by which they, or the Israelite laypeople, access, assess, and propagate God's will.[28]

---

26. Deuteronomy 17:18–20.

27. Christine Hayes, *What's Divine about Divine Law?: Early Perspectives* (Princeton University Press, 2017), 35. This assumption is supported by biblical descriptions of court proceedings during the period of kingship. On the whole, there is little indication that kings appealed to, or cited, written texts. That is not to say that they were not versed in the laws of the Torah. But it does seem to point to the fact that, whereas in later times, the text of Torah becomes the basis for legal interpretation and expansion, in the early biblical period, the kings relied on their ability to "seek" God through various prophetic and oracular means, and on their innate "understanding [of] good and evil" (II Sam. 14:17). For more examples, see II Samuel 15:1–5, I Kings 3:16–28.

28. The topic of text cannot be separated from the topic of literacy, as literacy levels have direct bearing on a given society's relationship to the written word. Scholars have debated the topic of literacy in ancient Israel, with some contending that literacy was widespread, while others maintain that a high level of literacy did not develop until later. See, for example, Alan R. Millard, "The Question of Israelite Literacy," *Bible Review* 3, no. 3 (1987): 22–31; Susan Niditch, *Oral World and Written Word: Ancient Israelite Literature* (Louisville: Westminster John Knox, 1996); Ian M. Young, "Israelite Literacy: Interpreting the Evidence, Parts I–II," *Vetus*

ASSESSING GOD'S WILL IN THE FIRST TEMPLE PERIOD

The night before his death on the battlefield, King Saul consults a necromancer and requests that she summon the already-dead prophet Samuel.[29] His decision, which is quite startling,[30] is also given context. Early in the chapter, we are told that "the Philistines gathered, and they came and set up camp in Shunem, while Saul gathered all of Israel and encamped at Gilboa" and that when Saul sees the Philistine camp, "his heart shuddered with fear." Saul does what any biblical king would have done in such a situation: he tries to commune with God.[31] Unfortunately, his attempts prove unsuccessful. The text then tells us that "Saul inquired of the Lord, but the Lord did not answer him, neither in dreams nor through the Urim nor through prophets." In desperation, Saul tells his servants, "Seek out a necromancer for me, and I shall go to her and consult through her."[32] The verse that recalls Saul's failed attempts helps explain his otherwise inexplicable decision to visit a necromancer, but it does something else as well: it sketches the three primary means by which people in the early biblical period discover God's will, namely, through dreams, the Urim, and prophecy.[33]

Testamentum 48 (1998): 239–53, 408–22; William M. Schniedewind, *How the Bible Became a Book: The Textualization of Ancient Israel* (Cambridge University Press, 2004); Christopher A. Rollston, *Writing and Literacy in the World of Ancient Israel: Epigraphic Evidence from the Early Iron Age* (Society of Biblical Literature, 2010); James D. Moore, *Scribal Culture in the Ancient Near East,* Oxford Biblical Studies Online, https://www.oxfordbiblicalstudies.com/ (2014); Andre Lemaire, "Schools and Literacy in Ancient Israel and Early Judaism," in *The Blackwell Companion to the Hebrew Bible* (2001), 201–17; Karel Van Der Toorn, *Scribal Culture and the Making of the Hebrew Bible* (Harvard University Press, 2009), 2–26.

29. I Samuel 28.
30. Consultation with any such medium is prohibited (Lev. 19:31, 20:6, 27; Deut. 18:11; Is. 8:19). Saul himself leads a crusade against the witches that operate within the Land of Israel (I Sam. 28:3).
31. See, for example, I Kings 22:1–28. Other examples are referred to below.
32. I Samuel 28:4–7.
33. Three technical terms used to describe the actions undertaken by humans to learn God's will are *saal, daras,* and *biqqer*. For a full discussion of the nuances of prophetic vocabulary, see Diana V. Edelman and Ehud Ben Zvi, *The Production of Prophecy: Constructing Prophecy and Prophets in Yehud* (Routledge, 2014).

Dreams, perhaps the most straightforward of the modes, are believed to be revelatory, either of what the future holds or of God's will. God Himself affirmed dreams as a valid method of divination in His declaration of Moses's inimitability. "Now listen to My words," God says to Miriam and Aaron. "When there is a prophet among you, I make Myself known to him in a vision; I speak to him in a dream."[34] Not surprisingly, divine dreams are a prominent motif in the patriarchal stories of Genesis.[35] Gideon the judge receives a revelatory dream on the eve of a decisive battle,[36] and the prophet Samuel seems to have received his first prophecy in a dream-like state.[37] At Gibeon, God "appeared to Solomon in a dream,"[38] and in the Book of Daniel, Daniel, like Joseph, is both a dreamer and a dream interpreter, who makes clear that his substantiated abilities are divinely controlled.[39]

In addition to dreams, the Urim and Thummim, which is worn inside the "breast piece of judgment" of the high priest,[40] function as an oracular device within Israel that determines God's will in specific matters. Joshua, for example, is told to "stand before Elazar the priest, who shall seek the decision of the Urim before the Lord on his behalf. By this word they will go out and by this word they will return, he and all Israel, the entire community."[41] The verse indicates that military decisions will be made by God as they were in the days of Moses, but, beginning with Joshua, those decisions will be disclosed through oracle rather than direct communication. In fact, Joshua seems to use the Urim

---

34. Numbers 12:6–7.
35. See, for example, Genesis 20:3, 28:10–22, 31:10–13, 37:5–9, 40:5, 41:1.
36. Judges 7:13–15.
37. I Samuel 3:3–10.
38. I Kings 3:5–15.
39. Daniel, chapters 2, 4, 7. Interpreters are often needed to make sense of the vision, and both Joseph and Daniel, the quintessential dream interpreters, make clear that "interpretation belongs to God" (Gen. 40:8). Like other forms of prophecy, dreams and their interpretations can be falsified, and as such, the Israelites are warned to steer clear of such phenomena. See, for example, Jeremiah 23:25–28, 27:9, 29:8; Zechariah 10:2.
40. Exodus 28:30; Leviticus 8:8.
41. Numbers 27:21.

to determine the identity of Akhan,[42] the man guilty of looting Israel's enemies. After Joshua's death, Israel seems to employ it to decide which tribe should lead them out to war.[43] Samuel seems to use the Urim to identify Saul as God's chosen,[44] Saul to discover which of his soldiers breaks their vow,[45] and David to obtain God's strategic guidance on more than one occasion.[46]

Prophecy, the last of the categories attempted by King Saul, is perhaps the best-known means of contact between God and Israel. Direct communication with God, the likes of which the Israelites experience at Sinai, terrifies them. Moses quotes the Israelites at Horeb as saying, "If I hear the voice of the Lord my God anymore, or continue to see this great fire, I will die,"[47] to which God offers the prophets as a solution: "I will raise up for them a prophet like you from among their own people. I will put My words in the prophet's mouth and he will tell them all that I command."[48] Prophecy is meant to replace the "abhorrent practices" of the Canaanites, which include trials by ordeal, spell casting, consulting augurs, diviners, soothsayers, sorcerers, ghosts, spirits, and oracle seeking from the dead.[49] Because prophets communicate God's will to the Israelites, the Israelites do not need to resort to the unacceptable means employed by their neighbors. Therefore, prophets in Israel function in

---

42. Joshua 7:13–18.
43. Judges 1:2.
44. I Samuel 10:20–24.
45. Ibid. 14:41.
46. I Samuel 23:2–9; II Samuel 5:23. This type of divination is used, for the most part, for ad hoc decisions and should be distinguished from legal decisions. In most cases, while the words "Urim" and "Thummim" are not explicit in the text, it is assumed that at this stage in history, when someone (with access to a priest) "asked (*shaal*) the Lord" a relatively simple or binary question, the Urim was utilized. Exactly what the Urim and Thummim looks like and how it functions remain a mystery although more recent scholarly discussions drawing from ancient Near Eastern parallels offer fascinating suggestions that are supported by the biblical text. See, for example, Victor Avigdor Hurowitz, "True Light on the Urim and Thummim," *Jewish Quarterly Review* 88, no. 3/4 (1998): 263–74.
47. Deuteronomy 18:16. In addition to their fear, individuals throughout Tanakh express similar trepidation. See, for example, Genesis 32:31; Exodus 3:6; Judges 6:22, 13:22.
48. Deuteronomy 18:18.
49. Ibid., vv. 9–14.

various capacities. They are consulted to reveal concealed information,[50] predict future outcomes or events,[51] advise and reproach kings,[52] perform miraculous deeds on behalf of the Israelites,[53] intercede on the Israelites' behalf with God,[54] and deliver God's messages of both rebuke and comfort to the people.[55]

EFFECTS OF ORAL COMMUNICATION

Since the Israelites rely on priests and prophets to orally communicate God's law and will, the written text seems to occupy less space in Israel's collective imagination and routine practices than we might imagine. The prophets often speak of the Torah, particularly Israel's spurning of it,[56] but the written text itself, with one exception, does not appear in the narratives from this period. That absence is significant, because it conveys the sense that the ideal interface between orality and text envisioned in the Torah does not play out as such in the early biblical period. Instead, the overwhelming majority of narratives from that period indicate that the oral transmission of God's will dominates the religious-instructive experience.

Nowhere is this more evident than in the episode of the discovered Torah scroll in the days of Josiah.[57] The episode recounts the incidental

---

50. See, for example, I Samuel 9:6.

51. See, for example, I Kings 14, 22:2–6; II Kings 3:11–20.

52. See, for example, I Samuel 13:14, 15:22–23, 19:18; II Samuel 7, 12; I Kings 1, 12:22–24.

53. See, most famously, the extended Elijah-Elisha narrative (I Kings 17–II Kings 13:21).

54. See, for example, I Samuel 12:23; Jeremiah 27:18. For a fuller discussion of the topic of intercessory prayer as it appears in Tanakh, see Samuel E. Balentine, "The Prophet as Intercessor: A Reassessment," *Journal of Biblical Literature* 103, no. 2 (1984): 161–73; and Daniel F. O'Kennedy, "Were the Prophets Really Intercessors?" *Old Testament Essays* 13, no. 3 (2000): 329–47.

55. The major classical prophets, including Isaiah, Jeremiah, and Ezekiel, as well as the minor ones listed in the Trei Asar. For a fascinating discussion about the roles and responsibilities of Israelite prophets, see Yochanan Muffs, "Who Will Stand in the Breach? A Study of Prophetic Intercession," in *Love and Joy: Law, Language and Religion in Ancient Israel* (Jewish Theological Seminary of America, 1992), 9–48.

56. See, for example, Jeremiah 2:8; Ezekiel 7:26; Habakkuk 1:4; Zephaniah 3:4.

57. 640–609 BCE.

discovery of a Torah scroll in the Temple, the interpretation of the find by Huldah the prophetess, and the public covenant renewal ceremony enacted by Josiah to ward off the dire fate Huldah says the scroll signifies.[58] The significance of the episode for our discussion is that only when we read that the "king went up to the House of the Lord, along with all the men of Judah and all the inhabitants of Jerusalem, the priests and the prophets and all the people, from the smallest to the greatest. And he read out to them all the words of the scroll of the covenant that had been found in the House of the Lord,"[59] do we realize that, despite what Deuteronomy projects, no king in Israel is ever recorded performing such a ceremony.[60] Furthermore, the fact that the Torah scroll is "found" speaks to an apparent lack of veneration accorded it to begin with.[61] Perhaps most significantly, a scribe is required to read the scroll and a prophet has to be sought to construe the implications of the words that the king should have been reading from daily.

At the same time, though, unlike her contemporaries, Huldah's prophetic rebuke is anchored in the Torah text. Her pronouncement, which began with the familiar "Thus says the Lord: I am about to bring disaster upon this place and its inhabitants," is followed with the unfamiliar: "Fulfilling all the words of the scroll that the king of Judah read."[62] While earlier prophets base their rebukes on doctrine found in the Torah, Huldah's prophecy is inextricably linked to the words of the Torah scroll itself. This episode could have easily remained an anomaly within the early biblical period, but hindsight indicates that Huldah's actions mark the beginnings of a subtle but significant shift from the oral-dominated culture to one in which the text begins to reoccupy its rightful place within Israel. That shift reaches its full expression in the days of Ezra-Nehemiah when the Torah text is once again used as the

---

58. II Kings 22.
59. Ibid. 23:1–3.
60. The last time we heard of such a ceremony is the days of Joshua (Josh. 24).
61. II Chronicles 34–35 contains a different ordering of the events recorded in Kings. According to Chronicles, the scroll would have been found during the repair of the precincts, further supporting the assertion that the scroll was disregarded earlier.
62. II Kings 22:16.

basis for understanding God. But that shift takes decades and a conflu-
ence of historical, cultural, and religious factors to materialize.

INCREASING FOCUS ON THE WRITTEN WORD

While the Huldah episode and its emphasis on the written text is unique
within the narrative portions of Kings, it is consistent with a trend perceived in some of the prophetic works from the latter half of the monarchic period in which the written word seems to reemerge as a critical
component of divine instruction. Prophets from this later period, more
than earlier prophets, emphasize the commitment of their prophecies to
writing, Isaiah being one of the earliest examples.[63] Habakkuk, proph-
esying on the eve of the Babylonian destruction,[64] is told to write his
"vison onto the tablets so that all may read it readily."[65] When Jeremiah
is unable to orally deliver his prophecies, either because he is barred by
the king[66] or too far from the exiles,[67] he too has his words consigned
to the text. Once his prophecies are written down, destruction of those
texts is taken by God as a rejection of God Himself.[68]

Ezekiel, too, is told to inscribe his prophecies, both those of rebuke
and of consolation.[69] Perhaps most evocative of the shift is a vision at
the beginning of Ezekiel. There, the prophet is told to eat the scroll
he sees spread out in front of him. Describing the experience, Ezekiel
writes, "I opened my mouth, and He fed it to me, this scroll, and said to
me: 'Man, feed your stomach; fill your insides with this scroll that I am

---

63. See, for example, Isaiah 8:16, 30:8–11.

64. Precise dating is not entirely clear, but his prophecies seem to indicate a date beginning after 612 BCE. See Adele Berlin et al., eds., *The Jewish Study Bible: Jewish
Publication Society Tanakh Translation* (Oxford University Press, 2004), 1226.

65. Habakkuk 2:2.

66. Jeremiah 36.

67. Ibid., chapter 29.

68. Ibid., chapter 36. Robert Carroll views Jehoiakim's burning of Jeremiah's scroll as
a negative reflection of the Josiah episode, the former displaying derision for the
text and the latter utmost respect. Robert P. Carroll, *Jeremiah* (A & C Black, 2004),
663–64.

69. Ezekiel 4:1–3, 37:15–22.

giving you.' I ate it, and in my mouth it had the sweetness of honey."[70] Ezekiel is then told to speak to Israel the words he ingested, and from that point on, as Ellen Davis explains, "there is no longer any ambiguity about the form in which the prophet receives the edible revelation. It comes to Ezekiel as a text. This is the form in which he must claim his inheritance and the basis on which he must make his own contribution to the tradition of faithful witness."[71] Ezekiel's ingestion of the text characterizes the phase in which the written text and spoken prophecy become indistinguishable.

It should therefore come as no surprise that Zechariah, like earlier prophets, receives his prophecy in a vision. But unlike other prophets, Zechariah's vision is of none other than a "flying scroll twenty cubits long and ten cubits wide," which, in addition to serving as witness to the evil that will befall the people, is also presented as the agent of the "curse emerging all over the land."[72] Taken together, these visions mark a turning point in Israel's consideration of text. As Hindy Najman points out, "The effects of the prophecy are inscribed in the form of an earthly (Ezekiel) or heavenly (Zechariah) written revelation. ... However, there is no independent oral revelation that precedes the written revelation. Rather the prophecy itself is revealed as sacred writing and the power, inalterability, and efficacious warning are all part of such a written revelation."[73] Thus, the gradual re-ascent of writing's prominence within Israelite thought began. Or, as James Kugel puts it, "People increasingly conceived of God's authority as bound up with writtenness."[74]

This shift, as with most historical and cultural developments, is the result of several factors. One of the most obvious is the increase in

---

70. Ibid. 3:1–3.

71. Ellen F. Davis, *Swallowing the Scroll: Textuality and the Dynamics of Discourse in Ezekiel's Prophecy*, vol. 21 (A & C Black, 1989), 51.

72. Zechariah 5:1–3. As Kugel writes, "God's mighty arm has now taken on the contours of a book; it is the book that indicts and the book that punishes. What greater literalization could there be of 'the word of God in action'?" James Kugel, *The Great Shift: Encountering God in Biblical Times* (Houghton Mifflin Harcourt, 2017), 247–48.

73. Hindy Najman and Judith Newman, eds., *The Idea of Biblical Interpretations: Essays in Honor of James L. Kugel*, vol. 83 (Brill, 2002), 172–73.

74. Kugel, *The Great Shift*, 248.

general literacy spreading throughout Israel. In discussing this link, William Schniedewind explains that "as literacy became more prevalent, textuality became more plausible."[75] The text is effective as a mode of communication only if the intended audience can read its content. Another possible contributing factor is tied to the desire of the later prophets to ensure that their words outlive them and the impending cultural destruction they foretell. These later prophets and their contemporaries who hear their words would not exist forever. But they hope that their words, once committed to writing, would.[76] And of course, the dispersion of Israelites beyond the boundaries of Israel means that a new form of communication has to develop if the prophecies are to reach places beyond the range of word-of-mouth communication.[77]

It is important to note that the increased emphasis in these books of the Later Prophets on God's written word is not identical to the Huldah episode in which the prophet draws directly from the words of the Torah, nor is it a direct precursor to Ezra's program. These smaller changes are components of a broader shift that comes to a head in Ezra-Nehemiah. As Hindy Najman states, "We are concerned here not with a dichotomy

---

75. Schniedewind, *How the Bible Became a Book*, 113. This "spread of literacy," according to Schniedewind, can be traced to several factors, most notably the increased literacy that accompanies imperialism and the centralized urbanization of Judah after the fall of the Northern Kingdom (see pp. 91–117). Some scholars disagree with Schniedewind, arguing that the degree of literacy Schniedewind claims existed is overstated. See, for example, David M. Carr and Gary Knoppers, "Response to W. M. Schniedewind, *How the Bible Became a Book: The Textualization of Ancient Israel*," *Journal of Hebrew Scriptures* 5, no. 18 (2005): 1–19.

76. As David Carr writes, "Unlike people, writing is immortal. Writing makes language permanent, depersonalizes language, decontextualizes expression, and adds normativity. Writing formalizes, generalizes, and perpetuates features and intentions of language – cutting it loose from momentary and context-bound utterance." David M. Carr, *Writing on the Tablet of the Heart: Origins of Scripture and Literature* (Oxford University Press, 2005), 10.

77. For a fuller discussion of this point, see David, *Swallowing the Scroll*, 41–43. In earlier times, the Temple and local sanctuaries were the loci of prophecy (see, for example, Amos 7:13; Jeremiah 7:2) and the prophet's words naturally spread by word of mouth throughout the land. Already in Jeremiah 29, a new vehicle for the spread of prophecy beyond the borders of Israel is necessary.

between an oral culture and a literate culture, but with complex econo-
mies of orality and literacy that shifted subtly over time."[78]

THE WANING OF PROPHECY AND THE
PROPHETS' LAST WORDS

This increase in literacy and emphasis on the written text coincides with
another important watershed of post-exilic history. The waning of prophecy and its eventual disappearance from the human experience[79] seems
to begin in the aftermath of exile. In fact, an inversely proportional relationship between text and prophecy emerges in the post-exilic period.
That is to say, as prophecy declines, the text grows in prominence. It
is not coincidental that Ezekiel, the prophet who ingests God's written word, also receives some of the most important prophecies of his
career through angelic mediation rather than the direct word of God.[80]
Zechariah, too, not only speaks through angels but relies, on multiple
occasions, on their interpretations of his visions rather than on his own
intuition and spiritual aptitude.[81] Prophecy in its latest phase exists in
a diminished capacity.

Perhaps the clearest indication of the finality of this shift is found in
the book of Malachi. Malachi, the last of the biblical prophets, spends
his documented career urging his audience of Judean repatriates to
improve their behavior. In one of the book's final verses, Malachi urges
his audience to "remember the teaching of Moses My servant, which I
commanded to him at Horeb, statutes and laws for all of Israel."[82] Mala-

78. Najman, *The Idea of Biblical Interpretation,* 144.
79. For a discussion of the relevant rabbinic texts that address both the reasons for
and the process of the cessation of prophecy, see Frederick E. Greenspahn, "Why
Prophecy Ceased," *Journal of Biblical Literature* 108, no. 1 (1989): 37–49 and Sommer, *Did Prophecy Cease?*
80. See, for example, Ezekiel 40:3–4.
81. See, for example, Zechariah 1:7–14, 2:2–7, 4:1–5, 11, 5:5–11, 6:4–5. Daniel, too (7:13–17,
8:15–17), depicts reception of this sort through angelic intermediary.
82. Malachi 3:22. One of the opinions brought down in the Talmud (Megilla 15a) claims
that Malachi is, in fact, Ezra. While it is a minority opinion and not adopted in later
Jewish traditions, it points to the transition we are tracing between oral prophecy
and Ezra's focus on the fixed text of the Torah.

chi prods those listening toward the text of the Torah. The importance of that directive appearing as one of the last verses of biblical prophecy cannot be overstated. It preemptively prescribes how the people should continue to find God once He is no longer directly communicating with them. They are to replace hearing with reading, and their dependence on God's spoken word should be replaced with the interpretation of His revealed text.[83]

This revolution, pronounced by Malachi, materializes in Ezra-Nehemiah. While many First Temple Jews eschew the word of God,[84] many that return to the land understand by virtue of their exiled history the dangers of not heeding it. They know enough history to recognize that their ancestors "turned a stubborn shoulder and closed their ears so that they could not hear; they set their hearts like adamant so as not to hear the Torah and the words sent through the earlier prophets by the spirit of the Lord of Hosts." And they also know that because of that obtuseness, "a terrible fury arose from the Lord of Hosts" and that He "blew them away to all the nations who do not know them," leaving in their wake "a land barren of wayfarers."[85] One of the (intended) consequences of their recent history is an unprecedented receptiveness to the word of God. But, ironically, that receptiveness coincides with the waning of the same means of communication they took for granted for centuries.[86]

Prophecy extends for a few decades into the Second Temple period, but by the time Ezra and Nehemiah emerge on the scene of Jewish history, God's voice is no longer being heard through prophets,[87] and His will is no longer being divulged through the Urim and Thummim.[88] The

---

83. The prophet also tells the people that "those who fear the Lord spoke one to another, and the Lord listened and He heard, and it was written – a book of remembrance before Him for those who fear the Lord and keep His name in mind" (3:16), further pointing to this shift.

84. This is why the exile happened in the first place.

85. Zechariah 7:8–14.

86. See, for example, Isaiah 30:9; Jeremiah 6:9, 11:10, 17:23, 25:4, 5, 7–11, 29:19, 35:15.

87. In fact, those referred to as prophets in Ezra-Nehemiah are suspect (Neh. 7–14). For references to rabbinic and scholarly sources that deal with the cessation of prophecy in Israel, see above, chapter 1, note 18.

88. Ezra 2:63 and Nehemiah 7:65 both mention the unknown whereabouts of the Urim and Thummim as well as the hope for its ultimate return.

people, who are finally ready to hear and internalize God's word, are left in silence. Like Saul, the people Ezra leads need to find an alternative mode of determining God's will. Unlike Saul, they do not turn to a witch. Instead, with Ezra's help, they make their way back to the divinely revealed text their ancestors disregarded, and, through that text, they know, once again, what God expects of them.[89]

CODIFICATION OF LAW IN THE PERSIAN PERIOD

Ezra's public reading of the Torah and the discourse that follows set in motion a religious revival that anchors those listening to long-forgotten laws documented in the text. But, as with all evolutions in Jewish history, those found in Ezra-Nehemiah do not take place in a vacuum. Rather, the interaction between the internal needs of the community and the external realities impacting that community generate the changes. Ezra's ability to fill the void of prophecy with Torah learning is facilitated by certain conditions and imperial policies.

The Persian Empire, the largest of its kind in the ancient world, employs several strategies for managing and "compressing" its vast empire.[90] Among those strategies are the establishment of a highly sophisticated network of roads and storehouses, an efficient postal system, the

---

89. For an interesting take on the distinction between prophecy and the later intellectual endeavors required to understand the Torah, see Yaakov Elman, "R. Zadok Hakohen on the History of Halakha," *Tradition: A Journal of Orthodox Jewish Thought* 21, no. 4 (1985): 1–26. In his article, Elman uses the teachings of Rav Tzadok to "account for the lack of halakhic rules and decisions in the prophetic books, and why the worlds of the prophet and sage seem so distant." As Elman explains, "Prophecy, though surer in result, is nevertheless seriously limited in directions which the human intellect is free to explore. The prophet can perceive only what he is shown; he cannot use his revelation to achieve greater insights (*medammeh milta lemilta*)."

90. Henry Colburn discusses the notion of "space-time compression" as one phenomenon of globalization. While he acknowledges that the Persian Empire may not have been "global" in the modern sense of the word, he explains that globalization's main features "existed in earlier periods as well, albeit on reduced geographical scales." One of those main features is "a perceived reduction in geographical and chronological distance as a result of increased connectivity." Henry P. Colburn, "Globalization and the Study of the Achaemenid Persian Empire," in *The Routledge Handbook of Archaeology and Globalization* (Routledge, 2016), 895–908.

employment of Aramaic as the official administrative language, and the standardization of the calendar.[91] These measures create consistency and the potential for connectivity between distant portions of the empire, allowing all citizens to feel included in, and loyal to, the empire. At the same time, though, the empire also encourages diversity among the various ethnic groups over which it rules. The numerous reliefs from royal palaces and tombs, depicting the empire's loyal subjects in distinctive clothing, are a testament to this imperial ideology that espouses inclusion and diversity[92] and garners allegiance through its tolerance of people's ancestral religions and traditions.[93]

That said, Persian rulers understand that the varying religious traditions they tolerate need to be systematized if order is to be maintained throughout the empire. For Persian governors to rule effectively in the empire's various provinces, they need to be informed about the preexisting civic and religious laws they enforce. So, when Darius I assumes the throne, one of the projects he inaugurates is the codification and translation of local laws into Aramaic.[94] In places like Babylon, where local religious law codes already exist in Aramaic, translation is

---

91. While many of these features exist in earlier empires, the Persians employ them on a broader geographical scale than ever before. Colburn, "Globalization," 874.

92. Gojko Barjamovic, "Propaganda and Practice in Assyrian and Persian Imperial Culture," in *Universal Empire: A Comparative Approach to Imperial Culture and Representation in Eurasian History* (2012), 43–59.

93. For extant evidence of this position, see Joseph Blenkinsopp, "The Mission of Udjahorresnet and Those of Ezra and Nehemiah," *Journal of Biblical Literature* 106, no. 3 (1987): 409–21.

94. Scholars seem to agree that Darius's thinking is influenced by an attempt to prevent religious and cultic blunders like those his predecessor Cambyses committed through ignorance of local laws. And while the bulk of the evidence is from Egypt, logic and piecemeal evidence suggest that the project is widespread. See Richard C. Steiner, "The mbqr at Qumran, the Episkopos in the Athenian Empire, and the Meaning of lbqr in Ezra 7: 14: On the Relation of Ezra's Mission to the Persian Legal Project," *Journal of Biblical Literature* (2001): 623–46. The *Demotic Chronicle* from Egypt, for example, provides information as to the different phases of the project and how long it took to complete. For a summary of the extant evidence of the multiphase program, see Peter Frei, "Persian Imperial Authorization: A Summary," in *Persia and Torah* (2001), 5–40.

unnecessary. But in places like Egypt and Judah, both steps are required, and ancient texts from the time give us insight into how those steps ensue.[95]

After the laws are codified, officials versed in their native laws are sent from Persia to their homelands to enforce the "new order." The men chosen for this work are described, in the Egyptian context, as "wise men ... among the military men, the priests, and the scribes of Egypt."[96] Not coincidentally, the epithets used to describe Ezra when he is first introduced include "high priest," "scribe," and "expert in the Torah of Moses."[97] These titles do more than earn the trust of the work's audience; they explain why Ezra is sent from Persia in the first place. He is sent, in Artaxerxes's own words, "to oversee Judah and Jerusalem, in accordance with the law of your God which you uphold."[98] Ezra's role is not, politically speaking, all-encompassing. In fact, he likely has less political authority than Zerubbabel and Nehemiah, who hold the title of governor.[99] Ezra's official duty is to ensure that the Jewish laws that were translated for the sake of Persian legislation are being properly upheld by the citizens in Judah.[100] Of course, Ezra could not single-handedly fulfill such a task, so Artaxerxes instructs him to "use the wisdom of your God

---

95. Blenkinsopp, *Mission of Udjahoressnet.*
96. Steiner, "The mbqr at Qumran," 636. See also on the page, historical support for rabbinic claims about Ezra's belonging to "the Great Assembly" and changing of the Torah's script.
97. Ezra 7:6.
98. Ibid., v. 14. The word *levakara* found in the verse is a source of debate among scholars. Utilizing contemporaneous philological evidence, Steiner claims the word is best translated as "to exercise the office of temporary overseer/visiting commissioner." Steiner, "The mbqr at Qumran," 626.
99. Ezra 5:14; Nehemiah 5:14, 18, 12:26.
100. This codification and translation likely took years. It is not surprising that while the project may have begun during the reign of Darius, Ezra is only sent in the days of Artaxerxes, once the project is complete. It has been posited that codification of Jewish law may have taken longer than other provinces as the Torah's ban on idolatry and idolaters may have been offensive to many Persians, so there might have been opposition to the official sanctioning of Jewish law. Echoes of this suggestion can be found in Esther 3:8, where Haman's attempt to provoke the king's wrath is cloaked in the charge "whose laws are different from those of all the other peoples." Steiner, "The mbqr at Qumran," 634.

to appoint judges and magistrates who will dispense judgment to all the people in the province beyond the River." Those men, Artaxerxes elaborates, must be "men with knowledge of the laws of your God." Together, Ezra and his appointees are to "provide instruction to those who do not know them." And, the king warns, "anyone who fails to obey the laws of your God and the laws of the king shall be sentenced promptly to death, corporal punishment, fine, or imprisonment."[101] In this new reality, violators of Torah law and Persian law are equally indictable.[102]

EZRA'S PUBLIC READING OF THE TORAH

As per Artaxerxes's charge, Ezra makes his way back to Jerusalem. There, he encounters a community of people struggling with the withdrawal of prophecy. With the Torah in hand and royal authorization to enforce it, Ezra fills that silence with the closest thing available to God's spoken word: God's written word.

In Nehemiah 8, we are told that the people in Jerusalem "assembled together in the open plaza" and called upon Ezra "to bring out the scroll of the Torah."[103] So Ezra "brought the Torah before the congregation – men and women and all who could understand what they heard." The scene depicts the people as hungry for divine directives and Ezra as satisfying that hunger. In stark contrast to the first law giving at Sinai, which was initiated by God, accompanied by awe-inspiring natural phenomena, and marked by the people's fear of death,[104] Ezra's law giving is characterized by the community's willing participation. The setting is mundane, and, as opposed to Moses, who ascends Mount Sinai to receive the revelation, only to reappear forty days later, Ezra's presence throughout the experience is constant. If there is any distance at all between him and the people, it is never more than the height of his "wooden platform erected for the occasion."[105] This time around, God's

---

101. Ezra 7:25–26.
102. Scholars debate whether Ezra's jurisdiction extends beyond Judah.
103. Nehemiah 8:1.
104. Exodus 20:14–17.
105. Nehemiah 8:4.

voice does not thunder from the clouds. Instead, Ezra reads from the Torah from morning until midday, "and the ears of all the people were attuned to the Torah scroll."[106]

But Ezra is not alone. "Next to him, on his right, stood Mattithiah, Shema, Anaiah, Uriah, Hilkiah, and Maaseiah, and on his left were Pedaiah, Mishael, Malchijah, Hashum, Ḥashbadanah, Zechariah, and Meshullam."[107] "Jeshua and Bani and Sherebiah, Jamin, Akkub, Shab-bethai, Hodiah, Maaseiah, Kelita, Azariah, Jozabad, Hanan, Pelaiah"[108] stand by as well. And after Ezra blesses the people, those men, along with the Levites, "explained the Torah to the people, who all the while remained standing."[109] They "read from the scroll of God's Torah while explaining and clarifying each detail to render the readings understandable."[110] Reading the words of the Torah, the work tells us, is the first step. But it does not suffice. For those words to be intelligible and implementable, the reading must be followed by interpretation, which is precisely what Ezra and the other scholars offer the people.

On the most rudimentary level, these teachers are likely interpreting words or idioms that had fallen out of use over the centuries, explaining unfamiliar or antiquated terms and concepts. But beyond the basic level of intelligibility, they are likely also contending with interpretive challenges that their ancestors likely encountered and with which their descendants would continue to wrestle. One of those challenges is the apparent internal inconsistencies that arise in the text.

RECONCILING THE TEXT WITH ITSELF

Imagine, for example, that Ezra reads aloud the verse from Exodus that demands that the Passover sacrifice not be "raw or boiled in water," but rather "roasted over fire."[111] Continue to imagine that he then reads the verse from Deuteronomy where the Israelites are instructed to "cook and

---

106. Ibid., vv. 2–3.
107. Ibid., v. 4
108. Ibid., v. 7.
109. Ibid.
110. Ibid., v. 8.
111. Exodus 12:9.

eat" that same sacrifice.[112] Without interpretation, the people would not know how to prepare their Passover sacrifices.[113] In a similar vein, the people would need help making sense of whether a slave who does not want to leave his master shall, as Exodus claims, "remain his slave forever"[114] or would, as Leviticus insists, automatically go free in the Jubilee year.[115] The people would probably be confused as to whether "the needy" among them should partake of the food left in the fallow fields during the *Shemitta* year[116] or whether the entire community should partake, as per the stipulations in Leviticus.[117] Judicial appointment is presented differently in Exodus and Deuteronomy,[118] and at first blush there does not appear to be consensus in the Torah regarding Israel's ideal geographical boundaries.[119] Even the obligation to rest on Shabbat is ascribed one reason in Exodus[120] and a different one in Deuteronomy.[121] All of these cases, and more, would require the knowledge and expertise of Ezra and the interpreters.

While the text of Ezra-Nehemiah and the Persian backdrop both seem to point to the law as the primary focus of the Torah's public reading, we know that the legal portions of the Torah are interspersed with narratives. In certain instances, the narrative portions of the Torah also seem to recount slightly different versions of the same episode, so those discrepancies, too, would require explication.[122]

---

112. Deuteronomy 16:7. II Chronicles 35:13, claiming that the people "cooked the Passover sacrifice with fire, as required," is likely an attempt at resolution. For this and more examples of resolutions already found in the book of Chronicles, see David W. Halivni, *Revelation Restored: Divine Writ and Critical Responses* (Routledge, 2019) 25.

113. Not coincidentally, II Chronicles 35:12–13 tells us that "as written in the book of Moses…they cooked the Passover sacrifice in fire."

114. Exodus 21:6.

115. Leviticus 25:40–42.

116. Exodus 23:11.

117. Leviticus 25:6–7.

118. Exodus 18; Deuteronomy 1.

119. Genesis 15:18; Numbers 34; Deuteronomy 11:24.

120. Exodus 20:8–11. There, the mitzva of Shabbat is connected to God's rest after the sixth day of Creation.

121. Deuteronomy 5:12–15. There, the Torah emphasizes the social aspect of Shabbat.

122. The Creation accounts (Gen. 1–2), the conflicting details within the flood story

In addition to the legal and narrative details that Ezra and his companions help clarify are the theological and philosophical truths the people need to grasp to rebuild a community rooted in faith. In the first version of the Ten Commandments, for example, God proclaims, "Those who hate Me, I hold the descendants to account for the sins of the father to the third and fourth generation."[123] The sentence is simple enough to understand. But then, as Ezra continues reading, he arrives at the verse in which God claims that He "repays with destruction those who reject Him, requiting them in a moment."[124] Naturally, the people assembled would want to know whether God punishes people immediately for their sins or defers that punishment, even intergenerationally. Likewise, when the people hear Ezra proclaim, "Not man is God, to lie; no mortal, to change His mind. Would He speak and not fulfill; would He promise and not keep?"[125] they would wonder how such a claim aligns with the narrative of the Golden Calf, in which "the Lord relented from the evil He had spoken of doing to His people."[126] The people, eager to behave correctly this time, would then turn to Ezra and the scholars[127] to understand the Torah they are now accepting for the second time.

INTERPRETATION AND APPLICATION OF TORAH LAWS

There is another layer to biblical interpretation that is as old as the Torah itself and undoubtedly demands the interpretive energies of Ezra and the scholars as well. That layer does not simply look at what the words of the Torah are saying but at how those words can be expanded upon and thus applied to unprecedented scenarios. When Moses is still alive

---

(Gen. 6–7), the sin of the spies (Num. 13; Deut. 1), and the sin of the Golden Calf (Ex. 32; Deut. 9) are among the more famous examples of such conflicting narrative portraits.

123. Exodus 20:4.
124. Deuteronomy 7:10.
125. Numbers 23:19.
126. Exodus 32:14.
127. Both Jeremiah (31:29) and Ezekiel (18:20) take a stand on the matter. Whether Ezra utilizes their prophecies as an interpretive tool is not known, but the long tradition of people addressing the topic may point to interpretive discrepancies that exist until that point.

and such scenarios arise, Moses simply asks God how to proceed. When the daughters of Zelophehad pose a question about inheritance laws that the Torah does not explicitly account for, for example, Moses consults God, and the verdict He declares becomes "a decree of law for the Israelites" from that day forward.[128] Similarly, when people who were barred from bringing the Passover sacrifice because of impurity due to contact with a corpse approach Moses wanting to partake, Moses waits for God to rule. Once He does, telling the petitioners to sacrifice the following month, that ruling is integrated as law.[129] But when God is no longer adjudicating directly through Moses and unprecedented situations arise, it falls on religious leaders to apply earlier conceptual precedents to those cases.

The book of Chronicles records just such an instance. It tells of the occasion in the days of King Hezekiah when, just before Passover, the priests become impure and the people are not able to gather in Jerusalem.[130] As a result, it is decided that Passover will be postponed by a month for the entire nation.[131] The scenario Moses rules on is not identical to the case that presents itself in the days of Hezekiah, but, as Michael Fishbane states, since "the latter scenario is related analogically to its Pentateuchal source," Hezekiah draws on that precedent. Like the landmark case in the desert, in Hezekiah's case, ritual defilement and distance from the Temple are the factors that interfere with celebrating. Of course, in Hezekiah's day, not only a handful of people are affected, but rather "the people...from Be'er Sheva to Dan,"[132] who had not celebrated properly. So, as Fishbane goes on to explain, "on the basis of the clause 'for you and your future generations' (Num. 9:10) the Pentateuchal provision for a delayed Passover feast was applied to a later

---

128. Numbers 27:1–11 and chapter 36. The case of the blasphemer (Lev. 24:10–23) and the man who gathers wood on Shabbat (Num. 15:32–36) are two additional cases in which Moses has to consult with God. But those cases are slightly different as they arise on their own, not within the context of extant laws.

129. Numbers 9:8–14.

130. II Chronicles 30:1–4.

131. II Chronicles 29:17 tells us that the Temple was not completely purified until the sixteenth of the month, which would have been reason to postpone the festival.

132. Ibid. 30:3–5.

historical occasion, and also generalized so as to serve the exigencies of a national crisis – not simple individual circumstances."[133] The laws of the Torah are binding. At the same time, those laws must be expounded and cultivated to be pertinent to new realities as they surface.[134]

RIGID ELASTICITY

That need to expound on preexisting laws and concepts to contend with novel scenarios is typified in Ezra's response to the intermarriage crisis of his day. The reality of a Diaspora creates unprecedented challenges and needs in the broader Jewish community, to which Ezra responds by drawing upon concepts from the Torah and applying them to those new circumstances. We saw, for example, how the term "holy seed," which serves as the basis for limitations on priestly marriages in the Torah, is applied in Ezra's time to the entire congregation of Israel.[135] We also saw how that seemingly simple extension served as the foundation for Ezra's anti-intermarriage campaign.[136]

Despite the innovative application of the term, Ezra and his associates do not consider themselves innovators, nor are they perceived as such by their contemporaries. Ezra's distinctive reputation is rooted in his scribal abilities, which denote his knowledge of and fidelity to the written text. When he first sets out on his journey it is with the explicit intent of "expounding the Lord's Torah and observing it; he wished

---

133. Michael Fishbane, "Revelation and Tradition: Aspects of Inner-Biblical Exegesis," *Journal of Biblical Literature* 99, no. 3 (1980): 343–61.

134. There is textual evidence that prior to this period, biblical authors were aware of and employing other biblical works. See Benjamin D. Sommer, *A Prophet Reads Scripture: Allusion in Isaiah 40–66* (Stanford University Press, 1998), 6–31. Still, inner-biblical allusions and even exegesis are not the same as legal interpretation and expansion.

135. Christine Hayes, "Intermarriage and Impurity in Ancient Jewish sources," *Harvard Theological Review* 92, no. 1 (1999): 3–36.

136. The fact that the people seem to employ the legal innovations that developed during this period (see, for example, Ezra 9:1–2) can indicate that some exegetical activity was taking place prior to Ezra's arrival or, more likely, that the author placed those innovations in the mouths of the speakers for the sake of ideological consistency.

to teach Israel its laws and precepts."[137] In fact, the Sukkot celebration initiated by the people after Ezra reads from the Torah is plainly presented as an observance "as prescribed" and "ordained by the law."[138] Later, in Ezra-Nehemiah, subtle revisions and developments of earlier Torah laws are evident as well, but it is their conformity to the text that is the work's focus. Rather than waiting for their tithes to be brought to the Temple as Deuteronomy instructs, for example, it is declared in Nehemiah 10 that the Levites will collect those tithes from depots in rural towns throughout Judah.[139] The law of the first fruits is expanded to include fruits from trees in addition to the already-established produce from the ground.[140] Buying wares on Shabbat is explicitly prohibited for the first time in that same chapter.[141] Yet all of the behaviors the community institutes are classified as laws "as is written in the Torah."[142] The people's (re)commitment to those laws is conceived as inherent to the process to which they consent: to "keep and observe all the commandments of the Lord … His laws and precepts."[143] From the perspective of Ezra and his community of students, text and the interpretation are not two separate things. Rather, text and its exegesis are one and the same.

That perspective springs from the simultaneous belief in God's eternal, fixed text and its inherently elastic character. Ezra understands from his own experiences in a post-prophetic world that for God's word to be practiced, it must be relevant. He also understands that the written

---

137. Ezra 7:10.
138. Nehemiah 8:18. For more examples of this sort of exegesis in Ezra-Nehemiah, in which earlier biblical verses are combined, see Sara Japhet, "What May Be Learned from Ezra-Nehemiah about the Composition of the Pentateuch?" in *The Formation of the Pentateuch* (2016), 543–60.
139. See Deuteronomy 14:23–26 and Nehemiah 10:38–40.
140. See Deuteronomy 26:2 and Nehemiah 10:36.
141. Nehemiah 10:32. Jeremiah 17:19–27 prohibits carrying burdens on Shabbat, and Amos 8:5 refers to the prohibition against selling on Shabbat. But only Nehemiah 10 extends the concept of "work" to include selling wares. For a fuller discussion of the exegesis evident in Nehemiah 10, see David J. Clines, "Nehemiah 10 as an Example of Early Jewish Exegesis," *Journal for the Study of the Old Testament 6*, no. 21 (1981): 111–17.
142. Nehemiah 10:35, 37.
143. Ibid., v. 30.

words are now required to guide the people. But for that to happen, those written words must resonate. They must be presented so that the people feel empowered to turn to them when questions arise and when they feel disoriented. The written Torah, Ezra shows them, contains the answers and the religious direction they are looking for; they just need to know how to find it.

In the same breath that Ezra re-presents the Torah to the Jewish people, he also gives them the tools they need to decipher and creatively employ its text. David Halivni writes that Ezra "imparted a fledgling canon of oral law." In that canon, he goes on, "were the antecedents of an ever-expanding network of Oral Tradition."[144] Rooted in the belief that God's text contains infinite revelatory possibilities, that Oral Tradition persistently turns to the written text as its springboard for legal, homiletic, and exegetic analyses. It insists on the immutability of the Torah, and, at the same time, relies on the text's resilience in the face of millennia of interpretive excavation. Eventually, the Oral Tradition Ezra championed would be the single most important mechanism by which the Jewish people would succeed in maintaining unwavering religious conviction despite history's unpredictability.

But beyond Ezra's content is his leadership style, toward which the people gravitate. Ezra, the priest and scribe, does not chastise the people for their lack of familiarity with the text, nor does he intimidate them. Instead, he shows them that their ability to access God's words should be celebrated.[145] This methodology seems to work. As the narrative progresses, so does the people's familiarity and comfort with their long-forgotten text and traditions.[146] Initially, "the ears of all the people were attuned to the Torah scroll" from which Ezra read,[147] and then they turned to the leaders as they were "explaining and clarifying each detail

---

144. David W. Halivni, *Revelation Restored: Divine Writ and Critical Responses* (Routledge, 2019), 48. It is possible that Ezra draws on oral traditions that were passed down through the generations.

145. Nehemiah 8:10–11.

146. Michael W. Duggan, *The Covenant Renewal in Ezra-Nehemiah: (Neh. 7:72b–10:10): An Exegetical, Literary, and Theological Study* (Society of Biblical Literature, 2001), 295–99.

147. Nehemiah 8:3.

to render the readings understandable."[148] By the twenty-fourth day, the people themselves "read from the scroll of the Lord their God's Torah."[149]

Whereas forty days after the first Torah-giving, Moses finds the people dancing around the Golden Calf, proclaiming "These Israel, are your gods who brought you out of Egypt,"[150] days after Ezra reintroduces the Torah to the people, they return to Ezra to "ponder the words of the Torah."[151] Through their learning, they are inspired to reinstate laws and festivals they "had not done since the days of Joshua son of Nun."[152] In those moments, centuries of neglect are redeemed.

WHAT FOLLOWS ACCEPTANCE OF THE TORAH

In chapter 7 we examined those ways in which authoritarian leadership models of the past are replaced in Persian-period Judah by collective, grassroots leadership, a trend that is especially evident in Ezra's law giving. Ezra presents the Torah to the "men and women and all who could understand what they heard."[153] It passes from him through the Levites to the heads of the ancestral families, and finally to Israel as a whole. This movement through the "hands of an expanding circle"[154] literally represents the social-religious trend that is underway. This is a trend that hands back the Torah to the masses by teaching them how to read and interpret the text that had always been intended for them.[155]

That education-for-all has a profound effect, because, for the first time in Israelite history, religious reform is not being spearheaded by a singular leader or by irate prophets but rather by the people themselves. For the first time, the people understand on their own that changes have to be made if they are to avoid the pitfalls in which their ancestors were

---

148. Ibid., v. 9.

149. Nehemiah 9:3 shows both increased literacy and interest in the text, which go hand in hand.

150. Exodus 32:4.

151. Nehemiah 8:13.

152. Ibid., vv. 10, 14–17. Japhet, "What May Be Learned," 550.

153. Nehemiah 8:2.

154. Duggan, *The Covenant Renewal in Ezra-Nehemiah*, 296.

155. See Deuteronomy 30:11–14.

so easily ensnared. Also for the first time, the people voice that awareness and articulate a plan. In the coming chapter, we will explore ways in
which the community, newly educated, institutes lasting change through
the historical precedents it draws from, the future it conceives, and the
shape of the newly imagined covenantal community.

Chapter Nine

Covenant Renewal

WRITING AND DESTINY

Increased emphasis on the written word, part of a broader cultural shift within the Persian Empire, has had a direct and conspicuous impact on the Judean community and its relationship to the written text of the Torah. But the religious-legal corpora discussed in the last chapter are not the only arenas in which the written word takes on heightened significance. Writing in general, specifically edicts written by political figures, become revered in the Persian period. The binding nature of written documents become a centerpiece of post-exilic works, and often they determine the progression of the work's plot.[1] In the Book of Esther, for example, a work preoccupied with power and its volatility, written documents function as a motif, marking critical turning points in power dynamics and the consequences that follow.[2] Similarly, in the

---

1. Their binding nature is taken as a given in earlier biblical works such as Deuteronomy 24:1–3 and Jeremiah 32:10–44. But post-exilic works highlight their import with added emphasis.

2. See Esther 1:19, 22, 2:23, 3:9, 12, 14, 4:8, 6:1, 8:5–13, 9:20–32. The preposterousness of a world in which kings are bound against their will by letters they themselves wrote is characteristic of the satirical nature of Esther. Still, the mockery is based on a well-known reality in which written royal decrees are binding.

book of Daniel, a written edict by King Darius and Daniel's subsequent defiance of it set in motion a dramatic chain of events that culminate in an additional edict publicly declaring Daniel's righteousness and God's supremacy.[3] Interestingly, on a number of occasions, the book of Chronicles mentions written documents in its narrative retelling earlier events, even when no such document is mentioned in the episode's original account,[4] further highlighting the augmented importance that such documents are accorded in the Second Temple period.

Like these other post-exilic works, Ezra-Nehemiah takes the importance of written documents as a given. But as we will see in this chapter, while documents revolving around Persian policy and governance pervade much of the work, a second sort, crafted in Nehemiah 10, signifies an important turning point in the history of the Judean community.

GOD'S HAND AND WRITTEN TEXTS

If in other post-exilic works, documents influence the narrative's plotlines, in Ezra-Nehemiah they are the very building blocks upon which the work takes shape.[5] As by now we well know, the opening of Ezra-Nehemiah is a quotation of Cyrus's written edict that both prompts

---

3. Daniel 6.
4. See, for example, I Kings 5 and II Chronicles 2:10. Chronicles references a letter exchange between Hiram and Solomon that is not mentioned in Kings. Likewise, in II Chronicles 21:12–15, Elijah is said to engage in a form of long-distance prophecy, sending a letter to King Jehoram of Judah, but no such exchange is mentioned in II Kings 8. And II Chronicles 32:17 tells of a letter deriding God that Sennacherib purportedly sends to Israel to intimidate them. Similar intimidation attempts in the book of Kings are remembered as having occurred orally by Sennacherib's messengers (II Kings 18:17–37). For more examples and a fuller elaboration on this topic, see Susan Niditch, *Oral World and Written Word: Ancient Israelite Literature* (Westminster John Knox Press, 1996), 91–94.
5. This stands in stark contrast to other biblical works in which speech is the narrative's chief storytelling medium. As Robert Alter points out, "Quantitatively, a remarkably large part of the narrative burden is carried by dialogue, the transactions between characters typically unfolding through the words they exchange, with only the most minimal intervention of the narrator." Robert Alter, *The Art of Biblical Narrative* (Basic Books, 2011), 182.

the people's return and vests the first generation of Judean leadership.[6] After that, the successes and (temporary) failures of the Temple building project are determined by both new and preexisting texts that were rediscovered.[7] The unique missions of both Ezra and Nehemiah are likewise governed by written texts,[8] as is membership within the community and eligibility for the priesthood.[9] In addition, the religious revival that characterizes the era is inspired by the text of Moses that Ezra is charged to bring with him from Persia to Jerusalem.

Readers of Ezra-Nehemiah come to understand that not only do written texts carry an unprecedented weight in the Persian period but that, in Ezra-Nehemiah specifically, they are the means by which the community's fate is determined. As Tamara Cohn Eskenazi argues, the carefully preserved documents "demonstrate Ezra-Nehemiah's view about the power and propriety of written texts as causative principles and significant forces in human events."[10] To be sure, this power attributed to documents does not by any means supplant God's power. Rather, written texts in Ezra-Nehemiah are seen as the conduit through which God's will is both verified and actualized. The work's inaugural decree, for example, is composed after God "stirred the spirit of Cyrus,"[11] a fact of which we are reminded with the words "they built the House and completed it according to the command of the God of Israel and in keeping with the edict of Cyrus, Darius, and King Artaxerxes of Persia."[12] At the conclusion of Artaxerxes's letter promoting Ezra, we find a similar reminder of this collaboration between royal texts and God's will. There, Ezra blesses God and thanks Him for "turning the king's heart toward the cause of beautifying the House of the Lord in Jerusalem. And for

6. As discussed in chapter one, whether the words are a direct quotation of his edict or a stylized paraphrase is less important than the fact that the prime motivating force identified at the outset of the work is a written document.

7. Ezra 4–6.

8. Ibid. 1:8, 7:13–28; Nehemiah 2:7–9.

9. Ezra 2, 8; Nehemiah 7, 12. For the priestly pedigree specifically, see Ezra 2:62.

10. Tamar Cohn Eskenazi and Cheryl Exum, "Ezra-Nehemiah: From Text to Actuality," in *Signs and Wonders* (1989), 165–98.

11. Ezra 1:1.

12. Ibid. 6:14.

showing me kindness in the eyes of the king and his ministers and all his valiant officers."[13] Nehemiah, too, notes the tight link between God's will and texts in his tallying of the community. "Then my God inspired me," he recalls, "to gather the nobles and officials and the people to register their genealogy, and I found the genealogical records of those who first came up."[14] What is clear to Ezra and Nehemiah becomes clear to us as well through their devout words. In this new era, God's plan for history is transcribed by those open to hearing it and then fulfilled by those who rightfully know to revere such documents. That assumed dynamic plays an important role in Nehemiah 10, because the community there will attempt to resolve a primary concern by drawing on the reverence of written texts that Ezra-Nehemiah promotes.

LINGERING TRAUMA

The community of repatriates in Ezra-Nehemiah deals with a range of issues that the rebuilding of a state demands. Many of those issues fall into the realm of what we might call practical or technical concerns. The construction projects, community assemblage, and educational reforms, for example, are solutions to some of those practical matters that arise during the various stages of rebuilding. But there is another, less tangible concern that the community carries with it from the moment it returns to the land, and that concern is not resolved by any of the above-mentioned accomplishments. Simply put, the community that returns to the land (rightfully) worries that, at any moment, exile could strike again.

Writing on the "afterlife of loss," Eva Hoffman notes that one of the characteristics of post-trauma is that "the past continues to overwhelm and overshadow the present and the mourning never lifts."[15] While subtle, this post-trauma influences Ezra-Nehemiah. By Nehemiah 9–10, the forced-Babylonian exile is long over [16] but far from forgotten. The

---

13.   Ibid. 7:27–28.

14.   Nehemiah 7:5.

15.   Eva Hoffman, "The Long Afterlife of Loss," in *Memory: Histories, Theories, Debates* (2010), 406–15.

16.   While the majority of the Jewish people continue to live in Babylon, their presence

experience of those who returned is colored by their trauma, specifically because those who returned had internalized that their existence on the land was not unconditionally guaranteed. As we discussed in chapter three, the pre-exilic prophets tried for centuries to impress that message upon the people, but their efforts were in vain. In post-exilic Judah, however, the after-effects of that truth persist.

When Ezra reintroduces the Torah to the people, those feelings of uncertainty are only exacerbated. As the Judeans listen to Ezra read Moses's words, they can identify the mistakes their ancestors made that led to their exile. Nehemiah 9 begins by telling us that the people "convened, fasting and in sackcloth with earth on themselves." They then "separated themselves from all those of foreign descent," and "confessed their sins and the wrongdoings of their ancestors." They "read from the scroll of the Lord their God's Torah for a quarter of the day," we are told, and "for another quarter-day they confessed and prostrated themselves before the Lord, their God."[17] Such a reaction suggests that, in addition to learning the specific laws outlined in the Torah, the people also internalize its broader and more fundamental precepts which teach that their fortune is inextricably linked to their behaviors and consequent relationship with God.

In fact, a close reading of the continuation of the chapter supports that assumption. The chapter contains a confessional retrospective of sorts in which the community declares God's inimitable power, compassion, and commitment to His people. The God that they now understand "created the heavens…the earth and all upon it,"[18] is also the God "who chose Abram, bringing him out of Ur-Kasdim and changing his name to Abraham."[19] He is the God who, in response to the cries of His people in Egypt and at the Sea of Reeds, "performed signs and wonders against Pharaoh," splitting the sea for Israel and "hurling their pursuers into the

---

there is no longer compulsory as it was prior to Cyrus's declaration. As such, Jewish presence in Babylon is no longer a consequence of exile so much as a choice to remain in the Diaspora. For more on this distinction see, chapter ten.

17. Nehemiah 9:1–3.
18. Ibid., v. 6.
19. Ibid., v. 7.

depths like a stone into raging waters."[20] He is also the God who, after guiding the Israelites through the treacherous desert "descended on Mount Sinai" and "charged them with commandments, statutes, and teachings."[21] But God's kindness to His people, the community learns, is not met with the unwavering gratitude it deserves. Their forefathers "acted in willful wickedness, stiffening their necks…refusing to listen," and they "turned their heads to return to slavery."[22] The Judeans learn that forty days after their ancestors receive the Torah, they "made themselves a molten calf, declaring, 'This is your god who brought you out of Egypt,' and aroused great anger." The Judeans also learn that despite that grave sin, God never abandons their ancestors.[23] His "cloud column did not cease guiding the way by day, nor did the nocturnal fire column cease illuminating the way for them to walk."[24] Reading the wilderness narratives consecutively, from the Exodus through their entry into the land, must be shocking for many of those listening. The degree of ingratitude and lack of faith displayed by the wilderness generation is jarring for anyone not familiar with the events. And yet, as they continue to study, they learn that the ingratitude does not stop there.

The nucleus of the retrospective found in Nehemiah 9 consists of the community's confession of its ancestors' abysmal failures. The speakers openly acknowledge that God brings their ancestors to the land, "subdued the Canaanite inhabitants before them," and bestows upon them "a rich fertile land full of all good things," including "hewn cisterns and vineyards, olive groves, and plentiful fruit orchards." Their ancestors "ate and were satisfied, growing rich and fat, luxuriating in Your great goodness."[25] But, like the wilderness generation before them, those in

---

20. Ibid., vv. 9–11.
21. Ibid., vv. 12–15.
22. Ibid., vv. 16–18.
23. In an in-depth analysis of Nehemiah 9, Rolf Rendtorff points out the importance of the way in which "the text alternates between Israel's bad deeds and God's merciful reactions," as that alternating, he argues, holds the key to the theological contributions of the chapter. Rolf Rendtorff et al., "Nehemiah 9: An Important Witness of Theological Reflection," in *Tehillah le-Moshe* (1997), 111–17.
24. Nehemiah 9:18–19.
25. Ibid., vv. 22–25.

the land "disobeyed and rebelled," only repenting temporarily when God "gave them into the hands of their oppressors." And "as soon as they were again at ease," they resort to their wicked ways. [26] The Judeans recognize that God gave their ancestors "laws ... by which a person shall live," but that instead of living by them, their ancestors turned "a stubborn shoulder, they stiffened their necks, and would not listen." So, eventually, God "delivered them into the hands of the peoples of the lands."[27] That delivery into their enemies' hands continues to haunt the repatriates despite their newfound freedom.

In addition to haunting them, the Bible's fusion of divine teachings and historical narratives does something else as well. It enables the Judeans to recognize patterns in their history and create a coherent portrait from their difficult past. When they put the pieces together, they understand, finally, that the horror of exile that their ancestors bore is not a stroke of bad luck, nor is it the result of unpreventable historical circumstances. Instead, the Torah learning in which the Judean community engages cements the conception that maintaining a presence in the land has always been in their hands.[28]

OWNING THEIR FATE

On the topic of inherited trauma, Hoffman goes on to explain that "the necessary task, for those who come into the inheritance of loss, is in a sense to liberate themselves from the thrall of the past sufficiently not to mistake our ancestors' history for our own."[29] From a collective, emotional perspective, this is certainly true. For people to progress beyond their painful past, they must disassociate sufficiently from it. But the community reflected in Nehemiah 9 also understands that for that emotional liberation to transpire, it must first identify and then disassociate from the behaviors that wrought that pain.

---

26. Ibid., vv. 26–29.
27. Ibid. 9:29–30.
28. For more on the basis of their realization, see Daniel J. Elazar, "Judaism as a Theopolitical Phenomenon," in *The Blackwell Companion to Judaism* (2003), 415–40.
29. Hoffman, *The Long Afterlife of Loss,* 411.

That realization is reflected in both the content and the grammar of Nehemiah 9. The chapter contains three primary subjects: God, the speakers' ancestors, and the community of speakers itself. The beginning of the chapter focuses on the people's ancestors and their defiance of the covenant that only intensifies with time. Making it clear that God is their intended audience, the speakers say things such as: "You heard their cries,"[30] "You guided them…and spoke to them from heaven,"[31] "But they and our fathers acted in willful wickedness, stiffening their necks and disobeying your commands."[32] Then, just before the end of the chapter, we note a swift transition from "them" to "we" and "us." That transition, so easily overlooked, links the speakers' experience with that of their ancestors. Still speaking to God, they say "You have been just throughout all that has come upon us, for You have dealt in truth while we have committed evil."[33] They, like their ancestors have sinned. And, like their ancestors, they "are indeed in dire trouble and distress."[34]

But the essence of the chapter lies in the fact that the parallels end there.[35] The speakers make clear that whereas their ancestors turned "a stubborn shoulder," and "stiffened their neck and would not listen,"[36] they now know better. Like their ancestors, they directly encounter the written word of God, but, unlike their ancestors, the current speakers choose unequivocally to embrace the demands of that written word, which brings with it a renewed sense of empowerment and will ultimately prove to be the salve for their lingering post-traumatic angst.

---

30. Nehemiah 9:9.
31. Ibid., vv. 12–13.
32. Ibid., v. 16.
33. Ibid., v. 33.
34. Ibid. v. 37. A reference to their ancestors' experience and its similarity with their own is also made in Ezra.
35. As Eskenazi notes, "The prayer thus diverges from the other confessions of penitence. It recites transgressions of earlier generations to account for how the plight came about. But it puts a definite distance between those earlier generations of sinners for whom God did so much and the community now in distress." Tamara Cohn Eskenazi, "Nehemiah 9–10: Structure and Significance," *Journal of Hebrew Scriptures* 3 (2001): 16.
36. Nehemiah 9:29.

BIBLICAL COVENANTS

That sense of empowerment is rooted in Tanakh's unique application of bilateral covenants and implications for human volition. The bilateral covenant, once prevalent in the ancient Near East is, in Tanakh, the framework upon which divine-human relationships are based. Understanding it enables the Judeans to believe that they can do better than their ancestors. As the term indicates, "bilateral covenants" assert that both sides must fulfill their obligations. While, in a relationship between Israel and God, this necessarily obligates the Israelites, it also galvanizes them. In a monotheistic world in which God's powers go unchallenged, Israelite adherence to or defiance of her covenant with Him becomes the sole determinant of her fate, and in the unpredictable world in which Israel exists, that assumption is extremely encouraging.[37]

It is evident from the Judeans' comments in Nehemiah 9 and their behavior in Nehemiah 10 that, in the course of their Torah studies, they relearn the parameters of the divine-Israelite bilateral covenant. Through that process, they come to understand the basic tenet of which God reminds the Israelites throughout their time in the desert. "The land is Mine," He says to the Israelites, lest they get the wrong idea. "You are merely migrants and visitors to Me."[38] The land He brings them to, God makes clear, is a gift, not a right. He reminds them that they did nothing to earn the land, and as such should never make the false claim that "it is because of my righteousness that the Lord has brought me in to take possession of the land."[39] That fact is evinced in rulings such as the one that declares: "All tithes from the land, whether seed from the ground or fruit of the tree, belong to the Lord"[40] and in the law demanding that every seven years "shall be to the land a Sabbath of complete rest, a Sabbath to the Lord."[41] The prohibition of working the land during

---

37. The perennial issue of theodicy is addressed throughout Tanakh as well (see, for example, the discussion in chapter four). But in its most basic form, the covenantal nature of the God-Israel relationship provides a sense of order and rationality to the human experience.
38. Leviticus 25:23–24. See also Deuteronomy 6:10–12.
39. Deuteronomy 9:4.
40. Leviticus 27:30.
41. Ibid. 25:2–7.

the Sabbatical year is a tangible reminder to the Israelites that they are beholden to God's land, not the other way around.

Still, while the people have no natural or intrinsic rights to the land, the Judeans also learn that out of a deep and abiding love for their forefathers,[42] God gifts them with it. And, perhaps more importantly, after doing so, He tells them what they need to do to retain their residential status. As we mentioned in chapter four, at Sinai and in the law giving that follows,[43] God outlines the stipulations of the covenant to which Israel is to consent.[44] Lists of blessings the Israelites would enjoy are introduced with phrases such as, "If you follow My decrees, keep My commands, and fulfill them, then I shall …"[45] Likewise, the list of curses they could bring upon themselves is preceded by sentences like, "But if you do not listen to Me and do not carry out all these commands – if you spurn My decrees and despise My laws, not keeping all My commands; violating My covenant – then I will do this to you."[46] The punishments enumerated include a list of nightmare scenarios including starvation, consumption, and death by enemy sword. But what likely would resonate most with the scrutinizing Judeans is that, of all the punishments listed,

---

42. Deuteronomy 4:37, 7:8.

43. It could be argued that the concept that Israel's behaviors could impact her fate is introduced in Exodus 12, where the people are told that if they fulfill certain commandments, they will be spared death on the night of the Exodus. But while the first Passover and some of its associated commandments are a onetime event, the Sinaitic covenant is relevant for all time.

44. Covenants, broadly speaking, are bilateral agreements that outline the features of the relationship they create. Conditional and unconditional covenants were ubiquitous in the ancient Near East. They existed between individuals, kings and subjects, nation-states, and other such liaisons. The theologically revolutionary demand that God made with the words "Have no other gods than me," (Ex. 20:1–2) is presented to Israel in the context of known covenantal templates so that the new divine-human relationship He demands would be intelligible to Israel. See René Lopez, "Israelite Covenants in the Light of Ancient Near Eastern Covenants," *Chafer Theological Seminary Journal* 9, no. 2 (2003): 92–111; Moshe Weinfeld, "The Covenant of Grant in the Old Testament and in the Ancient Near East." *Journal of the American Oriental Society* (1970): 184–203.

45. Leviticus 26:3.

46. Ibid., vv. 14–15. Similar formulations are found in Deuteronomy 28:1–45 and 29:24–27.

the one that has the most space allotted in the text is exile.[47] It states unmistakably that they have control over the phenomenon they most fear and that, just as their original entry into the land is not accidental,[48] neither is their banishment from it. The algorithm is straightforward: if they keep up their end of the deal, God will keep His. In such a situation, neither human enemies nor supernatural forces of evil will have any bearing on that arrangement.[49] If they do not, exile will ensue, but the choice is theirs to make.

ETHICAL MONOTHEISM

That choice involves more than other ancient religions demanded.[50] In obligating the Israelites to worship Him exclusively, God also implicitly

---

47. See, for example, Leviticus 26:27–33.
48. As Eryl W. Davies explains, the promise of the land, which is introduced in the days of Abraham, "emphasized the fact that the people did not dwell in a land to which the changes and chances of history just happen to have brought them, but in a land which had been destined for them by God before Israel even became a nation." Eryl W. Davies and Ronald E. Clements, "Land: Its Rights and Privileges," in *The World of Ancient Israel* (1991), 349–69. See also the first Rashi in Genesis, which claims that the entire record of creation proves a similar point.
49. On the topic of how monotheism changed humanity's conception of evil, Christine Hayes points out that "in the polytheistic worldview...just as there are good gods who might protect human beings, there are also evil gods who seek to destroy both humans and other gods. Death and disease are consigned to the realm of these evil demons or these impure evil spirits, but they are siblings with the good gods. Human beings are basically powerless...in the continual cosmic struggle between the good gods and the evil demons unless they can, utilizing magic and divination, tap into the powers of the metadivine realm and circumvent the gods who might be making their lives miserable.... Evil is a metaphysical reality." Monotheism, she further asserts, challenges that notion, leaving God in control. Christine Hayes, Yale University Intro to the Bible Series, Lecture 2, Monotheism, p. 4.
50. This is not to suggest that other ancient Near Eastern societies did not have sophisticated law codes, many of which ensured the protection of the weak within society. There is evidence from Egypt, Mesopotamia, and Ugarit that the protection of society's weak was the will of the god and the responsibility of the people. However, in polytheistic religions, the characteristics of justice and compassion are ascribed to one god in the pantheon whereas, in the Torah, the One and only God makes such demands of His people. As such, the Bible makes clear that there is no such thing as religious worship devoid of social ethics. Or, as Jeremiah Unterman

demands that they worship differently, following what scholars refer to as ethical monotheism. This concept may be obvious to students of the Bible, but it was not always internalized and implemented by earlier generations of Israelites.[51] Ethical monotheism, which equates ritual and ethical commandments, asserts that the One supreme God of the universe cares equally how people treat Him and how they treat each other.

Building on the pioneering work of Yehezkel Kaufmann,[52] Christine Hayes points out that while most people think that monotheism's theological contribution was its reconceptualization of the number of gods it construed, its most transformative contribution was actually its reconceptualization of the character of the One God. The gods of the ancient pantheons were depicted as capricious and, at times, cruel, but "biblical monotheism assumes that this God is inherently good, just, and compassionate and that human morality consists in conformity to His will."[53] Justice and compassion can be seen in God's expectation that His people treat each other justly and compassionately. For that reason, the Sinaitic covenant is comprised of both religious and civic laws, with no clear distinction between the two. The Decalogue, for example, demands that the people worship God exclusively and that they not covet their neighbor's wife. It prohibits them from creating graven images and also

---

puts it, "religious ritual is both secondary to ethics and dependent upon moral behavior for its validity." Jeremiah Unterman, *Justice for All: How the Jewish Bible Revolutionized Ethics* (University of Nebraska Press, 2017), 180. See also Charles F. Fensham, "Widow, Orphan and the Poor in Ancient Near Eastern Legal and Wisdom Literature," *Journal of Near Eastern Studies* 21, no. 2 (1962): 129–39.

51. See, for example, Isaiah 1:11–16; Hosea 6:6–7. The prophetic critique of the internally inconsistent use of cult has been misunderstood by many as a confrontation between priests and prophets. Actually, the prophets are not deriding the cult as an institution; they are simply trying to communicate that one without the other is futile.

52. Yehezkel Kaufmann, *History of the Religion of Israel, Volume IV: From the Babylonian Captivity to the End of Prophecy* (Ktav, 1977).

53. Christine Hayes (Yale); Intro to the Hebrew Bible; Lecture 2, p. 8. For a thorough and nuanced discussion of the concept of God's will and its impact on legal development in Israel, see Christine Hayes, *What's Divine About Divine Law? Early Perspectives* (Princeton University Press, 2015).

from murdering.[54] Sins against humanity, the biblical system proclaims, are sins against God.[55]

Beyond simply prohibiting violence, the Torah's entwining of ethics and ritual is designed to engender a society where people display their devotion to God through their kindness to others, particularly to the vulnerable and downtrodden. Those lucky enough to be on the receiving end of God's bounty, for example, are obliged to care for those who are not. The stranger, widow, and orphan are to be supported by the community,[56] as are the landless Levites.[57] At the time of harvest, produce is to be left behind in the fields for those without fields of their own,[58] and every third year the people are to "bring out the full tithe of your produce for that year, and leave it within your towns, so that the Levites, who have no share or inheritance as you have, together with the migrants, orphans, and widows in your towns, may come and eat and be satisfied."[59] Precisely because "there will never cease to be poor people in the land," God told His people, "I command you: open your hand generously to your kinsmen, your poor and needy, who share your land."[60] Likewise, God expects Israel to lend money without exacting

54. Exodus 20:1–13, Deuteronomy 5:6–17. This concept is expressed within narrative portions of the Bible as well.
55. For this reason, Israel, unlike her neighbors, is not allowed to pardon people for civic sins. In Babylonian, Assyrian, and Hittite adultery laws, for example, if a man chooses to pardon his wife, and by extension the paramour, no punishment would be exacted. In biblical law, because God is the offended party, no such option exists (see Lev. 20:10; Deut. 22:22–24). This concept is evident in the narrative and poetic portions of Tanakh as well. When Abimelech is prevented from violating Sarah, Abraham's wife, we are told that he is kept from sinning against God (Gen. 20:6). Joseph, likewise, refuses Potiphar's wife's advances, claiming he cannot "sin against God" (Gen. 39:9). And in Psalms 51, David prays to God for forgiveness for his sin with Bathsheba, proclaiming, "I sinned against You alone; I committed what is evil in Your eyes" (v. 6). For more on this idea and its distinction from ancient Near Eastern laws, see Moshe Greenberg, "Some Postulates of Biblical Criminal Law," in M. Haran, ed., *Yehezkel Kaufman Jubilee Volume* (Jerusalem, 1960).
56. Deuteronomy 26:12.
57. Ibid. 14:27.
58. Ibid. 24:19–21.
59. Ibid. 14 :28–29.
60. Ibid. 15:11.

interest and to give back any clothing collected as collateral because if a man is poor enough to borrow money, "what else does he have in which to sleep?"[61] God does not recommend altruism in the Bible; He legislates it. And a religious, God-fearing society is one rooted in the understanding that while disparities in wealth and power will always exist, human behavior must be regulated in such a way as to minimize the impact of those inequities. As Jon Levenson explains, "The covenant relationship... is not polar but triangular. At the top stands God, and at each of the two angles of the base stand Israelites. Each of them relates to his neighbor through the norms decreed by God.... In Israel, covenant becomes a basis of social ethics."[62]

In numerous instances, God demands compassion by invoking Israel's own experiences of vulnerability. "Do not oppress a stranger or exploit him," they are told, "for you yourselves were strangers in the land of Egypt."[63] Likewise, a person donating his first fruits to God at His Temple declares upon dedication, "My ancestor was a wandering Aramean. He went down into Egypt and lived there as a stranger, just a handful of souls, and there he became a nation – large, mighty, and great. And the Egyptians dealt cruelly with us and oppressed us, subjecting us to harsh labor. We cried out to the Lord, God of our ancestors. And the Lord heard our voice and He saw our oppression, our toil, and our enslavement. The Lord brought us out of Egypt with a mighty hand and His arm stretched forth, with terrifying power, with signs, and with wonders. He brought us into this place and He gave us this land, a land

---

61. Exodus 22:24–26. See also Deuteronomy 23:20.

62. Jon D. Levenson, *Sinai and Zion: An Entry into the Jewish Bible* (Harper & Row, 1987), 53–54. This does not obviate the responsibility that Israelites have toward non-Israelites. A basic tenet of biblical thought is respect for all of humanity and human life. But because the Sinaitic covenant outlines specifically what Israelite society will look like, its focus is those standing at Sinai and their committing to its terms. Furthermore, as Michael Walzer points out, "In principle, the covenant of law is open to anyone prepared to accept its burdens; hence it isn't entirely implausible to say that there is no chosen people, only people who choose." Michael Walzer, *In God's Shadow: Politics in the Hebrew Bible* (Yale University Press, 2012), 3.

63. Exodus 22:20. In keeping with this discussion, it is not surprising that the law regulating treatment of strangers is juxtaposed with the warning that "whoever sacrifices to any other deity shall be utterly destroyed" (v. 19).

flowing with milk and with honey. And now I am bringing the first fruit of the land that You, O Lord, have given me." The worshipper's gratitude to God does not end with his sacrifice; rather, he is to then "set the basket down before the Lord your God, and then bow down low before the Lord your God. *Then you, with the Levites and the migrants who live among you, shall rejoice in all the good that the Lord your God has bestowed on you and on your household.*"[64] The true display of gratitude to God is not the sacrifice alone but the inclusive society built in the wake of a conscious awareness of one's gratitude. God redeems His people from slavery. But, as the various biblical laws note, the ultimate goal of the Exodus is not simply about bringing the Israelites to Canaan; it is about the Israelites ensuring that Canaan does not become another Egypt.[65] Therefore, in Israel, slaves are granted respite every Shabbat along with all members of the household,[66] and every seven years the Israelites are obligated to grant their slaves freedom and cancel all monetary debts.[67] Draw from the painful experiences of your past, God instructs the Israelites, and build a society rooted in that empathy.

God not only mandates the way the Israelites should interact with the unfortunate among them; He also avenges any mistreatment. His call to "not abuse a widow or an orphan," is followed by His threat that "if you do abuse them, if they cry out to Me, I will unquestionably heed their cry. My anger will flare and I will kill you by the sword – and then your wives will be widows and your children orphans."[68] God similarly

---

64. Deuteronomy 26:5–11.
65. As Michael Walzer so beautifully puts it: "Conceived in territorialist terms, the promise of milk and honey has a temporal end point: sooner or later, the people will cross the Jordan and enter the land. Conceived in ethical terms, the promise is temporally uncertain, for its achievement is not a matter of where we plant our feet but of how we cultivate our spirits." Michael Walzer, *Exodus and Revolution* (Basic Books, 1986), 108.
66. Exodus 20:9; Deuteronomy 5:13–14.
67. Exodus 21:2; Deuteronomy 15:1–2, 12. In the ancient world, as Adriel Jost points out, "small farmers were always very close to indebtedness to a wealthy creditor." Granting them freedom from their debts also granted them, by extension, freedom from potential servitude. Adriel Jost, "A New Start for the Monetary System: A Theological Perspective," in *Revista Procesos De Mercado* (2022), 367–92.
68. Exodus 22:21–23.

tells the people that if they subvert justice for any reason, He will "not acquit the wrongdoer."[69] To thrive in the land, the Israelites are told, they must adhere to God's vision of what society in that land should be. Or, as E. W. Davies puts it, "The law was … both the norm of Israel's life in the land … and the primary condition of its occupation."[70]

LOSING AND THEN REGAINING SIGHT OF THE INTERPLAY BETWEEN ETHICS AND RITUAL

This is why, earlier in the work, when Nehemiah discovered that the Judeans with means are not going out of their way to ensure that those without can keep their fields and provide for their families, he is incensed. In his memoirs, Nehemiah records the outcry of the Judeans against their fellow countrymen. "We must mortgage our fields, our vineyards, and our homes to buy grain to stave off starvation," they cry. "Is our brother's flesh not like ours?" they persist, "Their sons akin to our own? And yet we must force our sons and daughters into servitude, and some of our daughters have already been forced in that way while we stand helplessly by."[71] So, in Nehemiah's words, "I upbraided the nobles and officials, saying to them, 'You are exacting exorbitant payments from your own brothers!'" Then, after shaming them into silence, Nehemiah makes clear that they are not only wronging their fellow Judeans but they are doing wrong because they should "walk in fear of our God."[72] Long after the Temple is rebuilt and sacrifices resumed, the exact scenario that biblical laws are intended to avoid has become a reality. The Temple is being financed, but local farmers are not. Nehemiah understands that the people are returning to their old, problematic ways. Modeling the change the community needs to institute, Nehemiah cancels all debts and then, following his lead, the creditors likewise promise, "We will restore it all and demand no more of them."[73]

---

69. Ibid. 23:7.
70. Davies, *The Land: Its Rights and Privileges*, 352.
71. Nehemiah 5:1–5.
72. Ibid., v. 9.
73. Ibid., v. 12.

But students of Tanakh recognize that top-down change enforced by a solitary, charismatic figure, while often successful in the short term, rarely endures.[74] If Ezra-Nehemiah has taught us anything, it is that for true change to happen, it must come from the people,[75] which is why the *amana* of Nehemiah 9–10 represents the turning point for the Judean community. It signifies the first time the community convenes and pledges to create a society based on ethical monotheism. Uttering aloud that they are nothing more than residents on God's land, the people collectively articulate for the first time that to remain, they must follow the rules outlined by their Host.

THE COMMUNITY'S REALIZATION AND THE WRITING OF THE *AMANA*

Nehemiah 9 is the lyrical expression of those realizations, and Nehemiah 10 is the community's reaction to them. These two chapters together mark the point at which the Jews who rebuild after exile make sense of their harrowing past and choose to evolve beyond it. In that imaginary moment between chapters 9 and 10, the newly educated Judeans make a critical decision. They decide that they will not allow stubbornness and impiety to become congenital conditions; they will differ from the generations that preceded them. Because of the culture in which they live, the Judeans know that the best way to fortify that resolve is with a written document of their own.

After recapitulating their ancestors' mistakes in Nehemiah 9 and conceding that they are "in dire trouble and distress,"[76] the Judeans write that document. In the opening words of Nehemiah 10, they declare "amid all this we commit to a faithful covenant and put it in writing under the seal

---

74. See, for example, the attempted religious revolutions of Elijah (I Kings 18), Hezekiah (II Kings 18–20; II Chr. 29–32), and Josiah (II Kings 22:1–23:30).
75. In chapter six, for example, we showed the grassroots efforts behind the various building projects, and in the previous chapter we looked at those ways in which the law giving initiated by the people differed drastically from the first law giving of Moses.
76. Nehemiah 9:37.

of our leaders, Levites, and priests."[77] The names of the signatories and all the leaders representing the community are then listed, followed by their "oath, under the penalty of a curse, to follow in the way of God's teaching as given into the hand of God's servant Moses."

Not surprisingly, while the community commits in that preamble to "keep and observe all the commandments of the Lord our Master and His laws and precepts,"[78] what follows that introduction is a sampling of biblical laws to which the community promises to adhere.[79] That sampling weaves seamlessly between ritual and ethical commandments. It shifts from the signatories' vow not to "give our daughters to the peoples of the land nor take their daughters for our sons," to their abstention from making purchases "on the Sabbath day or on any holy day." Then, without skipping a beat, they pledge that "in the seventh year we will forgo the crops as well as each person's debt."[80] Additionally, the people vow to bring "the first fruits of our land and all the first fruits of all trees each and every year, also the firstborn of our sons and of our animals," at which time, as the ritual demands, they will have recalled their paltry beginnings and been inspired to build the equitable society God intends. Like the Decalogue, the *amana* demands a devotion that extends both horizontally and vertically. And, like the Decalogue, rather than being a comprehensive list of commandments, the *amana* juxtaposes specific commandments that, when integrated correctly, maintain the all-important God/land/man triad.[81]

Rather than transcribing letters to Persian officials or cataloging lists of repatriates, in Nehemiah 10 the Judeans write a new type of document. This in-house text is written and signed by "all those who had separated

---

77. Ibid. 10:1.

78. Ibid., v. 30.

79. For a discussion of the early interpretive methods evident in the specific framing of the laws listed, see David J. A. Clines, "Nehemiah 10 as an Example of Early Jewish Biblical Exegesis," *Journal for the Study of the Old Testament* 6, no. 21 (1981): 111–17.

80. Nehemiah 10:31–33.

81. For a fuller discussion of the internal structure of the *amana*, and the various opinions regarding clauses found within it, see David A. Glatt-Gilad, "Reflections on the Structure and Significance of the'ªmānāh (Neh. 10, 29–40)," *Zeitschrift für die Alttestamentliche Wissenschaft* 112, no. 3 (2000): 386–95.

themselves from the peoples of the lands to be with God's Torah."[82] With that written oath, they take a step forward in Jewish history.

WHAT ABOUT THOSE WHO DO NOT LIVE ON THE LAND?

While initially the fate of the Judeans in Ezra-Nehemiah was shaped and controlled by texts written about them or on their behalf, the Judeans' embrace of their own texts changes that. After coming together as a community to learn from the paramount text of the Torah in Nehemiah 8 and recognizing its implications aloud in Nehemiah 9, the Judeans write a text of their own. The community rightfully believes that if adhered to, that document, more than any other, has the potential to define their future.

That outlook, which so profoundly shapes the Judean community in the Land of Israel, raises important questions for Jews not living on the land. Ezra-Nehemiah clearly emphasizes the movement from beyond the land inward, and the critical document from Nehemiah 10 sees life on the land as a core component of the religious experience. Nonetheless, we know that in the Persian period, the majority of the Jewish people lived outside the Land of Israel. Therefore, in the next chapter we will consider how the author of Ezra-Nehemiah addresses the chasm between the two communities and the potential to bridge it through his careful formulation of center and periphery.

---

82. Nehemiah 10:29.

Chapter Ten

Center and Periphery

WHAT IS SAID BY THAT WHICH IS NOT SAID

At the outset of this study, we discussed the three communities that developed in the aftermath of the Babylonian destruction of Jerusalem:[1] those who remained in the land after its conquest, those forcibly exiled to Babylon, and those who went down to Egypt, seemingly by choice rather than coercion.[2] Then, in the following chapters, we focused on the Land of Israel, specifically on its community of returnees and their efforts to reconstitute what was lost. We have paid only minimal attention to Jewish communities outside the borders of the land, and the few non-Judean Jews mentioned eventually ended up making their way to the land. This partiality was not accidental. Our study follows the text of Ezra-Nehemiah and, as such, delves into the details included about

---

1. Chapter two.
2. For a listing of some of the smaller, lesser-known communities, see Sara Japhet, "People and Land in the Restoration Period," in *From the Rivers of Babylon to the Highlands of Judah: Collected Studies on the Restoration Period* (Eisenbrauns, 2006), 99–100. For more on these communities and helpful footnotes, see John Kessler, "Persia's Loyal Yah-wists: Power Identity and Ethnicity in Achaemenid Yehud," in *Judah and the Judeans in the Persian Period* (2006), 91–121.

the community that Ezra-Nehemiah depicts.[3] That said, as students of Tanakh, we know that what is omitted from a text can reflect a work's ideology as much as what is included. So, in the penultimate chapter of this study, we shift our attention to what is *not* in the text of Ezra-Nehemiah and do our best to glean the ideological implications of those omissions.

PARTIAL RETURN AND RESPONSES TO IT

Early Israel's conception of God and, by extension, of sacred space, is influenced and redefined by the experience of exile. Prior to the exile, God is primarily conceived as dwelling in the Land of Israel, leaving prophets like Jeremiah and Ezekiel to emphasize God's universal character, and, in doing so, preventing the theological crisis that Israel's severance from the land could have potentially wrought. Those prophets remind the exiled Israelites that God is not restricted to their recently destroyed Temple, nor was He ever hemmed in by the land's geographical boundaries. "I shall be accessible to you," Jeremiah reassures the exiles on God's behalf.[4] That idea is likewise enforced by Ezekiel.[5] Those same prophets clarify from the outset that their words of solace are pertinent for only a limited time. "When you call upon Me and follow and pray to Me, I will hear you," Jeremiah consoles his audience. "And when you search you will find Me, if you seek Me with all your heart. I shall be accessible to you," he declares, quoting God. But those words of comfort are immediately followed by the ultimate consolation: "I shall bring back your captives and gather you from all the nations and from all the places to which I have driven you…I will bring you back to the place from which I have exiled you."[6] The prophets highlight that God's omnipresence enables the exiles to maintain a connection with Him regardless of where they are in the world, but they make equally clear that when the

---

3. The reverse partiality can be seen in the Book of Esther, for example, in which concern for the community of Jews in Israel is essentially undetectable.
4. Jeremiah 29:14. This prophecy (written between 597 and 586 BCE) is sent to those who are exiled with Jehoiachin (597 BCE) prior to the destruction of the Temple (see II Kings 24:8–17; II Chr. 36:9–10).
5. Ezekiel 11:16.
6. Jeremiah 29:12–14. See also 3:18, 16:14–15, 23:7–8, 29:10, 50:17–20, 28, 51:1–10, 45–53.

ideal reality is restored, God will be back in His land with His people.[7] Ezekiel's final prophecies, for instance, include a vision of God's rebuilt Temple in His land, alongside the charge that "this shall be the border according to which you shall give the land as inheritance to the twelve tribes of Israel."[8] Transmitting God's message, Isaiah refers to Cyrus as "My shepherd, fulfilling all My will, that he should tell Jerusalem, 'She shall be built,' and the Sanctuary, 'Let her be founded.'"[9]

This dual notion of God's presence in exile and His intention to return with His people to the land is alluded to in the opening of Ezra-Nehemiah. There, a foreign king's spirit is "stirred" by God, and that king is inspired to proclaim that "whoever is among you from all His people, may his God be with him, and let him go up to Jerusalem, in Judah."[10] Despite prophetic design, relatively few Jews actually return. Whether Cyrus anticipates the low response rate is not known. However, what we do know is that his charter accounts for those who choose to remain: "As for anyone left behind in the place where he lives, his townsmen shall aid him." As instructed, those who do not return to build the Temple support those who do "with vessels of silver, gold, supplies, beasts of burden, and precious goods, aside from gifts which had been donated."[11]

---

7. Jeremiah, for example, speaks about topics including the restoration of Israel and Judah (Jer. 30:1–17), the rebuilding of Jerusalem (Jer. 30:18–31:1, 38–40), the repopulation of the land (Jer. 31:2–25), a renewed covenant between God and the people (Jer. 31:31–34), Jeremiah's redemption of family property (Jer. 32:6–15), and the restoration of Davidides and Levitical priests (Jer. 33:14–26). Ezekiel, too, speaks of the installation of a Davidic leader (Ezek. 34:17–31), the repopulation of the hills of Israel (Ezek. 36:1–15), rejuvenation of the people (Ezek. 37:1–14), the reunification of Israel and Judah under David (Ezek. 37:14–26), a new Temple (Ezek. 40:1–47:12), and new tribal allotments and tribal locations (Ezek. 47:13–48:3). For more extensive coverage of this topic, see Gary Knoppers, "Exile, Return and Diaspora: Expatriates and Repatriates in Late Biblical Literature," in *Texts, Contexts and Readings in Postexilic Literature* (2011), 29–61.
8. Ezekiel 47:13.
9. Isaiah 44:28.
10. Ezra 1:1–3.
11. Ibid., v. 6.

For some Second Temple authors, just as the meager Temple and lack of political sovereign proves disappointing, so does this partial return. Since the prophets speak of a mass return in which God will "gather in the scattered ones of Israel from all four edges of the world,"[12] and "the children of Judah and the children of Israel will gather together,"[13] and since they speak of a time when both Israel and Judah will be gathered by God "from the ends of the earth"[14] and Jerusalem will once again be "densely populated" by the "whole House of Israel,"[15] the fractional return of the Jewish people feels inadequate. Just as they respond to the other restoration-period disappointments by claiming that the true redemption has not yet manifested,[16] some Second Temple authors employ the same approach to contend with the incomplete restoration.[17] Zechariah, for example, attempts to console his audience by claiming that while a complete ingathering has not yet transpired, in the future God will "strengthen the House of Judah and deliver the House of Joseph."[18] God, Zechariah assures them, will bring His people back "from the land of Egypt; from Assyria ... gather them in and bring them to the land of Gilad and Lebanon."[19] And when He does, the prophet assures his disillusioned audience, "the city squares will be full and alive

---

12. Isaiah 11:11–12. In those verses, Jeremiah speaks of the ingathering of "those who remain, from Assyria and Egypt, from Patros and from Kush, from Eilam and from Shinar, Hamat and the islands of the sea," referring to places as far as Egypt, Iran, Mesopotamia, and Syria.

13. Hosea 2:2.

14. Jeremiah 30–31 envisions a mass return marked by divine blessing, repopulation, prosperity, and national unity.

15. Ezekiel 36:10. See also chapter 37 and chapters 47–48.

16. See chapter four.

17. Michael Knibb suggests that some Second Temple works point to a belief that even after they return, the Jews remain in a spiritual state of exile. In such a conceptual framework, the people could be both in the land and in exile simultaneously. Michael A. Knibb, "The Exile in the Literature of the Intertestamental Period," in *Essays on the Book of Enoch and Other Early Jewish Texts and Traditions* (2009), 191–212.

18. Zechariah 10:6.

19. Ibid., v. 10.

with young boys and girls playing."[20] The full, final return, Zechariah insists, is yet to come.

Some scholars, going a step further, identify a critique of this Jewish inaction within certain Second Temple works.[21] John Kessler, for example, argues that Zechariah's heavy emphasis on geography in his first eight chapters shows the prophet implicitly condemning the people's lack of desire to return. In Kessler's opinion, "Geographical designations serve as highly significant markers of identity and ultimate destiny. In a profound way, they define the people of God in terms of where they are, where they have come from, and where they ultimately will be." As Kessler sees it, from the perspective of Zechariah, "Diaspora is a fundamentally aberrant phenomenon – a manifestation of the brokenness of the relationship between God and his people. As such, no other destiny is feasible than its ultimate dissolution by a full and definitive return to Zion on the part of all Diaspora members." [22] The Jews who remain in Babylon after Cyrus's decree would not fulfill this charge.

In a similar vein, Isaiah encourages the Babylonian community to "go forth from Babylon,"[23] following that exhortation with a rendering

---

20. Ibid. 8:5–8, 10:6–12.
21. There is certainly evidence that the Rabbis and later commentators are critical of this partial return. See, for example, the claim in Yoma 9b that the reason the *Shekhina* (Divine Presence) does not reside in the Second Temple is due to the failure of all the Jews to return. Rabbi Judah HaLevi similarly blames the less-than-ideal conditions of the Second Temple on the people's apathy. In his famous work the *Kuzari,* he writes, "Divine providence was ready to restore everything as it had been at first if they had all willingly consented to return. But only a part was ready to do so, while the majority and the aristocracy remained in Babel, preferring dependence and slavery, and unwilling to leave their houses and their affairs" (*Kuzari*, II:24). The Malbim goes so far as to claim that had all of the Jews returned, Zerubbabel would have been the Messiah (Malbim, Hag. 1:1).
22. For more on this topic and evidence of this critical theme and its messaging, see John Kessler, "The Diaspora in Zechariah 1–8 and Ezra-Nehemiah: The Role of History, Social Location, and Tradition in the Formulation of Identity," in *Community Identity in Judean Historiography* (2009), 119–45. There, Kessler develops the idea that the "foundational narrative continuum" in Zechariah "is thus: sin > judgment > dispersion > partial return to the land > cataclysmic intervention of [God] > full return and end of Diaspora" (p. 137).
23. Isaiah 48:20.

of the ideal exilic community.[24] That ideal community, as Antti Laato explains, is depicted as one "whose mission is to restore Israel and exhort other exiles who have not yet put their confidence in God's salvation to return to Zion."[25] While Isaiah does not explicitly condemn those who do not return, they clearly fall short. Even the Book of Esther, which seems indifferent to the affairs in the Land of Israel, has been interpreted by some scholars as a satirical reproof of the Jews who fail to return to Israel and build the Temple.[26]

EZRA-NEHEMIAH'S (UN?)CHARACTERISTIC RESPONSE

Ezra-Nehemiah makes no such claims. The opening of the work records that only a portion of those who hear Cyrus's decree go back to the land, and that fact is not followed with any critical assessment. Some Jews return to the land, Ezra-Nehemiah tells us, and some stay behind in Babylon, but the incomplete nature of the return does not hinder the program of restoration. Likewise, those who do not return are not condemned; they are simply recorded as a matter of fact.

It is not surprising that the work does not gauge its depicted reality relative to earlier prophecies. One of Ezra-Nehemiah's distinguishing features, which we have examined already, is its choice to focus on its

---

24. Ibid., chapter 49.
25. Antti Laato, "The Composition of Isaiah 40–55," *Journal of Biblical Literature* 109, no. 2 (1990): 207–28.
26. See, for example, the thesis of Menachem Leibtag, "Megillat Esther and Its Hidden Message," Tanach Study Center, https://tanach.org/special/purim/purim51. htm; and Jonathan Grossman, *Esther: The Outer Narrative and the Hidden Reading* (Penn State University Press, 2011). We also must keep in mind that in addition to the Jews who return because they believe the exile has ended and those who stay behind and initiate an exile-by-choice is a third group. That third group likely stays because they are convinced that, despite Cyrus's decree, the exile has not in fact ended. For more on this, see chapter four. For a contrasting view to this approach, see the writings of Aaron Koller in *Esther in Ancient Jewish Thought* (Cambridge University Press, 2014) and "Negotiating Empire: Living Jewishly under the Achaemenids in Persia and Palestine," in *Iran, Israel, and the Jews: Symbiosis and Conflict from the Achaemenids to the Islamic Republic*, ed. Aaron Koller and Daniel Tsadik (Pickwick, 2019), 3–23.

period's latent potential rather than its shortcomings.[27] At the same time, though, the work does not hesitate to critique its audience. Therefore, on issues over which the people have no control, such as sovereignty, economic stability, and the splendor of the Temple, rather than passing judgment, the work encourages its audience to make the most of an imperfect scenario. On the other hand, when it comes to intermarriage, lack of biblical literacy, and callous treatment of the poor, the work makes clear that the people must do better. These verdicts, sometimes explicit, sometimes subtle, are not reserved for express violations of Torah laws. They are found equally in cases where the people simply do not fall in line with the ideals the work esteems. When Nehemiah arrives in Jerusalem and sees the "dismal state with Jerusalem in ruins and her gates having been put to the torch,"[28] for example, he rallies the people to rebuild the wall and prevent further degradation in the eyes of their adversaries. Nehemiah does not quote a biblical ruling to support the undertaking, but students of Ezra-Nehemiah discern from the tone of his memoir that the community's ability to defend itself is a virtue, and those that accept Judean susceptibility as a norm are implicitly censured.[29] Along similar lines, those who move from the outskirts of Jerusalem inward are candidly evaluated by their peers. Toward the end of the work, we learn that "the people blessed all those who volunteered to settle in Jerusalem,"[30] thus communicating to the reader that living in and protecting Jerusalem is highly regarded.

That is why it *is* surprising that Ezra-Nehemiah assumes a neutral stance in regard to those who choose to remain in Babylon, particularly because the work asserts on more than one occasion that a return to the land denotes the fulfillment of God's promise to His people. In fact, the book's opening words give voice to that very contention.[31] Just before Nehemiah embarks on his journey back to the land, he similarly

---

27. See chapter four.
28. Nehemiah 2:17.
29. That credo is further supported when Nehemiah invokes God as he galvanizes the people to "fight for your kinsmen, for your sons and daughters, your wives, and your homes" (Neh. 4:8).
30. Nehemiah 11:2.
31. "In the first year of Cyrus, king of Persia, when the Lord's word pronounced by

concedes to God that "I and my father's house have also sinned. We have injured You grievously and have not kept the commandments, statutes, and laws with which You charged Moses, Your servant." Nehemiah then recalls the charge God issues, saying, "You will break faith; I will disperse you among the nations – yet you will return to Me; you will keep My commandments and observe them. If you should be expelled to the farthest of horizons, even from there I will gather them, bringing them to the place where I have chosen to house My name."[32]

The notion that going to the land is commendable, regardless of prophetic fulfillment, is also indicated in the work. In his memoirs, Ezra explains why he does not ask for a royal escort to protect him and his entourage on their journey toward the land. He writes, "I was ashamed to ask the king for a detachment of soldiers and cavalry to protect us from enemies on the journey, since we had already said to the king: 'The hand of our God is upon those who seek Him in their favor,'"[33] implying that if God protects those who fulfill His wishes, then a royal escort for those returning to the land would be extraneous because the act of return itself would garner the necessary protection. While Nehemiah's job compels him to live near the Persian throne,[34] the fact that the book records that he twice requests leave so that he can go to Jerusalem likewise indicates that in the minds of the two men for whom the book is named, living in the land is ideal. In depicting the experience of being allowed back to their land, Ezra writes, "Our God has rekindled the light in our eyes."[35] The historical retrospectives offered by both Ezra and Nehemiah concur that the Land of Israel is the ultimate destination of the Jewish people.[36]

Jeremiah had come to pass, the Lord stirred the spirit of Cyrus, king of Persia, and he issued a proclamation throughout his kingdom, by word of mouth and written word as well" (Ezra 1:1).

32. Nehemiah 1:6–10.

33. Ezra 8:22.

34. Nehemiah 2:6 and 13:6 make it clear that, unlike a majority of the Jews, he needs direct royal consent to leave his post in Persia.

35. Ezra 9:8.

36. See Ezra 9 and Nehemiah 9.

Despite their seemingly categorical outlook, at no point does either of those opinionated leaders disapprove of the Jews who remain behind in Babylon. Even in instances when a critique may seem fitting, none is apparent. On his way to Jerusalem, for example, Ezra mentions that he "noted the presence of Israelites and priests, but I did not find any of the Levites there." Rather than reacting accusatorily to that fact, Ezra goes on to explain that he "called upon Eliezer, Ariel, Shemaiah, Elnathan, Jarib, Elnathan, Nathan, Zechariah, and Meshullam, who were leaders, as well as Joiarib and Elnathan, who were teachers. I charged them with the task of approaching Ido, the master of a place called Casiphia. I placed words in their mouths to relay to Ido and his brother, Netinim in Casiphia, requesting that they send us men to serve in the House of our God."[37] The complacency of the Levites is insinuated but not denounced. Looking back at the earliest phases of the restoration, we similarly find that the inaugural leaders of the era, Zerubbabel, Jeshua, and Sheshbazzar, do not comment on the matter. The narrator of the work is equally silent throughout, which leaves readers of Ezra-Nehemiah wondering why a text so otherwise forthright about its ideals and values appears taciturn about the Jews that do not heed Cyrus's divinely inspired call.

SUGGESTED REASONS FOR A LACK OF CRITIQUE

Some scholars have suggested that this lack of reproach stems from the Judean community's dependence on its Babylonian counterpart. Drawing on a colonial model to depict the dynamic between the two communities, Peter Bedford claims that the relationship between the Judean and Babylonian Diaspora community was "an unequal relationship of parent community and colony." Bedford argues that "in Ezra-Nehemiah the community of repatriates is not in a position to develop an identity independent of its parent Diaspora community,"[38] and, as such, the work is careful not to offend or alienate its "parent community" by criticizing it. But this argument is unfounded. While select biblical texts do indicate

---

37. Ezra 8:16–18.
38. Peter Bedford, "Diaspora and Homeland Relations in Ezra-Nehemiah," *Vetus Testamentum* 52, no. 2 (2002): 147–65.

some degree of communication between the two communities,[39] as John Kessler rightly argues, there is no indication in Ezra-Nehemiah of "the Babylonian Diaspora community, which had its own inner governance structures, exercising the kind of managerial control over the Repatriate community that would be done in a full-blown 'colonial' context."[40]

Others suggest the opposite of that argument. They claim that the conspicuous silence of the work on the matter of return reflects a more generalized disinterest in the Diaspora community. Sarah Japhet, for example, claims that Ezra-Nehemiah "professes a distinct definition of 'we,' the community in which Israel's existence and survival is represented. This is the community of the 'Exile,' the people from Judah, Benjamin, and Levi who came to settle in Judah. Ezra-Nehemiah displays no interest in the fortunes of the Diaspora as such. The Jews of the Diaspora are referred to primarily as a 'source' of returnees."[41] Japhet's argument draws attention to the noteworthy fact that Ezra-Nehemiah does not inform its audience about goings-on in the Diaspora. But as we will see, this seeming lack of concern is anything but. The work's muted response to the sparse return from the Diaspora does not derive from its fear of isolation, nor does it stem from disinterest. On the contrary, the approach reflects a conscious attempt to simultaneously enfranchise the Babylonian Diaspora and unambiguously claim Jerusalem's eminence. That dual message, threaded throughout the work, reflects the author's awareness of the fragile line history created and the sensitivity with which it should be toed.

WHAT THE BABYLONIAN COMMUNITY MEANT TO THE PEOPLE

The fragility of that line is partially accounted for by the fact that the Babylonian exile, tragic and challenging as it was, had become a status

---

39. See, for example, Jeremiah 29, 51:59–60; Zechariah 2:10–17; Ezekiel 24:1–2, 26–27, 33:21.
40. Kessler, "The Diaspora in Zechariah 1–8 and Ezra-Nehemiah," 13–40.
41. Sara Japhet, "Post-Exilic Historiography: How and Why?" in *From the Rivers of Babylon*, 318.

symbol. That status was devised originally by pre-exilic and exilic prophets to deflect mistaken notions about those exiled and those left in the land. In time, it became integrated into the exiles' self-conception, taking shape shortly after the first wave of the Jerusalem exile in 597 BCE,[42] when Jeremiah receives a prophetic vision in which he sees "two baskets of figs placed before the Temple of the Lord.... In one basket were very fine figs, like well-ripened figs; in the other basket were very bad figs, so they could not be eaten."[43] Articulating the significance of the vision, God tells Jeremiah that "like these fine figs, so will I show favor to the exiles of Judah whom I have sent forth from this place to the land of the Chaldeans for their benefit. I will watch over them benevolently and bring them back to this land; I will build them up and not tear them down; I will plant them and not uproot them."[44] But, "of the bad figs," God explains, "like those I will make Zedekiah, king of Judah, his officers, and the remnant of Jerusalem that has remained in this land, and those who dwell in the land of Egypt. I will make them a horror, and evil, for all the kingdoms of the earth; a disgrace and an epithet, a sharp word and a curse, in all the places to which I shall banish them. And I will send against them the sword and famine and pestilence until they are finished off within the land which I gave them and their fathers."[45] Lest anyone think that the Jews who evade exile are the lucky ones or God's "preferred" people, Jeremiah's symbolic prophecy makes clear that the opposite is true. Those who are exiled will be watched over by God, while those who remain in the land will be neglected and ravaged by evil.

Ezekiel refutes the same mistaken assumption and, in doing so, perpetuates the polarity that Jeremiah establishes. Responding to the false claim that those who were exiled were "far from the Lord," Ezekiel reassures them that not only were they not rejected by God but that God would devotedly escort them into exile.[46] While Ezekiel's prophecy is

---

42. The exile includes the king along with a contingent of artisans and smiths (see II Kings 24:14).
43. Jeremiah 24:2.
44. Ibid., vv. 5–6.
45. Ibid., vv. 8–10.
46. Ezekiel 11:14–16. In Ezekiel's prophecy as well, the people left in the land assume that they are saved on merit, and as such they even go so far as to claim that "the

not initially explicit in his condemnation of those who remain in the land, he does mention that when the exiles return, they will have to "remove all the detestable things, all the abominations,"[47] implying that the population that remains in the land will continue the practices that brought about the exile in the first place. Or, as John Kessler summarizes the prophet's comments, "Through subtle implication the locus of hope is identified with those in exile, while the land is viewed as experiencing ongoing pollution until their return."[48]

In chapter 33, Ezekiel is far less subtle. There, after rebuking them for their unremitting sins, saying, "You eat with the blood, you lift your eyes up to your idols, you shed blood.... You stood by your sword, you practiced abominations, each of you defiled others' wives," the prophet turns to those who remain in the Land and sarcastically asks, "and you would inherit the land?"[49] He makes it abundantly clear that the only answer to his question is an unequivocal "no" and then continues: "So says the Lord God: As I live, those who are in the ruins will fall by the sword; those who are in the open field I will give over to animals as food; those who are in strongholds and caves will die by plague. I will hand the land over to waste and desolation, the majesty of her power will cease to be, the mountains of Israel will be desolate, none will pass through, and they will know that I am the Lord when I hand the land over to waste and desolation because of all the abominations they practiced."[50]

---

land has been given to us as a possession" (v. 15).

47. Ibid., v. 18.

48. John Kessler, "Images of Exile: Representations of the 'Exile' and 'Empty land' in the Sixth to Fourth Century BCE Yehudite Literature," in *The Concept of Exile in Ancient Israel and Its Historical Contexts* (De Gruyter, 2010), 309–51.

49. Ezekiel 33:25–26.

50. Ibid., vv. 27–29. Dalit Rom-Shiloni identifies the chronological development of the exile-remnant polarity within prophetic works. She distinguishes between those prophets who speak exclusively of the Jehoiachin exiles as the "people of God" and those that are more inclusive, taking the exiles from 586 BCE into account as well as those from the Northern Kingdom. For an extensive discussion of the different tendencies apparent during the various prophetic periods, see Dalit Rom-Shiloni, "Group Identities in Jeremiah," 11–46.

The aggregate of the prophets' messages is both conclusive and ironic: exile will save the people.[51]

The reason for that conclusion was discussed in chapter three. If obstinacy and hubris led the people to sin with abandon, never considering the ramifications of their choices, then rehabilitation would only come through the experience of utter vulnerability. And in fact, anticipating the exile, God depicts that process of tribulation and reformation: "I will bring such insecurity into their hearts in their enemies' lands that the sound of a windblown leaf will make them run as if they fled the sword; and they will fall, though no one is chasing them. They will stumble over one another as if fleeing the sword, when no one chases them. You will have no power to stand before your enemies. ... But if they confess their sins and those of their ancestors – their trespass against Me and their walking contrary to Me, which made Me walk contrary to them, bringing them into their enemies' lands – if their obstinate hearts are humbled and they atone for their sin, then I will remember My covenant with Jacob; and My covenant with Isaac and My covenant with Abraham I will also remember, and I will remember the land."[52] Jeremiah as well expresses a similar divine claim about the reparative effects of exile: "I will grant them heart to know Me, for I am the Lord. They will be My people, and I will be their God, for they will return to Me with all their heart."[53] Ezekiel, too, verbalizes God's avowal that after the people endure the exile, He will "remove the heart of stone from their flesh and give them a heart of flesh, so that they will follow My decrees and keep My laws and fulfill them; they will be My people, and I will be their God."[54] Exile, from the biblical perspective, is both a horrifying punishment and

---

51. It is interesting to note that the same sentiment is not applied to the community that ends up in Egypt. In fact, Jeremiah harshly condemns those who flee to Egypt for not submitting to Babylon as God commanded and for their corrupt religious practices (Jer. 42–44). If the prophets believe the exile to Babylon would be a corrective experience, the same is not assumed about Egypt.
52. Leviticus 26:36–42.
53. Jeremiah 24:7.
54. Ezekiel 11:19–20.

an unparalleled opportunity for religious maturation.[55] As such, those who withstand the remedial effects of exile constitute a distinct group.

THE DIFFERENCE BETWEEN EXILE AND DIASPORA AND THE CHALLENGE THAT DISTINCTION POSES

The moment Cyrus grants the exiles the opportunity to return to their native land, Jewish history as it exists until that point changes because, with Cyrus's decree, the reality of a forced exile ceases to exist. In its stead rises the unprecedented fact of Diaspora-by-choice.[56] To some, the distinction between exile and Diaspora may appear subtle enough to be insignificant. In fact, for the Jews who remain in Babylon, the new diasporic existence is largely indistinguishable from its exilic predecessor.[57] But from the perspective of biblical authors, sensitive to the theological import of exile and return, the two predicaments could not be more different. If exile is a religious phenomenon of God's making, the Diaspora is a historical reality bred by people's choice to remain outside their land.

That choice was clearly not endorsed by the prophets. But the author of Ezra-Nehemiah, writing when the Diaspora was an established way of life, has to take that reality into consideration. He cannot risk alienating the Diaspora with harsh critiques of its choices and their consequences. He knows that a group of people not anchored to its land can easily disappear within a few generations.[58] Therefore, an underlying objective

---

55. For a discussion of the ways in which the experience of exile influences a group's religious identity, see Daniel L. Smith-Christopher, *The Religion of the Landless: The Social Context of the Babylonian Exile* (Wipf and Stock, 2015), especially 128–59.

56. For a discussion of the distinction between the two, see James M. Scott, "Exile and Self-Understanding of Diaspora Jews in the Greco-Roman Period," in *Exile: Old Testament, Jewish, and Christian Concepts* (Brill, 1997), 173–218.

57. There is no reason to assume that the day-to-day lives of Jews in Babylon changed after the decree.

58. The northern tribes, for example, were largely lost to history within a short period of time. The community at Elephantine maintains ongoing contact with the community in Judah. For some interesting insights on the dynamic between the communities, see Lisa J. Cleath, "Colonial Identity in the Jedaniah Archive at Elephantine," (2019). This understanding of the need to tether a people to the land is visible in rabbinic literature as well. See, for example, Ze'ev Safrai, "The

of Ezra-Nehemiah is maintaining cohesion between the Judean and the Babylonian Diaspora communities.[59] For that reason, as we saw in chapter seven, Ezra-Nehemiah champions a recasting of Jewish identity to include those who live beyond the geographical boundaries of the land. But it goes further than that as well.

The work asserts that true religious leadership emanates from Babylon. All the restoration leaders extolled in Ezra-Nehemiah come from Babylon. In the first wave of return, Sheshbazzar brings the concrete, religious symbols that enable the Judeans to reinstate the cult and works alongside Zerubbabel and Jeshua who, together, restore political order and ritual to the land. Then, in the various phases of the second wave, the leaders bring with them the less tangible but equally important contributions of scriptural expertise, which inspires the Judeans' religious revolution. Ezra brings Torah law to a land depicted as an otherwise "lawless" state. And the very fact that he has a Torah to bring, as Gary Knoppers points out, "presupposes, of course, that the community in Babylon had a Torah scroll and that Ezra (and others) not only read (or recited) it but also made a point of studying it."[60] Whether the same can be said for the Judean community prior to Ezra's arrival is unknown, further accentuating what the work believes the Babylonian community has to offer.

Nehemiah, too, whose position is more political in nature, ensures that Torah law is upheld long after the group that gathers at the Water Gate has disbanded. Of course, the grassroots leadership made up of Judah's laity plays a critical role in all stages of the restoration. Still, the

---

Land in Rabbinic Literature," in *Seeking Out the Land: Land of Israel Traditions in Ancient Jewish, Christian and Samaritan Literature (200 BCE–400 CE)* (Brill, 2018), 76–203; Burton L. Visotzky, "Some Aspects of Rabbinic Literature on Holy Land and Covenant," *Studies in Christian-Jewish Relations* 8, no. 1 (2013).

59. No overt attention is paid to the Egyptian Diaspora in Ezra-Nehemiah. This could be attributed to the adoption of the aforementioned prophetic stance vis-à-vis those who fled to Egypt (see chapter two).

60. Gary N. Knoppers and Kenneth A. Ristau, eds., *Community Identity in Judean Historiography: Biblical and Comparative Perspectives* (Penn State University Press, 2009), 156.

principal characters formally appointed and acknowledged as the leaders of their generations are all of Babylonian origin.

This should not surprise us, because if the exile is a window in time in which people found their way back to God and to the fundamentals of Israelite belief, then those returning from Babylon should naturally possess the clarity of thought and purpose that developed during that exile. Ezra's inclination to fast and pray by the Ahava River[61] is a minor but pertinent indication of the evolution Jewish religion underwent in Babylon and of the potential impact those returning could have on the Judean community. It is an example of a "a certain kind of piety that is especially appropriate to an exilic setting but need not be exclusive to that setting,"[62] further confirming that the byproducts of exile are those most fit to lead.

BENEI HAGOLA: LITERAL AND FIGURATIVE "RETURNEES"

For that matter, Ezra-Nehemiah purports, they are also the ones most fit to rebuild Judean society, which is why various terms for the concept of "returned exiles" depict the people who rebuild Jerusalem, even if not all of them were ever actually in Babylon.[63] Noting this idiosyncratic

---

61. Ezra 8:21.
62. Expounding on this topic, Gary Knoppers writes: "Residing in Babylon over the generations, the Judean community had to make a number of adjustments. Ezra's immediate priestly predecessors were not able to serve at the Jerusalem Temple, yet they could maintain a priestly succession as if they still had access to the temple. Members of the Diaspora could not easily journey to the Jerusalem Sanctuary to bring offerings there, but they could send gifts and tribute to the Temple (Ezra 1:4, 6; 7:16; 8:25–30). Given Ezra's geographical location, it would not be feasible for Ezra to offer sacrifices at the Jerusalem Temple. Nevertheless, he is able to study sacrifices in the book that prescribes how sacrifices are to be offered (Ezra 7:10–11)." Knoppers, *Community Identity in Judean Historiography*, 157–58. Knoppers uses the word "exilic" where we might say "diasporic," as Ezra and Nehemiah return over a century after Cyrus's decree.
63. See, for example, Ezra 2:1, 3:8, 4:1, 6:16, 19–21, 9:4, 10:6–8, 16; Nehemiah 7:6, 8:17. Repatriates who had been in the land for three or four generations still identified as "those who had returned from exile."

terminological feature, Sara Japhet notes that "80 years after Cyrus and over 60 years after Darius, people settled in Judah and Jerusalem are designated 'the exiles.' The possibility of using such a designation at such a late date is of interest from the historical point of view, but all the more so for the understanding of the book's peculiar stand regarding the people's identity." To be sure, as Japhet acknowledges, "in the course of the story the people are also called 'Israel,' 'all Israel,' or 'the people of Judah and Benjamin,'" but as she goes on to clarify, those terms, "by being equated with the ones mentioned above, make the outlook of the book even clearer: The people of Judah and Benjamin, the people of Israel are exiles, that is – returnees from the Babylonian exile."[64]

That outlook helps explain why only Jews from Babylon are recorded as returning to Jerusalem, even though Cyrus issued his proclamation "throughout his kingdom."[65] It also explains why the census at the outset of the book only records "the people of the province, coming up from the captivity of the exile";[66] why, upon the Temple's completion in the days of Darius, we are told that the "returning exiles sacrificed the Passover offering on the fourteenth day of the first month";[67] and why, when Nehemiah arrives in Jerusalem and looks for a register of citizens, he finds and chronicles the "genealogical record of those who first came up."[68]

The author of Ezra-Nehemiah is well aware that the returnees are not the *only* people occupying the land during the restoration period. He is under no illusions about the presence of people in the land, nor does he try, through his historical retelling, to generate a "myth" that the land was completely devoid of Israelite descendants prior to the exiles' homecoming.[69] What he is mindful of, though, is the deep-rooted sentiment,

---

64. Japhet, "People and Land," 110.
65. Ezra 1:1–6.
66. Ibid. 2:1.
67. Ibid. 6:19.
68. Nehemiah 7:5.
69. For some of the diverging literature on this topic, see Robert P. Carroll, "The Myth of the Empty Land," *Semeia* 59 (1992): 79–93; Ehud Ben Zvi, "Inclusion in and Exclusion from Israel as Conveyed by the Use of the Term 'Israel' in Post-Monarchic Biblical Texts," in *The Pitcher Is Broken* (1995), 95–149; Hans M. Barstad, "The Myth

formulated by the prophets and internalized by the people, that only those who grappled with the exile are worthy of rebuilding in its wake.

Rather than allowing for a scenario where those who are left in the land are shunned by those returning, the author of Ezra-Nehemiah broadens the implications of "returnee" to include those who physically return from exile *and* those who, religiously speaking, return from their pre-exilic, apostate status. For example, the text stresses that the exiles commemorate their first Passover in the completed Temple, and that group celebrating includes the "Israelites who returned from the exile... along with all those who separated themselves from the impurity of the nations of the land and came to worship the Lord, God of Israel."[70]

---

of the Empty Land: A Study in the History and Archaeology of Judah during the 'Exilic' Period" (Oslo, 1996); Adele Berlin, "The Exile. Biblical Ideology and Its Postmodern Ideological Interpretation," in *Literary Construction of Identity in the Ancient World* (2010), 341–56; John Kessler, "Images of Exile: Representations of the 'Exile' and 'Empty Land' in the Sixth to Fourth Century BCE Yehudite Literature," in *The Concept of Exile in Ancient Israel and Its Historical Contexts* (De Gruyter, 2010), 309–51; Ehud Ben Zvi, "The Voice and Role of a Counterfactual Memory in the Construction of Exile and Return: Considering Jeremiah 40:7–12," in *Social Memory among the Literati of Yehud* (2019), 612–30; Ehud Ben Zvi, "Total Exile, Empty Land and the General Intellectual Discourse in Yehud," in *Social Memory among the Literati of Yehud* (2019), 599–611.

70. Ezra 6:21. Some explain the verse (and its parallel in Nehemiah 10:29–30) as referring to non-Judeans who left their pagan ways (see Kiddushin 70a; Japhet, "People and Land," 117; Kessler, "Persia's Loyal Yah-wists," 91–121). But that reading stands in opposition to a central ideological concern of the work. A more compelling explanation, and one that is more consistent with the exclusivist stance of Ezra-Nehemiah, uses the grammar, syntax, and context of the verse to prove that it is describing the separation of the returnees from the impurity of the nations and not their inclusion. This reading is based on the understanding of the *waw* in the verse to be as a *waw explicativum* rather than a coordinative *waw*. (A *waw explicativum* "introduces a clause or phrase that clarifies, expands, or paraphrases the clause that precedes it.") Thus, rather than the verse reading "And all the sons of Israel, who had returned from exile, *and* all who separated themselves from the impurity of the nations of the land, ate..." it would read, "And all the sons of Israel who had returned from the exile, *that is,* those who had separated themselves from the impurity of the nations of the land." The use of this *waw* is fairly common in Tanakh and is found in Ezra 6:9, 8:18. In addition to the grammatical evidence, the verse preceding 6:21 speaks of three groups for whom the Passover festival is prepared, and nowhere on that list are the proselytes mentioned, lending further proof to

Similarly, when Ezra reintroduces the Torah to the community, we are told that he "brought the Torah before the congregation – men and women and all who could understand what they heard."[71] In addition, when Nehemiah 10 describes the public oath taking, he includes the leaders "and the rest of the people and the priests, Levites, gatekeepers, singers, and Netinim, and all those who had separated themselves from the peoples of the lands to be with God's Torah, with their wives, their sons, and their daughters."[72]

Thus, contrary to those who claim that equating the term "returnees" with "Israel" and "Judah" is a tool employed by the exclusivist author of Ezra-Nehemiah to exclude non-repatriates,[73] what we find instead is that the words "return" and "exile" undergo a semantic evolution in Ezra-Nehemiah. Both words transcend their once strictly geographical connotations to include the religious experience of exile and return, regardless of physical location. In Ezra-Nehemiah, to be considered a "returnee from exile," one does not necessarily had to have left the country at all. While not ignoring the claims of Jeremiah and Ezekiel, Ezra-Nehemiah interprets their messages in a less literal way than they were originally understood, thus creating space for those who behave as if they have internalized the lessons of exile. As a result, those who would otherwise be excluded from the community of exiles extolled by the prophets are, in due course, incorporated into that "superior" community.[74]

---

the assertion that rather than speaking of two different groups, 6:21 contains two descriptions of the same group. For more on this, and a fuller understanding of the word אלהם in the context of this reading, see Matthew Thiessen, "The Function of a Conjunction: Inclusivist or Exclusivist Strategies in Ezra 6:19–21 and Nehemiah 10:29–30?," *Journal for the Study of the Old Testament* 34, no. 1 (2009): 63–79. See also David Janzen, *Witch-Hunts, Purity and Social Boundaries: The Expulsion of the Foreign Women in Ezra 9–10*, vol. 350 (A & C Black, 2002), 95.

71. Nehemiah 8:2.

72. Verse 29.

73. See, for example, Gary Knoppers, "Ethnicity, Genealogy, Geography, and Change: The Judean Communities of Babylon, and Jerusalem in the Story of Ezra," in *Community Identity in Judean Historiography* (2009), 147–71.

74. As Rom-Shiloni points out: "Incorporation (A + B = A) is a sociological strategy suggested by a community which considers itself dominant. While it is certainly an inclusive strategy, it maintains a clear hierarchical relationship between itself

Readers of Ezra-Nehemiah are thus left with an appreciation for the creative ways in which its author endeavors to unite the various groups of Jews that are no longer as organically cohesive as they once were. Prior to the exile, the people of Israel shared a land and a common history,[75] but exile creates a new "multicentric" reality.[76] In that new world, the once-Israelites find themselves in different lands and with different experiences, practices, and priorities.[77] Recognizing that new reality for the quandary that it was, the author of Ezra-Nehemiah attempts to integrate those who went to Babylon and stayed, those who went and came back, and those who never left in the first place. He does so by focusing on the features they share rather than on those they do not. As we saw in chapter seven, by redefining the parameters of Jewishness to include those who are genealogically Jewish, he ensures that the Jews living in Babylon are considered part of the people, regardless of the fact that they do not live in the land. By expanding the implications of the words "exiles" and "returnees," he further ensures that, regardless of their history, individuals of Israelite descent who want to partake in the community are deemed sufficiently rehabilitated to do so.

UNITED AROUND A CENTRUM

But if the work conveys, through its creative use of language and story-telling, that the two major communities at the time are parts of a whole, it also conveys that the epicenter of that whole is Jerusalem.[78] When

---

and its subordinate communities, and demands full acceptance of its own theology, worship, and political institutions." Dalit Rom-Shiloni, "Group Identities in Jeremiah," 26.

75. Jacob Wright points out that every phase in biblical history begins with an integrated, territorially bound Israel. For example, Joshua 3:1; Judges 1:1; I Samuel 8:4; II Samuel 5:1. For more on this point, see Kelle, *Interpreting Exile*, 107.

76. Talmon, "Exile and Restoration," 112.

77. For articles that address these changes, see Davies, *The Cambridge History of Judaism: Volume 1*.

78. It goes without saying that the work does not claim Jerusalem to be the center of Jewish political power. We already noted in chapter six that the non-autonomous Judean community is almost completely dependent on the legislations issued from the throne in Persia. Still, Persia is not a Jewish political center of power any more

we first open the book, of course, that is not the case. Beginning in Persia where the Jewish audience is located, the work implies that, for the duration of the exile, that was the center. Correspondingly, Judah, the "far-off" land to which they are allowed to return, is the implied periphery. But then, the work traces a series of movements by groups and individuals that effectively reverse those categories. The totality of Ezra-Nehemiah argues that while Judean identity has become "trans-temporal and international in scope" because of the exile,[79] post-exile, those international Jews should be moving toward the Land of Israel. Juha Pakkala, explaining the importance of the shift from Babylon to Judah, writes: "Centers and peripheries function as axes on which the events described in the story take place. When we are aware of these axes, we may better understand the background and context of the author."[80] To fully appreciate Ezra-Nehemiah, we must understand how the center becomes periphery and vice versa.[81]

---

than Israel is, as both communities are equally subject to the whims of the Persian emperors. One could argue that proximity to the seat of power grants power by extension, but there is no indication within the work that the community in Babylon is any better off than that in Israel. If anything, all we are told is that those with access to the throne use that access to help the Judean community.

79. Knoppers, *Priests, Prophets, and Promises,* 410.

80. Pakkala, "Centers and Peripheries," 170.

81. Whether the shift depicted in Ezra-Nehemiah is recognized by the Diaspora communities (or even by the Judeans themselves) is not known. But remains from extra-biblical documents may hold some clues. A fragmentary papyrus discovered in Elephantine known as "the Passover Papyrus" reveals an exchange between a Jerusalemite named Hananiah and Jedaniah, the head of the Jewish garrison in Elephantine. The letter, dated to 419 BCE, contains a reminder of the dates and stipulations of the festival. While much debate surrounds the content and motivation behind the letter, it seems to indicate that the community in Jerusalem sees itself as the center and feels responsible for the Jews in the Diaspora. Another letter dated to 407 BCE, known as the "Temple Papyrus," is sent from Yedaniah ben Gemariah, the leader of the Elephantine community, to the governor in Jerusalem asking him to intercede with the Persians on their behalf after their Temple has been destroyed. This letter too, seems to indicate a solidified Jerusalemite base. Stanley A. Cook, "The Significance of the Elephantine Papyri for the History of Hebrew Religion," *American Journal of Theology* 19, no. 3 (1915): 346–82; Bezalel Porten, *Archives from Elephantine: The Life of an Ancient Jewish Military Colony*

God Himself is the first and most important One in Ezra-Nehemiah to mark that shift. Referencing God in his proclamation, Cyrus declares, "The Lord, God of the heavens, has granted me all the kingdoms of the earth, and He has charged me to build Him a House in Jerusalem, in Judah."[82] In the next verse, he similarly proclaims, "the Lord, God of Israel, who is the God in Jerusalem."[83] The significance of the double epithet cannot be overstated.[84] As we recalled in the introduction to this chapter, the pre-exilic and exilic prophets make sure the Israelites know that while God is punishing them, He has not abandoned them. He had gone with them into exile,[85] and if they call to Him from wherever they are in the world, He will hear their prayers.[86] But if that theology is vital for the Jews who were uprooted from their homeland, it also carries the embedded risk of eliminating the need for a homeland altogether, which is why Cyrus's declaration at the opening of the work is so important: it acknowledges God's universal character without losing sight of His localized aspect emanating from Jerusalem. The movements the book traces follow that theological lead.

The first wave of returnees, for example, are described as "those whose spirit had been stirred by God," and the explicit motive for their departure is to "go up and build the House of the Lord, in Jerusalem."[87] And those people do not travel empty-handed. As we know, "their neighbors supported them,"[88] which is important as well. Within Persia at this time, there exists a "complex system of taxes, tribute, tolls, and gifts ... successfully employed by a succession of Achaemenid monarchs

---

(University of California Press, 1968), 128–33; Frank Moore Cross, "The Papyri and Their Historical Implications," in *Discoveries in the Wâdī ed-Dâliyeh* (1974), 17–29; Porten, *The Elephantine Papyri in English.*

82. Ezra 1:2.
83. Ibid., v. 3.
84. Elias Bickerman uses the "placement" of God in Jerusalem as proof of the text's authenticity, arguing that only a non-Jew would use the term "God of Israel" and confine that God to place. Elias J. Bickerman, "Edict of Cyrus," in *Studies in Jewish and Christian History* (Brill, 2007), 71–107.
85. Ezekiel 11.
86. Jeremiah 29.
87. Ezra 1:5.
88. Ibid., v. 6.

to enhance the prestige of their state and to direct largesse to the royal family and to those whom it favored in the aristocracy, the government, and the military."[89] In Ezra-Nehemiah, rather than that prestige returning to Persia, the gifts the Jews who remain give to those leaving for Jerusalem transfer the prestige in one direction only.[90] What is more, once those in Babylon hand over their donations, the scene shifts to Judah, where, with the help of the donations received, the people revive the center of Jewish ritual.

All subsequent waves of return follow that pattern. They begin in Persia, creating the initial sense that Persia is the center and Jerusalem the periphery. But then, a Jew or faithful group of Jews carries with them the goods, knowledge, or influence procured in Persia to reform, restructure, and enhance the homeland. Following their move, the Judean community they impact is discussed at length, whereas the community they left is almost entirely overlooked. When Ezra is introduced, for example, we learn about his Torah knowledge and scribal abilities, skills he undoubtedly learned in Persia. And yet we know nothing of how he uses those skills to contribute to Jewish life there. All we are told is that, as per Artaxerxes's directive, Ezra goes to Judah where he uses his education and training to transform the community.

Nehemiah's story is no different. It is obvious by the way he is introduced that he has a close working relationship with the most powerful man in Persia.[91] Yet, like Ezra, we are not told how he leverages that influence for Persian Jews. Instead, the first thing we learn about Nehemiah is that all the power and extravagances in the world are irrelevant to him so long as the fate of Judah is not secured. This is why, upon discovering that his brethren in Judah are "degraded and in dire stress," and that

---

89. Gary N. Knoppers, "The Construction of Judean and Diasporic Identity in Ezra-Nehemiah," *Journal of Hebrew Scriptures* 15 (2015): 13.
90. The work records the payment of taxes to the throne, but the fact that it opens with riches moving in the direction of Jerusalem is noteworthy from a literary perspective.
91. In Nehemiah 2:1–2, we learn that not only is Nehemiah Artaxerxes's wine bearer but also that the king knows him well enough to take an interest in him and ask what is troubling him when Nehemiah is preoccupied with the welfare of his brethren in Judah.

"Jerusalem's wall has been everywhere broken through, and her gates have been put to the torch,"[92] Nehemiah requests a leave of absence to help remedy the situation.

That backstory is exceptionally telling, both about who Nehemiah is and about what the author of Ezra-Nehemiah values in leaders. Many biblical heroes are introduced with backstories that help the reader understand why an otherwise unknown individual is fit for the task for which he or she is chosen. Moses, for example, displays exceptional sensitivity toward all humans and an intolerance of injustice,[93] critical traits in his role as liberator and law giver. David, who would become known as Israel's greatest warrior and most celebrated king, publicly proclaims his absolute dependence on God's powers and a desire to attribute his military victories to God rather than his own physical prowess.[94] Rebecca, Isaac's wife and the first woman to marry into Abraham's covenantal family, shows unmistakably that she, like her future father-in-law, is compassionate, welcoming, and open to self-sacrifice.[95] Like these and so many more, Nehemiah also has a backstory designating him worthy of leadership in the Persian period: his willingness to sacrifice what he has in the Diaspora to enhance the lives of the Jews in Judah.[96]

In each case, the community in Judah is depicted as deficient prior to the arrival of the leader or leaders. Before Sheshbazzar and Zerubbabel reach the land, there is no formalized worship. Prior to Ezra's arrival, the Judeans are religiously lawless. The political and security struggles that prompt Nehemiah's voyage are evident in the work as well. Nowhere in Ezra-Nehemiah is the claim made that life in Judah is perfect. Quite the opposite, in fact: throughout the rebuilding process in the text, the Judean community is rife with challenges and flaws. But the text also asserts that the skills, outlooks, and relationships cultivated in exile should be harvested and brought back to fertilize the renewed Jewish

---

92. Nehemiah 1:3–4.
93. Exodus 2:11–22.
94. I Samuel 17.
95. Genesis 24.
96. It is clear from the work that his leave of absence is necessarily temporary (Neh. 2:6, 13:6–7). Whether given the opportunity Nehemiah would have moved permanently is left to the reader's imagination.

center. As the work submits, just because the Jewish people and their religion can exist and even thrive outside of the land does not mean that they should.

Ezra is trained by what we must imagine are the great minds and religious teachers of the generation. Still, he leaves his birthplace because "he wished to teach Israel its [Torah] laws and precepts."[97] The combination of those two characteristics make him the uncontested hero of the work. As readers of post-exilic biblical history know, one can easily exist without the other. Torah can persist outside the boundaries of the Land of Israel,[98] and the people can live in the land while being ignorant of God's law.[99] But observing the Torah in the land, according to the author of Ezra-Nehemiah, constitutes the full Jewish experience.[100]

ANTICLIMAXES TO COME

As the book of Ezra-Nehemiah draws to a close, readers begin to feel confident that the returnees are well on their way to achieving all that they set out to accomplish. The Temple is standing and operational in a reinforced and populated Jerusalem, and the returnees have settled back into the land of their ancestors with the Torah as renewed religious companion. Rather than ending there, though, the last chapter of the work concludes on a very different note. While that conclusion may be disappointing for some, it is actually the perfect ending to Ezra-Nehemiah.

---

97. Ezra 7:10.
98. In addition to the texts mentioned earlier in this chapter, the book of Daniel also presents its hero as remaining staunchly loyal to the Torah's teachings outside of the land.
99. That seems to be the scenario until Ezra arrives. Of course, the work is also aware that such a scenario cannot endure and that another exile would be an inevitability in such a case (Neh. 9–10).
100. This outlook might account for the focus on Abraham in the historical retrospective of Nehemiah 9 rather than, for example, Moses. In Abraham, the author sees a model of someone who is both faithful to the covenant and migrated to the land. For more on the ways in which Abraham becomes a seminal figure in the imagination of Second Temple writers, see Ari Mermelstein, "When History Repeats Itself: The Theological Significance of the Abrahamic Covenant in Early Jewish Writings," *Journal for the Study of Pseudepigrapha* 27, no. 2 (2017): 113–42.

Chapter Eleven

Imperfect Endings

ANTICLIMAX

Had the work of Ezra-Nehemiah been only one chapter long, ending with the closing words of Ezra 1, "All vessels of gold and silver were five thousand four hundred in number; all were taken by Sheshbazzar when the returning exiles were brought out from Babylon to Jerusalem," some readers may have responded with the famous Hebrew phrase *Dayeinu!*[1] Literally translated "it would have been sufficient," the idiom would convey the notion that a foreign king empowering the people to return to their land and restore the Temple would have sufficed to show that, as predicted, the exile had ended and rebuilding would occur.[2] In an alternative hypothetical, the work could end with the close of Ezra 2, where we are told that "the priests, Levites, and others of the people,

---

1. The phrase is borrowed from a famous song from the Passover (Haggada) service, which is structured as a list of things God does for His people in the aftermath of the Exodus from Egypt. After each refrain, the singers claim, had He done only that one thing and no more, "it would have been sufficient." (For an explanation and translation of the Haggada, see Joseph Tabory, *The JPS Commentary on the Haggadah: Historical Introduction, Translation, and Commentary* [Jewish Publication Society, 2008].)
2. The book of Chronicles, for example, ends on this note.

the singers, gatekeepers, and the Netinim, settled in their towns, so that all Israel were in their towns." In such a scenario, readers could rest assured that both the return journey and the efforts to resettle the land were successful. Ezra 3, which ends with the raucous celebrations of the Temple's foundation laying might be another natural place to conclude, as would Ezra 6, which tells of the Temple consecration and festivities that follow. But the work does not end at any of those points. Ezra-Nehemiah is rife with potential "happy endings," yet the work does not conclude with any one of them. It does not conclude after issues of identity are settled,[3] and it does not conclude after the wall around Jerusalem is reinforced and the economy within overhauled.[4] Perhaps most surprisingly, the work does not even end after the resettled community accepts the Torah as its guide and pledges ongoing allegiance to it.[5] Instead, a work suffused with successes and numerous potential "highs" on which to leave us concludes with Nehemiah 13, a chapter in which old problems resurface, nemeses reappear, and the Judean leader tries to steer his people.

LOOSE ENDS LEFT LOOSE

Nehemiah 13, the last portion of Nehemiah's memoir, begins with Nehemiah's report of what he finds upon returning to Jerusalem after a twelve-year sojourn in Persia. He tells us at the outset that the people have broken up their mixed marriages and that he has expelled the foreigner Tobiah from the Temple.[6] He recounts the Levitical support that was neglected in his absence, and the Judeans who were "treading in winepresses on the Sabbath and those bringing heaps of produce and loading the donkeys with wine, grapes, figs, and all kinds of

---

3. Ezra 9–10 deals with the divorce of foreign wives and redefinition of Jewish identity. See chapter seven.
4. Nehemiah 2–7.
5. Ibid. 8–10.
6. Nehemiah 2:10 attributes Ammonite lineage to Tobiah, and the familial relations between Tobiah and Eliashib are delineated in Nehemiah 6:17–18. The fact that, as per Nehemiah's account, Tobiah is granted entry by the priest Eliashib further corroborates his claim that the problem of intermarriage persists.

burdens, then bringing them to Jerusalem on the Sabbath day."[7] Then, just before the work closes with Nehemiah's final prayer, Nehemiah tells us that "in those days I also saw those Jews who had brought home Ashdodite, Ammonite, and Moabite wives. As for their children, some spoke Ashdodite and could not even speak Hebrew, and so it was for each people in their native tongue."[8] The author has been chronicling the community of Judean returnees since Ezra 1, and the last thing we learn at the end of the work is that while the Temple and wall are still standing, the behaviors that will preserve the character of the community from within are not.

A close look at the violations listed in Nehemiah 13 seems to suggest that the promises the community made are not being upheld. As Ched Spellman asserts, the wrongdoings itemized in Nehemiah 13 "mirror the very aspects of the Mosaic covenant that the people hastily agreed to in Nehemiah 10."[9] The people in Nehemiah 10 vow to eschew mixed marriages, resist buying and selling goods on Shabbat, contribute to the maintenance of the Temple, and support the priesthood,[10] but twelve years later, Nehemiah confronts the breaching of those very vows, and in that very order, which is important because it is a product of authorial creativity, not chronological record. That is, rather than telling us how the final events of the work unfold, the author creates his own order of affairs, which structures the final chapter. At the chapter's outset, we are told that the people read the law and reform,[11] but then we follow the author back in time and learn about what the people are doing before their atonement.[12] In that flashback, Nehemiah lists their offenses and draws the work to a close in the depths of that nadir. This begs an obvious

---

7. Nehemiah 13:15.

8. Ibid. 13:23–24.

9. Ched E. Spellman, "Nehemiah's New Shadow: Reading and Rereading the Ezra-Nehemiah Narrative," *Southeastern Theological Review* 9, no. 1 (2018): 3.

10. Nehemiah 10:29–39.

11. The chapter opens with the words "On that day the book of Moses was read aloud to the listening people, and in it was found written that no Ammonite or Moabite shall be admitted to the congregation of God.... And when they heard the Torah, they separated all those of mixed lineage from Israel" (Neh. 13:1–3).

12. Some scholars maintain that the events go even further back in time, to before the community's pledge in Nehemiah 10. Williamson, *Ezra-Nehemiah*, 331; Zer-Kavod,

question: Why, rather than ending the work with the people's repentance, does the author present events non-chronologically and end with their sins? In other words, why, if there are so many gratifying ways to close the work, does the author not do so?

BIBLICAL ENDINGS

Ezra-Nehemiah is not the only biblical work to end on an anticlimactic note. A close look at the endings of the historiographical works of Tanakh reveals an interesting "anticlimactic trend." The book of Genesis, for example, whose primary focus seems to be the settlement and bequeathal of the land of Canaan to Abraham's descendants, could close with Jacob settled in the land surrounded by his twelve sons, leaving Exodus to pick up with their descent to Egypt. Israelite history would not have been any different, but the experience of closure we might derive from such an ending would be. Instead, Genesis ends beyond the borders of Canaan, where all of Jacob's sons are temporarily settled,[13] leaving its readers with a disheartening cliffhanger. In a similar vein, Exodus could conclude after Israel's acknowledgment of God's incomparability at the Song of the Sea[14] or after her famous proclamation that "all that the Lord has spoken we shall do and we shall heed."[15] The sins and tribulations of the wilderness could have been consigned to the book of Numbers, letting readers end Exodus relishing their ancestors' realization of religious sublimity. Instead, at the end of Exodus we are left with a people who had already sinned numerous times and had not yet made it to the Promised Land. Leviticus, Numbers, and Deuteronomy conclude similarly.

Ezra-Nehemiah, 141. The chronological portrait of Nehemiah 12:44–13:31 is difficult to establish with certainty as the temporal notices "on that day" (13:1), "previously" (13:4, 5), "throughout this period" (13:6), and "in those days" (13:23) are quite vague.

13. Genesis 50:14. The fact that Joseph and his brothers return to Canaan to bury Jacob but then go back to Egypt only exacerbates our frustrations.

14. Exodus 15.

15. Ibid. 24:7. These words, within rabbinic literature, became the symbol for absolute commitment to the commandments (see, for example, Shabbat 81a).

The book of Joshua tells of Israel's conquest of the land marked by improbable victories facilitated by ongoing miracles, and within the work are numerous places where a reader might hope the book will conclude. Instead, the book ends just prior to Joshua's death where he orders Israel to "purge the alien gods from your midst and direct your hearts toward the Lord, God of Israel,"[16] revealing that while the people are in their land, they are not yet living the way they should. Judges, too, with no shortage of heroic characters and feats,[17] ends at one of the lowest points in Israel's history.[18] And while Samuel could conclude with Saul's coronation and early successes[19] or with David's conquest of Jerusalem and institution of the Ark near his palace,[20] the book ends with the fallout of kings ensnared by unrestrained power. While readers might wish the book of Kings ended with the peace and prosperity that Solomon's successful reign yields[21] or the series of religious revivals that occur,[22] as it draws to its conclusion, readers confront the greatest "anticlimax" of all, in which everything history had been building toward since God's initial promise to Abraham is shattered.

Those endings are not accidental. The historiographical works of the Bible do not conclude in the short-lived instances of ideals realized, because that is not, the Bible seems to say, where the learning happens. The process by which we come to understand human nature and how that nature interacts with history and religious truth occurs in between those idyllic moments. It happens in the falls after the highs and in the efforts to climb back up. Had Genesis ended with a wealthy Abraham staking his claim in the land, we would never know the grit and resilience a life of faith demands. Had Exodus concluded with the people's acceptance of the Sinaitic covenant, we would never be warned of how easy it is to slip from spiritual ecstasy into old idolatrous habits. We only

---

16. Joshua 24:23.
17. See, for example, Judges 1:1–26, 3:9–11, 16–31, 4:15–24, 7:19–25.
18. Judges 21, the final chapter of the work, concludes after a brutal civil war almost wipes out the entire tribe of Benjamin.
19. I Samuel 10.
20. II Samuel 6:12–23.
21. I Kings 5:1–11.
22. See, for example, I Kings 18; II Kings 18:1–8, 23:1–25.

appreciate the perils of subjective morality because Judges allows us to see its consequences up close, and we learn the dangers of hubris and denial only by reading to the end of Kings and watching an Israel that had achieved everything hit rock bottom.

FRUSTRATION WITH A DASH OF HOPE

And yet, while we learn from the lows, we might also notice that sparks of hope are embedded in those lows. It is those sparks that keep us reading. While destruction and exile are the most notable events of the end of Kings, the work, in its last few sentences, gives us reason to be hopeful, incorporating its own ancient version of "to be continued." Despite all that had been lost and all the reasons to assume Israelite history had ended, the book of Kings tells us that the Judean king Jehoiachin has been granted a pardon, removed from prison, and given a permanent seat at the royal table.[23] On that note of latent potential, the work concludes. This is why readers of Kings want to keep reading and why we are eager for Israelite history to continue: we recognize the setbacks Israel suffers on account of her sins, and we trust the author who is telling us, through his choice of final scenes, that better is yet to come.

Genesis, too, which ends in Egypt, concludes with the words "Joseph remained in Egypt together with his father's family, and he lived one hundred and ten years. Joseph saw the third generation of Ephraim's children, and the children of Manasseh's son Machir were also born on Joseph's knees. Joseph said to his brothers, 'I am about to die. But God will surely take note of you and bring you out of this land to the land He promised to Abraham, Isaac, and Jacob.' Then Joseph bound the children of Israel by an oath: 'When God takes note of you, carry my bones up from this place.' Joseph died at the age of one hundred and ten. He was embalmed and placed in a coffin there, in Egypt."[24] Earlier in Genesis, God promises Abraham that his children will be enslaved in a foreign land and that only after their release will they return to inherit

---

23. II Kings 25:27–30.
24. Genesis 50:22–26.

their birthright.[25] When Genesis ends with all of Jacob's children living in Egypt, we are disappointed, but we are also simultaneously reassured. On the one hand, Abraham's family is not situated in the place where the book largely focused. On the other hand, we understand that the fact of nascent Israel outside of Canaan means that the fulfillment of the promise to Abraham has commenced, and it is only a matter of time until it is fully manifest.

Likewise, while Exodus ends in the desert, it ends with the sons of Israel transformed into a nation. That nation is not yet fully persuaded that God will provide for her, and she is punished for her faithlessness. But with the book's final words, "In all the journeys of the Israelites, when the cloud rose from the Tabernacle, they would set out. But if the cloud did not lift, they did not move on; they waited until it had lifted. The Lord's cloud was over the Tabernacle by day, and fire was in it at night, in view of all the House of Israel through all their journeys,"[26] we are reassured enough to continue reading. We know that the relationship between God and His people is being cultivated and that, while the learning curve may be steep, Israel is on it.

Leviticus ends in the wilderness, but it contains the laws that will structure Israel's life in the land. So when we read the work's final words, "These are the commands that the Lord gave Moses, on Mount Sinai, for the people of Israel," we are hopeful that that life is imminent. The reluctance of the Israelites to embrace that life is recorded in Numbers, as is the consequent deferment of it.[27] Still, Numbers's narrative, like the final narratives of the works that precede it, assures us that while protracted, Israel's development is still underway. Numbers's last narrative tells of the men from the tribe of Joseph who approach Moses to ensure that the land allocated to their tribe would not be reduced.[28] On its surface,

25. Ibid. 15:13–21.
26. Exodus 40:35–38.
27. Numbers 13–14.
28. In Numbers 26, a census of Israel is taken, and God declares that the land will be apportioned accordingly. But only men are counted in the census, so in Numbers 27, the daughters of Zelophehad, a man who had died without male heirs, approach Moses and the leaders asking if an exception can be made in a case like theirs. Moses consults with God, who answers in no uncertain terms that the daughters are correct

the concern of the narrative appears to be primarily administrative, but a closer look reveals that after forty years, the people finally believe that they are capable of entry and that the land is precious enough to fight for. Like the sins that appear at the end of Nehemiah, the final episode of Numbers likely occurs at an earlier time.[29] But the narrative, which marks the first-time Israelite men are concerned with the technicalities of life in the land, is the closing bracket of the book, because their request signifies that, despite a devastating delay, the people of Israel have learned to believe in their future. As believers, they will finally be ready to enter the land. Then, although concluding in that same wilderness, Deuteronomy relates that "Joshua son of Nun was filled with the spirit of wisdom."[30] That is, with Israel on the precipice, we mourn the unfortunate end to Moses's tenure while looking ahead toward Israel's conquest of the land.

The book of Joshua ends with its leader denouncing Israel's sins. Still, the last words the people speak to Joshua, "The Lord our God we shall serve, and His voice we shall obey!"[31] give us hope that in the next phase of history, they will live up to their potential. While those expectations are dashed by the social and religious ills that plague the book of Judges, particularly its final episodes,[32] the book of Judges, too, ends with a glimmer of hope: "In those days, there was no king in

---

for asking and that their case should set a legal precedent, allowing daughters of all heirless sons to become rightful heirs to their fathers' property. In Numbers 36, though, men from the tribe of Joseph, to which Zelophehad's daughters belong, voice their concern that if the daughters marry men from a different tribe, Joseph's landholdings will be diminished. God once again rules, declaring that the daughters must marry from within the tribe of Joseph.

29. Likely, the men from the tribe of Joseph would have approached Moses shortly after his ruling on Zelophehad's daughters.

30. Deuteronomy 34:9.

31. Joshua 24:24.

32. Chapters 17–21, known as the appendix to the book of Judges, contain a series of events that occur during but not necessarily at the end of the period. Unlike the rest of the work, the episodes in the appendix tell of events in the history of the tribes, specifically those of Dan and Benjamin, but unlike the rest of the work, do not contain stories of specific "judges." Internal evidence in those chapters, such as mention of Moses's and Aaron's grandsons (18:30 and 20:28), point to the fact that the events described occur earlier in the period.

Israel; everyone did what was right in his own eyes."[33] The moral fabric of Israel's society is coming apart at the seams, and yet, as we read the work's final words, we cannot help but wonder if perhaps kingship will be the panacea. The book of Samuel proves that it is not, but despite the shortcomings of the personalities that dominate the work, the narrative selected to close the book of Samuel depicts a devoutly monotheistic king, utterly devoted to his people and their future.[34] With that ending, we are left hopeful that the people may remain united and follow their king's lead. Their inability to do so brings us back to the book of Kings, the hopeful spark with which it ends, and the point from which Ezra-Nehemiah continues.

NEHEMIAH'S FINAL WORDS

Through its records of Israel's recurrent ups and downs, Tanakh concedes that Israel will never be perfect. Humanity was created with the ability to choose between good and evil, and while that ability enables human creativity and productivity, it is also what makes them fallible. God gave the Israelite people laws to curtail their imperfect nature and equip them with the tools and ideals to build an optimal society. At times, they adhered to those laws, and their accomplishments reflect that adherence. Other times, they did not and they slipped backward developmentally. Still, despite those seeming regressions, the net movement of the Israelite people was always in a positive direction. The proverbial "three steps forward, two steps back" perhaps best characterizes Israel's development. The endings of Tanakh's historiographical works suggest that this net positive has everything to do with the fact that Tanakh presents Israel's setbacks with candor, allowing them to deduce lessons from past mistakes while communicating a need and creating space for advancement. For that reason, it is the study of Tanakh itself

---

33. Judges 21:25.
34. Like the book of Judges, II Samuel also contains an appendix comprised of numerous events from throughout David's reign, likely placed at the end of the work for ideological reasons.

that enables us to continue netting advancement despite the fact that we have never been, nor will we ever be, perfect.[35]

This notion is expressed in Nehemiah's final words, "Remember me favorably, O my God."[36] Nehemiah's request reveals that behind the stalwart, untiring politician[37] is a man who has studied his people's thorny history and, as such, expects the period in which he is leading to be no less complex.[38] His request reveals a man well aware that progress demands that hard choices be made, implemented, and reinforced when opposition surges or conviction dwindles,[39] and his request acknowledges that even when we believe ourselves to be on the right side of history, ultimately that is for God to decide. Nehemiah believes his harsh measures and obstinate stance are necessary for the Judeans to move forward and realize their dream of restoration. But as a student

---

35. This differs from the Christian arrangement of the Bible, which extends from Creation to redemption. As Michael Walzer puts it: "The Jewish version reflects an unfinished engagement with history." Walzer, *In God's Shadow*, xvi.

36. Nehemiah 13:31. This is not the first time Nehemiah makes such a request, nor is he the first biblical personality to ask such a thing of God. See Nehemiah 5:19, 13:14, 22; Judges 16:28; Jeremiah 15:15; Psalms 106:4; Job 14:13; II Chronicles 6:42.

37. At times, Nehemiah could even be described as overly harsh or zealous. See, for example, Nehemiah 13:25.

38. The phrase, when it appears in Tanakh, seems to suggest that a leader is asking God to remember him favorably, as he is doing what he believes to be correct while faced with real or anticipated opposition from within his own community. In Jeremiah 15:15, for example, the prophet begs God to remember him in the face of those persecuting him, and in Samson's famous last speech (Judges 16:28), Samson begs God to restore his strength despite his being despised by both his own Israelite people and the Philistines who hold him captive. When Nehemiah makes his similar requests of God, the text does not explicitly describe the antipathy of the people, but it is safe to surmise from context that the measures he institutes are not all unanimously accepted by the people. His request in Nehemiah 13:31, which appears after his harsh verbal and physical repudiations of the people's sins, further supports this assertion. As such, the request indicates an awareness that while (or because) the leader does not have the support of the people, he is asking for God's support of his efforts.

39. See, for example, chapters seven-nine where we discuss the difficult decisions about inclusion and exclusion that leaders have to make, the reticence of some of the people to implement those decisions, and the abandoning of ideals.

of Jewish history,[40] Nehemiah is also humble enough to recognize that even good intentions can be erroneous. Despite the recurrent sins mentioned at the end of the work, as we leave the courageous returnees and their leaders, we are filled with hope, not because things are perfect but because, in the imperfect world, there exist leaders just unsure enough of themselves to ask God for help, and there exist people who prove that even though change is difficult, they are open to it.

---

40. Nehemiah 9 and 10 demonstrate that in addition to his use of the Torah for its legal teachings, Nehemiah used it as a book of lessons to be gleaned from Israel's history.

Epilogue

Humanity, created from the earth and animated with God's breath, was commanded in Genesis to "be fruitful and multiply" and to "fill the earth and subdue it."[1] And while there is no formal covenant between humanity and the land, there is an unspoken set of expectations regarding their relationship. Humans are meant to be innovative, productive, and generative, while the land is meant to produce humanity's sustenance.

Given these parameters, the Bible's first recorded act of interhuman violence results in a rupture of that relationship. After Cain kills his brother Abel, God says to him: "The voice of your brother's blood cries out to Me from the land! Now you are cursed, more so than the land that has opened its mouth to receive your brother's blood from your hand. When you work the land, it will no longer grant you its powers. You will be a fugitive wanderer over the land."[2] As God's admonishment of Cain makes clear, the land does not tolerate inhumanity. When humans harm or destroy life rather than perpetuate it, the synergistic relationship between people and

---

1. Genesis 1:28.
2. Ibid. 4:10–12.

land is marred. Because of Cain's actions, he is doomed to be uprooted and insecure, never settled in any one place. He will never know what it means to identify with a place, and for that place, in turn, to solidify his identity.[3] Cain failed humanity, so the land failed him.

This concept, presented on a universal level at the beginning of Genesis, is honed in the Abraham narratives. There, God establishes a covenant with Abraham, promising him a great nation *in* the Land of Israel.[4] God's choice of Abraham is not explicit from the outset, yet it becomes clear a few chapters in: "For I have chosen him," God declares, "so that he may direct his children and his household after him to keep the way of the Lord by doing what is right and just, that the Lord may bring about for Abraham what He spoke of for him."[5] Abraham, who will be the "father of a multitude of nations,"[6] is promised land specifically because God trusts that Abraham will be faithful to God's ways of righteousness and justice. That lifestyle, God indicates, merits Abraham's ability to inherit and dwell in his land.

A more particularistic rendering of this concept is presented to the Israelites in the wilderness. There, on their way back to the land of Abraham, the Israelites are taught, in painstaking detail, what life on that land demands.[7] Ritual and ethical imperatives, as we have seen,[8] serve as the basis for the ideal society they are to build and the means by which their

---

3. Ironically (or not), Cain also builds the first city recorded in the Bible and names it for his son (Gen. 4:16–17).

4. For an in-depth analysis of biblical covenants and the nature of God's covenant with Abraham, see Menahem Haran, "The Berit 'Covenant': Its Nature and Ceremonial Background," in *Tehillah le-Moshe: Biblical and Judaic Studies in Honor of Moshe Greenberg* (1997), 203–20.

5. Genesis 18:19. That righteousness is displayed on more than one occasion. Abraham risks his life to save his nephew Lot from captivity, refusing payment and choosing instead to glorify God's name (Gen. 14:22–24); he attempts to save any innocent people that might be living in Sodom after God reveals His intention to the destroy the city (Gen. 18:20–33); and he prays for Abimelech after he is stricken with illness (Gen. 20:17).

6. Genesis 17:5.

7. The laws the Israelites receive during that time appear throughout the books of Exodus, Leviticus, Numbers, and Deuteronomy.

8. See chapter nine.

potential as God's chosen people is to be realized.[9] On more than one occasion, the Israelites are reminded that the choice between adherence to those provisions accompanied by life in the land and defiance of them accompanied by exile is theirs to make.[10]

Unfortunately, like Cain, the Israelites fail to live up to their potential, and, in 586 BCE, after hundreds of years' worth of offenses, the land rejects them. But that rejection is temporary, as God promised it would be,[11] and the efforts to rebuild what was lost are recounted in Ezra-Nehemiah. As this study has attempted to illuminate, those efforts are met with significant challenges. Yet, despite those challenges, the people and their leaders endeavor to build something that, the second time around, will endure. And it does, for over five hundred years. In time, however, the people once again lose sight of their national imperative and, in doing so, forfeit their rights to the land. Ultimately, sectarian violence and a series of failed revolts against Rome (66–135 CE) lead to the destruction of the Second Temple, the sacking of Jerusalem, and the loss of Jewish statehood.

After the destruction of the Second Temple, some Jews remain in the Land of Israel, but most end up in Babylon and smaller communities throughout the Mediterranean. For the ensuing two thousand years, Jews spread across the globe, sometimes voluntarily and at other times under duress. In a manner reminiscent of Jeremiah's counsel to their forefathers,[12] the Jews do their best to flourish in the lands in which they find themselves. Still, the dream of a return to their ancestral homeland remains a central fixture of Jewish liturgy, rituals, and life-cycle events. Then, finally, after two millennia of yearning, that dream is realized.

And now, here we are once again: a people returned to its ancestral homeland after several thousand years of wandering.[13] Once again, we

---

9.   See, for example, Deuteronomy 7:6, 14:2, 26:18–19.
10. See, for example, Deuteronomy 27–28.
11. See, for example, Deuteronomy 30:1–10; Isaiah 40:1–5, 44:28–45:5; Jeremiah 25:11–12, 29:10–11.
12. Jeremiah 29. See chapter three.
13. This author recognizes that she, like the biblical authors, is telescoping large swaths of Jewish history and focusing on the Jewish experience within the Land of Israel. See chapter two.

are attempting to rebuild, and once again we are filled with determination to make this return our final one. Ezra-Nehemiah teaches us that
to do so, ironically, requires a sustained recognition of the precarious-
ness of our tenancy. Only by remembering our need to earn the land's
tolerance, the book implies, will we manage to do so.[14]

But restoration, Ezra-Nehemiah makes clear, is not a simple task,
particularly when the "dream fulfilled" is teeming with disappointments,
setbacks, and conflicts. It is tempting, when reality proves imperfect, to
contend that the dream has yet to manifest. Such a contention allows
people to hold on to the fantasy of an idyllic future while waiting pas-
sively for it to materialize. Equally difficult to resist is the inclination
to become mired in the challenges that abound while overlooking the
abundant blessings with which those difficulties coincide. But those
two approaches, the leaders of Ezra-Nehemiah assert, lead to stagnation,
even regression. True progress, according to them, requires faith in two
things: in God's mercy, evidenced by the fact of our momentous return,
and in our community's ability to acknowledge its shortcomings while
using every tool at its disposal to rectify them. If negotiated properly,
Ezra-Nehemiah suggests, the challenges of restoration can, rather than
inhibiting evolution, serve as its point of departure.[15]

For that to happen, though, the past must be employed as a guide as
it is in Ezra-Nehemiah. We must not rely on a sterilized version of our
past that focuses only on the high points in our history but on an honest,
sober version that delineates our failures alongside our triumphs. History, in Ezra-Nehemiah, is depicted as an uninterrupted flow of achieve-
ments, lapses, errors, and emendations.[16] Our forebears' mistakes are
our cautionary tale. Thus, as we rebuild, it is from those missteps that
we endeavor to learn.

Not repeating past mistakes, though, is easier said than done, because
while our external environment is constantly shifting, human nature
remains unchanged. There will always be, for example, those who abuse
the power they are granted. Ezra-Nehemiah responds to that truth by

---

14. See chapter three.
15. See chapter four.
16. See chapter five.

promoting a new model of leadership rooted in the notions of God's universal control and ongoing intervention in human affairs.[17] It is not a foolproof model, as subsequent Jewish history attests. But the promotion of it evinces the courage to pursue new solutions to age-old problems, and that courage is essential for a people striving to move forward.

Also essential to that forward movement are the collaborative efforts of the populace. After all, a society is only as strong as the people who comprise it. Ezra-Nehemiah depicts laypeople inspired to perpetuate the ideals their leaders espouse and build upon the foundations their leaders have laid.[18] But such a reality can only be forged when the leaders themselves are confident enough to empower their populace and sincere enough to be believed by them. It is generated when the individuals imbued with authority prioritize the needs of those they are leading over their own grip on power. And it endures when leaders are conscious of their transience and choose to invest in what will outlive them.

In addition to courageous, empowering leaders and an inspired populace, restoration also requires an awareness within the community of where its boundaries lie. Ezra-Nehemiah reminds us that a community in the process of restoration is necessarily vulnerable, and, because of that vulnerability, it must remain cohesive.[19] Cohesion does not require homogeneity or consensus. But it does speak to a shared appreciation for what is required of its members and an insistence that those requirements be met. "Particularism" is not an invective, and it is not to be confused with racism or xenophobia.[20] Rather, particularism speaks to the understanding that for a community to maintain its unique identity and sense of purpose, the porousness of its borders must be moderated.

Of course, those included must have a clear understanding of what the community to which they belong stands for. Belonging, after all, is only meaningful if one takes part in the community and contributes to its success. In Ezra-Nehemiah, the Judeans become proficient in the

---

17. See chapter six.
18. See chapter six.
19. See chapter seven.
20. For a thoughtful articulation of this theme, see Tikva Frymer-Kensky, "Judaism and Pluralism," *Journal of Ecumenical Studies* 52, no. 1 (2017): 34–38.

essential features of their community by virtue of Ezra's Torah education. Through his public reading of the written word, the people learn what the Torah demands of them and what makes them unique.[21]

In addition to the law codes, Ezra also conveys to the people that for the Torah to remain relevant and for the community that learns that Torah to be resilient, the Torah needs to be expounded upon. Its words need to be learned and relearned, and new, relevant interpretations must be applied to the words that are traced back to Moses himself.[22] Stasis, Ezra demonstrates through his creative exegesis, is not a Jewish value. Adaptation rooted in the biblical text, though, is a necessity.

So, Ezra, the consummate pedagogue, teaches Torah in a way that disarms his students. He encourages rather than chastises and invites them to partake in the communal return to Jewish literacy. But it is the outcome of their learning, perhaps even more than the process, that encompasses the mechanism for a successful restoration. The Judeans who learn at Ezra's feet sign a treaty in which they vow not to repeat the mistakes of those who preceded them. Torah learning, Ezra-Nehemiah illustrates through the scene, is not theoretical; it is the prelude to implementing the Torah's laws with the aim of creating a more just, compassionate, religiously conscious society. The content of the treaty reveals that, unlike those who incurred exile, those penning the treaty recognize the inextricable link between their relationships with God and with their fellow man and will thereby revere each. Perhaps most importantly, the treaty demonstrates the people's realization of the paramount truth that they, and only they, determine their fate in their homeland.[23]

That homeland, Ezra-Nehemiah contends, is the place toward which all Jews should strive to move, not because the conditions there are favorable or society as it stands is irreproachable but because it is ours. It is the land to which Abraham was told to go and the land to which our forefathers returned after years of exile in Egypt and, later, Babylon.

---

21. See chapter eight.
22. See chapter eight.
23. See chapter nine.

It is the place where biblical commandments can be observed to their fullest and which God chose "as a dwelling for His name."[24]

By the same token, Ezra-Nehemiah also acknowledges the reality of a Diaspora and the ensuing truth that there must be unity between the Jews of the Diaspora and those in Israel. That unity may prove challenging at times, as interests may clash, values may not perfectly align, and each community may feel a sense of superiority to its counterpart for a myriad of conditioned reasons. Nonetheless, Ezra-Nehemiah argues, Jewish solidarity is vital.[25] As such, we must wield language carefully and compose our national narrative in such a way that all factions know that they are an integral part. The Jewish story is not perfect but, like the land, it is ours, *all* of ours.

There is a designated epicenter for the Jewish people. That notion is axiomatic in the Bible. And for thousands of years that epicenter exerted a centripetal pull on the souls of Jewish people throughout the world. But now, the heart of that epicenter is beating once again. Once again, the Jewish people can ask the question Ezra-Nehemiah poses: What does it take to thrive in our revived homeland?

The answers have already been written. Our blueprint is in hand. We simply need to begin reading.

---

24. Deuteronomy 12:11.
25. See chapter ten.

Bibliography

Aberbach, David. *Major Turning Points in Jewish Intellectual History.* Springer, 2003.

Ackroyd, Peter R. *Exile and Restoration: A Commentary.* Westminster John Knox, 1968.

Albertz, Rainer. *Israel in Exile: The History and Literature of the Sixth Century B.C.E.* Society of Biblical Literature, 2003.

Alstola, Tero. *Judeans in Babylonia: A Study of Deportees in the Sixth and Fifth Centuries BCE.* Brill, 2020.

Alter, Robert. *The Art of Biblical Narrative.* Basic Books, 2011.

Arnold, Bill T. "The Use of Aramaic in the Hebrew Bible: Another Look at Bilingualism in Ezra and Daniel." *Journal of Northwest Semitic Languages* 22, no. 2 (1996): 1–16.

Aune, David E., and Eric Stewart. "From the Idealized Past to the Imaginary Future: Eschatological Restoration in Jewish Apocalyptic Literature." In *Restoration,* edited by Peter R. Ackroyd, 147–77. Brill, 2001.

Aviezer, Nathan. *In the Beginning: Biblical Creation and Science.* Ktav, 1990.

Balentine, Samuel E. "The Prophet as Intercessor: A Reassessment." *Journal of Biblical Literature* 103, no. 2 (1984): 161–73.

Barjamovic, Gojko. "Propaganda and Practice in Assyrian and Persian Imperial Culture." In *Universal Empire: A Comparative Approach to Imperial Culture and Representation in Eurasian History,* 43–59. Cambridge University Press, 2012.

Barkay, Gabriel. "Additional View of Jerusalem in Nehemiah Days." *New Studies in the Archaeology of Jerusalem and Its Region (Collected Papers)* 2 (2008): 48–54.

Barstad, Hans M. *The Myth of the Empty Land: A Study in the History and Archaeology of Judah during the "Exilic" Period.* Scandinavian University Press, 1996.

Bedford, Peter. "Diaspora and Homeland Relations in Ezra-Nehemiah." *Vetus Testamentum* 52, no. 2 (2002): 147–65.

Beeri, Ron, and Dror Ben-Yosef. "Gaming Dice and Dice for Prognostication in the Ancient East in Light of the Finds from Mount Ebal." *Revue Biblique* 117, no. 3 (2010): 410–29.

Ben-Yosef, Erez, Elisabeta Boaretto, Yuval Gadot, Oded Lipschits, Ron Shaar, Nitsan Shalom, and Yoav Vaknin. "Destruction by Fire: Reconstructing the Evidence of the 586 BCE Babylonian Destruction in a Monumental Building in Jerusalem." *Journal of Archaeological Science* 157 (2023): https://doi.org/10.2139/ssrn.4441154.

Ben Zvi, Ehud. "Inclusion in and Exclusion from Israel as Conveyed by the Use of the Term 'Israel' in Post-Monarchic Biblical Texts." In *The Pitcher Is Broken*, edited by Steven W. Holloway and Lowell K. Handy, 95–149. Sheffield Academic Press, 1995.

Ben Zvi, Ehud. "The Book of Chronicles: Another Look." In *History, Literature and Theology in the Book of Chronicles*, 20–41. Routledge, 2014.

Ben Zvi, Ehud. "Memory and Political Thought in the Late Persian/ Early Hellenistic Yehud/Judah: Some Observations." In *Leadership, Social Memory and Judean Discourse in the Fifth–Second Centuries BCE*, edited by Diana V. Edelman and Ehud Ben Zvi. Equinox, 2016.

Ben Zvi, Ehud. *Social Memory Among the Literati of Yehud*, De Gruyter, 2019.

Berlin, Adele, Marc Zvi Brettler, and Michael Fishbane, eds. *The Jewish Study Bible: Jewish Publication Society Tanakh Translation.* Oxford University Press, 2004.

Berlin, Adele. "The Exile: Biblical Ideology and Its Postmodern Ideological Interpretation." In *Literary Construction of Identity in the Ancient World*, 341–56. Eisenbrauns, 2010.

Berman, Joshua. "The Narratological Purpose of Aramaic Prose in Ezra 4.8-6.18." *Aramaic Studies* 5, no. 2 (2007): 165–191.

Berquist, Jon L. Book review of *A History of the Jews and Judaism in the Second Temple Period. Volume 1, Yehud: A History of the Persian Province of Judah*, by Lester L. Grabbe. *Journal of Biblical Literature* 125, no. 3 (2006): 579–81.

Bickerman, Elias J. "The Edict of Cyrus in Ezra 1." In *Studies in Jewish and Christian History*, edited by Amram D. Tropper, 71–107. Brill, 2007.

Blenkinsopp, Joseph. "The Mission of Udjahorresnet and Those of Ezra and Nehemiah." *Journal of Biblical Literature* 106, no. 3 (1987): 409–21.

Blenkinsopp, Joseph. *Ezra-Nehemiah: A Commentary*. Westminster John Knox, 1988.

Blenkinsopp, Joseph. "The Babylonian Gap Revisited. There Was No Gap." *Biblical Archaeology Review* 28, no. 3 (2002).

Bloch, Yigal. "Was the Sabbath Observed in Āl-Yāḫūdu in the Early Decades of the Babylonian Exile?" *Zeitschrift für die Alttestamentliche Wissenschaft* 132 (2020): 117–20.

Block, Daniel I. "Divine Abandonment: Ezekiel's Adaptation of an Ancient Near Eastern Motif." In *The Book of Ezekiel: Theological and Anthropological Perspectives*, edited by Margaret S. Odell and John T. Strong. Society of Biblical Literature, 2020.

Boda, Mark J. "Confession as Theological Expression: Ideological Origins of Penitential Prayer." In *Seeking the Favor of God*, vol. 1, 21–50. Eisenbrauns, 2006.

Boda, Mark J., Daniel K. Falk, and Rodney Werline, eds. *Seeking the Favor of God, Vol 2: The Development of Penitential Prayer in Second Temple Judaism*. Society of Biblical Literature, 2007.

Boda, Mark J. "Flashforward: Future Glimpses in the Past of Ezra 1–6." In *Let Us Go Up to Zion*, edited by Iain Provan and Mark J. Boda, 245–60. Brill, 2012.

Boyarin, Daniel. "Rethinking Jewish Christianity: An Argument for Dismantling a Dubious Category (to Which is Appended a Correction of My *Border Lines*)." *Jewish Quarterly Review* 99, no. 1 (2009): 7–36.

Brenner-Idan, Athalya. "Confession as Theological Expression: Ideological Origins of Penitential Prayer." In *Seeking the Favor of God*, vol. 1, 21–50. Eisenbrauns, 2006.

Brenner-Idan, Athalya, *The Israelite Women: Social Role and Literary Type in Biblical Narrative*. Bloomsbury Publishing, 2014.

Briant, Pierre. *From Cyrus to Alexander: A History of the Persian Empire.* Penn State University Press, 2002.

Bryan, Steven M. "The End of Exile: The Reception of Jeremiah's Prediction of a Seventy-Year Exile." *Journal of Biblical Literature* 137, no. 1 (2018): 107–26.

Carr, David M. *Writing on the Tablet of the Heart: Origins of Scripture and Literature.* Oxford University Press, 2005.

Carr, David M., and Gary N. Knoppers. "Response to W. M. Schniedewind, *How the Bible Became a Book: The Textualization of Ancient Israel.*" *Journal of Hebrew Scriptures* 5, no. 18 (2005): 1–19.

Carroll, Robert P. "The Myth of the Empty Land." *Semeia* 59 (1992): 79–93.

Carroll, Robert P. *Jeremiah.* A & C Black, 2004.

Cataldo, Jeremiah. "Utopia in Agony: The Role of Prejudice in Ezra-Nehemiah's Idea for Restoration." In *Worlds That Could Not Be: Utopia in Chronicles, Ezra and Nehemiah.* Bloomsbury, 2016.

Cataldo, Jeremiah W. *Imagined Worlds and Constructed Differences in the Hebrew Bible.* Bloomsbury, 2019.

Cleath, Lisa J. "Colonial Identity in the Jedaniah Archive at Elephantine." *Faculty Publications – George Fox School of Theology* (2019).

Clines, David J. "Nehemiah 10 as an Example of Early Jewish Exegesis." *Journal for the Study of the Old Testament* 6, no. 21 (1981): 111–17.

Clines, David J. *What Does Eve Do to Help? And Other Readerly Questions to the Old Testament.* Sheffield Academic Press, 1990.

Cogan, Mordechai. *Bound for Exile: Israelites and Judeans Under Imperial Yoke: Documents from Assyria and Babylonia.* Carta Jerusalem, 2013.

Cohen, Shaye. "From the Bible to the Talmud: The Prohibition of Intermarriage." *Hebrew Annual Review* 7 (1983): 23–39.

Cohen, Shaye J. D. *The Beginnings of Jewishness: Boundaries, Varieties, Uncertainties.* Vol. 31. University of California Press, 1999.

Colburn, Henry P. "Globalization and the Study of the Achaemenid Persian Empire." In *The Routledge Handbook of Archaeology and Globalization,* edited by Tamar Hodos, 895–908. Routledge, 2016.

Collins, John J. *Daniel: A Commentary on the Book of Daniel.* Hermeneia, 1993.

Cook, Stanley A. "The Significance of the Elephantine Papyri for the History of Hebrew Religion." *American Journal of Theology* 19, no. 3 (1915): 346–82.

Corfield, Penelope J. *Time and Shape of History.* Yale University Press, 2007.

Cross, Frank Moore. "The Papyri and Their Historical Implications." In *Discoveries in the Wâdī ed-Dâliyeh,* edited by Paul W. Lapp and Nancy L. Lapp, 17–29. 1974.

Davies, Eryl W., and Ronald E. Clements. "Land: Its Rights and Privileges." In *The World of Ancient Israel,* edited by R. E. Clements, 349–69. Cambridge University Press, 1991.

Davies, Gordon F. *Berit Olam: Ezra and Nehemiah,* edited by David W. Cotter. Liturgical Press, 1999.

Davies, William D., and Louis Finkelstein, eds. *The Cambridge History of Judaism: Volume 1, The Persian Period.* Cambridge University Press, 1984.

Davis, Ellen F. *Swallowing the Scroll: Textuality and the Dynamics of Discourse in Ezekiel's Prophecy.* Vol. 21. A & C Black, 1989.

Dewald, Carolyn, and Rosaria Vignolo Munson, eds. *Herodotus: Histories Book I.* Cambridge University Press, 2022.

Dozeman, Thomas B. "Geography and History in Herodotus and in Ezra-Nehemiah." *Journal of Biblical Literature* 122, no. 3 (2003): 449–66.

Duggan, Michael W. *The Covenant Renewal in Ezra-Nehemiah (Neh. 7:72b–10:40): An Exegetical, Literary, and Theological Study.* Society of Biblical Literature, 2001.

Duguid, Iain. "Nehemiah – The Best King Judah Never Had." In *Let Us Go Up to Zion,* edited by Iain Provan and Mark J. Boda, 261–71. Brill, 2012.

Edelman, Diana V., and Ehud Ben Zvi. *The Production of Prophecy: Constructing Prophecy and Prophets in Yehud.* Routledge, 2014.

Elazar, Daniel J. "Judaism as a Theopolitical Phenomenon." In *The Blackwell Companion to Judaism,* edited by Jacob Neusner and Alan J. Avery-Peck, 415–40. Blackwell, 2003.

Eliade, Mircea. *Patterns in Comparative Religion.* University of Nebraska Press, 2022.

Elman, Yaakov. "R. Zadok Hakohen on the History of Halakha." *Tradition: A Journal of Orthodox Jewish Thought* 21, no. 4 (1985): 1–26.

Eskenazi, Tamara Cohn. *In an Age of Prose: A Literary Approach to Ezra-Nehemiah*. Scholars, 1988.

Eskenazi, Tamara Cohn. "Ezra-Nehemiah: From Text to Actuality." In *Signs and Wonders*, edited by J. Cheryl Exum, 165–98. Scholars, 1989.

Eskenazi, Tamara Cohn. "Nehemiah 9–10: Structure and Significance." *Journal of Hebrew Scriptures* 3 (2001): 16.

Eskenazi, Tamara Cohn. "From Exile and Restoration to Exile and Reconstruction." In *Exile and Restoration Revisited: Essays on the Babylonian Persian Period in Memory of Peter R. Ackroyd*, edited by Gary N. Knoppers and Lester L. Grabbe, 78–93. T & T Clark, 2009.

Eskenazi, Tamara Cohn. "Imagining the Other in the Construction of Judahite Identity in Ezra-Nehemiah." In *Imagining the Other and Constructing Israelite Identity in the Early Second Temple Period*, edited by Ehud Ben Zvi and Diana V. Edelman, 230–56. Bloomsbury T & T Clark, 2014.

Fensham, Charles F. "Widow, Orphan, and the Poor in Ancient Near Eastern Legal and Wisdom Literature." *Journal of Near Eastern Studies* 21, no. 2 (1962): 129–39.

Fensham, F. Charles. *The Books of Ezra and Nehemiah*. William B. Eerdmans Publishing, 1982.

Finkel, Irving L. "In Black and White: Remarks on the Assur Psephomancy Ritual." ZA 85 (1995): 271–76.

Finkel, Irving. New Translation of the Edict of Cyrus. https://www.britishmuseum.org/collection/object/W_1880-0617-1941

Fishbane, Michael. "Revelation and Tradition: Aspects of Inner-Biblical Exegesis." *Journal of Biblical Literature* 99, no. 3 (1980): 343–61.

Fisher, Daniel Shalom. *Memories of the Ark: Texts, Objects, and the Construction of the Biblical Past*. PhD diss., UC Berkeley, 2018.

Flavius, Josèphe, *Flavius Josephus: Translation and Commentary, Volume 10: Against Apion*. Brill, 2000.

Fleishman, Joseph, "An Echo of Optimism in Ezra 6: 19–22." *Hebrew Union College Annual* (1998): 15–29.

Fox, Michael V. *Character and Ideology in the Book of Esther*. 2nd ed. The Library of Biblical Studies. Jewish Theological Seminary of America, 2001.

Fox, Michael V. *A Time to Tear Down and a Time to Build Up: A Rereading of Ecclesiastes*. Wipf and Stock, 2010.

Frei, Peter. "Persian Imperial Authorization: A Summary." In *Persia and Torah: The Theory of Imperial Authorization of the Pentateuch*, edited by James W. Watts, 5–40. Society of Biblical Literature, 2001.

Fried, Lisbeth S. "Something There Is That Doesn't Love a Wall (around Jerusalem) – Why Would a Simple Wall Create Such a Crisis?" *Transeuphratene* 39 (2010): 79–89.

Frye, Northrop. "Varieties of Literary Utopias." *Daedalus* (1965): 323–47.

Frymer-Kensky, Tikva. "Judaism and Pluralism." *Journal of Ecumenical Studies* 52, no. 1 (2017): 34–38.

Funkenstein, Amos. *Perceptions of Jewish History*. University of California Press, 1993.

Glatt-Gilad, David A. "Reflections on the Structure and Significance of the'ªmānāh (Neh 10, 29–40)." *Zeitschrift für die Alttestamentliche Wissenschaft* 112, no. 3 (2000): 386–95.

Glatt-Gilad, David A. "The Root Kn' and Historiographic Periodization in Chronicles." *Catholic Biblical Quarterly* 64, no. 2 (April 2002): 248–57.

Glatt-Gilad, David A. "Chronicles as Consensus Literature." In *What Was Authoritative for Chronicles*, edited by Ehud Ben Zvi and Diana Edelman, 67–75. Eisenbrauns, 2011.

Gnuse, Robert Karl. *No Other Gods: Emergent Monotheism in Israel*. A & C Black, 1997.

Grabbe, Lester L. *Ezra-Nehemiah*. Psychology Press, 1998.

Grabbe, Lester L. *A History of the Jews and Judaism in the Second Temple Period. Volume 1: Yehud – A History of the Persian Province of Judah*. T & T Clark, 2021.

Greenberg, Moshe. "Some Postulates of Biblical Criminal Law." In *Yehezkel Kaufman Jubilee Volume*, edited by Menahem Haran. Magnes Press, 1960.

Greenspahn, Frederick E. "Why Prophecy Ceased." *Journal of Biblical Literature* 108, no. 1 (1989): 37–49.

Grosby, Steven E. "Once Again, Nationality and Religion." *Genealogy* 3, no. 3 (2019): 48.

Grossman, Jonathan. *Esther: The Outer Narrative and the Hidden Reading*. Penn State University Press, 2011.

Hadad, Eliezer. *The Status of Minorities in the Jewish State: Halakhic Aspects.* Israel Democracy Institute, 2010.

Halbertal, Moshe, and Stephen Holmes. *The Beginning of Politics: Power in the Biblical Book of Samuel.* Princeton University Press, 2017.

Halivni, David W. *Revelation Restored: Divine Writ and Critical Responses.* Routledge, 2019.

Hallo, William. "The First Purim." *Biblical Archaeologist* 46, no. 1 (Winter 1983): 19–29.

Halpern, Baruch. The *First Historians: The Hebrew Bible and History.* Penn State University Press, 2010.

Hanson, Paul D. *The Dawn of the Apocalyptic.* Fortress, 1975.

Haran, Menahem. "The Berit 'Covenant': Its Nature and Ceremonial Background." In *Tehillah le-Moshe: Biblical and Judaic Studies in Honor of Moshe Greenberg,* edited by Mordechai Cogan, Barry L. Eichler, and Jeffrey H. Tigay, 203–20. Eisenbrauns, 1997.

Hasegawa, Shuichi, Christoph Levin, and Karen Radner, eds. *The Last Days of the Kingdom of Israel.* De Gruyter, 2018.

Häusl, Maria. "Jerusalem, the Holy City: The Meaning of the City of Jerusalem in the Books of Ezra-Nehemiah." In *Constructions of Space V: Place, Space and Identity in the Ancient Mediterranean World,* edited by Gert. M. Prinsloo, and Christl M. Maier, 87–106. Bloomsbury, 2013.

Hayes, Christine. "Intermarriage and Impurity in Ancient Jewish Sources." *Harvard Theological Review* 92, no. 1 (1999): 3–36.

Hayes, Christine. *Gentile Impurities and Jewish Identities: Intermarriage and Conversion from the Bible to the Talmud.* Oxford University Press, 2002.

Hayes, Christine. *What's Divine About Divine Law?: Early Perspectives.* Princeton University Press, 2017.

Hayes, Christine. *Yale University Introduction to the Bible Series,* Lecture 2, Monotheism, p. 4.

Hoffman, Eva. "The Long Afterlife of Loss." In *Memory: Histories, Theories, Debates,* edited by Susannah Radstone, and Bill Schwarz, 406–15. Fordham University Press, 2010.

Hundley, Michael B. *Gods in Dwellings: Temples and Divine Presence in the Ancient Near East.* Society of Biblical Literature, 2013.

Hurowitz, Victor Avigdor. "Spanning the Generations: Aspects of Oral and Written Transmission in the Bible and Ancient Mesopotamia."

In *Freedom and Responsibility: Exploring the Challenges of Jewish Continuity*, edited by Rela M. Geffen and Marsha Bryan Edelman, 11–30. Ktav, 1998.

Hurowitz, Victor Avigdor. *I Have Built You an Exalted House: Temple Building in Light of Mesopotamia and North-West Semitic Writings*. A & C Black, 1992.

Hurowitz, Victor Avigdor. "Urim and Thummim in Light of a Psephomancy Ritual from Assur (LKA 137)." *Journal of the Ancient Near Eastern Society* 21, no. 1 (1992): 65–90.

Hurowitz Victor Avigdor. "True Light on the Urim and Thummim." *Jewish Quarterly Review* 88, no. 3/4 (1998): 263–74.

Janzen, David. *Witch-Hunts, Purity and Social Boundaries: The Expulsion of the Foreign Women in Ezra 9–10*. Vol. 350. A & C Black, 2002.

Japhet, Sara. "Sheshbazzar and Zerubbabel – Against the Background of the Historical and Religious Tendencies of Ezra-Nehemiah." *Zeitschrift für die Alttestamentliche Wissenschaft* 95, no. 2 (1983).

Japhet, Sara. "Theodicy in Ezra-Nehemiah and Chronicles." In *Theodicy in the World of the Bible*, edited by Antii Laato and Johannes de Moor, 429–69. Brill, 2003.

Japhet, Sara. *From the Rivers of Babylon to the Highlands of Judah: Collected Studies on the Restoration Period*. Eisenbrauns, 2006.

Japhet, Sara. *The Ideology of the Book of Chronicles and Its Place in Biblical Thought*. Penn State University Press, 2009.

Japhet, Sara. "What May Be Learned from Ezra-Nehemiah about the Composition of the Pentateuch?" In *The Formation of the Pentateuch*, edited by Jan C. Gertz, Bernard M. Levinson, Dalit Rom-Shiloni, and Konrad Schmid, 543–60. Mohr Siebeck, 2016.

Jigoulov, Vadim S. "Administration of Achaemenid Phoenicia: A Case for Managed Autonomy." In *Exile and Restoration Revisited: Essays in Memory of Peter R. Ackroyd*, edited by Gary N. Knoppers, Lester Grabbe, and Dierdre Fulton, 138–51. T & T Clark, 2011.

Jonker, Louis C. *Texts, Contexts, and Readings in Postexilic Literature: Explorations into Historiography and Identity Negotiations in Hebrew Bible and Related Texts*. Mohr Siebeck, 2011.

Josephus, Flavius. *The Antiquities of the Jews*. Simon and Schuster, 2023.

Josephus, Flavius. *The War of the Jews*. Simon and Schuster, 2014.

Jost, Adriel. "A New Start for the Monetary System: A Theological Perspective." *Revista Procesos De Mercado* (2022): 367–92.

Kahn, Dan'el. "The Date of the Arrival of the Judeans at Elephantine and the Foundation of Their Colony." *Journal of Near Eastern Studies* 81, no. 1 (2022): 139–64.

Kaufmann, Yehezkel. *History of the Religion of Israel, Volume IV: From the Babylonian Captivity to the End of Prophecy*. Ktav, 1977.

Kelle, Brad E., Frank Richard Ames, and Jacob L. Wright, eds. *Interpreting Exile: Displacement and Deportation in Biblical Modern Contexts*. Brill, 2012.

Kessler, John. "Persia's Loyal Yah-wists: Power Identity and Ethnicity in Achaemenid Yehud." In *Judah and the Judeans in the Persian Period*, edited by Oded Lipschits and Manfred Oeming, 91–121. Eisenbrauns, 2006.

Kessler, John. "The Diaspora in Zechariah 1–8 and Ezra-Nehemiah: The Role of History, Social Location, and Tradition in the Formulation of Identity." In *Community Identity in Judean Historiography*, edited by Garpy Knoppers and Kennet A. Ristau, 119–45. Eisenbrauns, 2009.

Kessler, John. "Images of Exile: Representations of the 'Exile' and 'Empty Land' in the Sixth to Fourth Century BCE Yehudite Literature." In *The Concept of Exile in Ancient Israel and Its Historical Contexts*, edited by by Ehud Ben Zvi and Christoph Levin, 309-51. De Gruyter, 2010.

Klawans, Jonathan. *Impurity and Sin in Ancient Judaism*. Oxford University Press, 2000.

Knoppers, Gary N. "Nehemiah and Sanballat: The Enemy Without or Within?" In *Judah and the Judeans in the Persian Period*, edited by Oded Lipschits and Manfred Oeming, 305–22. Eisenbrauns, 2006.

Knoppers, Gary N., Oded Lipschits, and Rainer Albertz, eds. *Judah and the Judeans in the Fourth Century BCE*. Penn State University Press, 2007.

Knoppers, Gary. "Ethnicity, Genealogy, Geography, and Change: The Judean Communities of Babylon, and Jerusalem in the Story of Ezra." In *Community Identity in Judean Historiography*, edited by Gary Knoppers and Kenneth Ristau, 147–71. Eisenbrauns, 2009.

Knoppers, Gary N., and Kenneth A. Ristau, eds. *Community Identity in Judean Historiography: Biblical and Comparative Perspectives.* Penn State University Press, 2009.

Knoppers, Gary. "Exile, Return, and Diaspora: Expatriates and Repatriates in Late Biblical Literature." In *Texts, Contexts, and Readings in Postexilic Literature,* edited by Louis C. Jonker, 29–61. Society of Biblical Literature, 2011.

Knoppers, Gary N. "Periodization in Ancient Israelite Historiography." In *Periodisierung und Epochenbewusstsein im Alten Testament und seinem Umfeld,* edited by Josef Wiesehöfer and Thomas Krüger, 121–45. Franz Steiner, 2012.

Knoppers, Gary N. "The Construction of Judean and Diasporic Identity in Ezra-Nehemiah." *Journal of Hebrew Scriptures* 15 (2015): 13.

Knoppers, Gary N. *Prophets, Priests, and Promises: Essays on the Deuteronomistic History, Chronicles, and Ezra-Nehemiah.* Vol. 186. Brill, 2021.

Koller, Aaron. *Esther in Ancient Jewish Thought.* Cambridge University Press, 2014.

Koller, Aaron. "Negotiating Empire: Living Jewishly Under the Achaemenids in Persia and Palestine." In *Iran, Israel, and the Jews: Symbiosis and Conflict from the Achaemenids to the Islamic Republic,* edited by Aaron Koller and Daniel Tsadik, 3–23. Wipf and Stock, 2019.

Korpman, Matthew. "Was Noadiah a Trustworthy Prophet? The Demise of Prophecy in the Second Temple Period." *Zeitschrift für die Alttestamentliche Wissenschaft* 135, no. 1 (2023): 52–70.

Knibb, Michael A. "The Exile in the Literature of the Intertestamental Period." In *Essays on the Book of Enoch and Other Early Jewish Texts and Traditions,* edited by Michael A. Knibb, 191–212. Brill, 2009.

Kugel, James. *The Great Shift: Encountering God in Biblical Times.* Houghton Mifflin Harcourt, 2017.

Kuhrt, Amelie. *The Persian Empire: A Corpus of Sources from the Achaemenid Period.* Routledge, 2013.

Kutsko, John F. *Between Heaven and Earth: Divine Presence and Absence in the Book of Ezekiel.* Eisenbrauns, 1999.

Laato, Antti. "The Composition of Isaiah 40–55." *Journal of Biblical Literature* 109, no. 2 (1990): 207–28.

Laato, Antti, and Johannes C. De Moor, eds. *Theodicy in the World of the Bible*. Brill e-Books, 2003. https://ci.nii.ac.jp/ncid/BA67809329.

Langille, Timothy, "Reshaping the Persistent Past: A Study of Collective Trauma and Memory in Second Temple Judaism" PhD diss., University of Toronto, 2014.

Leibtag, Menachem. "Megillat Esther and Its Hidden Message." Tanach Study Center, https://tanach.org/special/purim/purims1.htm.

Lemaire, Andre. "Schools and Literacy in Ancient Israel and Early Judaism." In *The Blackwell Companion to the Hebrew Bible*, edited by Leo G. Perdue, 201–17. Blackwell Publishers, 2001.

Levenson, Jon D. *Sinai and Zion: An Entry into the Jewish Bible*. Harper & Row, 1987.

Levin, Yigal. "Judea, Samaria and Idumea: Three Models of Ethnicity and Administration in the Persian Period." In *Judah to Judaea, Socio-Economic Structures and Processes in the Persian Period*, edited by Johannes Unsok Ro, 4–53. Sheffield Phoneix Press, 2012.

Levin, Yigal. "Bi-Directional Forced Deportations in the Neo-Assyrian Empire and the Origins of the Samaritans: Colonialism and Hybridity." *Archaeological Review from Cambridge* 28 (2013): 217–40.

Levine, Baruch A. "The Netînîm." *Journal of Biblical Literature* (1963): 207–12.

Levine, Baruch A. "On the Presence of God in Biblical Religion." In *Religions in Antiquity: Essays in Memory of Erwin Ramsdell Goodenough*, edited by Jacob Neusner, 68–87. Wipf and Stock, 1968.

Levine, Baruch A. "Assyrian Ideology and Israelite Monotheism." *Iraq* 67, no. 1 (2005): 411–27.

Lipschits, Oded. "Judah, Jerusalem and the Temple (586–539 BC)." *Transeuphratène* 22 (2001): 129–42.

Lipschits, Oded. "On the Titles 'bd hmlk and 'bd yhwh." *Shnaton – An Annual for Biblical and Ancient Near Eastern Studies* 13 (2002): 157–172.

Lipschits, Oded. "Demographic Changes in Judah Between the Seventh and the Fifth Centuries BCE." In *Judah and the Judeans in the Neo-Babylonian Period*, edited by Oded Lipschits and Joseph Blenkinsopp, 323–76. Eisenbrauns, 2003.

Lipschits, Oded. *The Fall and Rise of Jerusalem: Judah Under Babylonian Rule*. Eisenbrauns, 2005.

Lipschits, Oded, and Manfred Oeming. *Judah and the Judeans in the Persian Period.* Eisenbrauns, 2006.

Lopez, René. "Israelite Covenants in the Light of Ancient Near Eastern Covenants." *Chafer Theological Seminary Journal* 9, no. 2 (2003): 92–111.

Mallek, Raanan. "Historical Developments of the Term Ger Toshav and the Halakhic Implications Therein for Relating to Non-Jews." In *Jews in Dialogue,* edited by Magdalena Dzjaczkowska and Adele Valeria Messina. Brill, 2020.

Mason, Steve. "Jews, Judeans, Judaizing, Judaism: Problems of Categorization in Ancient History." *Journal for the Study of Judaism* 38, nos. 4–5 (2007): 457–512.

May, Natalie Naomi, ed. *Iconoclasm and Text Destruction in the Ancient Near East and Beyond.* Vol. 8. Oriental Institute of the University of Chicago, 2012.

Mazar, Eilat. "The Wall That Nehemiah Built." In *Biblical Archaeology Review* 35, no. 2 (2009).

Mermelstein, Ari. "When History Repeats Itself: The Theological Significance of the Abrahamic Covenant in Early Jewish Writings." *Journal for the Study of Pseudepigrapha* 27, no. 2 (2017): 113–42.

Meyers, Eric. "Exile and Restoration in Light of Recent Archaeology and Demographic Studies." In *Exile and Restoration Revisited: Essays on the Babylonian and Persian Periods in Memory of Peter R. Ackroyd,* edited by Gary N. Knoppers and Lester L. Grabbe, 166–73. Bloomsbury, 2011.

Middlemas, Jill. *The Troubles of Templeless Judah.* Oxford University Press, 2005.

Milgrom, Jacob. *Leviticus 1–16.* Doubleday, 1991.

Millard, Alan R. "The Question of Israelite Literacy." *Bible Review* 3, no. 3 (1987): 22–31.

Moore, James D. *Scribal Culture in the Ancient Near East,* Oxford Biblical Studies Online, https://www.oxfordbiblicalstudies.com/

Muffs, Yochanan. *Love and Joy: Law, Language and Religion in Ancient Israel.* Jewish Theological Seminary of America, 1992.

Myers, Jacob M. *Ezra-Nehemiah: Anchor Bible, Vol. 14.* Doubleday, 1965.

Na'aman, Nadav. "A New Outlook at Kuntillet 'Ajrud and Its Inscriptions." *Maarav* 20, no. 1 (2013): 39–51.

Najman, Hindy, and Judith Newman, eds. *The Idea of Biblical Interpretations: Essays in Honor of James L. Kugel*, vol. 83. Brill, 2002.

Niditch, Susan. *Oral World and Written Word: Ancient Israelite Literature.* Westminster John Knox, 1996.

O'Kennedy, Daniel F. "Were the Prophets Really Intercessors?" *Old Testament Essays* 13, no. 3 (2000): 329–47.

Oeming, Manfred. "'See, We Are Serving Today' (Nehemiah 9:36): Nehemiah 9 as a Rheological Interpretation of the Persian Period." In *Judah and the Judeans in the Persian Period*, 571–88. Eisenbrauns, 2006.

Oeming, Manfred. "The Real History: The Theological Ideas Behind Nehemiah's Wall." In *New Perspectives on Ezra-Nehemiah: History and Historiography, Text, Literature, and Interpretation*, edited by Isaac Kalimi, 131–50. Eisenbrauns, 2013.

Olyan, Saul. "Purity Ideology in Ezra-Nehemiah as a Tool to Reconstitute the Community." *Journal for the Study of Judaism* 35, no. 1 (2004): 1–16.

Pakkala, J. K. "Centers and Peripheries in the Ezra Story." In *Centres and Peripheries in the Early Second Temple Period*, edited by Ehud Ben Zvi and Christoph Levin, 135–155. Mohr Siebeck, 2016.

Porten, Bezalel. *Archives from Elephantine: The Life of an Ancient Jewish Military Colony.* University of California Press, 1968.

Porten, Bezalel, "Aramaic Papyri and Parchments: A New Look." *Biblical Archaeologist* 42, no. 2 (1979): 74–104.

Porten, Bezalel, and Ada Yardeni, eds. *Textbook of Aramaic Documents from Ancient Egypt: Ostraca and Assorted Inscriptions.* Vol. 4. Hebrew University, Department of the History of the Jewish People, 1999.

Porten, Bezalel. *The Elephantine Papyri in English: Three Millennia of Cross-Cultural Continuity and Change.* Brill, 1996.

Porten, Bezalel. "Elephantine." *Shalvi/Hyman Encyclopedia of Jewish Women*, 31 December 1999. Jewish Women's Archive.

Pritchard, James B., ed. *The Ancient Near East: An Anthology of Texts and Pictures.* Princeton University Press, 2011.

Pritchard, James B., ed. *Ancient Near Eastern Texts Relating to the Old Testament with Supplement.* Princeton University Press, 2016.

Rainey, Anson F. "The Satrapy Beyond the River." *Australian Journal of Biblical Archaeology* 1.2 (1969): 51–78.

Reiss, Moshe, and David J. Zucker. "Chronicles as Revisionist Religious History." *Asbury Journal* 68, no. 2 (2013): 9.

Rendtorff, Rolf. "Nehemiah 9: An Important Witness of Theological Reflection." In *Tehillah le-Moshe*, edited by Mordechai Cogan, Barry L. Eichler, and Jeffrey H. Tigay, 111–17. Eisenbrauns, 1997.

Rollston, Christopher A. *Writing and Literacy in the World of Ancient Israel: Epigraphic Evidence from the Early Iron Age*, No. 11. Society of Biblical Literature, 2010.

Rom-Shiloni, Dalit "Group Identities in Jeremiah: Is It the Persian Period Conflict?" In *A Palimpsest: Rhetoric, Ideology, Stylistics, and Language Relating to Persian Israel*, edited by Ehud Ben Zvi, Diana Edelman, and Frank Polak, 11–46. Gorgias, 2009.

Rosen-Zvi, Ishay, and Adi Ophir. "Goy: Toward a Genealogy." *Dine Israel* 28 (2011): 69–122.

Safrai, Ze'ev. *Seeking Out the Land: Land of Israel Traditions in Ancient Jewish, Christian and Samaritan Literature (200 BCE–400 CE)*. Vol. 32. Brill, 2018.

Sarna, Nahum M. *Understanding Genesis: The World in Light of History*. Schocken Books, 1970.

Schaper, Joachim. "The Jerusalem Temple as an Instrument of the Achaemenid Fiscal Administration." *Vetus Testamentum* 45, no. 4 (1995): 528–39.

Schiffman, Lawrence H. "Jewish Identity and Jewish Descent." *Judaism* 34, no. 1 (1985): 78–84.

Schniedewind, William M. *How the Bible Became a Book: The Textualization of Ancient Israel*. Cambridge University Press, 2004.

Schniedewind, William M. *A Social History of Hebrew: Its Origins through the Rabbinic Period*. Yale University Press, 2013.

Schroeder, Gerald. *Genesis and the Big Bang Theory: The Discovery of Harmony Between Modern Science and the Bible*. Bantman, 2011.

Schwartz, Daniel R. *Studies in the Jewish Background of Christianity*. Mohr-Siebeck, 1992.

Schwartz, Seth. "How Many Judaisms Were There?: A Critique of Neusner and Smith on Definition and Mason and Boyarin on Categorization." *Journal of Ancient Judaism* 2, no. 2 (2011): 208–38.

Schweitzer, Steven J., and Frauke Uhlenbrush. *Worlds That Could Not Be: Utopia in Chronicles, Ezra and Nehemiah*. Bloomsbury, 2016.

Scott, James M. *Exile: Old Testament, Jewish, and Christian Concepts.* Brill, 1997.

Shalom, Daniel. "Was Noadiah a Trustworthy Prophet? The Demise of Prophecy in the Second Temple Period." *Zeitschrift für die Alttestamentliche Wissenschaft* 135, no. 1 (2023): 52–70.

Shatz, David. "Is There Science in the Bible? An Assessment of Biblical Concordism." *Tradition* 41, no. 2 (2008): 198–244.

Shepherd, David. "Prophetaphobia: Fear and False Prophecy in Nehemiah VI." *Vetus Testamentum* 55, no. 2 (2005): 232–50.

Shinan, Avigdor, and Yair Zakovitch. *From Gods to God: How the Bible Debunked, Suppressed, or Changed Ancient Myths and Legends.* University of Nebraska Press, 2012.

Smith-Christopher, Daniel L. *The Religion of the Landless: The Social Context of the Babylonian Exile.* Wipf and Stock, 2015.

Smith, Gary V. "The Concept of God/the Gods as King in the Ancient Near East and the Bible." *Trinity Journal* 3, no. 1 (1982).

Sommer, Benjamin D. "Did Prophecy Cease? Evaluating a Reevaluation." *Journal of Biblical Literature* 115, no. 1 (1996): 31–47.

Sommer, Benjamin D. *A Prophet Reads Scripture: Allusion in Isaiah 40–66.* Stanford University Press, 1998.

Sommer, Benjamin D. *The Bodies of God and the World of Ancient Israel.* Cambridge University Press, 2009.

Spellman, Ched E. "Nehemiah's New Shadow: Reading and Rereading the Ezra-Nehemiah Narrative." *Southeastern Theological Review* 9, no. 1 (2018): 3.

Steiner, Richard C. "The mbqr at Qumran, the Episkopos in the Athenian Empire, and the Meaning of lbqr' in Ezra 7: 14: On the Relation of Ezra's Mission to the Persian Legal Project." *Journal of Biblical Literature* (2001): 623–46.

Steiner, Richard C. "Bishlam's Archival Search Report in Nehemiah's Archive: Multiple Introductions and Reverse Chronological Order as Clues to the Origin of the Aramaic Letters in Ezra 4–6." *Journal of Biblical Literature* 125, no. 4 (2006): 641–85.

Stern, Efraim. "The Babylonian Gap Revisited. Yes There Was." *Biblical Archaeology Review* 28, no. 3 (2002).

Sternberg, Meir. *The Poetics of Biblical Narrative: Ideological Literature and the Drama of Reading*. Indiana University Press, 1987.

Tabory, Joseph. *The JPS Commentary on the Haggadah: Historical Introduction, Translation, and Commentary*. Jewish Publication Society, 2008.

Tadmor, Hayim. "'The Appointed Time Has Not Yet Arrived': The Historical Background of Haggai 1:2." In *Ki Baruch Hu: Ancient Near Eastern, Biblical, and Judaic Studies in Honor of Baruch A. Levine*, edited by Robert Chazan, William W. Hallo, and Lawrence H. Schiffman, 401–8. Eisenbrauns, 1999.

Talmon, Shemaryahu. "The Judean Am Ha'ares in Historical Perspective." In *Fourth World Congress of Jewish Studies*. Vol. 1, 71–76. World Union of Jewish Studies, 1967.

Talmon, Shemaryahu. "'Exile' and 'Restoration' in the Conceptual World of Ancient Judaism." In *Restoration: Old Testament, Jewish, and Christian Perspectives*, edited by James M. Scott, 107–46. Brill, 2001.

Talmon, Shemaryahu, *Literary Motifs and Patterns in the Hebrew Bible: Collected Essays*. Eisenbrauns, 2013.

Thiessen, Matthew. "The Function of a Conjunction: Inclusivist or Exclusivist Strategies in Ezra 6:19–21 and Nehemiah 10:29–30." *Journal for the Study of the Old Testament* 34, no. 1 (2009): 63–79.

Unterman, Jeremiah. *Justice for All: How the Jewish Bible Revolutionized Ethics*. University of Nebraska Press, 2017.

Van Dam, Cornelis. *The Urim and Thummim: A Means of Revelation in Ancient Israel*. Eisenbrauns, 1997.

Van Der Toorn, Karel. *Scribal Culture and the Making of the Hebrew Bible*. Harvard University Press, 2009.

Visotzky, Burton L. "Some Aspects of Rabbinic Literature on Holy Land and Covenant." *Studies in Christian-Jewish Relations* 8, no. 1 (2013).

Walzer, Michael. *Exodus and Revolution*. Basic Books, 1986.

Walzer, Michael. *In God's Shadow: Politics in the Hebrew Bible*. Yale University Press, 2012.

Water, Matt. "Cyrus and the Achaemenids." *Iran* 42, no.1 (2004): 91–102.

Weinfeld, Moshe. "The Covenant of Grant in the Old Testament and in the Ancient Near East." *Journal of the American Oriental Society* (1970): 184–203.

Weinfeld, Moshe. *Normative and Sectarian Judaism in the Second Temple Period*. T & T Clark, 2005.

Williamson, H. G. M. *Ezra-Nehemiah*. Vol. 16. *Word Biblical Commentary*. Zondervan Academic, 2018.

Woolf, Daniel, *A Concise History of History: Global Historiography from Antiquity to the Present*. Cambridge University Press, 2019.

Wuench, Hans-Georg. "The Stranger in God's Land – Foreigners, Stranger, Guest: What Can We Learn from Israel's Attitude Towards Strangers?" *Old Testament Essays* 27, no. 3 (2014): 1129–54.

Yerushalmi, Yosef Hayim. *Zakhor: Jewish History and Jewish Memory*. University of Washington Press, 2011.

Young, Ian M. "Israelite Literacy: Interpreting the Evidence, Parts I–II." *Vetus Testamentum* 48 (1998): 239–53, 408–22.

Zaia, Shana. "Godnapping in the Ancient Near East." ASOR. 2016. https://www.asor.org./anetoday/206/09/godnapping-ancient-near-east/.

Zer-Kavod, Mordechai. *Ezra-Nehemiah*. Mossad HaRav Kook, 2001.

Zerubavel, Eviatar. *Time Maps: Collective Memory and the Social Shape of the Past*. University of Chicago Press, 2003.

Zerubavel, Yael. *Recovered Roots: Collective Memory and the Making of Israeli National Tradition*. University of Chicago Press, 1995.

Other books in the Maggid Studies in Tanakh series:

Genesis: From Creation to Covenant
Zvi Grumet

Exodus: The Genesis of God's People
Zvi Grumet

Joshua: The Challenge of the Promised Land
Michael Hattin

Judges: The Perils of Possession
Michael Hattin

I Samuel: A King in Israel
Amnon Bazak

II Samuel (forthcoming)
Amnon Bazak

I Kings: Torn in Two
Alex Israel

II Kings: In a Whirlwind
Alex Israel

Isaiah: Prophet of Righteousness and Justice
Yoel Bin-Nun and Binyamin Lau

Jeremiah: The Fate of a Prophet
Binyamin Lau

Ezekiel: From Destruction to Restoration
Tova Ganzel

Joel, Obadiah, and Micah: Facing the Storm
Yaakov Beasley

Amos: The Genius of Prophetic Rhetoric
Yitzchak Etshalom

Jonah: The Reluctant Prophet
Erica Brown

Nahum, Habakkuk, and Zephaniah: Lights in the Valley
Yaakov Beasley

Haggai, Zechariah, and Malachi: Prophecy in an Age of Uncertainty
Hayyim Angel

Ruth: From Alienation to Monarchy
Yael Ziegler

Lamentations: Faith in a Turbulent World
Yael Ziegler

Ecclesiastes and the Search for Meaning
Erica Brown

Esther: Power, Fate, and Fragility in Exile
Erica Brown

Nehemiah: Statesman and Sage
Dov S. Zakheim

Maggid Books
The best of contemporary Jewish thought from
Koren Publishers Jerusalem Ltd.